EVIDENCE

Examples and Explanations

EVIDENCE

Examples and Explanations
Second Edition

Arthur Best

Professor of Law
University of Denver

ASPEN LAW & BUSINESS
A Division of Aspen Publishers, Inc.

To Hannah, Rachel, and Eli

Contents

Preface

Evidence law is full of simple rules, complex rules, hard problems with satisfying answers, and hard problems that can never be resolved to everyone's agreement. This makes the subject difficult, but rewarding. For a student beginning the course, "Participation precedes interest" might be a helpful slogan. Once you get involved with the course, you will like it and you will master its various levels of complexity.

This text is designed to make participation easy. For every topic, it presents questions of different degrees of difficulty. It also provides clear explanations of how to analyze the questions. I hope you like this text, and I hope you like your Evidence course. Because it affects all of law practice, developing your skills in Evidence is a project that deserves your attention.

Arthur Best

December 1996

Acknowledgments

I am grateful to colleagues for reviewing parts of the manuscript, for sharing reactions to the first edition, and for helping me to develop my understanding of Evidence Law in less formal ways as well. Thanks, very much, to Sheila Hyatt, Frank Jamison, and Randolph Jonakait. I also appreciate the intellectual example set by many friends, particularly Rosemary Kahn-Fogel, Nicholas Kahn-Fogel, David Korngold, and Ethan Kuhlmann. The fun, rigor, and imagination brought to the course by my Evidence professor, A. Leo Levin, remain an inspiration.

This book is influenced strongly by the scholarship of the casebook editors whose works I have used in teaching. For their vital, though indirect, guidance, I would like to thank Ronald L. Carlson, Edward J. Imwinkelried, Eric D. Green, the late John Kaplan, Edward J. Kionka, Laird C. Kirkpatrick, Richard O. Lempert, Leon Letwin, the late David W. Louisell, Christopher B. Mueller, Charles R. Nesson, Stephen A. Saltzburg, and Jon R. Waltz.

The support and skill of Little, Brown's editorial staff have been vital in the writing of this text. In particular, thanks are due to Richard Heuser, Elizabeth Kenny, and Carol McGeehan. Finally, I am grateful to the students who have used this book's problems in earlier versions. Their insights were essential to its development.

EVIDENCE

Examples and Explanations

1

The General Requirement of Relevance

Introduction

Learn a few simple rules and amaze your friends! There is much more than that to evidence law, but you do have to learn the basic structure to do well in an evidence course, the bar examination, or actual litigation. And it is only when you understand the explicit doctrines of evidence law that you can spot the sophisticated and complicated ambiguities that still remain even after the adoption of a code, the Federal Rules of Evidence.

The logical starting place in the study of evidence is the concept of relevance. In order to be admissible, information must be relevant to a disputed issue. This concept is the foundation of evidence law. If someone sued a police officer for alleged police brutality, could you imagine the defendant's lawyer asking the plaintiff, "Are you married?" That kind of question seems strange because the plaintiff's marital status has nothing to do with evaluating the police officer's conduct. Knowing whether the plaintiff is married cannot legitimately help the trier of fact decide whether the police officer used too much force against the plaintiff, so evidence law keeps that information out of the trial. The question is improper because it refers to something that has no reasonable connection to the substantive doctrines that govern a police brutality suit. Almost every issue in evidence law involves relevance — the idea that the party who seeks to have evidence admitted must specify what issue it relates to and show how it rationally advances the inquiry about that issue.

This chapter begins our consideration of evidence law by exploring the way it divides all the facts of the world into two categories in every case: relevant and irrelevant. Material must be relevant to be admitted into evidence at a trial. That highlights the importance of the relevance inquiry. But admissibility requires more than a showing of relevancy. There are important requirements for the form of testimony and the authentication of documents and about the degree of knowledge a witness must have concerning the topic of testimony, for example. Succeeding chapters discuss these rules as well as others that exclude relevant material for reasons based on social policies such as rules of privilege, which protect confidential communications, and the rule against hearsay, which avoids basing trial results on unreliable secondhand information. The Federal Rules of Evidence will be the main focus. They apply, of course, in federal courts. Additionally, more than 40 states have adopted evidence codes or rules modeled on the Federal Rules.

The Basic Standard and Its Application

The relevance rule restricts the trier of fact to considering only material that relates closely to facts that matter in the case. How close must the relationship be between an item of evidence and the proposition it is offered to support? The answer is necessarily vague: just close enough so the evidence could influence a rational fact finder in determining the truth or falsity of that proposition.

The Federal Rules have three main relevance provisions. Rule 402[1] requires that evidence be relevant to be admitted and that irrelevant evidence be excluded:

> All relevant evidence is admissible, except as otherwise provided by the Constitution of the United States, by Act of Congress, by these rules, or by other rules prescribed by the Supreme Court pursuant to statutory authority. Evidence which is not relevant is not admissible.

Rule 401 provides the following definition of relevant evidence:

> "Relevant evidence" means evidence having any tendency to make the existence of any fact that is of consequence to the determination of the action more probable or less probable than it would be without the evidence.

Another provision allows the trial judge to use discretion to avoid admitting evidence under certain circumstances even when its admission would seem to be required under Rules 401 and 402. That provision is Rule 403:

---

1. Throughout this book, Rule numbers will refer to provisions of the Federal Rules of Evidence.

Although relevant, evidence may be excluded if its probative value is substantially outweighed by the danger of unfair prejudice, confusion of the issues, or misleading the jury, or by considerations of undue delay, waste of time, or needless presentation of cumulative evidence.

The relevancy concept saves time. It narrows the topics that parties have to develop in preparation for trial. Finally, it increases the perceived legitimacy of trials by insuring that outcomes will be based on data most people would believe have something to do with the controversy.

Suppose a plaintiff sued the owner of an office building, claiming that he had fallen and hurt himself in the lobby and that inadequate maintenance of the lobby was the proximate cause of his injury. Should our trial system allow the plaintiff to show that the office building is one floor taller than the maximum height permitted by zoning regulations? The answer to this question depends on the substantive tort law that will govern the case. The evidence will be kept out because compliance with maximum height regulations has nothing to do with an owner's liability for injuries in a building's lobby. In technical terms it is immaterial since it does not involve one of the legal issues in the case. In the language of Rule 401, it does not deal with a fact that is "of consequence to the determination of the action." Could the plaintiff show that the lobby walls had once been painted pink but had been repainted yellow shortly before the injury? That evidence does relate to an issue at stake in the trial, the condition of the lobby, but it could not possibly influence a decision about the building owner's efforts to maintain a safe lobby. A court would keep it out, calling it irrelevant. How would a court treat evidence that the lobby was dimly lit? That information relates to an issue in dispute in a way that could help a fact finder decide rationally whether the owner had been adequately careful to provide a safe lobby. The evidence would be admitted.

For any relevance decision, the advocates and judge must have background information in mind, a context in which to evaluate whether the offered evidence has "any tendency," in the language of Rule 401, to affect the fact finder's resolution of a disputed issue. For example, in the lobby case, evidence that the lighting was dim seems relevant to us because we know (without its being proved or evidence about it being offered) that people trip and fall more often in dark places than in places that are brightly lit. This type of information about what the world is like is necessarily a part of every relevancy decision.

The judge decides questions of admissibility under common law and under the Federal Rules. Rule 104(a) provides:

Preliminary questions concerning the qualification of a person to be a witness, the existence of a privilege, or the admissibility of evidence shall be determined by the court, subject to the provisions of subdivision (b). In making its determination it is not bound by the rules of evidence except those with respect to privileges.

Subdivision (b) of the Rule is discussed later in this chapter. Because relevancy is a condition for admissibility, it is one of the issues the judge is intended to decide by himself or herself. Notice that evidence can clear the relevancy threshold with a very small showing: The judge must believe that a rational fact finder could be influenced by the material in deciding the existence of a fact. Strong influence is *not* required. The evidence only has to be capable of making determination of the fact more or less probable than it would be without the evidence. Thus, relevance is different from sufficiency. In McCormick's famous phrase, "A brick is not a wall."[2] Where the contribution an item of evidence could make is very slight, however, the possibility increases that a judge will exclude it under the authority of Rule 403 as wasteful of time or needlessly cumulative. In this field, judges have discretion and are rarely overruled because factual situations are so diverse and there can be a wide range of ideas about the rational relationships between various kinds of information and facts sought to be proved.

Unfair Prejudice

Evidence is subject to exclusion if the risk of unfair prejudice substantially outweighs its probative value. Rule 403 uses those terms to frame the judge's discretion. To understand this balancing, it is necessary to define both unfair prejudice and probative value. If evidence will help an opponent, parties try not to introduce it. In this sense, all evidence that a party introduces is intended to prejudice the opponent, since it is meant to help the proponent's side of the case and hurt the opponent. It is only when a factfinder might react to aspects of evidence *in a way that is not supposed to be part of the evaluative process* that the reaction is considered *unfair* prejudice.

For example, the victim in an assault case could introduce testimony that the defendant ran towards him shouting, "Get over here, I'm going to break your arm." Naturally, a juror might dislike a person who made such a statement and might therefore be prejudiced against him. This type of prejudice is proper because it comes from the juror's belief that the defendant committed the alleged aggression. On the other hand, if someone testified that the defendant said to the alleged victim, "I'm going to break your arm because I belong to a cult that worships violence," jurors might develop two kinds of ideas from learning about the defendant's worship of violence. They might relate the statement about religion specifically to the alleged crime and conclude that those words were part of the crime (in the sense that they reinforced the scary effect of the threat). Jurors might also develop negative impressions about the defendant based on their feelings of aversion to people who belong to weird cults. Those impressions would be an example of unfair

---

2. Charles T. McCormick, McCormick on Evidence 339 (John W. Strong, ed., 4th ed. 1992 (abridged ed.)).

prejudice since they are unrelated to the probative value the religion information has with respect to the charged crime. They flow from jurors' reactions to information about the person that would cause revulsion whether or
not it was linked to the events of an alleged crime, not from a belief that the
defendant did commit the crime. As Chart One illustrates, jurors who believed that the statement was made could simultaneously draw two ideas
from it. One would be that the defendant had committed the charged offense. The other would be that the defendant is a wretch and deserves to be
punished no matter what. Obviously our system intends to have only the first
kind of reaction, illustrated in the top row of Chart One, play a part in the
outcome of trials.

There is another type of unfair prejudice that the trial judge is authorized to consider under Rule 403. This is the risk that a juror will give undue
probative weight to an item of evidence. For example, if there was a dispute
in a products liability case about whether a plaintiff's injury had really occurred the way the plaintiff claimed, the plaintiff might seek to introduce evidence that someone else had been injured in that same way. If the defendant
argued that the plaintiff's claimed injury was impossible, letting the jury
know that someone else had been hurt that way would be proper since the
jury could use that information to evaluate the defense of impossibility. A different treatment would be sensible if the defendant admitted that the type of
accident claimed by the plaintiff was possible, but claimed that the plaintiff
just had not been injured in that way. In that case, proof that one other person had been hurt that way would have only a small bearing on the likelihood

CHART ONE
Simultaneous Inferences from Evidence that Defendant
Said "I'm Going to Break Your Arm, I Belong to a Cult
that Worships Violence."

Allowable Chain of Inferences

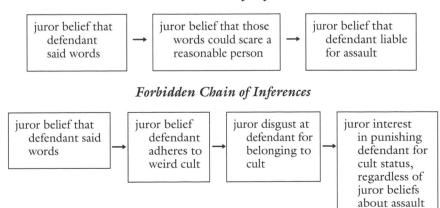

Forbidden Chain of Inferences

that the plaintiff's claim was true, but there is a risk that jurors might believe that because something happened one time it was highly likely to have happened another time. In a case where a defendant acknowledged that the plaintiff's theory was possible, admitting evidence about a single other incident of the type claimed by the plaintiff would subject the defendant to a risk that the jury would give it too much weight.

To determine whether the risk of unfair prejudice substantially outweighs the probative value of evidence, a judge is required to do some kind of weighing. This process is not literally a measurement since there is no scale on which degrees of probativeness and prejudice can be quantified. In the worshipping violence example the judge would consider the other evidence the prosecution had that connected the defendant to the crime. If the prosecution had other evidence that did not entail a reference to violence worship, the probative value of that violence reference would be slight. If the judge were to instruct the witness outside the hearing of the jury that the "break your arm" statement could be repeated but that the "cult" statement must be kept from the jury, this would ensure that the prosecution had access to an important part of its case against the defendant. Additionally, it would avoid the risk of providing the jurors with information that might affect them improperly.

EXAMPLES

1.   Why might rich defendants in civil cases or guilty defendants in criminal cases prefer an evidence system that did not impose a requirement that evidence be relevant?

2.   Imagine a patent infringement suit. The plaintiff claims that the defendant has begun to sell a pen with an ink supply system that copies a system patented by the plaintiff more closely than patent law allows. To prove patent infringement, can the plaintiff introduce testimony that the defendant company recently moved its headquarters from one city to another?

3.   Suppose the plaintiff in Example 2 offers testimony that the defendant's president bought one of the plaintiff company's pens, wrote with it, and said that he would like to invent a pen that worked as well. Would evidence of that statement be relevant?

4.   In Example 2's lawsuit, suppose that the defendant company's president had paid to have a sadistic thug beat up the plaintiff and make the plaintiff tell him how to set up a production line that could make pens using the plaintiff's patented design. Could the plaintiff testify about the beating?

5. X is on trial for stealing a 1957 DeSoto automobile worth about $5,000 to collectors of classic cars. To show motive to steal and knowledge of the DeSoto's value, can the prosecution introduce evidence that X has a collection of classic cars?

EXPLANATIONS

1.   In a system where irrelevant evidence as well as relevant evidence was admissible, trials could last forever since only a party's endurance or financial resources would limit the amount of evidence the party could present. Theoretically, a civil defendant in a suit where the cost of losing would be very high would find it in its interest to delay the end of trial for as long as possible. The same reasoning would apply to the guilty criminal defendant, who might well prefer daily attendance at court to serving a prison sentence.

On the other hand, the relevance principle can help defendants by preventing the jury from finding out facts about them which might make them seem unattractive: the immense wealth of a corporate defendant or a criminal defendant's long record of prior convictions.

2.   No. The location of the defendant's headquarters has nothing to do with how our legal system treats the right to use particular patented inventions, so the judge should reject the testimony. Note that the judge decides questions of relevance.

3.   This testimony does relate to the parties' pens. But would it help a jury decide whether the pen actually manufactured by the defendant made improper use of the plaintiff's patented invention? Its probative value is very low on the issue of patent infringement, and there might be a risk that a jury would fail to distinguish between a desire to imitate a product and a plan to misuse patented aspects of a design. Either decision made by a judge on this evidence — letting it in or keeping it out — would probably be affirmed on appeal.

4.   Yes. The fact that the defendant company sought information about how to use the patented design could logically support a conclusion that the product it eventually manufactured was very close in specifications to the patented product. The fact that the defendant hired an evil person to use force against the plaintiff might cause jurors to be inclined to rule for the plaintiff just to punish the defendant for the use of force rather than because of its evaluation of the patent law issues. Nevertheless, there is a strong argument for admitting this evidence. If the plaintiff's case had lots of other evidence about the patent infringement, then it is possible that under Rule 403, a judge might decide to exclude information about the beating. But because the beating is so closely related to the defendant's manufacturing plans, it is highly likely that testimony about it would be admitted.

5.   Yes. Proof that X collects cars would not support a verdict of guilty in the theft case if it were the prosecution's only evidence. But evidence does not have to be conclusive to be relevant. If X is interested in classic cars, does that make the propositions that he stole a classic car or that he knew the worth of the car more likely to be true than they would be without that information about X's interest? If the judge believes that the answer to this question is "yes," then the evidence is admissible.

Limited Admissibility

Sometimes an item of evidence is relevant to one issue in a case and *has no relationship at all* to another issue. In that circumstance, the evidence passes the relevancy hurdle since no single piece of evidence is expected to be relevant to all the disputed issues of a case. The situation is more complicated when a single item of evidence is relevant to one issue in a case and is a type of evidence *forbidden to be considered* with respect to another issue. For example, a specialized relevancy rule prohibits admission of evidence of an alleged tortfeasor's subsequent remedial measures to prove negligence. Such remedial actions can be relevant and admissible, however, on issues other than the quality of the defendant's care. They could relate, for example, to the issues of ownership or control of the site where the injury occurred.

If a tort plaintiff seeks to introduce evidence that qualifies for the permissible relevance of showing that the defendant had control of a place where the plaintiff was hurt, our legal system is placed in a difficult position. It must deal with the possibility that a jury will make use of that information not only for the permitted purpose but also for deciding the defendant's culpability — even though a specific rule prohibits introduction of this kind of evidence to show culpability. There are two possible resolutions of the circumstance where evidence has one permissible use and another impermissible use. We could keep the evidence out. This would guarantee that the jury would not make a wrongful use of the material but would also guarantee that the proper, permitted use of the information would not occur. The other choice, which is typically the choice made by trial judges, is to let the material in and give the jury a cautionary "limiting" instruction. The limiting instruction would tell the jurors to consider the information only with respect to the topic for which it is legitimately admitted. This allows the proper use of the information, consistent with the pro-admissibility trend of modern evidence law in general and the Federal Rules in particular, while it decreases somewhat the risk that the jury will use the information improperly.

Conditional Relevance

Sometimes an item of evidence *by itself* will have no relevance to any issue in a trial but would be relevant if the trier of fact also had some other information. Rule 104(b) governs this situation:

> When the relevancy of evidence depends upon the fulfillment of a condition of fact, the court shall admit it upon, or subject to, the introduction of evidence sufficient to support a finding of the fulfillment of the condition.

To illustrate, suppose in a murder trial the prosecution sought to show that the defendant owned a red hat with a blue feather. If an eyewitness saw the murderer run from the scene wearing that kind of hat, then information about the defendant's hat would be significant circumstantial evidence of guilt. Notice, however, that the relevance of hat ownership is only apparent if there is testimony from the eyewitness. This is called "conditional relevance." The relevance of the testimony about the defendant's hat comes from the context provided by the information from the eyewitness. Judges are supposed to admit evidence of this kind if its proponent has already produced the other material that shows its relevance to the trial or if the proponent promises to produce that contextual information later. We leave it to the jury to decide whether the underlying context has been proven adequately to support consideration of the conditionally relevant information.[3] This process is mandated in Rule 104(b), which defines the situation as one in which "the relevancy of evidence depends on the fulfillment of a condition of fact."

In the red hat illustration, the jury will make a decision about the reliability of the eyewitness testimony. If it believes that the murderer really did wear a red hat with a blue feather, it will go on to consider whether it believes the testimony which stated that the defendant owns a hat like that. If the jury does not believe that the eyewitness saw that kind of hat, it will pay no attention to the testimony it heard about the defendant's hat. Knowing that the defendant had a peculiar hat would be of no interest to a juror who did not believe that such a hat was seen at the time of the murder.

The judge does continue to have a role in the conditional relevance situation if it turns out that the proponent of the conditionally relevant information fails to produce the extra material that relates the conditionally relevant information to the case. In the red hat illustration, if the prosecutor failed to introduce eyewitness testimony about the murderer having worn a red hat, then the judge could instruct the jury to ignore whatever it had heard about the defendant's possession of a red hat. This instruction, of course, would only tell the jury to do what it would most likely have done without a specific warning, since ignoring the defendant's red hat would be natural if there was no testimony that made a red hat important to any aspect of the case.

EXAMPLES

1. In a suit between an ice cream company and the creator of a special recipe, the recipe creator claims that the ice cream company paid too little in royalties and falsified its reports of the costs of manufacturing and sales. To

---

3. Conditional relevance is recognized in the Rules, and judges and litigators are usually comfortable with the concept. Nevertheless, some scholars argue that the concept is analytically unsound. They point out that the relevance of *any* evidence depends on other items of evidence or other information. Whether information about the defendant's hat should be part of the jury's consideration in the hypothetical murder case is left to the jury, under the Rules. The jury will decide whether or not to think about it. In contrast, if evidence of a hatred between the defendant and the victim were introduced, the relevancy decision would not be treated as involving the Rules' concept of conditional relevance. The judge would admit it unconditionally, relying on his or her own belief that hatred is often a motive for murder.

show that the company defrauded him, the recipe creator wants to introduce a tape recording which he claims contains a discussion by two officers of the company about the amount of profits from "this season's big project." The company objects to admission of the tape recording, claiming that "this season's big project" meant a new kind of packaging, not a recipe, and that therefore the tape is not relevant to the plaintiff's case. Discuss how the plaintiff might argue for admissibility of the tape.

2.   The use of coerced confessions in criminal trials is prohibited. If a defendant objects to the admission of a confession on this basis, should the judge treat the question of whether the police used coercion as a conditional relevance issue that the jury should resolve?

3.   In a rape case, the alleged victim testifies that the defendant said, "Come with me and do what I say. I'm not kidding, I've already been in prison for rape twice before." Is this testimony relevant to any issue in a rape case? Does it raise problems of unfair prejudice?

EXPLANATIONS

1.   The plaintiff would have to be able to tell the judge in good faith that he had some additional evidence showing that the conversation really involved his recipe. If the people talking on the tape were discussing packaging, then the tape would have nothing to do with the current case. If the taped executives really were discussing the plaintiff's recipe, then the information would be relevant. This is an example of conditional relevance, and the judge would properly admit the tape recording. The fact finder would consider the tape recording only if there was also persuasive evidence supporting the plaintiff's claim about what the speakers meant by "this season's big project."

2.   This objection involves a factual issue about the making of the confession. But the objection does not involve the concept of relevance since the defendant is not, for the purpose of this objection, contending that the confession lacks a relationship to guilt or innocence. The defendant, for this objection, is claiming inadmissibility on the basis of a particular rule that keeps coerced confessions out of trials. The judge would decide whether the circumstances of the making of the confession were legitimate or involved forbidden coercion. If the judge decides that there was coercion, the confession would stay out and the jury would never hear about it.

   If this were mistakenly treated as a conditional relevance situation, there would be an absurd result. The jury would be asked to decide whether a confession had been made voluntarily and would then be told to ignore the confession if it decided that the confession had been coerced. Notice that this puts the jury in a difficult position. A juror would be told to ignore a confession he had learned about if he decided that a preliminary factual condition our system imposes — voluntariness — was not satisfied. A juror might be able to do that, but it would require extraordinary concentration and dedication to the values on which the constitutional rule is based.

In a true conditional relevance situation, jurors are never asked to do anything counterintuitive. When they are supposed to ignore information it is highly likely they will do so, because the information will not seem to them to have anything to do with the case. In the analysis of Example 1, no juror would think about the tape recording in connection with the current suit unless the juror thought the information on it involved the plaintiff's recipe. Otherwise it would not make any sense to use information about packaging to think about profits from the plaintiff's recipe. Confession cases are different. In those cases, it *would* make sense to think about the confession even if it had been coerced because some coerced confessions are accurate. That is why we protect defendants from being tried by jurors who have heard about their confessions in a case where the confession was coerced.

3.   If there is dispute about whether the victim consented to intercourse, testimony that the defendant used coercive language would be relevant. Since the defendant's own words happen to reveal facts about his past that could cause the jury to want to punish him for that past rather than for the crime for which he is being tried, there is a possibility of unfair prejudice. The balancing test, weighing the probative value of the information against the risk of unfair prejudice, would lead to admission of the evidence, because there is not likely to be any way to prove the method of coercion other than by proving what words the alleged rapist said. Thus, the probative value of the words would be great. The risk of unfair prejudice would be treated with a limiting instruction, telling the jury to consider the words only on the issue of coercion and prohibiting the jury from considering whether or not the defendant had actually been imprisoned for rape in the past. (The problems presented by evidence of past convictions are covered by a set of specialized rules, which are discussed later in this chapter.)

Recurring Situations

Some factual propositions are involved in so many trials that precedents have developed for handling the kinds of evidence parties seek to introduce about them. Examples of these relevance inquiries are: an effort to suggest that a person is guilty of a charged crime by showing that he fled the jurisdiction when arrest was imminent, or fled after arrest; use of similar occurrences to show what happened on a particular occasion; and use of statistical probabilities to prove that an event occurred.

Flight

Courts usually reason that fleeing the jurisdiction supports an inference that the defendant believed he or she was guilty, and that this supports another inference that the defendant in fact was guilty. On this analysis, flight is usually admitted as relevant to guilt. Counterarguments that are not usually successful maintain that flight should be excluded because it may show only fear of wrongful conviction, and because even a belief in guilt may not truly indicate guilt under the detailed substantive standards applicable to any given crime. A similar approach is taken to evidence about destroying evidence or trying to obtain perjured testimony.

Similar Happenings

Evidence of similar happenings is sought to be admitted in many trials. In criminal trials, prosecutors may seek to introduce evidence that a defendant has committed prior acts that are similar to the charged offense. This issue is treated in connection with "character evidence," at pages 33-36.

In tort cases, typically an accident victim will offer testimony that other people had been injured in the same way on previous occasions. This information might be relevant in a variety of ways depending on the underlying theory of the plaintiff's case. This can be illustrated with the case of a plaintiff who claims he was injured when the cap of a soft drink bottle flew off under pressure as he opened it. Proof of a significant number of similar past occurrences involving bottles sold by the defendant would support the plaintiff's contentions that: 1) his injury actually was caused by a bottle cap; 2) the bottle cap was dangerous; 3) the defendant had notice of the dangerousness of the product; and 4) the defendant had an opportunity to correct the problem. Note that all of these theories of relevancy would apply in a case based on negligence, but some of them would not work in a strict liability case. Since strict liability will be imposed regardless of a defendant's notice or "wrongful conduct" in not correcting a dangerous situation, the plaintiff could not argue for the relevance of information about past injuries by claiming it showed notice to the defendant or that it supported a claim that the defendant should have acted to correct the problem. In all relevance situations, the basic substantive law or the proponent's theory of the proponent's case will have a major effect on the judge's decision on admissibility.

In determining the relevancy of similar occurrences evidence, a court will examine the surrounding circumstances of the previous incidents to compare them with the alleged facts of the incident that is the subject of the trial. If the earlier events took place under conditions with characteristics that were similar to the conditions present at the time of the event that is the basis of the suit, information about them will be considered relevant. The proponent's legal theory will affect which and how many characteristics in the past events and the litigated event must be similar to each other.

In the bottle cap example, a plaintiff who seeks recovery on negligence grounds could claim that past incidents were relevant with regard to notice. On that theory, the degree of similarity between the event that harmed the plaintiff and other earlier events could be less than would be required if the past events were claimed to be relevant to show how the plaintiff's injury occurred or to show that the product feature that harmed the plaintiff was negligently designed. If the plaintiff pleaded only a strict liability case, the plaintiff would have no basis for arguing that the past injuries were relevant to show notice. They could only be relevant to show that the plaintiff's injury really occurred in the way the plaintiff claims (by showing that the plaintiff's description of how the injury took place matched the details of past occurrences) and that the product design was hazardous. For those purposes, a high degree of similarity between the plaintiff's incident and the prior incidents would be required.

Information about similar past occurrences raises a subtle issue of the distribution of decisionmaking between the judge and jury. This evidence is really an example of conditional relevance since information about the past events will be relevant only if a certain factual proposition is proved adequately: the similarity of settings between the past and litigated events. On this analysis, then, the judge should let the material into the trial if a juror could reasonably decide that the past event and the event being litigated are similar enough so that information from the past event could help the juror decide what really happened in the event being litigated. In theory, jurors will ignore what they learn about past mishaps if they consider them unrelated to the event examined in the trial. Even where proof of the closeness of circumstances is weak, the conditional relevance analysis leads to the idea that the judge should give the jury an opportunity to evaluate the evidence.

A further analysis is based on the fact that evidence of past injuries may be highly prejudicial. Jurors who hear about injuries to people other than the plaintiff may be inspired to make the defendant pay money to the plaintiff even if they are not persuaded there really was negligence in the plaintiff's instance. This argues against adopting a generally pro-admissibility stance on the issue of past occurrences. So even though evidence of past occurrences could be treated as an instance of conditional relevance, with most of the decisionmaking left to juries, judges properly exclude the evidence unless they are persuaded that the showing of similarity of conditions is strong.

Statistical Proof

Another type of evidence that parties sometimes seek to introduce is testimony by experts about the probability of events. In the most famous case of this type, *People v. Collins*,[4] a married couple were criminal defendants charged with robbery. The husband was a black man who sometimes wore a beard, and the wife was a white woman with blond hair. Eyewitness testimony supported the contention that the robbers were a black man with a beard and a white woman with blond hair. An expert in statistics testified for the prosecution about the probability of occurrence of many factors in the

---

4. 68 Cal. 2d 319, 66 Cal. Rptr. 497 (1968).

case, such as a couple being composed of two people with the combination of racial and other physical appearance attributes of the defendant couple.

The California Supreme Court found a number of problems with this. First, in calculating probabilities, it is necessary to have some empirical basis for assigning values to any event. The expert witness in *Collins* merely made guesses about the frequency of occurrence of the attributes he used for his calculations, such as how many black men have beards and how many do not. Another problem was that in calculating probabilities of combinations of different variables, the variables must be "independent." That requirement was not met in the expert's testimony. Finally, the court was concerned that jurors might improperly confuse the probability of a couple possessing the traits possessed by the defendants with the probability that the defendants were not guilty.

All of these concerns led the court to be strict about the requirements of scientific accuracy in this kind of testimony because there is a strong likelihood that it will be very impressive to juries. Most courts are cautious with regard to scientific or technical material when they think members of a jury will have difficulty in adopting a critical stance toward it. This leads them to scrutinize the relevancy of probability evidence more closely than the relevancy of other types of evidence.

An additional reason for reluctance to admit probability evidence on issues such as the identity of wrongdoers is that in criminal cases the fact finder is supposed to be persuaded beyond a reasonable doubt, while probability evidence by its nature incorporates some degree of doubt. Even in civil cases, where the standard of proof is a preponderance of the evidence, some courts may believe that probability evidence cannot be weighed fairly with other types of information.

EXAMPLES

1.   A plaintiff who claimed he had been injured on the defendant's ship planned to introduce a statement from a sailor who said he had seen the injury occur. The plaintiff, the plaintiff's lawyer, and the defendant's lawyer all participated in obtaining a deposition from the sailor. On the day after taking the deposition, the defendant located crew lists showing that the "eyewitness" had not been on board the ship on the day of the injury. The plaintiff's lawyer then informed the court that he would not seek to introduce the "eyewitness" statement. The *defendant* then stated that he wanted to introduce it to show "fraud." The court replied:

> Well, I'm not going to permit you to do that. I'm going to say that if this person perjured himself then we can do one of several things, one of which we can report it to the United States Attorney for perjury, for purposes of perjury, because it was done to influence the outcome of this case. I think that's the appropriate procedure. I don't think we

> are going to start introducing a document which you think is incorrect and intentionally incorrect in this case. . . . If it is not brought in [by the plaintiff] then I don't say it's an issue in this case for this jury to consider whether or not the plaintiff is involved. I don't know whether the plaintiff is involved in this matter. That's whose case we're trying. We're trying the plaintiff's case.[5]

The judge was wrong. Why?

2.   Warren Webster seeks damages from an amusement park, claiming that his arm was broken when one of the amusement park rides came to a sudden stop and threw him against the side of one of its cars. Webster claims that the ride was carelessly designed and carelessly operated. He also claims that the defendant amusement park should have known about the risks that the ride presented and was negligent in failing to warn about them or correct them. If Webster had evidence that other people had been hurt on the ride in the same way he claims he was hurt, it would be admissible provided that the circumstances of the earlier injuries were similar to the circumstances of Webster's injury. What if the amusement park's manager knows that in ten years of operation no one besides Webster has claimed to have been injured by the ride, and the manager knows of no other injuries? How would you argue for admissibility of this evidence of prior safety?

3.   The plaintiff was hit by a carelessly driven armored truck. Unfortunately, the driver drove away from the scene of the accident. The plaintiff could not see a company's name on the truck, but remembers that it was blue. There are two companies using blue armored trucks in the area where the accident occurred; one of them has 90 trucks and the other has ten trucks. The plaintiff sues the 90-truck company claiming that there is a 90 percent chance that one of its trucks hit him. If there is no other evidence about the identity of the truck in the accident except the victim's testimony about its color and evidence showing that 90 percent of the blue armored trucks in use belong to the defendant, should the plaintiff's case get to the jury or is the defendant entitled to a directed verdict?

EXPLANATIONS

1.   If the jury believed that the plaintiff had known that the "eyewitness" statement was phony, the jury could infer from that belief that the plaintiff considered his case so weak that it needed help from perjured testimony. That inference could properly assist the jury in deciding whatever disputed issues of fact were involved in the case.

The judge might have been on firmer ground if he or she had ruled that the evidence was relevant but inadmissible because without a strong link

---

5. *McQueeney v. Wilmington Trust Co.*, 779 F.2d 916, n.3 (3d Cir. 1985).

between the plaintiff personally and the attempted perjury, there are risks of wasting time and confusing the jury.

2.   For the prior safe operation of the ride to be admissible evidence, the manager would have to establish that the circumstances at the time Webster claims to have been injured were highly similar to the circumstances during all the prior period about which the manager has knowledge. "Similarity" here must be interpreted to mean that the prior circumstances and the circumstances when Webster was hurt did not differ in ways that could affect safety. If that similarity is established, then safe operation in the past is directly relevant on the issue of notice since it would have suggested to the defendant that the ride was safe (not that the ride was dangerous as the plaintiff claims).

Safe operation in the past also would support a claim by the defendant that the plaintiff is mistaken or lying about how or where his injury occurred, because a history of safe operation suggests (although it does not prove conclusively) that the ride does not cause injuries the way the plaintiff claims it did. Finally, it could support the amusement park's general contention that the ride is reasonably safe even if it did cause harm to the plaintiff on one occasion.

3.   Some courts would let this plaintiff get to the jury on the probability theory. There is not really any risk that the "statistical" evidence will be overpoweringly technical and too hard for jurors to refute with their own common sense. And information about which company with blue armored trucks owns the most blue armored trucks does relate to the question of which company's truck was involved in the accident. Yet some courts would hold that the inference one could base on the statistics is so slight that the evidence should be treated as not relevant. They might also treat the information as relevant but subject to a significant risk that the jury will give it inappropriately heavy weight; this would unfairly prejudice the defendant and could be a separate rationale for excluding the evidence.

Courts may be reluctant to create a situation in which a judgment is entered in a case which might seem entirely theoretical or suppositional to the general public. That point of view ignores the fact that most cases involve only evidence that is subject in varying degrees to error or that is based on implicit estimates of probability. Nonetheless, while a case based on eyewitness testimony may be more likely to produce the wrong result than a case based on 90 percent odds such as the problem case, many courts tolerate the risk in the eyewitness case but would be reluctant to acknowledge that probability evidence has equal reliability. (In *Kaminsky v. Hertz Corporation,* 288 N.W.2d 426 (Mich. Ct. App. 1979), the court faced a problem like the one in this question, but its task was made easier because the plaintiff remembered seeing the defendant's name on the truck. Even though some trucks with that name were not owned by the defendant, the court relied on substantive theories connected with the obligations an enterprise must bear if it allows its name to appear on trucks other than those it owns.)

2

Specific Exclusions of Relevant Material

Introduction

Judges have great discretion in applying the relevance requirement and the safeguard that excludes relevant but unfairly prejudicial information. However, in certain specific circumstances they are required to keep evidence out despite its logical relevance. These are situations where the likelihood of unfair prejudice from particular types of evidence is considered so extreme that it cannot be risked or where social goals unrelated to the truth-finding process are more important than the contribution that particular types of evidence could make to that process.

Insurance

The rule regarding evidence of insurance is one of the simplest of these specialized relevance rules, so it is a good one to consider first. Rule 411 states:

> Evidence that a person was or was not insured against liability is not admissible upon the issue whether the person acted negligently or otherwise wrongfully. This rule does not require the exclusion of evidence of insurance against liability when offered for another purpose, such as proof of agency, ownership, or control, or bias or prejudice of a witness.

This rule is based on a fear that jurors who know a party has insurance may find that party liable only because they believe the liability will be cost-free to the party, or that jurors will increase the amount of damages they find, secure in the belief that only an insurance company will be affected adversely. It

17

could be argued that proof that a party has insurance does have logical relevance to the question of how carefully the party acted on a specific occasion, if one believed that people who know that they will not be financially responsible for injuries they might inflict might be more willing to take chances than people who expected that they would have to pay personally for harms they caused. That likelihood is probably slight, however. This possible logical relevance is outweighed by the fear that insurance information will distort a jury's willingness to assign liability according to a fair-minded evaluation of evidence in terms of the judge's instructions.

As a matter of fact, jurors may well have suppositions about parties' insurance, and if that is so, it might be more sensible to give them accurate information than it is to leave them to their own guesswork. This argument strikes at the reasonableness of the exclusionary rule. In circumstances where insurance information comes out at trial by error, appellate judges who decide whether the error was significant enough to require retrial may be influenced by this possible weakness in the rationale for the rule. However, at common law and under the Federal Rules, the doctrine is clear, and compliance with it is not a matter of judicial discretion.

The Rule does not prohibit all possible uses of evidence about a party's insurance coverage. If it can support findings about topics other than negligent or wrongful conduct, evidence of insurance coverage is permitted to be introduced. For example, if a defense witness works for the defendant's insurance company, information about the witness's possible financial bias would be permitted to be introduced, despite the fact that it would inform the jury about the defendant's insurance coverage.

Subsequent Remedial Measures

In negligence cases the plaintiff must show that the defendant's conduct before the plaintiff's injury was careless, and that it was a proximate cause of the accident. One technique a plaintiff might like to use to show the negligence of the defendant would be to introduce evidence that after the accident, the defendant made a repair or changed a procedure. This approach is forbidden under common law and under Rule 407. That Rule states:

> When, after an event, measures are taken which, if taken previously, would have made the event less likely to occur, evidence of the subsequent measures is not admissible to prove negligence or culpable conduct in connection with the event. This rule does not require the exclusion of evidence of subsequent measures when offered for another purpose, such as proving ownership, control, or feasibility of precautionary measures, if controverted, or impeachment.

If this rule did not exist, would evidence about subsequent repairs meet the test of the general relevance standard under Rule 401? For example, if a plaintiff claims she slipped on the defendant's loose rug, evidence that after the accident the defendant tacked down the rug would suggest that the rug had been loose at the time of the accident, and that the defendant considered it risky to leave the rug as it had been. On the other hand, the defendant's repair could have been an instance of excessive caution and therefore not a clue that the defendant was negligent in the rug's earlier maintenance. Negligence law does not require people to be extraordinarily careful, just reasonably careful. So evidence of subsequent repairs can be ambiguous, but that does not mean that it will always be unhelpful and therefore irrelevant.

Exclusion of subsequent repairs evidence involves two significant policy considerations. Proponents of the doctrine have believed that if plaintiffs were able to let jurors know about changes defendants make in response to injuries, individuals and organizations would be deterred from responding to accidents by increasing their precautions. It also seems unfair, to some, for a defendant to be penalized at a trial for taking the socially desirable action of decreasing risks.

In the language of Rule 407, evidence of subsequent remedial measures taken after an event "which, if taken previously, would have made the event less likely to occur . . . is not admissible to prove negligence or culpable conduct." There are two slightly complicated additional aspects of this exclusionary rule. First, the prohibition does not apply if evidence of subsequent repairs is offered to show something other than culpable conduct. For example, information about subsequent repairs would be admissible to show that the defendant owned or controlled the thing or the place that was involved in the accident. Evidence of subsequent remedial measures may also show that it was possible to improve whatever harmed the plaintiff; this rationale is only available, however, if the defendant controverts the feasibility of improvements.

The second complication is that decisions interpreting the federal rule and analogous state provisions disagree about whether the shield should apply in strict liability cases. A California decision[1] was the first to hold that the doctrine's policy foundation of encouraging remedial measures has no application in modern strict liability cases since manufacturers have a huge incentive to make improvements whether or not those improvements will be reported to juries in tort cases — they want to continue to sell products and they want to cut down the number of future injuries caused by their products. In addition to this functional analysis, under Rule 407 there is a strong argument that its literal words limit its application to negligence cases and prevent its application to claims based on strict liability. Under the law of most states, strict liability claims for product-related injuries do not involve

---

1. *Ault v. International Harvester Co.*, 13 Cal. 3d 113, 117 Cal. Rptr. 812, 528 P.2d 1148 (1974).

any required showing of culpable conduct since the quality of care or care-lessness is not a factor under the substantive definition of "defective product." This interpretation of the substantive law of products liability would eliminate any role for Rule 407, since by its terms it applies only to showings related to "negligence or culpable conduct." Nevertheless, the majority of states and circuit courts take the position that Rule 407 and the general common law prohibition of evidence about subsequent repairs does apply in strict liability cases. They reach that result primarily by emphasizing the aspects of strict liability theory that are functionally quite similar to negligence doctrines.

Compromises and Offers to Compromise

Another important exclusion of material that would otherwise be relevant and admissible concerns compromises and settlements. Statements made in negotiating settlements, and the fact of an accomplished settlement itself, are kept from the knowledge of the trier of fact even though many settlement offers are probably a good indication that the party that offered the settlement believed that the opponent's claims were valid. In the terms of Rule 408:

> Evidence of (1) furnishing or offering or promising to furnish, or (2) accepting or offering or promising to accept, a valuable consideration in compromising or attempting to compromise a claim which was disputed as to either validity or amount, is not admissible to prove liability for or invalidity of the claim or its amount. Evidence of conduct or statements made in compromise negotiations is likewise not admissible. This rule does not require the exclusion of any evidence otherwise discoverable merely because it is presented in the course of compromise negotiations. This rule also does not require exclusion when the evidence is offered for another purpose, such as proving bias or prejudice of a witness, negativing a contention of undue delay, or proving an effort to obstruct a criminal investigation or prosecution.

The purpose of this rule is to encourage settlements. If it did not exist, people involved in disputes might be reluctant to talk about them for fear that their words would be used against them in later trials. The proponent of this rule's application must show that there was a disputed claim. This means that Rule 408 does *not* prevent the admission of an offer of payment like, "I know I made a mistake and there's about $500 worth of damage to your car, but I'll only pay $200." Those words admit responsibility and also concede the amount of harm caused. Unless a judge were somehow persuaded that "I'll only pay $200" was really a modification of the admission that the damage amounted to $500, Rule 408 would allow testimony about the statement.

There is a distinction between: 1) offers to pay or payments; and 2) statements made in connection with negotiating for a payment. The Federal

Rule shields evidence about settlements or offered settlements *and* evidence about "conduct or statements made in compromise negotiations." In some jurisdictions statements made in settlement talks may be admissible unless the speaker or writer accompanies them with phrases like "this is hypothetical" or "for purposes of settlement only." The Federal Rule does not have any requirement of this type because the pro-settlement rationale of the rule is served best by a straightforward approach that does not trip up the unwary.

Under Rule 408, however, the protection for *conduct and statements* related to settlements is phrased in connection with "compromise negotiations." It may sometimes be difficult to know, for example, whether a conversation was part of regular business contacts between two parties or was part of something that can properly be considered compromise negotiations. The rule is meant to facilitate settlements by shielding statements made in working them out, but it is not meant to apply to statements made in non-settlement activities. If one party has sued or threatened to sue another, then it is easy to characterize their later discussions as being part of compromise negotiations. If litigation has not been mentioned, then conversations between parties are likely to be characterized as part of ordinary business give-and-take, and the things parties say in those conversations are likely to be treated as outside the coverage of Rule 408.

It is important to remember that the purpose for which a party seeks to introduce evidence relating to a settlement can be crucial. Under Rule 408, if the proponent of testimony that would reveal the fact that some parties had agreed on a settlement can show that the information is relevant in a way other than in connection with the validity of the settled claim, the information is admissible. One such use would be in a situation where the benefits of a settlement might have made a person biased in favor of the party who agreed to the settlement. If the beneficiary of the settlement became a witness in a trial and gave testimony that benefitted the provider of the settlement, a party who opposed that testimony could have the jury learn about the settlement. The settlement would be treated as relevant to the truthfulness of the witness but not as relevant to the merits of the case.

There is another important limitation to the effect of this rule. Although Rule 408 prevents a party from telling the trier of fact that his or her opponent said a particular thing during settlement talks, a party is entitled to bring the substance of that information into the trial if it is relevant and was obtainable other than in the settlement talks. Illustratively, a party cannot testify, "My opponent told me in settlement talks that his company's trucks had suffered 50 similar brake failures before the accident that hurt me." However, that party would be allowed to introduce evidence of the prior brake failures as long as he or she did not refer to the settlement talks, even if it was the opponent's disclosures during settlement talks that gave the party the idea of obtaining that evidence. A party cannot immunize information from introduction into a trial merely by mentioning it in settlement talks.

Payments of Medical Expenses

People involved in an incident that causes an injury may sometimes be motivated to pay the victim's medical expenses. Insurance companies have an incentive to provide medical care for an accident victim to decrease the magnitude of the victim's injury if they think they may ultimately have financial responsibility for the harm. These payments might not be kept secret under Rule 408 since that rule applies only where there is a disputed claim. However, a different rule facilitates this type of humanitarian payment. Rule 409 provides that:

> Evidence of furnishing or offering or promising to pay medical, hospital, or similar expenses occasioned by an injury is not admissible to prove liability for the injury.

Under this rule, proof about medical payments or offers of medical payments made outside of settlement negotiations is not admissible to show liability for the injury. In contrast to the broad protection provided in Rule 408 for conduct and statements related to compromise negotiations, Rule 409 offers no protection for statements made in connection with the payments. This difference in the scope of exclusion between Rules 408 and 409 is inconsequential to professionals, such as lawyers or employees of insurance companies, because they know about it and are guided by it in what they say or do not say. For individuals who have no counsel or who are inexperienced in the legal aftermath of accidents, the difference may not matter because their decision to pay for medical care is based not on legal considerations but on genuine humanitarian feelings.

Nolo Contendere and Withdrawn Guilty Pleas

The Federal Rules of Evidence, in parallel to Federal Rule of Criminal Procedure 11(e)(6), seek to facilitate plea bargaining by providing confidentiality for statements made in plea bargaining, for pleas of nolo contendere, and for guilty pleas that are later withdrawn. Rule 410 states:

> Except as otherwise provided in this rule, evidence of the following is not, in any civil or criminal proceeding; admissible against the defendant who made the plea or was a participant in the plea discussions:
> (1) a plea of guilty which was later withdrawn;
> (2) a plea of nolo contendere;
> (3) any statement made in the course of any proceedings under Rule 11 of the Federal Rules of Criminal Procedure or comparable state procedure regarding either of the foregoing pleas; or
> (4) any statement made in the course of plea discussions with an attorney for the prosecuting authority which do not result in a plea of guilty or which result in a plea of guilty later withdrawn.

However, such a statement is admissible (i) in any proceeding wherein another statement made in the course of the same plea or plea discussions has been introduced and the statement ought in fairness be considered contemporaneously with it, or (ii) in a criminal proceeding for perjury or false statement if the statement was made by the defendant under oath, on the record and in the presence of counsel.

The purpose of this rule is to afford significant confidentiality to an individual's statements made in the course of negotiating a plea. However, many law enforcement officials are able to avoid the rule's effects by refusing to negotiate unless the individual waives his or her rights under the rule. The United States Supreme Court has upheld the effect of such waivers, despite arguments that Congress did not intend the rule to be waivable and that allowing it to be waived may, as a practical matter, withdraw the rule's provisions from most plea negotiations.[2]

This rule has some significant details. A guilty plea that becomes the basis for a conviction is not protected from other uses. The policy of facilitating plea bargaining is not strong enough to support a doctrine insulating convictions based on plea-bargained guilty pleas from use in other contexts. For a statement to be covered by the rule, it must have been made to a prosecutor. This is meant to prevent a defendant who makes statements to detectives or other investigators from later characterizing them as part of plea bargaining to have them excluded from admission by this rule.

Compared with the rules on compromises and payments of medical expenses, Rule 410 treats the negotiating defendant differently than the negotiating civil party or the good samaritan who pays an injured victim's expenses. For example, while Rule 410 applies only where a prosecutor has been involved in negotiations, for civil compromises or payments of medical expenses there are no similar limitations on the identity of those who must be involved in negotiating or handling a medical expenses payment.

If the plea bargaining leads to a nolo contendere plea or to a plea of guilty that is later withdrawn, evidence of those pleas is inadmissible to show criminal liability for the charged offense. This may facilitate plea bargaining, and the grant of secrecy is consistent with the secrecy provided to support the pro-settlement stance of Rule 408 and the pro-humanitarian payment approach of Rule 409. However, evidence of the pleas may not even be admitted to show bias or for any other purpose different from showing criminal liability for the charged offense. This is more restrictive than parallel provisions for compromises and payments of medical expenses.

Statements made in connection with plea bargaining cannot be admitted to show liability for the charged offense. This is equivalent to Rule 408's provisions for compromises, barring use of such statements to show liability. For

---

2. *United States v. Mezzanatto*, 115 S.Ct. 797, 130 L.Ed.2d 696 (1995).

payments of medical expenses, however, any statements that may accompany the payment or offer of payment are admissible under Rule 409. Also, according to Rule 408, statements made in compromise negotiations are not barred from admission if they are relevant for a purpose other than showing liability for the original claim or injury. In the criminal law context of Rule 410, there is a much more limited treatment of the use of bargaining statements for purposes other than proving liability for the underlying offense. Statements made during plea bargaining are admissible only to complete partial disclosures that the defendant may make and in certain perjury prosecutions. The following chart summarizes the important aspects of Rules 408, 409, and 410.

CHART TWO
Admissibility of Settlements, Payments, or Pleas (or Offers to Make Them) and Related Statements and Conduct

Points of Comparision	Civil Settlements	Payments and Offers to Pay Medical Expenses	Nolo Contendere and Withdrawn Guilty Pleas
Federal Rule	408	409	410
Must there be a dispute for rule to apply?	Yes	No	Impliedly
With whom must party with potential liability deal?	Anyone who can settle disputed claim	Anyone who can accept payment	Prosecutor (not police)
Can offered or actual settlement payment or plea be admitted to show liability?	No	No	No
Can offered or actual settlement payment or plea be admitted for uses other than to show liability?	Yes	Yes	No
Can related statements or conduct be admitted to show liability?	No	Yes	No
Can related statements or conduct be admitted for uses other than to show liability?	Yes	Yes	To complete partial disclosures by defendant; also certain perjury cases

EXAMPLES

1. Consider the following chronology:

    March, 1993: a carpenter bought a power tool

    April, 1993: the tool company redesigned that product, incorporating a finger guard

    May, 1993: the carpenter's fingers were injured while she was using the tool

In a suit against the tool company, seeking damages under negligence and strict liability theories, can the carpenter introduce evidence of the April product improvement to show that the product as sold to her was defective or carelessly designed?

2. A customer says to a used car dealer, "I'm sorry I haven't made the last payment, and I have to admit the car runs fine, but I just can't afford it. I owe you $800 more, but will you accept $450?" In a later suit for the full $800, the customer claims he should not have to pay anything because the car was defective. To establish that there was nothing wrong with the car, can the dealer testify that the customer told him the car was fine?

3. Plaintiff sues defendant for money she claims is due under the terms of the settlement of a prior suit. How can the plaintiff establish her claim in the light of Rule 408's prohibitions about evidence of settlements?

4. In a malpractice case, the plaintiff wants to establish that the defendant doctor made a mistake in an operation by testifying that when the doctor looked at an X ray of the plaintiff taken after the operation, he said, "This makes it look like I did the whole operation wrong." The defendant doctor objects to the testimony, claiming that it should be excluded under Rule 408 because when he said it he suspected that the patient might sue, and he wanted to establish a rapport that would help reach a compromise. Should this testimony be kept out under Rule 408? Should the judge or the jury make the decision?

5. After an accident at a railroad crossing, the state highway department cut down trees that obstructed the view of the tracks from the road. The person injured in the accident sues the railroad, claiming that the intersection was dangerous and that therefore the railroad should have instructed its engineers to slow down when they approached it. Can the plaintiff introduce evidence about the highway department's action as relevant to the dangerousness of the intersection prior to the accident?

6. In a products liability suit, the plaintiff seeks to establish that a machine's design was unreasonably dangerous. If the manufacturer added a safety feature after the plaintiff's injury, Rule 407 prohibits introducing evidence of the change to establish negligence or culpable conduct. Suppose a

witness for the manufacturer states that the product's safety features, as present in the model that injured the plaintiff, were "the best possible" or "of the highest quality." Could that provide an avenue for bringing information about the subsequent changes into the trial?

7.   Andrew First and Bertha Second were walking across an intersection when they were both hit by a truck operated by defendant Cash Corporation. They were each hospitalized, and each accepted payments from Cash Corporation for the medical expenses. First later sues Cash. If Second testifies at the trial that Second and First were talking while they crossed the street and were not particularly attentive, could First introduce evidence that Cash paid Second's medical bills?

8.   In a medical malpractice case, an expert testifies that in his opinion, based on an examination of the plaintiff, the defendant never injured the plaintiff. If the expert works for an insurance company that would be responsible for paying a judgment against the defendant doctor, can the plaintiff bring that fact to the attention of the jury?

EXPLANATIONS

1.   This example concerns the general prohibition against using evidence of subsequent remedial measures to prove negligence or other culpability. The problem is complicated because the design change was made *after* the purchase but *before* the injury. So, was the design change a *subsequent* remedial measure? Courts have split on this issue, with the majority relating the time of the remedial measure to the time of the purchase of the product to apply the rule's prohibition against admissibility. This choice is consistent with the view that litigation risks are very important to manufacturers and that shielding them as much as possible from introduction into evidence of information about improvements or modifications will serve the public policy of encouraging sellers to continually upgrade their products. To support the contrary position, some courts have reasoned that fear of consequences in lawsuits will not deter companies from making changes if they are considering the changes before any injuries have occurred that might ultimately be the subject of suit.

    The example also serves as a reminder that strict liability actions are thought by some courts (a small minority) to be outside the coverage of Rule 407. The language of the Federal Rule is ambiguous with respect to strict liability actions. In part the responses of courts to this problem have reflected their general point of view on the underlying issue of whether evidence rules can have an important effect on willingness to adopt safety measures. The courts that believe the exclusionary rule really affects people's and companies' plans for remedial measures will be inclined to apply the rule broadly to negligence and strict liability cases. In a jurisdiction that applies the rule only to negligence cases, the material could be admitted with an instruction that the jury ignore it in deciding the strict liability aspects of the case.

2.   Yes. Attempting to whittle down the amount of an acknowledged debt is *not* the kind of conversation the rule against disclosure of settlement talks seeks to encourage. Rule 408 covers only statements and conduct in connection with claims that are disputed either as to validity or amount. In this example, there is no dispute about the quality of the car or about the total amount ($800) that is owed.

3.   The plaintiff is entitled to introduce evidence of the settlement agreement. Rule 408 only precludes admission of evidence about settlements or settlement talks if the evidence is introduced as relevant to the validity or invalidity of the underlying claim that is the subject of the negotiations. In this example, the claim is not based on whatever dispute led to the settlement. It is based on a contractual undertaking (the settlement), which can be interpreted and enforced by a court without any attention to the original dispute that it was intended to resolve.

4.   This is a reminder that the judge ordinarily has the responsibility to make preliminary rulings personally. Here the judge will decide whether the conversation is within Rule 408's characterization of compromise negotiations. If this task were assigned to the jury, jurors would listen to evidence about the challenged statement and the context in which it was made. Then the judge would tell them about Rule 408 and would tell them to ignore the statement if they concluded that it was made in the context of compromise negotiations. It might be hard for a juror to forget about the doctor's words, even if the juror did conclude that they had been spoken in settlement talks.

The evidence should be admitted. The only suggestion that the doctor's words were part of settlement negotiations comes from the doctor's statement that he suspected a suit might someday be filed. This does not satisfy the requirement in Rule 408 that a dispute be involved. Furthermore, compromise negotiations must take place in order for Rule 408's protections to be invoked. If the doctor's own predictions about litigation were permitted to turn his words into protected statements for the purpose of settlement, just about any words anyone ever says to a person who later sues him would be inadmissible at trials.

This is *not* a conditional relevance situation where the judge is required to let the jury do part of the work of deciding the fundamental relevance question. For conditional relevance, an item of evidence could be relevant to the trial as long as some additional condition was believed to have existed. Conditionally relevant evidence has a place in the trial if the result of some factual inquiry provides a logical link between the offered evidence and an issue at the trial. This is different from the Rule 408 problem, in which the doctor's words could be let in or kept out depending on the outcome of the factual issue about whether they were spoken in a compromise effort. There is a difference between: a) conditional relevance where the jury gets the initial item of evidence and then decides itself whether to use it; and b) most preliminary admissibility questions. For conditional relevance, if the additional required condition is not fulfilled, there is no risk that the jury will use the originally offered evidence, because it contradicts common sense to base a decision on nonrelevant information. In other situations, like those covered by Rule 408, it would definitely not contradict common sense or human nature for a juror to base a decision on significant words, even if principles based on independent social policies led the judge to instruct the jury to ignore them.

5.   Yes. Ordinarily evidence of subsequent remedial measures cannot be introduced to support contentions about the quality of an actor's conduct at the time of an earlier injury. However, in this situation, the remedial measures were carried out by someone other than the defendant. Keeping them secret from the jury would not serve the public policy goal of avoiding "penalizing" those who make post-accident repairs. For that reason, most courts would admit the evidence.

6.   Yes. Rule 407 prohibits the use of information about subsequent remedial measures to show culpability or negligence. It states explicitly, however, that this kind of material may be introduced for other purposes. One of the purposes listed is to show the feasibility of precautions when the defendant disputes or controverts that feasibility. The analysis of this example depends on whether the statements "highest quality" or "best possible" are equivalent to claims that there were no feasible alternatives. Many courts would characterize them that way and allow the plaintiff to introduce evidence of subsequent improvements to demonstrate that the prior design was not the "best possible" or of the "highest quality." On the other hand, if the defendant's witnesses had merely described the prior design as "good" or "excellent," it would be difficult for the plaintiff to contend that they had controverted the feasibility of alternatives.

7.   Yes. The point of introducing the evidence would be to show that Second might be biased in favor of Cash Corporation. This use of the payment information is not barred by Rule 409 even though it does exclude evidence of medical payments if the evidence is introduced to show liability for the injury. Here the rationale for introducing the evidence is to show possible motivation for Second to lie or shade the testimony favorably to Cash. The evidence would be admissible, and Cash would be entitled to a limiting instruction telling the jury that it could not infer from the fact of payments to Second that Cash was responsible for the accident.

8.   Yes. This would be a reference to insurance not to show culpability but to show that the witness might be biased to give testimony that favors his employer, the insurance company.

Character Evidence

If you wanted to hire someone to take care of a child, would you pay attention to information about the person's temperament? If you knew that an applicant was mean, nasty, or dishonest, would that affect your hiring decision? Most people would answer these questions "yes" since character traits do affect how we act. For instance, a dishonest person will commit more illegal acts than an honest person would. Experience suggests that it is reasonable to make inferences from a person's character traits to a person's likely conduct. However, evidence law often prohibits that use of information about a person's "character." In evidence law, "character" means the type of person someone is — honest, dishonest, generous, selfish, friendly, nasty, careless, cautious, hot-headed, or calm, for example. A basic rule (with some exceptions) is that evidence of a person's character may not be introduced to support an inference that the person acted on a specific occasion in conformity with that character.

Evidence law reflects deep ambivalence about the concept of character. Although there is an apparently broad prohibition against the use of character evidence, rules allow it to be used in many settings. The complex treatment of character is also reflected in rules about *how* character can be proved, which is an issue different from *whether* there is a role for character evidence in a particular case. This chapter and Chapter 5 on "Examination and Impeachment" cover the topic of character evidence. A brief overview of the ways in which evidence law controls proof about people's character will help put the various detailed explanations in context.

Character evidence to prove a person's action in conformity with that character is often prohibited. The basic rule is that information about a person's character may not be introduced to suggest that the person did something because of a propensity to do such things. The "propensity inference," that a person did something because he or she is the type of person who would likely have done it, is often forbidden. The next paragraph describes situations where evidence law does allow propensity inferences.

Character evidence to prove a person's action in conformity with that character is often allowed. In some situations, the propensity inference is explicitly allowed. First, a criminal defendant is allowed to introduce evidence about his or her own good character to support an inference that he or she did not commit a charged crime. Once a criminal defendant does this, the prosecution may introduce rebuttal evidence about the defendant's character to suggest that he or she is guilty. Second, also in criminal trials, the defendant may attempt to show that the victim was the aggressor by introducing evidence of the victim's character for violence. The prosecution may show that a murder victim had a peaceful character to rebut a claim made in any way that the victim was an aggressor. Third, relatively new provisions of the Federal Rules allow proof of a defendant's sexual propensities in sex offense trials. Finally, the process of impeachment is another circumstance where the propensity inference from character is permitted. Where an issue at trial is whether a witness has testified truthfully, evidence about that witness's character for truth-telling is permitted to be introduced to support the inference that the witness has acted at the trial in conformity with the witness's usual respect for truth. This use of character evidence, to show truthful or deceptive conduct at a trial, is explained in the chapter on "Examination and Impeachment."

Character evidence to prove a person's character is allowed. An element of a claim or defense can explicitly involve someone's character. For example, a defendant in a defamation case, accused of falsely describing the plaintiff as evil, would be permitted to prove that the plaintiff is, in fact, evil. In that type of case, evidence intended to show the nature of a person's character is allowed.

Evidence that seems like character evidence is allowed if its relevance does not depend on an inference involving a conclusion about a person's character. The propensity bar prohibits the introduction of character evidence to support inferences that because of a person's character, the person is more likely to have acted in a certain way usually linked to that character. Sometimes evidence that could support a conclusion about a person's character may have relevance independent of that type of conclusion. For example, evidence that someone charged with a crime has committed similar crimes in the past could lead a jury to think that the defendant is a criminally inclined type of person. If this were the prosecution's only justification for offering the evidence, it would be excluded by the general prohibition against propensity evidence. If the prosecution offered the evidence to show, for example, that participation in those past crimes gave the defendant skills that were specially needed in the offense for which the defendant is charged in the current trial, then admissibility would be possible. In this situation, the jury would not be asked to use the information about past conduct to determine what type of person the defendant is, but would be asked to use the information to determine that the defendant possessed a specific skill that made it more likely that he or she was the perpetrator of the charged offense.

Methods allowed for proof of character. A person's character traits can be conveyed to a finder of fact in a variety of ways. Testimony about the person's reputation or about a witness's opinion of the person is always allowed. In certain specific cases evidence about actual instances of past conduct is allowed to support inferences about a person's character. In some situations a questioner is allowed to ask about a person's past conduct to support an inference about the person's character, but is not allowed to introduce evidence (other than the response to the inquiry) about the specific past conduct.

The Propensity Inference

Suppose someone on trial for the robbery of a liquor store had robbed gas stations several times in the past. He might also have the reputation of being a thief. The propensity rule prohibits introduction of information about his reputation or the past robberies to support the inferences that he is a thief and that he therefore robbed the liquor store. Rule 404(a) establishes the general exclusion by stating:

> Evidence of a person's character or a trait of character is not admissible for the purpose of proving action in conformity therewith on a particular occasion [subject to exceptions].

This prohibition applies to civil cases with no exceptions and to criminal cases with a small number of exceptions. For civil and criminal *sexual offense* cases, however, Congress rejected this traditional analysis in 1994 legislation that added Rules 413, 414, and 415 to the Federal Rules. These provisions, discussed below, permit introduction of evidence of a defendant's past sex offense to support an inference that the defendant committed another offense of that type.

There are two main reasons for the prohibition in Rule 404(a). One is the belief that the propensity inference may lead to wrong conclusions. Another is a concern that the propensity inference would almost always be supported by evidence that carries a significant risk of unfair prejudice.

These reasons for excluding character evidence offered to show a person's propensity to act in a certain way can be examined using the liquor store robbery example. In that case, one might argue that the defendant's past crimes and reputation support an inference that he is a criminal type of person and disrespects private property, and that this supports an inference that he robbed a particular liquor store at a particular time. Rule 404(a) rejects this line of analysis. Chart Three shows this chain of inferences, highlighting the fact that it involves a middle conclusion about the defendant as a type of person.

The propensity inferences are questionable because "character" is a vague concept and because the effect of a person's character on a person's actions may be highly variable. Since character is likely to be multidimensional, and may mean different things to different people, it is difficult to be sure that evidence of gas station robberies really does support an inference that

CHART THREE
Prohibited Propensity Inferences

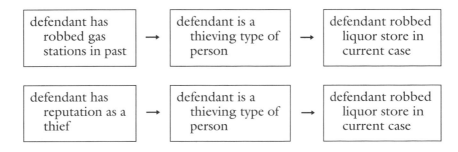

the robber is a thieving type of person (if there really is such a thing as a thieving type of person at all). Reputation evidence is similarly subject to a wide range of interpretations. It is also hard to know what a reputation for thievery really means in specific terms. Secondly, it is far from clear that people who are known to be thief-like rob liquor stores more often than other types of people do, since the external manifestations of any type of character by any particular person can be very varied.

Even though character evidence has only weak probative value, there is a large risk that jurors will be led to improper prejudice, since it is often evidence of *bad* character. For example, a juror may turn against a defendant who it learns has been a robber in the past and may wrongly convict in the current case just to impose additional punishment. A juror might also think that a weak prosecution case is good enough to support convicting a "bad" defendant, since convicting a past thief of a current crime does not blemish an otherwise clean record even if the conviction is mistaken.

For sexual offense cases, three specific rules take a position contrary to the general position of Rule 404(a). These rules specifically provide for admission of character evidence showing a person's propensity to act in conformity with his or her character. Rule 413(a) states:

> In a criminal case in which the defendant is accused of an offense of sexual assault, evidence of the defendant's commission of another offense or offenses of sexual assault is admissible, and may be considered for its bearing on any matter to which it is relevant.

Rule 414(a) states:

> In a criminal case in which the defendant is accused of an offense of child molestation, evidence of the defendant's commission of another offense or offenses of child molestation is admissible, and may be considered for its bearing on any matter to which it is relevant.

Rule 415(a) states:

> In a civil case in which a claim for damages or other relief is predicated on a party's alleged commission of conduct constituting an offense of sexual assault or child molestation, evidence of that party's commission of another offense or offenses of sexual assault or child molestation is admissible and may be considered as provided in Rule 413 and Rule 414 of these rules.

Rules 413 and 414 include definitions of "sexual assault" and "child molestation" that refer to federal and state criminal statutes and that describe various types of sexual activity. Rule 415 incorporates those definitions by reference. Rules 413, 414, and 415 also require the proponent of evidence admissible under their provisions to give notice to the party against whom it will be offered.

These rules reject the anti-propensity stance of Rule 404(a) and allow evidence of a defendant's past sexual offense to be admitted to show that the defendant has a propensity to commit that type of act. They are based on the belief that having committed a sexual offense in the past makes a person more likely to have committed another such offense than he or she would be absent that prior offense. A number of states have reached this same result under doctrines that treat evidence of "lustful disposition" as an admissible type of character evidence despite the general prohibition of character evidence as proof of action in conformity with character.

Non-propensity Uses of Character Evidence

Although proof of someone's character is kept out if offered to show action in conformity with that character on a specific occasion (except in sexual offense cases and certain other limited circumstances), it can be admitted if it is introduced for other purposes. Rule 404(b) provides illustrations of such uses:

> Evidence of other crimes, wrongs, or acts is not admissible to prove the character of a person in order to show action in conformity therewith. It may, however, be admissible for other purposes, such as proof of motive, opportunity, intent, preparation, plan, knowledge, identity, or absence of mistake or accident, provided that upon request by the accused, the prosecution in a criminal case shall provide reasonable notice in advance of trial, or during trial if the court excuses pretrial notice on good cause shown, of the general nature of any such evidence it intends to introduce at trial.

Imagine a case where a defendant, charged with manufacturing an illegal drug, claims he was conducting innocent science experiments and was unaware that the experiments produced drugs. Evidence that he had manufactured the illegal drug on other occasions would be admitted, not to show that he likes drugs or that he has the character trait of disobedience to law, but to show that he knew what he was doing. The past bad acts could show his knowledge, his intent, or "absence of mistake or accident" and would not

CHART FOUR
Comparison of Inferences Possible from Information About a Defendant's Past Wrongdoing

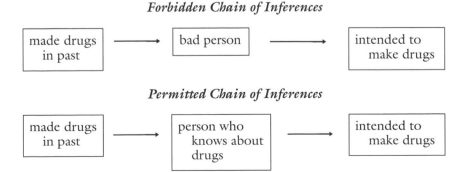

Forbidden Chain of Inferences

made drugs in past → bad person → intended to make drugs

Permitted Chain of Inferences

made drugs in past → person who knows about drugs → intended to make drugs

be prohibited by the Rule 404(a) propensity rule. Note that this chain of inferences does not require any conclusion about the defendant's character traits. Chart Four illustrates the idea that information about past drug manufacturing could be characterized as supporting a conclusion about character in general, which is forbidden, or as supporting a conclusion about the defendant's knowledge, which is permitted.

It is true that a juror who believes the defendant intentionally manufactured an illegal drug might also conclude that he is dishonest or evil. But a juror would, in theory, reach these conclusions about the defendant's character *after* deciding that he actually had violated the law on the occasion in question. Thus, the juror would not be using a belief about "character" to evaluate the person's conduct in connection with the charged offense. It cannot be said that the evidence about the defendant's past was introduced to support that forbidden train of thought. In Chart Five below, the first chain of inferences represents the forbidden "propensity" use of information about a person's character. The fact that the defendant made drugs in the past is shown as relevant to the proposition sought to be proved because it supports an inference that the defendant is a bad person. In the second chain of inferences, the information about past drug manufacturing is shown to be relevant in a way that evidence law permits. It supports an inference that the defendant knew about drugs, and that therefore he knew what he was doing.

The list in Rule 404(b) of non-propensity uses of people's past acts is not an exclusive list. It is a set of examples of types of uses that might be available for information that would otherwise seem relevant only to show that a person had a certain type of character and probably acted in conformity with that character. Information about these past acts can be presented in any form its proponent chooses. The special restrictions on style of proof that apply to character evidence have no force in a situation where evidence about a per-

CHART FIVE
Distinction Between Forbidden Character Inference and
Permitted "Surplus" Character Inference

Forbidden Chain of Inferences

Permitted Chain of Inferences, with "Surplus," Irrelevant, Inference About Character

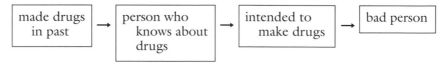

son's past conduct is introduced to support inferences about a topic *other than the person's character.*

When a party asserts a non-character rationale for introducing information about a person's past acts, the court must determine whether the claimed relevance is legitimate or is just a ploy to bring unfavorable information about that party to the jury's attention. For example, if a rare technique for disabling an alarm was used in a burglary case where the defendant claims some other person committed the crime, and the defendant had in the past committed burglaries using that unique method, information about the defendant's past acts would be relevant to establish her likely identity as the person who committed the charged offense. In this setting, the trial judge would have to make two determinations. One is whether a belief that the defendant committed the past crimes would or could reasonably support an "identity" inference that the defendant is the person who committed the charged offense. If the supposedly special technique is used by many people, then the fact that an unknown person used it to commit the charged offense does not really link the offense to the defendant. Second, the court must determine that there is adequate evidence to support a conclusion that the defendant really did commit the past acts sought to be described in the current trial as having been done by her. Each condition must be satisfied in order for the past acts information to be admissible against the defendant.

In a kidnapping case, evidence that the defendant had been convicted in the past for buying narcotics could be characterized as showing that the defendant had a motive to demand ransom because he needed money to support a drug habit. In a trial for bank robbery, evidence that a person stole a car might be admissible if the car was used to commit the robbery. These uses would be described as evidence of a past bad act admissible to show a plan. Chart Six illustrates some of the ways in which the links might be established between a defendant and past conduct, and between that conduct and conduct on the occasion under scrutiny in the trial. It shows that the proponent of evidence in this situation must always make at least two logical connections: one is between the defendant and the past conduct, and the other is between the past conduct and the charged offense.

Even if a defendant has been acquitted of past charged crimes, evidence of a possible connection with those crimes could be used against him or her in a new case. Acquittal, after all, means that the prosecution failed to prove its case beyond a reasonable doubt; it does not represent a finding that the defendant did not commit the alleged offense. So a defendant could be tried for committing a fraud through a unique set of representations and could be acquitted, yet information about the past accusations could be used in a new trial if the defendant were accused of perpetrating the same fraud against a new victim. The general relevance test — does the information make a significant fact more likely to be true than it would be in the absence of that information — is applied here, even though the ultimate decision in a criminal case is required to satisfy the beyond a reasonable doubt standard.

CHART SIX
Examples of Possible Links Between Defendant,
Past Acts, and a Current Charged Offense

Person	Type of Link	One Past Event	Type of Link	Another Past Event
Defendant	Convicted of past con- duct; or	Past Conduct	Marks the de- fendant as one with special knowledge or methods of action; or	Charged Offense
	Described (ad- equately for preponder- ance test) as connected with past conduct; or		Establishes mo- tive for committing charged offense	
	Acquitted of past conduct			

The proponent of past bad acts evidence has the burden of persuading the judge that the information has some relevance to the current trial other than to support a conclusion that the defendant is a bad person and therefore is more likely to have committed the charge offense. Additionally, because past bad acts evidence is so likely to involve a risk of unfair prejudice, the trial judge will consider the relationship between its probative value and that risk of unfair prejudice under Rule 403. In evaluating the probative value of the evidence, the court will be strongly influenced by the proponent's need for the evidence. If there are other ways to establish whatever the proponent says the past bad acts evidence will show, courts will ordinarily exclude the past bad acts and relegate the proponent to less inflammatory proof of that issue. Where other evidence is not available for the non-propensity purpose that the past bad acts evidence could serve, such as proof of a plan, a motive, or absence of mistake, then despite the risks of juror misuse of the information, the past bad acts material is properly admitted. Because evidence admitted under Rule 404(b) is often strongly damaging, and because analyzing its relevance may be difficult, the rule entitles criminal defendants to notice in advance if the prosecution intends to rely on Rule 404(b) for admissibility.

Note that Rules 413, 414, and 415, discussed above, allow introduction of evidence of a defendant's past sexual offenses to support an inference that the defendant committed another such offense.

"Character in Issue"

Other situations in which evidence about a person's character avoids the propensity bar are sometimes referred to as "character in issue" cases. For example, in a defamation case there may be a dispute about whether a description of the plaintiff was true. Each side can legitimately introduce evidence on that point without implicating the rule against using character evidence to support an inference that a person acts in conformity with his or her character. The point of introducing evidence about character in a case where, for example, a defendant is accused of defaming a plaintiff by describing him or her as "a thief" would be to show whether the plaintiff is a thief. This is different from using information about the plaintiff to support an inference about whether the plaintiff acted in conformity with thief-like character on any particular occasion. As Chart Seven illustrates, the chain of inferences involving character in a defamation case is different from the forbidden propensity inferences. In the defamation case, character is proved to show character. In the prohibited propensity use of character evidence, character would be used to show action in conformity with that character.

Instances are rare where data about a person's character can be relevant other than by supporting an inference about action in conformity with that

CHART SEVEN
Allowable Non-propensity Use of Character for "Character in Issue" Case Contrasted with Prohibited Propensity Use in Other Cases

Acceptable Chain of Inferences where Substantive Law Makes Person's Character Relevant by Itself and Not as a Means of Inferring Something About the Person's Actions

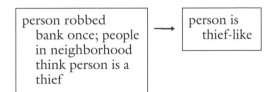

Forbidden Chain of Inferences where Actor's Character is Relevant Only is a Means of Inferring Something About the Person's Actions

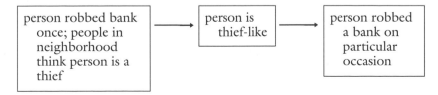

character. One other example would be the litigation about the tort of negligent entrustment, where a plaintiff alleges that the defendant was culpably careless in letting a particular individual operate a car or some kind of machine. To show that the defendant was negligent, the plaintiff could introduce evidence about the character of the operator to show not that the person drove badly or operated a machine badly on a specific occasion, but to show that based on what the defendant should have known about the operator, the defendant should not have let him or her be in control of the car or machine. (Proof that the operator really did do a poor job of driving or machine work would have to be made in some non-propensity way, such as through eyewitness testimony about what actually happened.) Negligent hiring cases may sometimes fit this description since a jurisdiction's substantive law may make it negligent, for example, to hire a violent person to work as a security guard.

Habit

A concept related to character is "habit." Knowing that a driver always comes to a full stop at stop signs and looks both ways would support an inference that the driver is a cautious and law-abiding individual. If information about that habit were introduced to support that inference about character, it would usually be excluded. But evidence of habits is considered relevant to how a person acted on a specific occasion in a way that does not involve consideration of the person's general character. Rule 406 describes evidence of habits, as well as routines of organizations, specifically and makes it clear that the propensity rule does not keep them out. It states, "[e]vidence of the habit of a person or of the routine practice of an organization . . . is relevant to prove that the conduct of the person or organization on a particular occasion was in conformity with the habit or routine practice." This makes sense, since a decision that a person with the habit of stopping for stop signs really did stop at a stop sign on a particular occasion need not be based on an inference about the person's character traits in a broad sense. Chart Eight illustrates this.

Where a way of acting is as specific and automatic as a "habit," the problems with ordinary character evidence disappear. There is very little ambiguity about proof that someone, for example, always locks his car door when he leaves his car. On the other hand, there is vast ambiguity about a trait such as calmness or honesty. And once a habit is proven as well as it can be, there is a strong relationship between a habit like door-locking (or obeying stop signs as illustrated in Chart Eight) in general and conduct on a specific occasion. In contrast, even if a general character attribute like honesty is proven, the relationship between the trait and conduct on a specific occasion is bound to be weak. For these reasons, evidence of habits is not excluded by the propensity

CHART EIGHT
Inferences from Evidence that a Person Has a Habit
of Stopping at Stop Signs

Permitted Inference

Forbidden, But Unnecessary, Inference

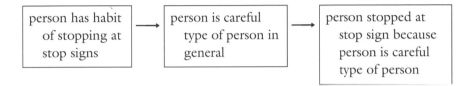

prohibition. Because of this, habit can be proved with any relevant evidence, including evidence about a person's specific past conduct.

In order for past conduct to be treated as habit evidence rather than as information that is relevant only as a basis for a general inference about the actor's character, a judge must be persuaded that the conduct in question is virtually automatic and has been repeated many times in the past. When that showing is made, the judge will treat the material differently from "character" evidence. "Stops at stop signs" and "quick to get angry" are examples, respectively, of habit and character evidence. In a sense, however, they are both ways of describing how a person acts in life. The main difference between them is that the stop sign conduct is easy to describe, can be demonstrated to have occurred repeatedly, and can be compared easily to whatever situation is in dispute at a trial. The conduct described as getting angry quickly may be much harder to describe accurately, and it may be difficult to show that it has been repeated in circumstances that are manifestly similar to the circumstances under study at a trial.

Form of Proof Related to Character

An important aspect of character evidence is understanding the methods of proof allowed in different contexts. Rule 405 defines the permitted techniques for proving character. This rule, it should be remembered, does not specify *whether* character evidence is legitimate in any particular circumstance. Rule 404 accomplishes that task. Rule 405 is subsidiary to Rule 404 and deals with *how* character can be proved in any situation where Rule 404 allows any attention at all to the topic of character. The rule states:

> (a) Reputation or opinion. In all cases in which evidence of character or a trait of character of a person is admissible, proof may be made by testimony as to reputation or by testimony in the form of an opinion. On cross-examination, inquiry is allowable into relevant specific instances of conduct.

> (b) Specific instances of conduct. In cases in which character or a trait of character of a person is an essential element of a charge, claim, or defense, proof may also be made of specific instances of that person's conduct.

This rule applies to "character in issue" cases and to certain instances of allowable character evidence defined in Rule 404(a)(1) and 404(a)(2). It does not apply to the propensity inferences that are forbidden by Rule 404(a). Since they are prohibited, there is no style of proof through which the character on which those inferences would be based can be proved. Where Rule 404(b) is a proponent's theory of relevancy, Rule 405 again has no application because it governs proof of character, while evidence is admitted under Rule 404(b) only on the premise that its relevancy does not depend on conclusions about a person's character. Habit evidence is also excluded from the coverage of Rule 405 since it is defined as something different from character evidence. Finally, Rule 405 does not control the method for proof of character allowed under Rules 413, 414, and 415, since those rules treat that issue explicitly.

"Character in issue" cases are an exceptional situation in which proof of character is permitted to be in the form of information about specific conduct (as well as in the forms of reputation and opinion testimony). Assume that a worker injures a plaintiff, and the plaintiff seeks damages from the worker's employer alleging that it was negligent for the employer to entrust someone like the worker with the job that led to the plaintiff's injury. In this type of case, the worker's character will be an essential element of the plaintiff's claim (fitting Rule 405(b)'s definition) since the plaintiff alleges that it was negligent to hire a person with the worker's particular character traits. Proof of character would be used to influence the fact finder to arrive at a conclusion specifically about the worker's character (a use which is not prohibited by Rule 404(a).

On the other hand, if the issue in that plaintiff's suit was not improper hiring but allegedly improper performance by the worker, evidence about the worker's character would not be essential to the plaintiff's claim. Its only relation to an issue at the trial would be the forbidden propensity relationship: Because the worker is a certain type of person, he or she probably acted carelessly when the plaintiff was hurt. There is no basis for the plaintiff, in this second version of the case, to say that the legal theory of the case requires the jury to form a conclusion about the worker's personal traits. In the first case, a conclusion on that topic is required because it is the employer's alleged disregard of those traits that is claimed to have been negligent.

EXAMPLES

1.   A 60-year-old man is on trial for sexual assault on a 14-year-old girl. The prosecution knows that he was once married to a woman significantly younger than he was, and that he has also had consensual sexual relations on several occasions with women much younger than himself. If the defendant denies committing the charged crime, can the prosecution introduce evidence about his past marriage and other sexual conduct?

2.   As part of its case in a bank robbery trial, the prosecution produces testimony of an eyewitness that the robbers fled the bank in a blue Chevrolet. The prosecution seeks to introduce evidence showing that the defendant had stolen a blue Chevrolet an hour before the bank robbery. In what context might this evidence be admissible, despite the general prohibition of propensity character evidence?

3.   In a defamation trial, the plaintiff seeks to prove that the defendant called him a barbaric skinflint, in order to recover damages for that defamation. The defendant admits having described the plaintiff that way, but asserts the defense of truth. May the defendant introduce evidence that the plaintiff has a reputation as a cheapskate? May the defendant introduce testimony about specific acts of cruelty the plaintiff has committed against animals?

4.   The treasurer of a charitable organization is accused of embezzlement. Large sums of money under her control have disappeared, and she has adopted a lifestyle seemingly far more costly than her earnings would allow. In a criminal prosecution for embezzlement, may the prosecution introduce evidence that the defendant has lied to a university in applying to graduate school and has been convicted of bigamy?

5.   The defendant is on trial for murder, accused of shooting the victim with a rifle. If there is evidence that a year earlier he had attempted to poison someone, can the prosecution plausibly argue that it should be allowed to introduce that evidence as relevant to the defendant's intent or identity?

6.   A patient sues a doctor, claiming that the doctor carelessly forgot to warn the patient about side effects from a prescription drug. The doctor claims that she did give the patient that information. Can the doctor testify that she is very careful in all her work and therefore must have given the proper warnings? Can she testify that whenever she hands a prescription to a patient she shows the patient the name of the drug on the prescription and discusses how to take the medicine and what risks are involved in it?

7.   *D* is on trial for shoplifting, specifically for stealing a magazine from a large drug store. He claims that he had bought a large number of items, and

that the owner of the store, after accepting payment for those items, said to him, "Help yourself to a magazine on the way out." He would like to introduce testimony from witnesses showing that in the past the owner had sometimes offered free boxes of candy to three or four customers in a single day. Is this "character" evidence? Is this evidence admissible?

8.   What if the defendant in Example 7 offered testimony that in the past the owner has offered free *magazines* to three or four customers in a single day? Would this evidence have a better chance of admissibility?

EXPLANATIONS

1.   The only logical relevance the information has to the prosecution claim is that it could lead a jury to think of the defendant as typically interested in sexual relations with women much younger than himself, and that this belief could support an inference that on a particular occasion the defendant acted in conformity with that interest. This would be an instance of the forbidden propensity inference and could not be a basis for admitting the evidence in federal court. In some states there is an exception to the propensity prohibition for evidence that shows characteristic sexual depravity. While those states will not allow evidence of past robberies to be introduced in a defendant's trial for a current robbery, in a trial for a sex offense they will admit evidence of past sexual offenses on the theory that they show something about the defendant's sexual character that can reliably be a basis for decision in the current case.

2.   Stealing a car could be treated as evidence showing a plan to rob a bank rather than as evidence which only has relevance to support an inference of the actor's bad character. The prosecution might be able to persuade the judge that the use of stolen cars in robberies is common enough so that a car theft can properly be linked to a later bank robbery as an element of a common plan.

     Additionally, if a witness saw the defendant steal the car and can thus identify the defendant in connection with that car, and if the witness to the robbery can identify the car but does not have the ability to identify the defendant, then the evidence linking the defendant to the car would be relevant as identification evidence. Showing the defendant's connection, then, to the earlier car theft would be for the purpose of providing circumstantial evidence of his identity as the person who robbed the bank.

3.   Yes. The point of using testimony about either reputation or past acts of the plaintiff would be to support a jury inference about his character. Since the plaintiff's character is itself an issue under the substantive law of defamation, the propensity rule has no impact on the case. Note that the theory of relevance rejected by the propensity rule would be the following: After the jury concluded something about the plaintiff's character it then went on to infer that because the plaintiff had a certain character the plaintiff probably

acted in conformity with it on a specific occasion. That conclusion is not required for the defendant's defense of "truth" in the defamation case. The possibility that the jurors might reach such conclusions does not eliminate the legitimate possible use of the material that is justified by the relevance of character in defamation.

4.   No. A common mistake in this situation is to notice that embezzlers are usually corrupt and deceitful people and to jump to the wrong conclusion that "deceitful character" is an element of the charged crime. To put you in jail for embezzlement, the prosecution does *not* have to show that you are generally a lying or stealing type of person. All the prosecution is required to do is show (beyond a reasonable doubt) that you took money that didn't belong to you. People of generally honest character may sometimes be embezzlers and so may people of criminal dispositions. But no principle of substantive criminal law establishes, as an element of the crime of embezzlement, that "bad character" is required to be shown to support a conviction. Therefore, Rule 404(a) prohibits use of this evidence.

5.   The only way the past poisoning attempt would show "intent" on the occasion of the shooting incident would be if the jury reasoned that a person who tries to poison someone has an evil or murderous character, and that having such a character makes it likely that on another occasion he acted in conformity with it. This is the prohibited propensity inference. Another facet of this example that makes its resolution easy is that the issue of intent can be dealt with clearly from the explicit facts of the case, namely the use of a rifle for shooting at the victim. Where conduct is ambiguous, there may be greater latitude for allowing introduction of earlier instances of similar conduct to shed light on the probable facts of the conduct on the specific occasion that is being evaluated at the trial.

Facts about the past poisoning attempt can identify the defendant as the shooter only if the jury makes the propensity inference. The past poisoning incident by the defendant makes it likely that he was involved in the shooting only if it is used by the jury as a basis for a belief that the defendant is a murdering type of person. Information about past acts known to have been committed by someone accused of a new offense can show the identity of the accused as the actual wrongdoer only if the new offense and the past acts have very strong similarities. Thus, if someone who has in the past committed crimes with a distinctive method or "signature," that fact will be admissible in a trial where he or she is accused of committing a new crime in that specific way. It shows the defendant's likely participation in the new crime without requiring a jury to reason that because he or she committed the past crimes, the defendant probably has character traits that support an inference of guilt.

6.   Testimony that she is "always careful" would be kept out. It describes the doctor's character trait of being responsible and non-negligent, and for that reason is excluded from the trial if sought to be introduced to support

the conclusion that on a specific occasion the doctor acted in conformity with that character. Could "being careful" be treated as a habit? To do that would be to eliminate almost all of the propensity bar since most traits of character could be described as habitual ways of being. The second kind of testimony in this problem, that the doctor gives warnings when she hands patients prescriptions, describes what the Federal Rules intend to characterize as a habit. The conduct is routine, repeated often, and does not involve reflection.

7.   This testimony could support an inference that the owner is generous. If the defendant wanted the trier of fact to infer from the owner's generosity the idea that he acted generously on a specific occasion, this is precisely the type of inference the propensity rule prohibits. Could this evidence be treated as "habit" testimony? That approach would fail since the process of offering free candy involves a lot of conscious volition, was apparently infrequent, and was not shown to be a nearly automatic response to virtually every occurrence of a particular circumstance. Furthermore, the defendant is not interested in establishing that the defendant offered him candy since he is charged with stealing a magazine.

8.   There may be a category of evidence of conduct in between habit and character. Here the defendant's argument for admissibility would fail if he claimed that the information about past gifts of magazines indicated a habit. (The gifts involved free will, were not frequent, and were not a uniform response to all instances of a particular stimulus.) Admissibility would also be barred if the evidence was offered to establish the forbidden propensity inference. A chain of inferences from "past gifts of magazines" to "generous nature" to "probably did offer a free magazine to defendant" would be prohibited by the propensity rule because it involves reasoning from a belief about the type of person the storekeeper is. However, it is possible that the defendant can point to another chain of inferences: from "past gifts of magazines" to "frequent although not habitual magazine giver" to "probably did offer a free magazine to defendant." The defendant would have to persuade a judge that the middle conclusion, "frequent although not habitual magazine giver," is quite different from the middle conclusion, "generous type of person," which clearly implicates the rule against character evidence used to show action in conformity with character.

Some of the reasons character evidence is kept out include: Descriptions of personality attributes are sometimes very vague or likely to mean different things to different people; and it is hard to be sure what kinds of specific conduct are probably related to people's possession of various personality, or character, attributes. Here these problems loom large if the middle conclusion is "generous." The problems are much smaller if the middle conclusion is "person who sometimes gives away magazines." The effort to persuade the trier of fact that the owner really has the trait of giving away magazines sometimes is straightforward and does not involve ambiguity. The notion that past magazine giving is related to magazine giving on a specific later occasion is also fairly direct. A juror could reasonably use information about past magazine giving to evaluate the claim that the owner offered a free magazine to the defendant without reaching any conclusion about the owner's overall character trait of generosity. It is also important to notice that there is no risk of unfair prejudice here. Jurors are not likely to have feelings one way or the other about magazine giving. Also, any prejudice that might be felt would be against one of the prosecution's witnesses (the owner) and not about the defendant. Prejudice against the defendant is much more serious than prejudice against a witness in a case.

In circumstances like these, courts are frequently willing to use the nonpropensity examples of Rule 404(b) quite generously. Perhaps the past magazine giving would be admitted under the theory that it negatived a possible mistake by the owner or that it showed a plan or method of doing business. Using these descriptions this way distorts them but serves the beneficial result of letting the evidence in.

Character of the Accused and the Victim

A defendant is allowed to introduce evidence of his or her own character to support the inference that he or she did not commit a charged crime. This permitted inference (good character shows the defendant did not commit the crime) is analytically identical to the ordinarily prohibited propensity inference (bad character shows the defendant did commit the crime). The fact that defendants control whether the propensity inferences can be used at their trials shows our system's fundamental interest in giving defendants ample opportunities to protect themselves from being found guilty. Three complications go along with this defendants' option. First, the defendant is permitted to introduce this type of character evidence only through the testimony of witnesses who state an *opinion* about the defendant's general character or report on what *reputation* the defendant has in some community. Second, the prosecutor is entitled to cross-examine these character witnesses by asking whether they have heard or know about specific past actions by the defendant. Third, when a defendant chooses to introduce testimony about his or her character, the prosecution may respond with its own witnesses about the defendant's character.

Notice that evidence law *forbids* the use of inferences from general character to conduct on specific occasions, *but allows* a criminal defendant to use that precise chain of inferences to disprove guilt, *and allows* a prosecutor to use it, too, if the defendant does first. The defendant's ability to inform the jury about his or her character is sometimes called the "mercy rule." A defendant must prove character by *reputation* or *opinion* evidence instead of with information about specific instances of past conduct, but a prosecutor may bring in the defendant's *past conduct* by asking the defendant's character witnesses about it. This is a confused welter of illogical rules, described by the Supreme Court in the famous *Michelson* case as "archaic, paradoxical, and full of compromises and compensations by which an irrational advantage to one side is offset by a poorly reasoned counter-privilege to the other."[3]

Understanding the Federal Rules treatment of evidence about the character of an accused and a victim requires another look at Rule 404(a). That Rule states:

> Evidence of a person's character or a trait of character is not admissible for the purpose of proving action in conformity therewith on a particular occasion, except:
>
> (1) Character of accused. Evidence of a pertinent trait of character offered by an accused, or by the prosecution to rebut the same;
>
> (2) Character of victim. Evidence of a pertinent trait of character of the victim of the crime offered by an accused, or by the prosecution to rebut the same, or evidence of a character trait of peacefulness of the victim offered by the prosecution in a homicide case to rebut evidence that the victim was the first aggressor;
>
> (3) [impeachment uses of character evidence].

A criminal defendant is entitled to introduce evidence of his or her "pertinent" character traits. The policy that supports this exception from the general rule excluding propensity inferences is that criminal defendants may sometimes have a very hard time refuting mistaken eyewitness testimony or developing other avenues of exculpatory proof. Recognizing these difficulties, common law tradition has allowed defendants the opportunity to have a jury know that they have acquired good reputations. At common law, a defendant's character witness can testify that the defendant has a generally decent, law-abiding character. The Federal Rules requirement that the trait be pertinent suggests, for example, that evidence of a defendant's trait of nonviolence would not be admitted in an embezzlement case. In a trial for theft, evidence about the defendant's honesty and typically careful treatment of other people's property would clearly be admissible. Additionally, testimony that a defendant is generally law-abiding may be treated as pertinent to any criminal charge.

Under common law, the defendant's character evidence was required to be in the form of testimony about the defendant's *reputation*. The Federal Rules have liberalized this to a slight extent, with Rule 405(a) permitting testimony based on *reputation or opinion*. A witness may have a basis for a personal opinion about the defendant, even if that defendant is not well-known enough in a community to have a reputation in it. The defendant is forbidden to introduce evidence of specific conduct to support inferences about his

---

3. *Michelson v. United States*, 335 U.S. 469, 487 (1948).

or her character. Even though a jury might develop a more accurate idea of how a person acts by learning about actual past actions (rather than by hearing summaries of reputation or opinions held by others), that type of evidence is prohibited. Besides making character evidence easier for defendants to obtain by allowing opinions as well as reports of reputations, the Federal Rules make one other pro-defendant change from the common law: A witness may describe the defendant's reputation in a particularized community such as a workplace instead of being required to report on reputation in a city or town.

Once a criminal defendant "opens the door" by introducing character evidence, the prosecutor is permitted to cross-examine the defendant's character witnesses and to introduce rival character witnesses. In cross-examining the defendant's character witnesses, the prosecutor is allowed to "inquire into" any "relevant specific instances of conduct" by the defendant (Rule 405(a)). This means that the prosecutor may ask a character witness for the defendant questions like "Have you heard that the defendant once hijacked a school bus?" or "Did you know that the defendant once hijacked a school bus?" This is a marked contrast to the rules governing the defendant's treatment of the character witness since the defendant is prohibited from asking about specific past events. However, while the prosecutor is allowed to ask about events, the prosecutor is not allowed to introduce independent proof about them and is required to accept whatever answer the character witness gives. The somewhat tortured rationale for this assortment of privileges and restrictions is that the prosecutor's questions are not intended to bring the facts of the past acts to the attention of the jury as a basis for the jury's evaluation of the *defendant*. They are meant to give the jury a basis for evaluating the *defendant's character witness* by showing how well that witness really knows the defendant's reputation or by showing what kinds of standards that witness has in mind when describing a person as having good qualities.

To respond to a defendant's character evidence, the prosecutor is also permitted to introduce testimony from other character witnesses. When this happens, the form of testimony by the prosecutor's witness is required to be the same as the form of testimony from witnesses for the defendant. That is, the witness can only report the defendant's general reputation in some community or locale and can give his own opinion of the defendant's character, but is forbidden to discuss specific instances of past acts by the defendant.

A few additional rules apply generally in criminal cases. Under Rule 404(a)(2), the defendant is entitled to introduce evidence about the character of the victim, and the prosecution is then entitled to respond with its own character evidence about the victim. This provision applies mainly to situations where someone accused of assault claims self-defense. That allegation leads to two issues for which character evidence is relevant. The first is the factual question of whether the victim actually did assault the defendant. The defendant is allowed to introduce evidence showing that the victim had an aggressive or violent character to support an inference that the victim was the aggressor. In this instance, the usually forbidden propensity inference is allowed. Character evidence can also support a defendant's self-defense claim by persuading the jury that the defendant could reasonably have feared the victim because the defendant knew the victim had a reputation for violence. When a defendant introduces character evidence on either of these rationales, the prosecution can then introduce contrary character evidence to refute the defendant's showing. In homicide cases, the prosecution is sometimes entitled to introduce evidence about the victim's character even if the defendant chooses not to use that kind of material. It will be given that right if the defendant introduces non-character evidence suggesting that the victim was the aggressor. Rule 405 requires that all of this material be in the form of reputation or opinion testimony since the character of the victim is relevant only as a stepping stone to the ultimate inference about the victim's conduct.

For sexual offense cases, Rule 413 states that "evidence of the defendant's commission of another offense or offenses of sexual assault is admissible." Rule 414 has similar language for child molestation, and Rule 415 has similar language for civil cases involving sexual assault or child molestation. The legislative history of these rules indicates that the proponent of this type of proof must introduce evidence of specific instances of conduct, rather than reputation or opinion evidence. A criminal defendant would be entitled to respond to evidence of his or her past acts with reputation or opinion evidence, under Rule 404(a)(1).

The Rule 415 provision allowing evidence of a party's past acts in civil suits involving sexual assault or child molestation is the only provision in the Federal Rules that allows introduction of character evidence in a civil case as relevant to someone's conduct out of court. It is not clear whether a civil party would be entitled to use reputation or opinion evidence in response to evidence of specific acts introduced by his or her opponent under Rule 415. Rule 404(a)(1) allows an "accused" to introduce evidence of pertinent character traits, but it does not apply to civil cases.

Character of the Sexual Assault Victim

It was once common for the defendant in a sexual assault prosecution to introduce evidence about the alleged victim's character to suggest that because she was sexually experienced ("unchaste") she had probably lied while testifying or had probably consented to sexual contact. Under the Federal Rules and in most states now, there is special treatment for this type of character evidence, typically with requirements meant to shield alleged victims from personal questions that have only slight relevance to the case. The Federal Rules allow evidence about an alleged sexual assault victim's past sexual behavior only in limited circumstances. Rule 412 provides:

(a) Evidence generally inadmissible. The following evidence is not admissible in any civil or criminal proceeding involving alleged sexual misconduct except as provided in subdivisions (b) and (c):

(1) Evidence offered to prove that any alleged victim engaged in other sexual behavior.

(2) Evidence offered to prove any alleged victim's sexual predisposition.

(b) Exceptions.

(1) In a criminal case, the following evidence is admissible, if otherwise admissible under these rules:

(A) evidence of specific instances of sexual behavior by the alleged victim offered to prove that a person other than the accused was the source of semen, injury or other physical evidence;

(B) evidence of specific instances of sexual behavior by the alleged victim with respect to the person accused of the sexual misconduct offered by the accused to prove consent or by the prosecution; and

(C) evidence the exclusion of which would violate the constitutional rights of the defendant.

(2) In a civil case, evidence offered to prove the sexual behavior or sexual predisposition of any alleged victim is admissible if it is otherwise admissible under these rules and its probative value substantially outweighs the danger of harm to any victim and of unfair prejudice to any party. Evidence of an alleged victim's reputation is admissible only if it has been placed in controversy by the alleged victim.

(c) Procedure to determine admissibility.

(1) A party intending to offer evidence under subdivision (b) must:

(A) file a written motion at least 14 days before trial specifically describing the evidence and stating the purpose for which it is offered unless the court, for good cause requires a different time for filing or permits filing during trial; and

(B) serve the motion on all parties and notify the alleged victim or, when appropriate, the alleged victim's guardian or representative.

(2) Before admitting evidence under this rule the court must conduct a hearing in camera and afford the victim and parties a right to attend and be heard. The motion, related papers, and the record of the hearing must be sealed and remain under seal unless the court orders otherwise.

The logical premise of this rule is that evidence of a person's past sexual conduct is rarely relevant to a question about how the person acted sexually on a specific occasion. This may conflict with the underlying premise of Rules 413, 414, and 415, which require admission of evidence of a defendant's past sexual offenses as relevant to the question of the defendant's sexual conduct on a specific occasion.

Rule 412, for criminal cases, does allow introduction of evidence of an alleged victim's past sexual conduct if it could support a claim that someone other than the defendant was the source of an injury or of semen connected with the alleged assault. If the past conduct involved the accused, evidence about it can be admitted to support a claim that the alleged victim consented to sexual behavior, or to support a claim that the defendant had engaged in a pattern of misconduct with the alleged victim.

The rule also states, for criminal cases, that evidence of an alleged victim's sexual behavior in additional circumstances may be admitted if the constitution requires it to be admitted (of course, constitutional requirements would supersede the rule's restrictions whether or not the rule stated that possibility explicitly).

The rule's provision for civil cases is less detailed than its provision for criminal cases. Rule 412(b)(2) sets up a general balancing test that compares probative value of any kind of sexual conduct proof with the dangers of unfair prejudice and harm to the alleged victim, instead of referring specifically to proof about physical injury, semen, or consent. This balancing test is different in two ways from the usual balancing test set out in Rule 403. Harm to the alleged victim is a relevant factor under Rule 412(b)(2), although it is not mentioned in Rule 403. Also, the proponent of evidence under the balancing test in Rule 412(b)(2) must show that its probative value "substantially outweighs" its dangers, while evidence is admissible under Rule 403 unless its dangers substantially outweigh its probative value. This means that when the balance is close under Rule 412(b)(2), the judge must exclude the evidence. Rule 403 is written to favor admissibility when the balance is close.

The hearing provisions in this rule are consistent with its underlying intent to protect alleged sexual assault victims from being embarrassed by questions about personal subjects that cannot be justified as part of the trial process. The hearing on admissibility of evidence of the alleged victim's past sexual conduct or predisposition is held in camera, and the record is ordinarily kept sealed. If a judge believes on the basis of such a hearing that information the defendant wants to present about the alleged victim would be properly admitted if the information is true, this presents a situation of conditional relevance. The judge would allow introduction of the evidence, since Rule 104(b) requires the jury (not the judge) to decide whether some "condition of fact" has been fulfilled.

Constitutional Restrictions on Exclusion of Defense Evidence

In a well-known case, *Chambers v. Mississippi*,[4] the Supreme Court held that "[t]he rights to confront and cross-examine witnesses and to call witnesses in one's own behalf have long been recognized as essential to due process." The defendant had been convicted of murdering a police officer despite the fact that another man (Gable McDonald) had admitted committing the crime.

---

4. 410 U.S. 284 (1973).

State rules prohibited the defendant from impeaching McDonald when he testified that he had not confessed to the murder, and also prevented the defendant from introducing testimony from other witnesses about that confession. These prohibitions deprived the defendant of "a trial in accord with traditional and fundamental standards of due process." The court was influenced in reaching this conclusion by its beliefs that the rejected evidence had substantial circumstantial guarantees of trustworthiness and that the "voucher" rule, which prevented the defendant from impeaching the individual who had allegedly confessed to the crime, did not have a sound basis in policy.

Chambers does not provide clear guidance for evaluating the constitutionality of exclusion of defense evidence, in general, even though it does establish that some exclusions may be so poorly based or so strongly outcome-determinative that they are unconstitutional. In the context of rape shield statutes, the issues raised by *Chambers* may be significant. Where a strong argument about relevancy of a rape complainant's past sexual conduct is made, there is a possibility that the exclusionary provisions of Rule 412 may be unconsitutional. For example, if a defendant's knowledge of an alleged victim's reputation for consenting to sexual intercourse might affect a jury finding on the issue of intent to commit rape, *Chambers* might require that proof of that reputation be admitted if the defendant's evidence about the reputation was clear and detailed enough to support the argument for its relevance.

Another Supreme Court decision, *Crane v. Kentucky*,[5] held that it was unconstitutional for a state to prohibit a criminal defendant from introducing evidence intended to show that his confession had been coerced. The issue of coercion had been decided against the defendant, outside the hearing of the jury, in a judge's ruling on a motion to suppress the confession. The Supreme Court held that notwithstanding the trial court's ruling that the confession was voluntary enough to satisfy constitutional standards, the defendant's evidence supporting a contention that the confession had been coerced could have influenced the jury in evaluating the truthfulness or accuracy of the confession. In the absence of strong reasons to support the state court decision to exclude the defendant's evidence, the significant adverse impact of its exclusion on the defendant's case made the exclusion unconstitutional.

Summary of Permitted Uses of Propensity Evidence

The following chart summarizes the permitted uses of character evidence to show that a person acted in conformity with that character on a specific occasion. Not included in the chart are two other circumstances in which char-

---

5. 476 U.S. 683 (1986).

acter evidence is admissible. One is impeachment, covered in Chapter 5. The other is character evidence introduced to prove character rather than to prove actions in conformity with character. Where a person's character is an ultimate issue in a case, all methods of proving it are permitted. It is also important to remember that when a witness provides opinion or reputation

CHART NINE
Character Evidence Offered to Show Conduct in Conformity with that Character on a Specific Occasion: Summary

Evidence About	May be Introduced by	Reputation or Opinion Proof Allowed?	Extrinsic Specific Acts Proof Allowed
Defendant's traits inconsistent with commission of charged crime	Defendant. FRE 404(a)(1)	YES	NO
Defendant's traits consistent with commission of charged crime	Prosecution to rebut defendant's character evidence. FRE 404(a)(1)	YES	NO
Defendant's sex-related traits in sex offense or child molestation case	Plaintiff, prosecutor or defendant. FRE 404(a)(1), 413, 414, 415	YES, introduced by a criminal defendant or by the prosecution to rebut such proof. FRE 404(a)(1)	YES, introduced by any party. FRE 413, 414, 415
Victim's trait (usually trait of aggressiveness)	Defendant. FRE 404(a)(2)	YES	NO
Victim's trait (usually trait of non-aggressiveness)	Prosecution to rebut defendant's character evidence about victim or (only in homicide cases) other evidence that victim was aggressor. FRE 404(a)(2)	YES	NO
Victim's traits in sexual assault case	Prosecutor or defendant in specific relatively rare instances. FRE 412	NO	YES

testimony about someone's character, the opposing party may question that witness about specific acts believed to have been committed by the subject of that person's testimony.

EXAMPLES

1.   Can the defendant in a burglary trial seek to show that he did not commit the crime by having witnesses testify in the following ways?

Witness One: "He has a reputation in his neighborhood for being law-abiding."

Witness Two: "I've known the defendant for five years, and he seems honest to me."

Witness Three: "He has been a volunteer soccer coach for a junior high school for several years, and he's never missed a game or a practice session. The league also has him collect all the dues and handle all equipment purchases, and there's never been any problem about accounting for the money."

2.   In a murder trial, before any other prosecution witnesses are presented and before any witnesses are presented by the defendant, the prosecution seeks to show the defendant's guilt by having the defendant's neighbor testify that the defendant is violent and has a reputation in the neighborhood as hot tempered. Is this proper?

3.   In a criminal case where the defendant has used character testimony to show that he is fundamentally peaceful and thus did not commit the charged crime of violence, can the prosecution present a witness who testifies that she believes the defendant has a violent nature and has no respect for law and order, and that she has developed those opinions in the course of knowing the defendant as the defendant's parole officer?

4.   In a criminal trial for securities fraud, the defendant seeks to establish his innocence by presenting a witness who testifies that the defendant has a reputation for honesty. Can the prosecution ask that witness, on cross-examination, whether he has heard that the defendant was once convicted of car theft?

5.   If a criminal defendant who has been convicted in the past of offenses involving dishonesty introduces character testimony in his own behalf, what use can the prosecution make of the past convictions?

6.   The defendant in a criminal assault case admits using force against the victim, but claims that he was acting in reasonable self-defense. May he support that claim by testifying that the victim had a reputation for violence?

7.   If the case described in Example 6 was a civil suit for damages, could the defendant introduce the same type of character evidence about the victim?

8.   In a case where the defendant is accused of having sexually abused a young child, a social worker testifies that the child used terminology about sexual matters that is not usually used by children of such a young age, and that the child seemed unusually knowledgable about sexual intercourse. The defendant seeks to introduce evidence that the alleged victim had been sexually active with several adults other than the defendant, on the theory that this past experience could account for the child's familiarity with sexual matters. Does Rule 412 prevent the admission of this evidence?

EXPLANATIONS

1.   Each of the three witnesses' testimony is relevant to the defendant's character and would not have any other relevance to the case. Therefore, an initial point for analysis is *whether* character evidence can be used by the defendant in this situation. The answer to that inquiry is yes, since the defendant in a criminal case is exempted from the ordinary prohibition against use of the propensity inference if he wants to introduce character evidence about himself. Recall that the evidence must relate to a pertinent trait under the terms of Rule 404(a)(1). "Law-abiding" and "honest" are general traits, but they are well related to a defendant's likely guilt. Respect for equipment and accurate accounting for a team's finances are traits that reduce the likelihood that the defendant was a burglar, since burglary is a crime that involves disrespect for property.

Having dealt with the issue of *whether* character evidence regarding the defendant may be introduced, the second stage of analysis is the question of *how* it can be presented. Witness One's testimony is in the form of a report of the defendant's reputation. This is the most traditional form of character evidence and is totally acceptable. Witness Two's testimony illustrates opinion testimony. Opinion testimony is an allowable method of proving character. Only Witness Three's testimony would be excluded. It relates to character, and character is a permissible topic in this trial for presentation by the defendant, but the form of presentation is wrong. Witness Three's testimony attempts to support inferences about character on the basis of information about specific conduct by the defendant in the past. This kind of testimony about specific acts is not allowed for the purpose of showing character unless character itself is an ultimate issue in a case.

2.   The testimony is inadmissible. It must stay out because its only relevance depends on the forbidden propensity inference, and prosecutors are not allowed access to that inference until a defendant has "opened the door" by using it himself. If information about character were allowed in this situation, the form of the witness's testimony would have been acceptable because it is a combination of two permitted styles — reputation and opinion.

3.   Because the defendant has introduced character evidence, the prosecution is entitled to respond with its own character evidence. The form of this

testimony is all right because it involves the witness's own opinions. There is a risk of unfair prejudice, however, because in identifying herself as the defendant's parole officer, the witness unavoidably reveals that the defendant has been convicted of a crime and has been subject to parole supervision. Some judges might allow this testimony if there was a neutral way to describe the connection between the witness and the defendant. Others might find the risk of prejudice too great, particularly considering the low probative value of character evidence on the issue of whether the defendant actually did commit the charged offense.

4. Yes. In cross-examination of a character witness, questions that "inquire into" past conduct of the person who was the subject of the character testimony are permitted.

5. All the prosecutor can do is "inquire into" them in cross-examination of the defendant's character witnesses. Even if a character witness says he doesn't know or hasn't heard about the past convictions, the cross-examiner is required to accept that answer. Proof about the past convictions is not allowed.

6. Yes. This testimony makes two points. First, if the jury believes that the victim had a violent temperament, it may infer from that fact that the victim actually was the initial aggressor in the incident. Second, if the jury believes that the defendant was aware of the victim's reputation at the time of the incident, it can use that fact in evaluating the force the defendant used against the victim. The reasonableness of self-defense depends on the degree of threat perceived by the self-defender.

7. Rule 404(a)(2) explicitly permits this kind of proof in criminal cases and is silent about civil cases. That suggests that the normal bar to propensity uses of character material should govern. At common law, however, courts have sometimes held that the special character rules for criminal trials should be applied in a civil case if the underlying conduct could be part of a criminal case. The policy for this is that the same difficulties of proof that support the permissive attitude towards character evidence in criminal cases are present when the conduct that is involved in a civil suit is the same kind of conduct that could be the subject of a criminal prosecution. Also, a reason for allowing criminal defendants special privileges for introduction of character evidence is the idea that losing a criminal case is extremely serious both in terms of loss of liberty and loss of social respect. The social respect losses are equal in the kind of civil case where a potential result is equivalent to a finding that a person has been a criminal. Federal courts have followed this common law tradition despite the clearly opposite language of Rule 404(a)(2), for example, in cases involving civil rights actions claiming police brutality.

8. The detailed provisions of Rule 412 would require exclusion of this evidence since it involves sexual conduct by the victim with people other than the accused, and it does not relate to the source of semen or injury. However, *Chambers v. Mississippi* may require that the evidence be admitted on consti-

tutional grounds. If the jury does not learn of these other possible reasons for the child's knowledge of sex and terminology related to sex, it is very likely to assume that the knowledge came from the defendant's conduct with the victim. The strong relevance of the offered evidence suggests that it should be admitted despite the social policies inherent in Rule 412 intended to protect the privacy of sexual assault victims.

3

Defining Hearsay

Introduction

The myth of hearsay is that no one understands it, and students and practicing lawyers always make mistakes about it. It does seem sometimes that the people who understand the hearsay doctrine are a kind of secret society. They have learned something that confuses other people, and they know how to manipulate their knowledge of it. This dual nature of hearsay — its appearance of difficulty to "outsiders" and its relative simplicity to initiates — may be one reason that reform proposals have often been rejected. People who have mastered hearsay may not want to give up their advantage over people who are traumatized by it.

The truth is that the hearsay rules are based on some intuitive assumptions about what kinds of communications are likely to be the most accurate. You can organize your understanding of hearsay by remembering first that "hearsay" is a type of evidence that may not be admitted, and second that exceptions to the general rule of exclusion are available in many situations. This suggests that understanding hearsay requires a grasp of its basic definition, the reasons for our system's traditional aversion to it, and the factors that lead to tolerating its use in many common situations.

Basic Rule

Statements made by people out of court often relate to issues that are disputed at trials. However, even if words people have said or written out of court contain relevant information, they can be excluded from admission. Rule 801 provides the following definitions:

> (a) Statement. A "statement" is (1) an oral or written assertion or (2) nonverbal conduct of a person, if it is intended by the person as an assertion.
> (b) Declarant. A "declarant" is a person who makes a statement.

> (c) Hearsay. "Hearsay" is a statement, other than one made by the declarant while testifying at the trial or hearing, offered in evidence to prove the truth of the matter asserted.

Rule 802 gives a purpose to those definitions, stating:

> Hearsay is not admissible except as provided by these rules or by other rules prescribed by the Supreme Court pursuant to statutory authority or by Act of Congress.

Thus, out-of-court statements are defined as *hearsay* and are *inadmissible* if a party seeks to have them admitted to establish that their content is true. Unless there is an exception to the rule of exclusion, a party cannot have a witness quote what anyone ever said outside of court, and a party cannot introduce a document containing words written out of court. Information from such statements is kept out of trials because the original speaker's absence makes it hard for the jury to decide if the original speaker: 1) had an adequate opportunity to perceive or learn about the subject of the out-of-court statement; 2) had a clear memory of the subject of the out-of-court statement; 3) meant to tell the truth; and 4) understood the typical meanings of the words he or she used. If the original speaker is present, the jury can see him or her and draw some conclusions about these issues. Also, if the original speaker is present, cross-examination is possible. Many people think that cross-examination is a particularly strong technique for uncovering flaws in a person's perception, memory, honesty, and use of words.

Testimony that quotes an out-of-court statement is hearsay only if the out-of-court words are introduced to prove the truth of what they assert. For example, an issue at a trial was whether Mr. Driver had drunk beer at a party before driving a car. Testimony by a witness at the trial that while he was at the party he heard Mr. Host say, "Driver has been drinking beer all night" would be relevant because it supports the proposition that Driver had been drinking. This would be an example of hearsay since the purpose of offering proof that the out-of-court words were said would be to support the exact proposition that they assert — that Driver had been drinking before he drove. The idea behind the hearsay rule is that having someone repeat another person's out-of-court statements is a poor way to have the jury find out the truth about the subject of the out-of-court words.

Out-of-court words treated as hearsay can be written as well as spoken. If an issue at a trial was whether a patient had received morphine in a hospital, a statement in a hospital record showing that morphine was administered would be relevant evidence. But it would also be hearsay, since it is a written out-of-court statement conveying the idea that the patient received morphine, and the purpose of introducing it would be to support the conclusion that the patient received morphine.[1]

---

1. The record would be admissible under an exception to the hearsay exclusion. That admissibility, however, does not change the fact that evidence law doctrines would characterize the statement as hearsay.

The person who makes the out-of-court statement is usually referred to as the declarant. In the typical hearsay situation, a person testifies at a trial and seeks to repeat the declarant's words. Those words are the declarant's statement. When a declarant's statement is in writing, a litigant seeks to bring the out-of-court words into the trial by introducing the document that contains them rather than by having a person testify about having heard the declarant say the words. Suppose that a plaintiff sued a construction company, claiming that something had fallen from a building under construction and had damaged his car parked on the street below. If the car owner sought to establish what had happened by having a witness testify that a pedestrian who saw the event said later that an object had fallen from the building onto the plaintiff's car, the testimony would be hearsay and would be rejected. Note that the person testifying (the witness) is a witness not to the accident but to another event: the speaking by the pedestrian. In standard hearsay terminology, the pedestrian (who was a witness to the accident but who is not a witness in court) is called the declarant. If the pedestrian came to the trial, he or she would be allowed to testify about recollections of the event. However, bringing the pedestrian's knowledge into the trial by having another person quote some of the pedestrian's words violates the rule against hearsay.

Basic Rationale for Excluding Hearsay

Information you get from a person directly is likely to be more accurate than information you get from that person through an intermediary. If you wanted to know about an automobile accident, for example, and there was a person — Mr. Observer — who claimed to have information about it, what might you do? Your first choice would be to talk to Mr. Observer. In a conversation, you would find out how Mr. Observer initially saw or learned what he thinks he knows about the accident. You could evaluate the clarity of his memory. If he used words that were ambiguous or if he seemed to be using ordinary words in an unusual way, you could ask him to make his meaning clear. It is also possible that in talking with Mr. Observer, you could get an impression of his honesty. Mr. Observer might say, "The red car was going very fast, and it slammed into the blue car." You could ask him how he knew about the accident. He might tell you how close he was to the scene of the accident, and this would give you an idea about how clearly he might have been able to see what he thinks he saw. You could ask him to describe the weather at the time, or give you details about the style of the cars, to estimate how strong his memory is. Since words like "fast" and "slammed" are ambiguous, you could ask Mr. Observer questions that would give you an idea of what he really means when he says a car moves fast or slams into another car. Finally, by seeing Mr. Observer's style of responding to your questions, you might develop an opinion about how honestly he was reporting what he believed he knew.

Notice that the probing questions to determine the reliability of Observer's words involve checking on how well he saw the event and how well he remembers what he saw. These factors control the accuracy of whatever beliefs Observer has about the past event at the time he talks about it. The probes to check on Observer's sincerity and on the ambiguity of his language focus on another part of the communication process. They highlight the possibility that a person who has an accurate belief about some past event might still use words to describe it that convey a false impression of that accurate belief. *Perception, memory, sincerity,* and *ambiguity* are sometimes called the *testimonial infirmities.* They are called infirmities because they represent the possible sources for incorrect descriptions of past reality in testimony or in non-testimonial communications. Checking on all of them is possible when you have a firsthand communication with a speaker. If you have only another person's report of what a speaker once said, checking on the possible infirmities is much harder. At trials, the extent to which a statement's accuracy may have been impaired by any of the testimonial infirmities will be exposed, usually, through cross-examination.

Of course, an alternate method of getting Mr. Observer's information would be the indirect process of talking to someone else — Ms. Friend — who had talked to Mr. Observer. Ms. Friend could tell you what Mr. Observer had told her about the accident. For example, she could say, "Mr. Observer said to me, 'I saw the red car drive very fast and slam into the blue car' when we had lunch together last week." Getting Mr. Observer's information this way would deprive you of a chance to ask exactly how he saw the event and to ask questions that might test his memory, the meanings he intended to convey with the words he used, and his honesty.

This second method, where one person's knowledge about something is conveyed to a listener by a second person repeating or quoting what the first person has said, is prohibited in trials by the rule against hearsay. The jury must learn what people know by hearing them talk about their knowledge, and by hearing them respond to cross-examination that illuminates the possible weaknesses in their original perceptions, their recollection, their current choice of words, and their honesty. If Mr. Observer's information is relevant at a trial, it must (ordinarily) be presented at the trial by Mr. Observer testifying in person. Ms. Friend is not allowed to appear at the trial and tell the trier of fact what Mr. Observer once told her. In private life, a person who wanted to know about the automobile accident would prefer to learn about it from Mr. Observer directly, but might be satisfied to have Ms. Friend provide a secondhand version of Mr. Observer's knowledge by quoting him. Evidence law rejects that choice in general, on the theory that the opportunities for clarification and reliability checks that are lost when testimony quotes out-of-court statements are so valuable that the goals of fairness and accuracy in trials are best served by prohibiting the testimony.

The hearsay rule contradicts the general freedom that evidence law gives parties to select their own kinds of proof. A party can usually try to prove its case with any kind of evidence it can find, subject only to the requirement that the material be relevant. A witness with weak eyesight can testify about something he saw at a great distance. To suggest that a person stole something, circumstantial evidence is permitted that the object was in a place at one time and was missing from that place after the person had access to it. Our system relies on the self-interest of litigants to encourage them to use the most efficient and persuasive styles of proof. Also, we expect that adversaries will alert juries if the evidence their opponents choose to use is weak in terms of the conclusions it is presented to support. But the reliability problems of out-of-court statements are thought to be so great that common law decisions and the Federal Rules of Evidence take the position that a rule of exclusion will produce the fairest results overall.[2]

Despite the strong policy grounds for excluding hearsay, the Federal Rules and common law do allow it to be admitted in many circumstances covered by exceptions to the general principle of exclusion. The exceptions apply where there are reasons to think that the out-of-court statement was particularly likely to be accurate or truthful so that the impossibility of probing the original speaker's statements is not so harmful. An additional rationale for some exceptions is the belief that the risks that out-of-court words may convey a false meaning are outweighed by other factors. In a murder trial, for example, the dying victim's accusatory statement naming someone as the murderer is admissible since it has often been thought that people at the point of death have no motive to lie and may be afraid (for religious reasons) to lie. Also, the risks of using the out-of-court words are less severe than the unfairness of excluding from a trial a victim's last words identifying the murderer.

Detailed Analysis of Statements Typically not *Offered to Prove the Truth of What They Assert*

When an out-of-court statement is relevant without regard to whether it conveys accurate information, then the hearsay prohibition does not operate, and testimony about the statement is allowed. How can a litigant ever claim that an out-of-court statement is relevant without also claiming that the jury should believe the substance of what the speaker said? Suppose a party needed to prove that security guards were patrolling a warehouse on a particular evening. A janitor could testify that as he passed the warehouse door

---

2. There are some other examples of evidence doctrines that move away from relying on the competitiveness of litigation and the common sense of juries to protect against cases being decided on weak evidence. One is the original writing rule, discussed at pages 200-202. Others are the specialized relevance rules, controlling the use of evidence of subsequent remedial measures or of evidence of a person's past bad acts, discussed at pages 18-20 and 32-36.

he heard the guards talking to each other. The janitor would be permitted to quote the words the guards said because proof that the words were said is relevant to an issue at the trial (were the guards in the warehouse?), and using the words as relevant to that issue does not require that the *content* of the guards' statements be true or be believed by the jury. No matter what the guards said, and no matter whether it was true or false, the fact that they were speaking supports the proposition for which the janitor's testimony is sought to be introduced: The guards were present in the warehouse. The guards' words would be introduced not to show that what they asserted was true, but just to show that the words were said.

The plaintiff's case in a defamation suit provides another clear example. The plaintiff must prove that the defendant said something defamatory about the plaintiff, but when the plaintiff has someone testify about the defendant's out-of-court statement, the plaintiff is *not* seeking to have the jury believe that the statement was accurate. The plaintiff needs to have the jury believe that the allegedly defamatory words were uttered, not that they were a truthful report of some aspect of reality. The plaintiff's position is that *words were said*, not that the *words were true*. For this reason, the hearsay rule allows quotation of the defendant's out-of-court statement.

Warnings are another example of out-of-court words that are relevant because they were spoken whether or not they are "true." A defendant who is sued for carelessly failing to guard a dangerous machine might introduce evidence that she told the plaintiff, "Look out for the sharp edge." If the plaintiff's degree of care is relevant under the substantive law of the case, proof that the defendant gave a warning would be admissible. There is neither truth or falsity in the "look out" statement. It is important in the case merely because it was made. If the speaker meant to lie when she said it, that doesn't matter. If the speaker meant to say "pointed" instead of "sharp," that doesn't matter either. If the speaker had the impression that the machine had one kind of danger but was really mistaken about it, that misperception or lack of clear memory is also completely unimportant since on the question of the plaintiff's conduct and his response to words of warning, it is the fact that the words "look out for the sharp edge" were once spoken that provides information for the jury to consider. None of the testimonial infirmities are involved in this kind of testimony. The out-of-court speaker's perceptions, memory, sincerity, and possible use of words in an idiosyncratic way would have no impact on the significance of the fact, if the jury believes it to be a fact, that those warning words were once spoken by her.

The language of contracts is another instance of out-of-court words being used in a non-hearsay way. When a litigant introduces evidence that a party, out of court, wrote or spoke words that created a contract, the litigant is *not*, in theory, relying on those words to establish their own truth. If the contract is enforced, it will not be because the party's promise was taken as "true" by the court. The contract will be enforced if legal principles independent from the "truth" or "falsity" of the party's words require that those words once spoken or written constitute a contract.

The contracts example belongs to a category sometimes called verbal acts or verbal parts of acts. If you say, "This is a gift," and hand someone some money, it *is* a gift in some jurisdictions under property law doctrines. In those places, testimony that the donor said "this is a gift" would not be hearsay because the statement would be introduced merely to show that the words were said (the jurisdiction's substantive law takes over the task of converting the saying of those words to a decision about ownership of the money). In some other jurisdictions the money might only be a gift if the donor meant it to be a gift. Then, proof of what the donor said would be hearsay since it would be intended to support a conclusion about the donor's state of mind at the time he or she handed over the money. This hearsay would be admissible under an exception for statements reflecting a speaker's mental state.

Words introduced just to show their effect on the hearer or reader are another broad class of non-hearsay in which out-of-court words can be relevant without their proponent asking the trier of fact to treat them as true. Warnings are in this class, as are any other kinds of statements that are relevant just because a party was exposed to them. In a tort suit claiming that a manufacturer should have changed its design because it had received reports of injuries earlier than the plaintiff's injury, the reports of those other injuries would be relevant in two ways, of which one would constitute hearsay and one would be non hearsay. To show that the out-of-court reports accurately conveyed information about those past injuries, the reports would be hearsay, since that use depends on their information being true. To show that the manufacturer had received information that a reasonable manufacturer would investigate, the reports are *not* hearsay since that use does not require that the reports have contained accurate information; it only requires that there is a showing that the manufacturer actually did receive the reports.

Criticizing a manufacturer's response to reports of injuries does not require reliance on the accuracy of the reports, as long as it is shown that they apparently were made concerning the same kind of product that allegedly injured the plaintiff. This same analysis would apply where a person's motivation for committing a crime was at stake: If that person sought to establish that he was acting in response to a threat, testimony that someone once said to him "Commit this crime or I'll kill you" would be admissible. It would be significant in the trial because of the effect those out-of-court words allegedly had on the person charged with the crime, *not* because of the truth or falsity of the details of the threat.

Where proof that words were said is relevant in a trial, without regard to whether or not the content of the words provides a true account of some past reality, a witness may quote those words. Proof such as a witness's testimony that words of warning or words of a business agreement were said, when they are being introduced not to prove that they were true but just to prove that they were said, does not involve any hearsay problems. A witness can report to the jury that the words were uttered, just as a witness can report any other event that a witness has observed. Testimony that a witness heard a person say, "Look out," is just like testimony that a witness saw a person wearing a blue sweater or running across a street. The hearsay rule's preference for having the actual speaker present in court and available to answer clarifying questions has no application where the proponent's effort is to prove that words were *said* rather than that words were *true*.

Visual Aids

Visual aids may help in one of the crucial issues of hearsay analysis: whether the declarant's words are being offered into evidence to prove the truth of what they assert or merely to prove that they were said. This distinction defines hearsay, since the hearsay exclusion only operates when the out-of-court words are offered as evidence of their truth. A detailed analysis of the components inherent in people's communications may clarify this inquiry.

When a person talks about something she thinks she knows, her words reflect an effort to convey information about something she believes. Her belief, in turn, is formed (partly) by some aspect of reality she observed in the past. In analyzing statements people make (in court or out of court), three stages can be outlined.

1. The speaker's words about a past event;
2. The speaker's belief about the past event; and
3. The real past event.

Someone, for example, who once saw a ship sail might say, "I saw the ship sail." That statement would involve the speaker's choice of words to convey an idea. The speaker would have to mean by "ship" what most people mean by that word, and the speaker would have to intend to get that typical meaning across to his audience. If the speaker meant to be honest and used words carefully, the speaker's statement would be a full and clear version of his belief about having seen the ship. Does the fact that he believes he saw the ship sail mean that the ship really sailed? The speaker's belief is based on some past perception of reality and on his ability to remember that past perception. Depending on how clearly he was able to see what he thought was a ship sailing, and on how well he is able to remember things he has seen in the past, his belief about having seen the ship sail might or might not be an accurate report of past reality.

It is possible to think through what a juror does when he or she hears testimony, focussing on these same three factors: the speaker's current words, the speaker's current belief, and past events. The juror hears the speaker speak. The juror then must decide whether the speaker's *words* are an accurate reflection of what the speaker believes is true and whether the speaker's current *belief* really is an accurate reflection of a *past event*, taking into account how well the speaker was able to perceive what he was looking at and how well the speaker is able to remember what he saw. Chart Nine illustrates these stages of past perception, current belief, and current spoken words. It shows how a speaker may come to say certain words about a past event, and also how a juror who hears those words must inferentially work through the same process that the speaker used if the juror's purpose is to learn about the past event from the speaker. An expanded illustration, Chart Ten, also illustrates how issues such as lying, use of ambiguous words, poor memory, and poor original perception of an event can affect the accuracy of what a person says about an event. In the expanded version, the "testimonial infirmities" are inserted to show how they might affect the reliability of a speaker's words.

These charts can help solve the "truth of the matter asserted" issue in identifying hearsay. The hearsay rule only excludes out-of-court statements sought to be introduced as a basis for a finding that the information they contain is true. A way to remember this is to see that on the charts, depending on the way in which an out-of-court statement is claimed to be relevant, a jury will have to decide one or more of the following issues: 1) did a speaker make the statement someone says in court he made; 2) what was the out-of-court speaker's belief when he spoke; or 3) what did the out-of-court speaker perceive about something. If the only issue for which the out-of-court words are sought to be introduced is the first of these issues — whether the words were spoken or written — then the hearsay rule allows admission of the words.

CHART TEN
Links between Words and Perceptions

Relationship between observer's words and past reality	Relationship between hearing observer's words and forming a belief about past reality (juror)
SPEAKER	JUROR
Describes a recollection of ship	Hears speaker's words
Description is based on a belief	Decides if words truthfully and clearly portray what speaker remembers
Belief is based on past perception	Decides if speaker's past perception was likely to have been accurate and whether (if it was accurate) the speaker's current memory is a good reflection of that former accurate perception

CHART ELEVEN
Location of "Testimonial Infirmities" in the Steps between
Observer's Words and Past Reality

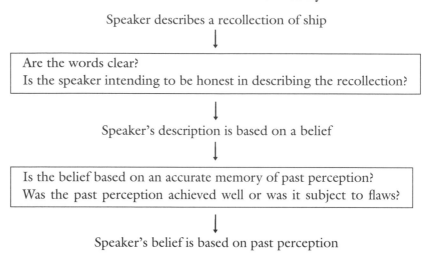

Speaker describes a recollection of ship

Are the words clear?
Is the speaker intending to be honest in describing the recollection?

Speaker's description is based on a belief

Is the belief based on an accurate memory of past perception?
Was the past perception achieved well or was it subject to flaws?

Speaker's belief is based on past perception

In that situation the words are not introduced to establish that their meaning is true, and as the charts illustrate none of the testimonial infirmities are involved.

The testimonial infirmities come into play only when the proponent of admission of the out-of-court words wants the jury to rely on them to form an opinion about what the out-of-court speaker believed or what the out-of-court speaker had perceived. In contrast, whenever a statement made out of court could illuminate an issue without the jurors deciding that it is an accurate representation of the speaker's belief or that it is an accurate report of some past reality perceived by the speaker, the hearsay rule does not apply. This makes sense because using words that fit this description avoids all four of the testimonial infirmities illustrated in the chart.

The stages of: 1) past perception; 2) current belief; and 3) communication about that belief are illustrated in these charts in a vertical column. You could also think of them in any of the ways shown in Chart Eleven.

All these visualizations incorporate the same fundamental idea. If the out-of-court words can be characterized as relevant at the trial without any requirement that they are an accurate representation of the speaker's belief or that the speaker's belief was an accurate representation of some past reality, then the hearsay issue disappears. If no consideration is required past the first point of the triangle, past the statement point on the horizontal row, or into the brain of the speaker in the human illustration, then the testimonial infirmities are not implicated and the policies inherent in the hearsay rules do not require exclusion of the statement.

CHART TWELVE
Round Up the Usual Diagrams

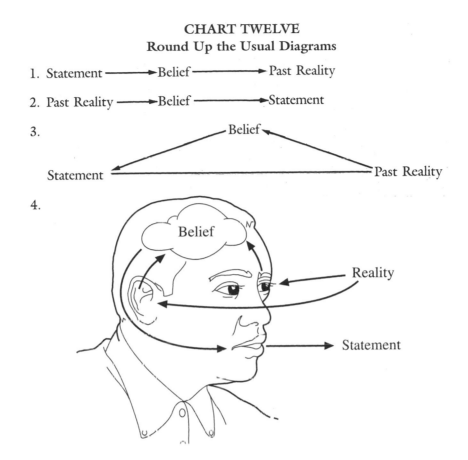

1. Statement ⟶ Belief ⟶ Past Reality

2. Past Reality ⟶ Belief ⟶ Statement

3.

Belief

Statement ⟷ Past Reality

4.

Belief

Reality

Statement

Detailed Analysis of What Constitutes a Statement

The hearsay prohibition applies to spoken and written words. It also applies to actions that are intended to convey a meaning. The Federal Rules call such actions "assertive conduct." In our society, nodding your head up and down is usually understood to convey the assertion of agreement or the meaning "yes." Head nodding is conduct primarily meant to express an idea. In contrast, most conduct is "nonassertive," intended to accomplish something but not to convey information. However, nonassertive conduct may still indicate what a person thinks about a subject. In some jurisdictions, but not those following the Federal Rules, testimony about conduct that was not intended to express an idea is defined as hearsay if it is relevant because the action indicates that the actor believed something to be true. The way noncommunicative action can be relevant at a trial is illustrated by an effort to prove that a ship was seaworthy by introducing testimony that an experienced ship captain examined it and then sailed on it. Would the report of that captain's actions be hearsay? Under the Federal Rules, the answer is no. Because the captain was intending to take a trip on a ship rather than make an assertion, the conduct can be described without any hearsay concerns. In jurisdictions that apply a broader definition of hearsay, testimony describing what the captain did would be called hearsay because in order to be relevant it must be treated as an expression of what the captain believed to be true about the ship.

The Federal Rules call it hearsay for a witness to testify that the captain once said, "This is a fine ship," but they allow a witness to say that he or she saw the captain examine the ship and then sail on it. This is because sailing on a ship is non-assertive conduct, conduct meant to accomplish something but not to effect a communication or make an assertion. The drafters of the Federal Rules believed that the risk of insincerity in *statements* by an out-of-court *speaker* is greater than the risk of insincerity in the *actions* of an out-of-court *actor*. A speaker is always conscious that his or her words relate to the topic they talk about. An actor, by contrast, may not be as clearly aware that others may interpret his or her actions as revealing what he or she believes to be true. Certainly, if one were interested in lying about a topic, one would lie about it while speaking on that subject. It is less clear that a person who wanted to lie about something would shape nonverbal conduct in ways that would produce deceptive impressions. Furthermore, where an actor's conduct is sought to be relied on in a trial as evidence of some fact the actor may have believed, the actor will usually have done something in real life that was consistent with the supposed underlying belief. The fact that actions expose people to consequences is an additional guarantee that actions will be based on an actor's honest beliefs about reality. These distinctions between words and actions are the main justification for the Federal Rules position in Rule 801(a) that excludes non-assertive conduct from the definition of hearsay. They mainly affect the testimonial issue of truthtelling, which suggests that of all the four aspects of conveying information (perception, memory, choice of words, and sincerity), the drafters considered sincerity (or truthtelling) to be the most important.

Since speech itself can be thought of as a kind of conduct, the Federal Rules treatment of nonassertive conduct requires analysis of another issue, the non-intended implications of people's assertions. Recall that the Federal Rules exclude from the definition of hearsay testimony about conduct that is relevant because of what it reveals about the actor's beliefs as long as the actor did not intend to be communicating about those beliefs. By implication, another exclusion from the Federal Rules definition of hearsay is testimony about an out-of-court statement that is offered to prove something the speaker did not intend to assert. Obviously, out-of-court words may sometimes be relevant for what they imply rather than what they assert directly. However, it may be difficult to distinguish between a statement claimed to be relevant because of a fact it asserts and a statement claimed to be relevant because it is circumstantial evidence of some fact.

For example, in a suit alleging that a landlord failed to obey a regulation requiring that apartments have adequate heat during winter months, the plaintiff might seek to introduce testimony about the following out-of-court statements made by people in an apartment as part of the plaintiff's proof that the apartment was very cold:

1. "It's very cold in here."
2. "This is a great place for polar bears."
3. "I need to put on a sweater."

Everyone would call the first of these statements hearsay, because the declarant stated that the apartment was very cold, and the statement is sought to be introduced to show that the apartment was very cold. The second statement ("polar bears") is also hearsay. Even though there are differences between the exact out-of-court words and the proposition they are offered to support ("polar bears" is not the same as "very cold"), everyone would agree that the sense of the declarant's words, the meaning the declarant meant to convey, was that the apartment was very cold. For that reason, the statement is hearsay when offered as proof that the apartment was too cold. A speaker's use of humor or metaphor does not prevent evidence law from analyzing the statement as being equivalent, for hearsay purposes, to a statement like the first example, "It's very cold in here."

The third statement, "I need to put on a sweater," would be relevant on the issue of the temperature of the apartment, because someone who plans to dress warmly probably is basing that plan on a belief that the apartment is cold. However, in line with the Federal Rules treatment on nonassertive conduct, it could be argued that the statement is *not* an assertion about the temperature of the apartment. Since its main subject was how the speaker would be dressed, the likelihood that the statement might be a false characterization of something else (the temperature of the apartment) is reduced. Under the Federal Rules, the statement about the sweater would be an example of what the Advisory Committee Note called "verbal conduct which is assertive but offered as a basis for inferring something other than the matter asserted."

A famous common law case, *Wright v. Doe d. Tatham*,[3] represents a point of view opposed to the Federal Rules position on this issue. To prove that a person had been of sound mind at the time he wrote a will, the proponent of the will sought to introduce letters that various individuals had written to the testator at that time. The explicit subject matter of the letters was not claimed to be relevant. The proponent of the will sought to introduce

---

3. 7 Ad. & E. 313, 112 Eng. Rep. 488 (Exchequer Chamber 1837).

them to support the inference that the writers believed that the person to whom they were writing was sane, since the letters were straightforward and friendly and involved routine matters of business. After a number of appeals, it was decided that admission of the letters was wrong. They were the equivalent of out-of-court statements by the writers that they thought the testator was sane. Since that was their claimed relevance, they were being offered as a basis for a finding that the writers' ideas about the testator's sanity were correct. If out-of-court statements by the writers like "I think the man is sane" would be hearsay, so too should out-of-court statements that use different words but carry with them the same implication. The Federal Rules reject this result on the theory that the risk of lying about a particular subject is greatest when an out-of-court statement is explicitly about that subject. If a conclusion about one subject can be drawn from a speaker's statements on another subject, the chances that the speaker made a false statement about the second subject to create a false impression about the first subject are slight.

Relevancy may be a problem where out-of-court words are introduced to support an inference that the speaker did not intend. If the statement is very similar to the proposition sought to be proved, then it will likely be considered hearsay as in the "polar bear" weather example about the apartment with allegedly inadequate heat. As the clear equivalence between the statement and the proposition that it is intended to support decreases, the statement is less likely to be classified as hearsay under the Federal Rules. However, the statement's relevance is likely to decrease as the link between its explicit content and the idea it is introduced to prove gets less and less direct. The statement, "I'm going to put on a sweater," would be safe from a hearsay objection under the Federal Rules if offered to support the inference that the speaker thought the apartment was cold. Notice, though, that there might be many reasons for planning to wear a sweater. The speaker might have been getting ready to go outside, the speaker might have thought that his or her shirt was ugly and should be covered up, or the speaker might have been wearing only a thin shirt and thus would have been too lightly dressed even in a warm apartment. The logical distance between the proposition sought to be proved and the surface meaning of the out-of-court statement introduced to prove the proposition helps the statement avoid being characterized as hearsay, but it may reduce the relevancy of the statement. If relevancy is extremely slight, the statement may be excluded.

Classic Hearsay Puzzles

Academic writers and occasional practicing lawyers and judges are familiar with a group of dilemmas about whether to classify certain statements as hearsay. Deciding whether the statements are hearsay usually has no practical significance because exceptions to the hearsay exclusionary rule often allow their admission. (If they are not hearsay, then no exception is required to permit their admission into evidence.) The following discussions describe these problems and typical approaches to resolving them.

> **Circumstantial use of the declarant's words to prove something about the declarant**: for example, quoting the statement "I am the King of Mars" to prove that the declarant was mentally ill at the time he said it.

This problem is more important in jurisdictions that treat nonassertive statements as hearsay than it is in a Federal Rules jurisdiction where a statement introduced for a meaning it does not assert is treated as outside the definition of hearsay. Logically, proof that someone said "I am the King of Mars" has no relevance to the person's sanity at the time he said it unless it supports the proposition that he believed he was a Martian when he said it. Therefore, for "I am the King of Mars" to be relevant as to the speaker's sanity, the proponent of the statement must argue that it is exactly equivalent to "I think I am the King of Mars." It would, in this analysis, be offered to prove that when the person said "I think I am the King of Mars," he or she really did think so. This is an instance of an out-of-court statement being admitted for the proof of what it asserts and should therefore be considered hearsay.

The usual analysis given to statements such as this is that the proponent of the statement is definitely not trying to use it to prove the truth of what it asserts, that the speaker was king of Mars. Since there is no effort to establish that the speaker was really king, the speaker's interest in lying, or the speaker's errors in the perception, memory, or use of language will all be of no importance. A court or lawyer using this analysis looks for a literal congruence between the out-of-court words and the proposition that they are introduced to prove. Only if that exact equivalence is found will they call the statement hearsay. Thus, "I *think I am* the king" would be called hearsay if introduced to show that the speaker *thought* he was the king. On the other hand, "I *am* the king," would typically avoid being called hearsay if it was introduced to show that the speaker *thought* he was the king since the statement was just "I am the king," and was not "I think I am the king." Treating the out-of-court statements "I am the king" and "I think I am the king" differently is traditional but is hard to support analytically. Under the Federal Rules, both "I think I am the king" and "I am the king" are non-hearsay if introduced to show that the speaker was mentally ill.

> **Circumstantial use of declarant's words to prove something about a place**: for example, to establish that an office was being used for illegal betting, evidence that someone called the phone at the office and said, "This is Bill, put $50 on Speedy to win in the fifth race."

Hearsay writers and courts have called statements like "$50 on Speedy," offered to show that a place is a bookie joint, either hearsay or not hearsay. The best support for "not hearsay" is that the statement is being used as circumstantial evidence, so that whether the speaker meant to bet or not, the fact that the call was made to the location is highly suggestive that the place is used for taking bets. In this analysis, the accuracy of the speaker's perceptions and the honesty of the speaker do not matter. On the other hand, if the speaker did not believe that he or she was making the call to a bookie joint, the fact that the call was received does not logically support the idea that the location of the phone actually was a bookie joint.

The statement could be treated as an example of an unintended assertion like the letters to the testator in *Wright*. Taken this way, it is assumed that the statement is relevant because it incorporates the idea, "I think this is a bookie joint," and the truthfulness and accurate perception of the speaker becomes important. Some common law jurisdictions would keep the statement out since it is only relevant to the extent that it incorporates the speaker's unstated belief, "this phone is used by a bookie." Under the Federal Rules, if the judge decided that the statement really meant something about placing a bet, and that this is different from a subsidiary inferable meaning that the speaker believed the location to be a bookie joint, then the statement would be outside the definition of hearsay. In this analysis, the speaker's statement is admissible as incorporating the speaker's actual belief that the phone is used for a bookie joint, but because the speaker did not explicitly articulate that belief there is an adequate guarantee of trustworthiness to justify treating it as non-hearsay.

In a famous case, *Bridges v. State*,[4] a defendant was accused of having committed a crime against a child. The trial court admitted testimony quoting the child's out-of-court description of the room in which the crime occurred. Proof was also introduced that the defendant lived in a room that met the child's description. Admission of the child's statement was approved in an opinion that characterized it as circumstantial evidence. It can be argued that the words show she had been in that room *not* because that is the meaning of her outof-court assertion, but because — regardless of the meaning attributed to her statement — her ability to say anything that contained a description of the room provided circumstantial evidence that she had been there. Testimony was introduced showing that the child would not have had any way to know about the room unless she had, in fact, been taken there by the defendant.

Monograms, inscriptions and commercial signage: for example, to prove that a hit-and-run vehicle belonged to ABC Pizza, testimony that writing on the side of the vehicle said "ABC Pizza."

---

4. 19 N.W.2d 529 (Wis. 1945).

If a hit-and-run victim wants to prove that he or she was hit by a truck owned by ABC Pizza, evidence that the truck said "ABC Pizza" on it would be relevant. Would it be hearsay? Since the words are equivalent to a statement, "This truck is operated by ABC Pizza," it is clear that they are sought to be introduced to prove the truth of what they assert. Therefore, the words meet the standard definition of hearsay. (If ABC Pizza is a party to the case, and the words are offered against ABC Pizza, then the hearsay rule will not be an obstacle. Under a hearsay exemption, discussed in Chapter 4, a party's own words are never barred by the hearsay rule when offered by the opposing party.) If the words are hearsay, how could the plaintiff ever have the jury find out that the truck had that writing on it? The trick is to find some way to argue that the words are not being introduced to rely on the truth of their assertion that the truck is operated by ABC Pizza. One approach would be to find evidence from some other source that trucks with the words "ABC Pizza" on them are operated by ABC Pizza. Then, testimony that the hit-and-run truck had "ABC Pizza" on it could be offered just to prove that the words were on the truck without any requirement that their underlying meaning be taken as true merely because of what the words say. Once it is established that the hit-and-run truck said "ABC Pizza" *and* that ABC Pizza did own trucks with that type of writing on them, the problem of trying to draw meaning from the out-of-court words disappears. The analysis becomes the same as if the victim saw a truck with blue and yellow spots, and there was testimony that the defendant operated trucks with blue and yellow spots. Where the identifying characteristics of a thing are a monogram or inscription, or someone's name, the hearsay rule is implicated if a party tries to use the writing to show that its meaning is true. If a party just uses a writing to show that the writing existed, and uses other proof to suggest that things with that writing have certain attributes (such as ownership by the person named in the monogram or inscription), there is no hearsay problem.

> **Surveys:** for example, to prove that the defendant manufacturer's product was deceptively similar to the plaintiff's, testimony that survey respondents identified the defendant's product as the plaintiff's.

It may violate trademark or unfair competition law for one company to make its product look too much like the product of another company. One element of the cause of action may be proof that the appearance of the defendant's product deceived customers into thinking that it was the plaintiff's. A plaintiff in a case like this will often commission a survey to discover if people in the marketplace think that the defendant's product is made by the plaintiff. The hearsay problem in this context involves testimony by the director of the consumer survey, stating that some percentage of survey respondents identified the defendant's product as the plaintiff's. Does this involve quotation of out-of-court statements? While there is no direct quotation, the testimony is entirely based on what other people (the survey respondents) have said out of court. For this reason, the hearsay problem cannot be avoided by a conclusion that the testimony does not involve the use of out-of-court statements. This leads to the next inquiry, whether the words are being used to prove the truth of what they assert. Here, in a manner similar to the "I am the King of Mars" problem, it could be argued that the words are *not* being introduced to prove that what they said was true, if what they said is characterized as "This product is made by the plaintiff." Recall that the plaintiff's effort is to show that products made by the defendant looked so much like the plaintiff's that people mistook the defendant's items for those manufactured by the plaintiff. So, if the words meant that the product in question was made by the plaintiff, there is no possibility that the truth of those words is the substance of what the plaintiff is trying to prove.

A better analysis would accept the idea that reports of what the respondents said to survey interviewers are relevant only if the respondents' statements are understood as equal to "I think that this product was made by the plaintiff." In this sense, the out-of-court words are indeed being used to support a conclusion that their contents are true, that what was said out of court about what the speaker believed really was a true report of what the speaker believed. This analysis would classify testimony based on surveys as hearsay. The testimony will be admissible, however, under exceptions covering statements of mental state or covering presentation of testimony by an expert witness.

> **Silence:** for example, can evidence of a person's failure to complain about an allegedly defective car be introduced as proof that he thought the car was all right?

Testimony about people's silence may be relevant in a variety of circumstances. Two frequent situations are: 1) lack of complaints by other buyers sought to be introduced as a defense by a seller accused of selling substandard goods to the plaintiff; and 2) the defendant's failure to mention an alleged business deal to colleagues, introduced to support a conclusion that the alleged deal was never made. The quick answer to the relationship between hearsay and these types of proof is that hearsay has no application because the testimony does not quote any out-of-court words.

Most courts decline to see a hearsay issue in this situation and admit the testimony that no complaints were made or no mention was made of a business deal, limiting this pro-admissibility approach by applying relevancy considerations. On relevancy grounds, they will exclude the evidence if there is only a small likelihood that other customers would have complained if they were dissatisfied, or that the person with whom the business deal was allegedly made could well have failed to mention it because of his usual pattern of topics of conversation. An argument that this testimony does implicate usual issues of hearsay could be made, since proof of silence will only be relevant if it supports a conclusion that the nonspeaker thought the merchandise was all right. The nonspeaker's ability to perceive the merchandise, ability to remember what it was like, and the significance he personally gave to silence are all topics that would affect the reliability of giving weight to his observations. If the out-of-court speaker had said something like "the merchandise is so-so," all courts would recognize hearsay if the words were sought to be introduced with respect to the quality of the goods. Where that same customer said no words, most courts ignore the issues of hearsay.

> **Information from animals and machines:** for example, can information from a radar speed detector be introduced to prove that a particular car was going as fast as the detector indicated?

If a radar detector "says" that a car was going at a certain speed, is that an out-of-court statement subject to definition as hearsay? The Federal Rules definition of "statement" in Rule 801(a) requires that a person make a statement in order for the statement to be hearsay. Therefore, readings from devices and other types of mechanical records are outside the definition of hearsay. Bloodhounds are sometimes used to track people thought to have committed crimes. When a dog's handler testifies that the dog found and pointed to a suspect, it is sometimes claimed that the handler's testimony is hearsay since he is quoting the dog's out-of-court statement. Under the Federal Rules, that argument would fail because a dog is not a person. Under common law, animal and machine evidence is usually protected from objection on hearsay grounds because the risks of insincerity, narration, memory, and perception are small and because the reliability of the mechanical or animal observations can usually be supported with evidence describing the workings of the machine or the training of the animal.

EXAMPLES

Underlying Policies

1. Walker claims that Driver's car went through a red light and hit him as he was crossing a street. To prove that Driver ignored the traffic signal, he seeks to testify that after the accident, a person came up to him and said, "That light was red when Driver hit you." Walker's quotation of what this person said is hearsay. Explain why it is desirable for our system of evidence law to reject Walker's testimony about the statement.

2. If the person in Example 1 who spoke to Walker had said, "Are you all right? What kind of driver just zooms across an intersection, even when the light is red?" how would that affect your analysis?

Basic Instances of Hearsay and Non-hearsay

3.   Homeowner's house is burned down in a fire that was caused by a defective lighting fixture. Homeowner thinks that the fixture was made by Waybright Corporation and sues that company for damages. A painter once said to Homeowner, while standing on a ladder near the light, "This is a Waybright fixture." On the issue of whether Waybright made the fixture, would it be hearsay for Homeowner to state what the painter said?

4.   Homeowner (from Example 3) puts the painter on the witness stand. The painter testifies: "Two years ago, when I was painting Homeowner's house, I saw her lighting fixture and I told her it was a Waybright fixture." Does this testimony contain hearsay?

5.   Could the painter (from Examples 3 and 4) testify that when he painted the room the fixture was in, it looked to him like the fixture was installed securely?

6.   An insurance company wants to prove that an insured believed he was suffering from arthritis at the time he applied for insurance that was only available to people who did not suffer from arthritis. Could a witness testify for the insurance company that she saw the insured sitting in a waiting room at a hospital's arthritis clinic on a date earlier than the date of the insurance application?

7.   Plaintiff sues Defendant for trespass. The plaintiff said to the defendant the day before the alleged trespass, "I'm glad to meet you, you're nice. You're never a trespasser on my land, and you can visit it whenever you want to." Would it be hearsay evidence for the defendant to testify that the plaintiff said "you're never a trespasser"?

8.   Mr. Victim was injured in an industrial accident and seeks damages from Mr. Maintainer, a self-employed contractor who allegedly did a negligent job of maintaining the machine that hurt him. Shortly after the injury, a government inspector checked the machine and said, "I'd never let that Mr. Maintainer do any work for me." Would testimony by Mr. Victim that the inspector said that be hearsay, if it was introduced to prove that Mr. Maintainer did bad work?

9.   Harry Hasty and Clarence Clever started an office-cleaning company that became successful. Hasty sold his share of the business to Clever and agreed not to contact any of the company's customers for a period of two years. Three weeks later, Clever suspected that Hasty was approaching customers of the business and offering to do their office cleaning. In a suit seeking damages for violation of the noncompetition agreement, Clever sought to show that Hasty solicited business from Clever's customers. Clever had a note written to him by one of his cleaning employees. It said, "Yesterday when I was cleaning the offices of Maximum Corporation, their office manager told me that Harry Hasty was calling them up and visiting them, trying

to get them to stop using our company and start hiring Hasty to do their cleaning." Would the note be hearsay, if introduced by Clever?

10.   Accused of negligently hiring an incompetent nurse, a doctor would like to testify that one of the nurse's former employers had stated in an employment reference that the nurse "does excellent work." Would the reference comment be hearsay on the issue of the doctor's reasonableness in hiring the nurse? Would it be hearsay on the issue of whether the nurse is skillful?

11.   To show that an extortion defendant knew the alleged victim, the prosecution seeks to introduce a piece of paper found in the defendant's apartment with the victim's address and telephone number on it. Is the note hearsay?

12.   Ms. Spectator sues the owner of a large field where a motorcycle race was held. She claims that she was hit by a motorcycle while watching the race from a hill that was marked out as safe for viewing. The defendant claims that she thought that spot was appropriate for spectators because the organizers of the race told her the race would be on flat parts of the land and never told her anything about using the hill. An investigator, hired by the owner, interviewed all the people who organized the race. Would it involve hearsay for the investigator to give the following testimony?

a)   "Based on my interviews, I conclude that when the race was rehearsed, all the riders stayed on the flat land"

b)   "No one I spoke to said anything about warning the owner that the racing motorcycles would go up the hill."

Written Statements as Hearsay and Non-hearsay

13.   Suppose that you parked your car in a shopping center and that after shopping you returned to find that another car had banged into it, crushing one of the doors. If a note on the windshield said, "I saw the accident, the car that hit you had license plate ABC-123," could you introduce that note in a suit against the owner of the car that had that license plate number?

14.   Patient sues a surgeon, claiming that medical negligence by the surgeon left him with severely decreased mobility in his hands that weakened them so much that he could no longer use eating utensils or hold a pen or pencil to write. To show that the patient did have the ability to write, the doctor seeks to introduce a note, written by the plaintiff one week before the trial, that says, "Thank you for your invitation, but I won't be able to come to the party Thursday because I'll be busy with my lawsuit." Is the note hearsay?

Conventional Non-hearsay Situations

15.   In a trademark infringement case, a food company claims that an electronics company has marketed a radio with a brand name that is confusingly

similar to one of the food company's brand names. The food company seeks to introduce testimony that it has received orders for the radios from many of its customers. Does this testimony include hearsay?

16.   Mr. Poor gives some money to Ms. Rich and says, "Here is the repayment of the loan you made to me so I could buy a car." Later, Ms. Rich sues Mr. Poor claiming that the money she received was a gift, and that Mr. Poor still owes her money to repay the car loan. May Mr. Poor quote his own out-of-court statement about the purpose of the payment, or would that be hearsay?

17.   A parking lot had a large sign stating "convenient to downtown." If a state consumer affairs department alleged that the lot was really not convenient to downtown and sued the company for false advertising, could the defendant offer testimony that no customer had ever made a complaint about the lot's location or about its advertising claim?

18.   To show that a Stanley Sportsfan was reckless (in a suit involving a claim that a defendant had been negligent to hire him for work where good judgment was required), the plaintiff seeks to introduce testimony showing that: Several hours after an important professional football game had been played, Sportsfan saw one of the players in a restaurant; the player was extremely large and strong and had a reputation for committing violent acts against strangers; Sportsfan said to the player, "I think you're a bum. You play like a little girl." Would testimony including the quotation of what Sportsfan said be defined as hearsay?

EXPLANATIONS

Underlying Policies

1.   The person Walker is quoting is not available for cross-examination. This makes it impossible to find out what the person meant by "light was red." The declarant might not have meant to imply anything at all about whether the light was in the driver's favor or the pedestrian's favor. Without having the speaker present in court, there is no way to determine what the words really meant. Even if it was somehow clear that the declarant meant to express the idea that the light had been red against the driver, there is also no way to assess the declarant's truthfulness. Also, there is no information about how well the declarant actually saw the accident. Perhaps the declarant arrived at the scene just after it happened and guessed or tried to figure out who had been in the wrong. Having the declarant available at the trial would allow Driver to expose fully the basis for the declarant's beliefs. One of the testimonial infirmities, poor memory, would not be a problem here, since on the facts of the problem very little time had passed between the declarant's perception of the event and the declarant's statement about it.

2.   If "What kind of driver just zooms . . . ?" was sought to be introduced to show that the light was red against Driver when Driver entered the intersection, some courts might state that the declarant's words are not hearsay because they are in the form of a question, and questions do not assert anything. A better analysis would be to interpret the out-of-court words as equivalent to the assertion, "Driver had the light against him when he entered the intersection," and treat them therefore as hearsay when they are introduced to support the conclusion that the light was against Driver.

Basic Instances of Hearsay and Non-hearsay

3.   Yes. The declarant is the painter. The out-of-court statement is "this is a Waybright fixture," and it is sought to be introduced to show that the fixture was a Waybright fixture. Thus, the statement's relevance depends on its meaning being true. In terms of the Federal Rules, it is sought to be introduced to prove the truth of the matter it asserts. This makes it hearsay.

4.   Yes. The out-of-court statement is the painter's report to Homeowner that the fixture was a Waybright fixture. Note that hearsay can be a direct quotation such as "I said 'This is a Waybright fixture,' " or an indirect quotation such as "I told her that it was a Waybright fixture." The declarant in this problem is the painter, he made his statement out of court, and it is offered to prove the truth of its contents. The unusual aspect of this example is that he is now repeating the statement in court while he is a witness. Self-quotation, in the opinion of some authorities, ought not to be considered hearsay. However, under the Federal Rules and in most places governed by other rules, even self-quotation can be hearsay.

5.   Assuming that this information is relevant, there would be no hearsay problem. The painter in this example, unlike question 4, is telling in court something he *saw*. This is different, for hearsay purposes, from telling what he once *said*.

6.   Yes. This testimony gets in, even though testimony by a witness that the insured had once said, "I have arthritis" would be hearsay.[5] The insured's conduct of sitting in a particular waiting room does not fit the Federal Rules definition of assertive conduct. Since it was not a statement and was not conduct meant to convey information, it is outside the scope of the hearsay definition.

7.   The testimony does not contain any hearsay. This is an example of out-of-court words that have independent legal significance. They are introduced

---

5. Remember that many out-of-court statements sought to be introduced to prove the truth of what they assert do escape the standard exclusionary result of the hearsay rules because they fit certain exceptions to the doctrine or because, under the Federal Rules, they fall within specialized exceptions to the definition of hearsay itself. The statement in this example is an admission and would therefore be safe from objection on grounds of hearsay.

by the defendant to support the proposition that he was not a trespasser, and they do include words saying that the defendant is not a trespasser. That equivalence of expression is a coincidence that does not make the out-of-court words hearsay. They are introduced by the defendant to prove just that they were said. If they were really spoken, they amount to permission to enter the plaintiff's land. The court and our substantive law will assign a meaning to them such as deciding that they constitute the defense of permission in the trespass case. This effect is provided to the words by our system of property law without regard to what the declarant might have thought, remembered, seen, or meant to say when he said them. The testimonial infirmities do not matter since the words are relevant if a reasonable person who heard them would consider them to constitute permission to enter the land. It doesn't matter, under standard property law, whether the plaintiff meant or did not mean them to have their standard meaning.

8.   The out-of-court statement is not exactly equal to the proposition for which it is sought to be introduced — that Mr. Maintainer did bad work. All the declarant said was that she would never have Mr. Maintainer do any work for her. Yet the statement is relevant, if at all, because it conveys the meaning that the inspector thought Mr. Maintainer did bad work. That meaning is so close to the explicit content of the out-of-court statement that the statement should be classified as hearsay. If there was an issue, for example, about whether the inspector had ever heard of Mr. Maintainer or whether Mr. Maintainer had worked on the machine, proof that she said something about Mr. Maintainer would not be hearsay because the ideas that the inspector knew Mr. Maintainer or that Mr. Maintainer had worked on the machine would be unintended implications of the inspector's words.

On the other hand, it strains the imagination to say that the idea, "Maintainer did bad work" was an *unintended* implication of the statement, "I'd never let that Mr. Maintainer do any work for me." Obviously, there is room for disagreement about whether the inspector's statement should be treated as intending or not intending to assert something about Mr. Maintainer's work. A court would be influenced in deciding whether or not to classify the statement as hearsay by the importance of the statement in the case and by the seriousness of the testimonial infirmities in the specific situation. If the words were ambiguous and they were the proponent's only proof on a crucial issue, there would be a tendency to exclude them.

9.   There are three out-of-court statements in this problem:

1.   Hasty to the office manager (words such as "I'd like your office-cleaning business");
2.   Office manager to Clever's worker (words such as "Hasty has been soliciting our business"); and
3.   Clever's worker to Clever (note with words such as "the manager said that Hasty had solicited business").

Hasty's words would not be hearsay because whether it was true or not that Hasty wanted Maximum's business, Hasty's saying those words violated Hasty's promise not to contact customers of the office-cleaning business. So if Clever had a witness who could testify that she heard Hasty make his offer to Maximum, that quotation of Hasty's words would not be hearsay.

Clever does not have a witness to testify that Hasty said the words. Clever has a piece of paper written by his employee. And the piece of paper quotes Maximum's office manager. The manager's words are hearsay since they state that Hasty had done something, and they are relevant only to prove that Hasty had done it (solicit business from Maximum). Similarly, the note from Clever's employee is hearsay. It is an out-of-court statement conveying the idea that Maximum's office manager had said certain things about Hasty to Clever's employee. Unless that information is accurate, the note is not relevant to the trial. It is sought to be introduced to prove that what it asserts is true: that Maximum's manager spoke to Clever's employee and told him that Hasty had solicited business from him.

10.   The reference comment ("does excellent work") is not hearsay on the issue of how reasonable it was for the doctor to hire the nurse. Used in connection with that issue, the truthfulness of the reference is not material. All that matters is that the words were communicated to the doctor because whether or not they were true, a doctor who gets such a reference and then employs the person described in the reference is probably acting reasonably.

On the issue of how competent the nurse really is, the out-of-court words *are* hearsay since they are relevant to that issue only if their assertion ("excellent") is true.

11.   The vast majority of courts and scholars agree that this note is not hearsay — it is used just to show that there is a connection between the defendant and the victim. It is not shown to prove what the victim's address is since presumably that will be established in some other way. A minority view is that this note is equivalent to a note in the defendant's handwriting saying, "I know victim." If the note really did say that, most courts would be more inclined to treat it as hearsay. However, in the recurring instances in which this problem is litigated, the conventional treatment is to call the writing just circumstantial evidence and decide that it raises no hearsay problems.

12.   a. The statement that the racers stayed on the flat land when they rehearsed is phrased as a conclusion from the witness's investigation. It is apparent, though, that it is entirely based on what people said to him. Since it is therefore equivalent to a quotation in court of what various people said about the events during the rehearsal, it is hearsay when introduced to support the idea that the rehearsal race did not use the hill.

b. To prove that no one gave a warning to the owner about use of the hill, the investigator states that no one mentioned warnings in his interviews. Should this be treated as silence that is not hearsay? That analysis fits usually where there is a good reason to think that a certain subject would be mentioned to the person who later testifies about it. Where an investigator is involved, it seems likely that people would answer questions and remain silent about other topics. Their silence ought not logically to be taken as implying anything about their ideas on the non-addressed topic.

If the investigator had asked, "Did you give warnings?" and people replied to that question, their answers would be hearsay if quoted by the investigator. In this problem, the investigator may not have asked any questions about warnings. If he did not ask about warnings, the lack of mention of warnings in his interviews probably does not prove anything about warnings and is therefore not relevant. If he did ask about warnings, then his reports of non-replies might best be characterized as reports of assertive conduct (silence in response to a direct question could be the same as a negative shake of the head) or as reports of conversations in which the totality of the speaker's comments added up to a statement that they gave no warnings. For these reasons, the investigator's testimony that no one said anything about warnings should be treated as not relevant (since it is based on conversations in which silence about warnings is not logically related to whether or not warnings were given) or should be treated as hearsay.

Written Statements as Hearsay and Non-hearsay

13.   No. The statement is hearsay. Hearsay can be written or spoken. In this instance, you would be seeking to use the written words to establish exactly what they stated: the license plate of the car that hit your car. This makes them hearsay. Another problem is that there is no way of knowing the identity of the declarant (the writer) and showing the source of his or her knowledge.

14.   This statement is not hearsay. Written words can be hearsay, just as spoken words can, but only if they are introduced to prove the truth of what they assert. Here the truth of whether the writer will be able to accept the invitation is irrelevant to the issues at trial. But the note is relevant in a non-hearsay way. The fact that it was written shows that the plaintiff did have the ability to do some writing.

Conventional Non-hearsay Situations

15.   Information that customers ordered the radio from the food company is relevant because it shows that people who saw the radio and knew its brand name assumed that it was manufactured by the plaintiff food company and not by the defendant electronics company. The standard analysis of this situation is to describe the testimony as non-hearsay. The proponent is not trying to show that the out-of-court statements (the orders) were accurate. The proponent, rather, is using them circumstantially as evidence that some con-

sumers acted in a way that suggests that the defendant's brand name was confusingly similar to the plaintiff's. A contrary result is logically supportable but rarely adopted: If the customers' orders are analyzed as statements that necessarily incorporated the idea, "I believe that you are the manufacturer of the following item," then introducing them to prove that the customers did believe that the food company was the manufacturer of the radio would make them hearsay.[6]

16.   Mr. Poor may quote himself in this instance because his out-of-court words are called a verbal act or a verbal part of an act. Without those words being introduced into the trial, the conduct of turning over money would be ambiguous. The reasoning here is similar to the reasoning that permits words of independent legal effect to be introduced without regard to hearsay problems. Some courts use the expression *res gestae* as a label for defining statements of this kind as non-hearsay since the words are permitted to be introduced as "part of the act" being described.

17.   Yes. Silence by a person (like each of the lot's customers) is not considered to be a statement made out of court. Since there is no statement, there can be no hearsay. Like so many issues in hearsay, this one could reasonably be analyzed to reach an opposite result. The witness is really basing testimony on a report of everything the customers have ever said to show that none of their remarks involved dissatisfaction with the location of the lot or the wording of its sign. This point is logically sound, but courts are satisfied to respond to situations like this one in a conventional way and admit the testimony. Incidentally, this example serves as a reminder that successfully avoiding hearsay objections is not a guarantee that evidence will be admitted. Other requirements, such as relevance, must also be met. Here, to establish that the customers' silence was relevant, the defendant would need to show that it would have been easy for a disappointed customer to find a way to present a complaint.

Would the words of the sign be hearsay? No. The state consumer affairs department is seeking to introduce them to prove that they were used by the defendant and to show that they are false. There would be a hearsay issue only if the words were used in an effort to state that the meaning they convey is true.

18.   This testimony does not fit a sensible definition of hearsay. The words by Sportsfan are relevant whether or not they are a true statement of Sports-

---

6. Defined as hearsay, this material would still be admissible under a state of mind exception to the hearsay exclusion to prove that the people giving the orders had the belief that the food company made the radios. Alternatively, expert testimony based on a properly conducted survey would be a method of establishing the plaintiff's showing of confusion in the marketplace that would completely avoid the hearsay problem discussed in this example.

fan's feelings about the player. The jury can use them to assess Sportsfan's recklessness or good judgment without the jury having to decide whether the words were an accurate representation of Sportsfan's beliefs. Even if the words were false, and Sportsfan did not believe what he was saying, he was probably reckless to say words that the player would likely consider to be insults. The fact that Sportsfan said the words is relevant to a judgment about whether he is a reckless type of person.

4

Exceptions to the Hearsay Exclusionary Rule

Introduction

The supreme irony of the hearsay doctrine is that a vast amount of hearsay is admissible at common law and under the Federal Rules. The full analysis of any hearsay problem, therefore, requires considering whether the offered evidence is hearsay and then, if it is hearsay, whether any exception to the rule of exclusion applies to it.

The exceptions give special treatment to recurring instances of hearsay. Many are based on longstanding tradition, while others are newer, justified by a belief that at least one of the testimonial infirmities is unlikely to be a factor in most of the instances they cover. The Federal Rules also provide for admission of hearsay as part of an expert's testimony even if no specific hearsay provisions would allow it, so long as the material is of a type usually relied upon by such experts.

Some types of hearsay statements are thought to be particularly free from the risk that the maker of the statement intended to lie. Statements of this kind are usually admissible, whether or not the declarant is available to testify. Other types of hearsay are thought to be particularly necessary in special circumstances. These types of statements are usually admissible only if the proponent shows that the declarant is unavailable. Finally, there is a third class of out-of-court statements offered to prove the truth of what they assert that universally is allowed into evidence despite the hearsay rule, even without a belief that the statement is likely to have been truthful when made or that the statement is particularly necessary to a party's case. This class of statements includes admissions, which are any statements ever made by a *party* in the current case if introduced against that party, and certain statements made out of court by a person who appears in court as a *witness*. The Federal Rules exceptions to the hearsay exclusion are organized, accordingly, in three categories: 1) hearsay exceptions that apply without regard to whether the declarant is available as a witness; 2) hearsay exceptions that apply only if the declarant is unavailable as a witness; and 3) exemptions from the definition of hearsay for certain out-of-court statements offered for the truth of what they assert.

Hearsay and the Confrontation Clause

Situations in which out-of-court statements are admitted as proof of what they assert involve an apparent conflict with the confrontation clause of the Constitution. The Sixth Amendment states that a criminal defendant "shall enjoy the right . . . to be confronted with the witnesses against him." If this clause were interpreted literally, exemptions and exceptions to the hearsay exclusion rule would be unconstitutional because they allow statements by absent "unconfronted" declarants to be introduced at criminal trials. As a matter of constitutional law, however, Supreme Court decisions indicate that use of out-of-court statements will rarely violate the confrontation clause so long as they fit within the exemptions and exceptions defined in the Federal Rules.

Mattox v. United States[1] held more than a century ago that the use of a declarant's dying declaration did not abridge the constitutional rights of the criminal defendant against whom it was introduced. A succession of Supreme Court cases has since considered a wide range of traditional exceptions to the hearsay exclusion. While it was thought for a period that the Constitution would be interpreted to prohibit use of these exceptions unless the declarant was shown to be unavailable, recent decisions have weakened that requirement considerably. In 1992 the Supreme Court decided *White v. Illinois*,[2] holding that there was no constitutional bar to the use of excited utterances and statements for the purpose of medical treatment against a criminal defendant, without regard to the availability of the declarant. Some decisions refer to a requirement that an exception be "firmly rooted."[3] Despite that language, in the 1980s and 1990s the Supreme Court has approved use of a

---

1. 146 U.S. 140 (1892).

2. 112 S. Ct. 736 (1992).

3. *Ohio v. Roberts*, 448 U.S. 56 (1980) held that the former testimony exception could be used only if the declarant was shown to be unavailable, relying on a characterization of the exception as "firmly rooted" as a basis for finding its use to be constitutional.

great many hearsay exceptions, including some in circumstances that cannot fairly be described as traditional or firmly rooted. The exception for coconspirator statements, for example, was found to be constitutional even when, as a matter of statutory interpretation, the court held that traditional requirements of independent corroboration of the conspiracy no longer applied.[4]

Statements Exempted from the Federal Rules Definition of Hearsay

Admissions

Perhaps the largest loophole in the hearsay doctrine is a category of statements called "admissions." An admission is anything a party has ever communicated (in speech, writing, or in any other way) sought to be introduced against that party at trial. At common law these statements are defined as hearsay and admitted under an exception to the hearsay exclusion rule. Under the Federal Rules they are specifically exempted from the definition of hearsay and thus are not barred by the prohibition against introducing hearsay evidence. The statement, at the time the party made it, could have been favorable to some interest of the party, or unfavorable, or neutral. The proponent of an out-of-court statement who seeks to take advantage of the admission rationale is only required to show that the statement was once made by the opposing party, and that it is relevant in the current trial.

There are two primary rationales for permitting statements defined as admissions to be used in evidence despite the concerns that underly the hearsay doctrine. First, it seems fair to many that people ought to be forced to live up to their own claims, promises, and statements. Allowing them into evidence when people become involved in lawsuits furthers this goal. Second, because admissions by definition are always statements by a party (or someone closely affiliated with a party), many hearsay dangers are obviated. If the statement was false at the time it was made, or if use of the statement at the trial might create a false impression because of discrepancies between the circumstances at the time at which it was made and circumstances at the time of the trial, the party is available to explain what the statement meant at the time it was made.

These justifications for exempting admissions from exclusion under the hearsay rule are imperfect at best. They may reflect a basic ambivalence about the hearsay rule. While excluding statements that meet the definition of hearsay seems highly desirable in the abstract, many classes of statements seem too good to ignore. This has led to the current structure of hearsay law

---

4. *Bourjaily v. United States,* 483 U.S. 171 (1987).

with its large number of exceptions rationalized on fairly questionable grounds.

The exemption of admissions from the definition of hearsay is accomplished by Rule 801(d)(2):

> A statement is not hearsay if . . . [t]he statement is offered against a party and is (A) the party's own statement, in either an individual or a representative capacity or (B) a statement of which the party has manifested an adoption or belief in its truth, or (C) a statement by a person authorized by the party to make a statement concerning the subject, or (D) a statement by the party's agent or servant concerning a matter within the scope of the agency or employment, made during the existence of the relationship, or (E) a statement by a coconspirator of a party during the course and in furtherance of the conspiracy.

Thus, five types of statements are defined as admissions by Rule 801(d)(2). The clearest example is a party's own past words, relevant at the time of trial to an issue in the trial. Illustratively, suppose *A* sues *B* for damages suffered in a collision allegedly caused by *B*'s bad driving. An issue concerns whether *B* drove through a red light. If *B* said after the accident, "I didn't see the traffic light," *A* would be entitled to introduce evidence of *B*'s statement as a basis for concluding that *B* did not see the light (which would be relevant to evaluating *B*'s driving).

Related to statements a party makes are "adoptive admissions." An adoptive admission is a party's reaction to a statement or action by another person when it is reasonable to treat the party's reaction as an admission of something stated or implied by the other person. In the automobile collision example, if someone said to *B* right after the collision, "You didn't stop for the red light," and *B* answered, "I'm sorry I didn't," *B*'s answer (together with the question to which it was a reply) would be an adoptive admission. Similarly, there are instances in which a party's silence will be treated as an admission if most people would have spoken to contradict something like a statement just made to the party. Silence as an admission might be applied if someone said to driver *B*, "Everyone saw that the light was against you," and *B* said nothing in reply.

Sometimes statements by a person other than a party can be treated as admissions when offered against a party. The statements of a person authorized to speak on behalf of someone who becomes a party to a lawsuit are admissible as admissions when offered against the party. A lawyer is the most common example of a person who is authorized to speak on another's behalf.

While a lawyer is a particular kind of agent, employed to provide legal representation, the Federal Rules definition of "admission" covers statements made by any type of agent or employee. A statement is an admission, usable against a party, if it is made by the party's agent or employee concerning something within the scope of agency or employment during the time of the agency or employment. Also, one coconspirator's statements are considered admissions when offered against another coconspirator so long as the statements were made during and in furtherance of their conspiracy. So if a truck driver working for a company was involved in a traffic accident and then said something about his or her driving, those words would be admissible in a suit against that company for damages for injuries arising out of the accident. This is true even though the truck driver is probably not authorized by the company to make statements about driving. The Federal Rules would define the driver's words as an admission, usable against the company, because they concerned the driver's employment and were made while the driver and the company continued to have an employer-employee relationship.

Some common law jurisdictions are more restrictive than this and would treat quotation of the driver's words as hearsay if used in a suit against the company. Their doctrinal analysis would state that the driver's job is driving, not making statements about driving, and that therefore use of the words against the company would be hearsay because the words were spoken outside the scope of the driver's employment. For these jurisdictions, the authorization to speak on a subject is crucial to deciding whether the speaker's words can be treated as an admission against someone other than the speaker.

Prior Statements by a Witness

The Federal Rules exclude one other group of statements in addition to admissions from the definition of hearsay. These are certain statements made outside of court by a person who then testifies at trial. The need for special treatment arises because under common law and the general Federal Rules definition of hearsay, a witness's own out-of-court words are hearsay even if they are quoted at trial by the witness, if their relevance depends on the truth of what the out-of-court words assert. Despite the applicability of the general definition, it is controversial to treat as hearsay out-of-court statements by a person who appears at a trial and testifies. After all, the fact that the witness and the out-of-court declarant are the same human being makes this situation different from most attempted uses of out-of-court statements. Where the witness's own past statements are involved, a jury would be able to observe the declarant's demeanor and to hear responses to cross-examination about the statements. Since the lack of these opportunities is the basis for excluding hearsay, it has seemed to some authorities that the hearsay rule should be completely withdrawn from past statements of a person who is a witness at the trial.

The Federal Rules mostly adopt the opposing view that a witness's own out-of-court words should be defined as hearsay. Those who believe that the hearsay exclusion can sensibly be applied even to the out-of-court words of a person who is a witness at the trial point out that cross-examination at trial time may be less effective than cross-examination would have been at the time the speaker made the statement. If out-of-court statements by people who become witnesses were generally admissible, well-organized parties would develop a practice of making records of interviews with prospective witnesses. There would be no cross-examination at the time they obtained these statements, and then they would seek to introduce them at a subsequent trial. At the time of the trial, opponents of this practice suggest, the person who gave the interview might be less willing to change or be self-critical of the recollection than he or she might have been if the recollection had been challenged when he or she first expressed it.

In the context of these opposed views, FRE 801(d)(1) treats selected types of statements by witnesses as outside the hearsay definition, under particular circumstances. The Rule states:

> A statement is not hearsay if . . . [t]he declarant testifies at the trial or hearing and is subject to cross-examination concerning the statement, and the statement is (A) inconsistent with the declarant's testimony, and was given under oath subject to the penalty of perjury at a trial, hearing, or other proceeding, or in a deposition, or (B) consistent with the declarant's testimony and is offered to rebut an express or implied charge against the declarant of recent fabrication or improper influence or motive, or (C) one of identification of a person made after perceiving the person.

Notice that there are three types of out-of-court statements by a witness: prior inconsistent statements, prior consistent statements, and statements identifying a person. For any of them to qualify for exclusion from the hearsay definition, there must be a showing that the declarant is "available for cross-examination" concerning the declarant's out-of-court statement. The "available for cross-examination" requirement may be very easy for the proponent of a witness's out-of-court statement to fulfill. It was satisfied in a case, binding on federal courts and suggestive authority elsewhere, where a witness remembered making a statement but did not remember the events that he had described in his statement and did not remember any circumstances involved in his making the statement.[5] Obviously, the opportunity for realistic cross-examination of such a witness would be very slight.

A prior inconsistent statement is any statement by a witness: 1) made out of court; 2) before the witness testifies; that 3) conflicts with something the witness says in testimony. At common law, these statements may be introduced for impeachment, that is, to support a conclusion that the witness testified falsely. This use does not violate the hearsay rule because, analytically, the out-of-court statement is being introduced to show its *contrast* with the in-court statement, not its *truth*. Prior inconsistent statements may not, at common law, be introduced to support a conclusion that the prior statement

---

5. See *United States v. Owens,* 484 U.S. 554 (1988).

was true. Under the Federal Rules, impeachment use of a prior statement is permitted since it raises no hearsay implications. Additionally, if the prior statement was made under oath at a proceeding, it may be introduced as proof of what it asserts.

A prior consistent statement is any statement by a witness made out of court before the witness's testimony that reinforces or supports the testimony. Under the Federal Rules, a prior consistent statement does not have to have been made under oath in a proceeding as is required for substantive use of a prior inconsistent statement. However, evidence that a prior consistent statement was made is permitted to be introduced only if the proponent shows: 1) that the witness's testimony has been attacked as recently fabricated or influenced by a motive to lie; and 2) that the witness made the prior statement before the time of the alleged fabrication or before the time that he or she was subject to the alleged motive to lie.

If a witness who testifies to a certain proposition is accused of lying or of slanting the testimony because of a motive favorable to one side in the trial, proof that the witness has said similar things prior to the trial would support a conclusion that the trial testimony was truthful. This logic is particularly strong if the out-of-court statements were made before a motive to lie arose. For example, Witness A testifies that Defendant D committed a crime. If D shows that the prosecution promised leniency to A in exchange for A's testimony, an implication would arise that A's testimony may have been untruthful in favor of the prosecution. Proof that A had said similar things about D prior to the time of A's deal with the prosecution would support the truthfulness of A's in-court testimony. Although Rule 801(d)(1)(B) does not explicitly state that the prior consistent statement must have been made before the witness had a motive to falsify his or her testimony, the United States Supreme Court has interpreted it to include that requirement.[6] Thus, a statement made *after* the speaker had a motive to testify falsely but before the witness testified in court would not be eligible for the non-hearsay treatment of Rule 801(d)(1)(B). In some states, a prior consistent statement made at any time is admissible for whatever weight the trier of fact may give it.

These two types of prior statements, inconsistent and consistent, have differing prerequisites under the Federal Rules for admission as substantive evidence of the information they assert. Consistent statements are admissible only to rebut specified types of attacks on the witness's in-court testimony. Inconsistent statements do not have to meet a similar requirement. However, inconsistent statements must have been made under oath in a proceeding to be entitled to substantive treatment, while substantive treatment is accorded consistent statements whether or not they were made under oath in a proceeding. The following chart illustrates these requirements.

---

6. *Tome v. United States,* 115 S.Ct. 696, 130 L.Ed.2d 574 (1995).

CHART THIRTEEN
Prior Statements by Witness

Type of Statement	Required to Have Been Made under Oath?	When Admissible?
Consistent	No	Only to rebut claimed improper influence or recent fabrication
Inconsistent	Yes	Always

Greater restrictiveness concerning inconsistent statements may make sense because the proponent of substantive use of a witness's prior *inconsistent* statement asks the jury to reject what it has heard in court and substitute a version of reality drawn from out-of-court statements. In contrast, the proponent of substantive use of a prior *consistent* statement seeks to reinforce a conclusion that what the in-court witness said was true. Belief in the content of the prior consistent statement evidence will lead a jury to conclude that the witness's testimony it heard originally is true. This is a less powerful use of out-of-court words than the use permitted by the Federal Rules for prior inconsistent statements. Because substituting out-of-court words for in-court words with an inconsistent meaning is so drastic, it is not surprising that the Federal Rules place significant requirements on the use of prior inconsistent statements as substantive evidence.

Under the Federal Rules, a witness's out-of-court statement identifying a person is admissible as substantive evidence of the identification. This is a change from common law treatment of the issue. Under the Federal Rules, for example, if a person sees a crime, later tells the police that the crime was committed by *X* and testifies at *X*'s trial, the out-of-court statement is admissible as substantive evidence that *X* committed the crime. If the person had identified *X* at a line-up or from mug shots, the same logic would apply. The rationale of the rule is that identifications of people made prior to trials are likely to be more accurate than identifications made during testimony, and for that reason should not be excluded from substantive use.

EXAMPLES

1.   Plaintiff claims that she was badly hurt by xanadite, an ingredient in a microwave pizza sold by the defendant manufacturer. To support a claim for punitive damages, the plaintiff wants to prove that xanadite is extremely dangerous. Discuss whether the plaintiff may introduce each of the following items of evidence to show that xanadite is dangerous. Remember that admissibility on the issue of *xanadite's dangerousness* is different from admissibility on other issues that might be part of the plaintiff's case, such as the *company's knowledge* about xanadite's dangerousness.

a. A letter from a university scientist found in the company's files, stating that the scientist has discovered that xanadite is very dangerous in microwave pizzas and asking to be hired by the company to do further research about it.

b. A memorandum written by the company's president to the company's chief scientist, saying that the president wanted him to start work immediately on a new formula for the company's pizza that would replace the xanadite with another ingredient because the xanadite is extremely dangerous.

c. A note written by the company president to the company's chief of public relations, with an attached copy of a scientific article, saying, "The attached article says that xanadite is dangerous in foods. We use it in our microwave pizza. This shows we've been selling something dangerous."

d. If the note in Example c did not say, "This shows we've been selling something dangerous," but said instead, "This shows we may be in serious trouble," what result?

c. Testimony that a worker in the manufacturer's pizza ingredients warehouse once said to a friend, "If you ever get a job here, be sure you don't get assigned to handling xanadite. That stuff is unbelievably dangerous. Most of the people who work with it lose their hair and get bad rashes."

f. An autobiography by someone who once was the president of the manufacturing company, written after retirement, describing xanadite as a dangerous ingredient.

2. In a variation of Example 1, if it was admitted that xanadite is extremely dangerous, but the manufacturer denied having had that knowledge at the time it made the pizza that hurt the plaintiff, could the evidence offered in parts a to f of Example 1 be introduced to show that the manufacturer did have that knowledge at the relevant time?

3. Manny and Moe are on trial for bank robbery. A witness has testified that she saw them enter the bank together carrying guns. The prosecution seeks to have a police officer testify that after he had been arrested, Manny told the officer that Moe was the other person involved in the robbery. Is this testimony admissible to show that Moe was one of the two robbers?

4. Eagle Enterprises sues Cybernetics Corporation, seeking damages on a claim that a computer program Cybernetics was supposed to produce by January 1, 1993, failed to operate as expected. Fred Micro, an independent computer engineer, testifies for Eagle that he examined the program in February, 1993, and that it did not work. May he testify further to show that the computer program did not work properly, that in February 1993 he told a group of Eagle's employees that the Cybernetics program did not work?

5. Paula Plaintiff was injured when a large bus she was riding in collided with another vehicle. She sought damages from the transit company that operated the bus. One of her witnesses was an expert at reconstructing

accidents. The accident reconstructionist testified that the collision probably occurred because the bus driver did not pay careful attention to oncoming traffic. The transit company contended that a defect in the brakes, for which the bus manufacturer would be responsible, was the cause of the collision. Could the transit company introduce evidence that the expert once testified in a similar case involving a bus collision and stated in the circumstances of that case that brake failure was the most likely cause of the incident? If it is admissible, could proof of the witness's earlier statements be used for any purpose other than impeachment?

6.   In a medical malpractice case, a nurse testifies that the defendant doctor followed standard procedures during an operation in which the doctor allegedly harmed the plaintiff. During cross-examination, the nurse admits that since the time of the operation, the defendant doctor has recommended him for several promotions. On re-direct examination, may the defendant have the nurse testify that he wrote a letter to a friend a few days after the operation, stating that the doctor had followed standard procedures?

7.   Someone ran up to Victim on a street and stole his wallet. Victim then hailed a passing police car and drove around in it, looking for the robber. As the police car went by Suspect, Victim pointed at him, started sobbing, and fainted. Suspect is now on trial, accused of stealing Victim's wallet. May a police officer describe how Victim pointed to Suspect?

EXPLANATIONS

1.   a. The letter is hearsay, since the plaintiff seeks to introduce it to prove that what it asserts is true, that xanadite is dangerous. It is not an admission, since it is not a statement by any employee or agent of the company. Further, it would not be an adoptive admission, since a company does not indicate agreement with an unsolicited letter just by filing it.

b. The letter is partly hearsay and partly not hearsay. The portion that is a command to the scientist could be classified as non-hearsay. Yet it might be treated as relevant on the issue of the dangerousness of xanadite since one of the main reasons why a company president might want an ingredient eliminated from a product would be that the ingredient is dangerous. What about the president's statement that xanadite is extremely dangerous? If it is sought to be introduced to prove the danger of xanadite in pizza, it is an out-of-court statement sought to be introduced to prove the truth of what it asserts. This would be hearsay under the common law, but the hearsay rule would not keep it from being introduced since it would be covered by the admission exception. It is a party's own statement, sought to be introduced against the party. Under the Federal Rules, the statement fits the description of admission. Thus, it is exempt from the definition of hearsay.

c. The plaintiff is seeking to introduce the note and the attached article as proof that xanadite is a dangerous ingredient. Therefore, the evidence will be hearsay under common law and will meet the Federal Rules definition of hearsay, too, unless it qualifies under the Federal Rules provision that removes admissions from the definition of hearsay. The evidence is admissible as an adoptive admission. It is an out-of-court statement by a party (the company president speaks for the company) accepting as true an out-of-court statement by another (the author of the scientific article). The note and the article are both admissible.

d. Changing the president's words from "we've been selling something dangerous" to "we may be in serious trouble" makes it harder to treat the president's note as an adoptive admission of the statements in the scientific article. The trial judge will accept or reject the adoptive admission rationale depending on what the parties persuade the judge the president may have meant by writing that the article meant the company was "in serious trouble." If that meant the president agreed with the attached scientific article, then the president's statement and the article would all be admissible under the rationale of adoptive admission. Understood that way, the president's out-of-court statement expresses agreement with (or adopts) the scientist's out-of-court statement. On the other hand, if the president's statement about being "in serious trouble" just meant that the company should anticipate negative publicity about the ingredient, then the trial judge would properly reject the adoptive admission argument for admissibility. Under Rule 104(a), it is the judge who decides whether the admissions rationale applies.

e. The out-of-court words would be an admission under the Federal Rules because they were spoken by one of the defendant's employees during the period of the employer-employee relationship, and they concerned something within the scope of the declarant's employment. In some common law jurisdictions, the words would be inadmissible hearsay since the company has not authorized the warehouse worker to make statements about the health risks of the materials the workers handle.

f. The autobiography is an out-of-court statement. Its only relevance is to support the plaintiff's contention that xanadite is a dangerous ingredient. Because that fact is what the autobiography asserts, it will be treated as hearsay and excluded unless it qualifies as an admission. Under the Federal Rules and common law, the book would be kept out. Because the book was written after the writer retired from the company, it does not meet the part of the Federal Rules definition of admission requiring that the statement be made during the course of the declarant's employment.

2.   a. The letter from the scientist would not be hearsay if it was introduced to show that the company had heard about a possible risk. In this use, the truth of the letter's contents is not the basis for admissibility. The argument for admissibility is that having received the letter, whether it was true or not, the company should have been stimulated to find out the details about the safety of xanadite.

b. The president's memo to the chief scientist, saying that xanadite is dangerous, would be admissible to show that the president knew that xanadite was dangerous. It reflects the declarant's then-current mental state, or could be said to be circumstantial evidence of his possession of knowledge. Since the facts about xanadite itself are established in some other way, this use of the president's memo does not involve the problems that would be present if the memo was sought to be used to show that xanadite is dangerous. To show that xanadite is dangerous, the memo's relevance depends on the truth of its assertions. To show that the president knew about xanadite, it is just necessary to show that the president was writing things about it.

c. The president's memo about the scientific article could be admitted without hearsay problems if its purpose was not to establish that xanadite is dangerous, but just to show that the president was aware of xanadite's dangerousness. The memo shows that the president acted in ways that are consistent with a belief that xanadite was dangerous. If the dangerousness of xanadite was shown in some other way, then there would be no risk in introducing the president's memo just to show awareness of that dangerousness.

d. The change in the president's words does not affect their applicability on the issue of notice and does not change the hearsay analysis.

e. The words by the warehouse worker are also non-hearsay if used just to show current knowledge of the problem rather than the fact that xanadite *is* a problem.

f. If the former president's autobiography did not say that the president had known about the xanadite problem while working as president, it would be irrelevant. If it did say that the president knew about xanadite's dangers while working as president, it would be hearsay. This would be a use to show that at some time in the past, the president, while employed by the manufacturer, knew about the danger of xanadite. That statement can be thought of as "A few years ago, I was aware that xanadite is dangerous." To be relevant, it would have to be understood as a truthful statement about the past event it describes. This is different from the warehouse worker's statement, for example, which shows relevant current knowledge by a company worker because it is made while the worker is connected with the company.

3. No. The statement, made out of court, is sought to be introduced to support a conclusion that its assertion — that Moe was one of the robbers — is true. The admissions rationale for statements by coconspirators requires that the statement be made in furtherance of the conspiracy and while the conspiracy is in effect. When Manny gave Moe's name to the police, the conspiracy, if any, clearly was no longer in effect, and Manny's statement cannot in any way be characterized as in furtherance of the goals of the conspiracy.

4. No. This would be an instance of a witness quoting his own out-of-court statement. Since the purpose of bringing Micro's out-of-court words into the trial would be to support the inference that the computer program did not work, it is clear that the words would be offered to prove the truth of what they assert. They are therefore hearsay. The Federal Rules provide spe-

cial treatment for some out-of-court statements by people who testify, but this situation does not meet any of the requirements for that treatment.

5. There are two possible uses the transit company might assert for the evidence of the accident reconstructionist's testimony in the earlier trial. One use is impeachment, where the jury would be permitted to learn that in a similar case the witness had given testimony that conflicts with his testimony in the current case. Where impeachment is the purpose for informing the jury about a witness's earlier statements, no hearsay problems arise because the prior statement is *not* being used to support a conclusion that it is true. It is used only to suggest to the jury that the witness's current testimony may be false.

The second purpose for which the transit company might want to introduce evidence of the accident expert's earlier testimony would be to support a conclusion that bad brakes were the cause of the accident involved in the current trial. This substantive use of the prior statements does involve the use of out-of-court statements to prove the truth of what they assert, but under the Federal Rules, the statements are treated as outside the definition of hearsay. They are prior statements by a witness; in particular, they are prior inconsistent statements given under oath at an earlier proceeding by a witness who is subject to cross-examination in the current trial. Therefore, under the Federal Rules, the testimony by the accident expert at the earlier trial would be admissible for both impeachment and substantive purposes.

6. The nurse's letter is an out-of-court statement. Under the Federal Rules, it can qualify for admission to prove the truth of what it asserts if it meets the requirements of the prior consistent statement portion of the Rules' definition of hearsay. That section excludes from the definition of hearsay a prior consistent statement of a witness if the witness is available for cross-examination, and if there has been an express or implied charge of improper influence or motive. The prior statement must have been made before the witness had a motive to lie in favor of the party whom his or her testimony supports. In this problem the plaintiff has brought out on cross-examination that the defendant, who is supported by the nurse's testimony, has helped the nurse obtain promotions. This suggests a motive for the nurse to slant his testimony in the doctor's favor. It also might suggest that the promotions were made in return for a promise to give favorable testimony. Either of those implications can be rebutted by evidence that the nurse made a statement consistent with his trial testimony, if the trial judge is persuaded that the nurse made the statement before the nurse and doctor had dealings related to the nurse's interest in being promoted. The Federal Rule makes clear that the prior statement may be treated as substantive evidence, and not merely as a basis for evaluating the truth of the in-court testimony.

7. The out-of-court conduct by Victim fits the definition of statement, under the Federal Rules, because it is clear that Victim meant it to convey information. (If Victim had only fainted and not pointed to Suspect, an

argument could be made that the fainting reaction is relevant to Suspect's guilt and is not a statement by Victim subject to analysis as possible hearsay.) Victim's out-of-court pointing is sought to be introduced to prove the truth of what it asserts, so it will be hearsay (and inadmissible unless an exception applies) unless it qualifies as a prior statement by a witness or as an admission. It cannot be an admission because it is not being introduced against the declarant. It does fit the Federal Rules definition of "identification of a person made after perceiving the person." Therefore, so long as the declarant is available for cross-examination, the out-of-court statement is admissible. If Victim is available at the trial and can be cross-examined, then the out-of-court assertive conduct (Victim's pointing to Suspect) can be described to the jury.

Groupings of Hearsay Exceptions under the Federal Rules

The Federal Rules define 27 specific types of out-of-court statements as *hearsay* that is *admissible* under exceptions to the hearsay exclusion. Additionally, the rules have "catch-all" exceptions that allow admission of hearsay in circumstances that are not covered in any of the other 27 exceptions. The exceptions are organized into two groups: exceptions for which the availability of the declarant is immaterial, and exceptions which are usable only if the declarant is unavailable. This separation of the exceptions into two classes indicates that the drafters of the Federal Rules believed that the risks inherent in admitting some of the types of hearsay were less than those connected with other types. For situations where the risks are minimal, the material can be used whether or not the declarant is available. For other situations, where the arguments supporting the exceptions are based on the necessity to use the out-of-court statements rather than on the likely truthfulness of the out-of-court declarant, the exception is allowed only if there is proof that the declarant is unavailable.

Statements Defined as Hearsay but Admissible Without Regard to the Declarant's Availability

Twenty-three specific categories of hearsay are admissible under the Federal Rules whether or not the declarant is available. Additionally, there is a "catch-all" provision. Each of these types of hearsay is described in its own subpart of Rule 803. This section defines and discusses the most important ones. Descriptions of *all* the exceptions are in the Appendix, "Federal Rules of Evidence with plain language explanations and review of important points added to the text of the Rules."

Present Sense Impressions

People sometimes describe things as they are seeing them or immediately after seeing them. Statements of this kind are called present sense impressions and are admissible to prove the substance of what they assert. They are defined in Rule 803(1):

> Present sense impression. A statement describing or explaining an event or condition made while the declarant was perceiving the event of condition, or immediately thereafter.

Problems of memory are extremely slight in these circumstances since the rule requires that the statement be made during or immediately after the event or condition it describes. In most of these statements, there will be some check on the accuracy of the speaker's perception because the speaker may be describing the event to someone else who is seeing it or may be speaking in the hearing of others who know what is going on. In most instances descriptions that are at variance with reality will be repressed by people's fear of seeming to be wrong or will be corrected by others who are present. It should be noted, though, that the rule does not require that the statement be made to anyone who was in a position to correct the statement if it was wrong.

Excited Utterances

Besides narrating descriptions of events that they see, people sometimes speak out of excitement, or shock, or in reaction to having been startled. The Federal Rules treat this type of statement slightly differently from present sense impressions. An "excited utterance" is defined in Rule 803(2):

> Excited utterance. A statement relating to a startling event or condition made while the declarant was under the stress of excitement caused by the event or condition.

In bar examinations and law school tests examples of excited utterances are usually statements that begin with the words, "Oh my God" or "Oh, no." They usually end with an exclamation point. The rationale of this exception is that any motive the declarant might have to lie will be overcome by the shock of the startling event, and that memory is not a problem because the statement must be made close in time to the event.

Present Sense Impression and Excited Utterance Compared

There are small differences between the Federal Rules treatments of the present sense impression and excited utterance exceptions. A statement covered by the present sense impression exception must "describe" something, while a statement covered by the excited utterance exception is required only to "relate" to the event that was startling. The present sense impression statement can be made during or immediately after the declarant sees its subject, while the excited utterance must be made while the declarant is under the stress or excitement that justifies the exception. A person who is injured and rendered unconscious may wake up and say something about the cause of the injury. That statement can be treated as an excited utterance despite the passage of a long period of time between the stimulus and the statement since there is no likelihood that the speaker's perception could have been affected by events that occurred while the speaker was unconscious. If a statement about a stress-inducing event is made in response to someone's question, some courts may rule that it was not the product of the speaker's stress.

Statements of Current Mental, Emotional, or Physical Condition

When people say what they think about something or say how they feel physically or emotionally, there are no perception or memory problems likely to diminish the accuracy of what they say. For that reason, the Federal Rules provide a hearsay exception for statements of "then existing mental, emotional, or physical condition." The definition is provided in Rule 803(3):

> Then existing mental, emotional, or physical condition. A statement of the declarant's then existing state of mind, emotion, sensation, or physical condition (such as intent, plan, motive, design, mental feeling, pain, and bodily health), but not including a statement of memory or belief to prove the fact remembered or believed unless it relates to the execution, revocation, identification, or terms of declarant's will.

This exception covers statements about what a person is feeling at the time he or she speaks, including both physical and emotional feelings. A statement like "I feel terrible" would be admissible for its truth — that is, that the speaker was feeling terrible at the time he or she spoke. A person's statements about a fact can show two different things: 1) the fact is something the speaker believes; and 2) the fact is true. The mental state exception allows proof of a person's statement of fact to show that the person believed the fact to be true but prohibits the use of a person's statements of feeling to prove that a remembered fact is true. Thus, proof that a declarant said, "I saw Bill yesterday," would be inadmissible if offered to prove that the declarant did see Bill on the day before he spoke. It would, however, be admissible to show that at the time the declarant said it, the declarant *thought* he had seen Bill on the previous day.

A statement of a person's plan or intention is considered an expression of then-existing mental state. It will be admitted as relevant on two issues: whether the declarant had that plan; and whether the declarant carried out the plan. In contrast, a statement about a past act will be hearsay if offered to prove that the past act occurred. For example, to prove that the declarant attended a movie on a Friday, an out-of-court statement on Saturday, "I went to the movies yesterday," would be excludable hearsay if offered to prove that the declarant did go to the movies the day before her statement. It would be a use of a statement of the mental state "memory" to prove the fact remembered and is explicitly prohibited by the Federal Rules. However, a statement on Thursday, "I plan to go to the movies tomorrow," is admissible as relevant to the issue of whether the declarant went to the movies on Friday.

A person's statement that he or she has already done something may seem far more probative on the question of whether he or she did it than the person's earlier statement about having a plan to do it. Yet a statement about a plan is acceptable evidence under this hearsay exception while the recollection of past conduct is not. One possible rationalization for this choice by the drafters is that both statements are the type of hearsay that incorporates many dangers of error, but that jurors who hear about a person's statement of a plan can be expected to be aware that plans are sometimes not accomplished, so that the risks of having them hear about the statement of plans are not great. If jurors hear that someone said he had actually done something in the past and are permitted to rely on that as support for the conclusion that he had done it, the natural skepticism about whether plans come to fruition would not have any place in the jurors' thinking. There is therefore a greater chance that the jurors would rely on the out-of-court statement as very strong evidence that the declarant actually did do what he said he had done.

The mental state exception permits the introduction of testimony that a declarant stated a plan to meet another person to show that the *other person* went to the location where the declarant said they would meet. This uses the declarant's statement of the declarant's intention as proof of the conduct of another person — to show that the other person acted as the declarant expected. Realizing that this type of proof depends on a large inductive leap, some courts have permitted it only when there is additional evidence suggesting that the declarant's belief about the future actions of the second person was accurate.

The mental state exception provides the practical solution for some of the standard hearsay dilemmas, namely "I'm the King of Mars" and "I think this product was made by Company *X*." For statements used to support an implication that the speaker was insane, a conclusion that the statement reflected the speaker's belief is all that the proponent seeks. This is permitted under the exception for "then existing mental condition." Similarly, most survey research is intended to develop information about what people think, not whether what they think is an accurate reflection of reality. Thus, proof that respondents articulated particular beliefs is admissible under the mental state exception.

Statements for Medical Diagnosis or Treatment

This exception, in the Federal Rules, overlaps the exception for statements of physical condition. It is defined in Rule 803(4):

> Statements for purposes of medical diagnosis or treatment. Statements made for purposes of medical diagnosis or treatment and describing medical history, or past or present symptoms, pain, or sensations, or the inception or general character of the cause or external source thereof insofar as reasonably pertinent to diagnosis or treatment.

This exception covers more types of statements related to physical condition than are covered in Rule 803(3)'s exception for statements of mental, emotional, or physical condition. Partly on the theory that people have compelling self-interest in speaking truthfully to those who provide medical services, the rule makes admissible statements of past medical history as well as current symptoms if they are made for the purpose of medical diagnosis or treatment. The exception's coverage also extends to descriptions of what caused the patient's problem so long as the descriptions are reasonably pertinent to diagnosis or treatment.

In a break from doctrines applied in some common law jurisdictions, statements made by the declarant to medical personnel involved in treating him and statements made by the declarant to medical personnel only involved in diagnosing his condition have identical status under this exception. Physicians who only see the declarant to make a diagnosis may be, and often are, physicians whose only purpose for seeing the declarant is to prepare expert testimony for a trial. In some common law jurisdictions, statements to non-treating physicians have no exception from the hearsay exclusion.

The exception does not require that the statements be made by the person who needs medical help since statements of that kind might be made by others on behalf of a sick or injured person. It does not specify that the statements must be made to a doctor; rather it requires that they be for the purpose of medical diagnosis or treatment. This means that many people involved in the delivery of health care could possibly be spoken to in statements that would be within the limits of this exception.

The exception's coverage of statements about the cause of a condition is a significant shift from more limited common law doctrines. Cases in which this portion of the exception has been litigated have typically involved statements made by people who bring an accident victim to an emergency room and say something about the circumstances of the injury. If they say, "He hurt his head diving into a swimming pool," all that information would probably be treated as admissible to show the circumstances of the injury because those details are significant to medical personnel. If the statement was something like, "He hit his head diving into a swimming pool that didn't have any warning signs about which end was the shallow end," the opponent of introduction of that statement would have a strong argument that the information about warnings was not closely enough related to the providing of medical care for it to be covered by the policies supporting this exception.

Past Recollection Recorded

Sometimes a witness at a trial may have no recollection about a relevant fact but may have made written notes about it at an earlier time. Those notes are admissible under the "recorded recollection" exception provided certain conditions are met. The exception is defined in Rule 803(5):

> Recorded recollection. A memorandum or record concerning a matter about which a witness once had knowledge but now has insufficient recollection to enable the witness to testify fully and accurately, shown to have been made or adopted by the witness when the matter was fresh in the witness' memory and to reflect that knowledge correctly. If admitted, the memorandum or record may be read into evidence but may not itself be received as an exhibit unless offered by an adverse party.

The proponent of the document (or other type of record) must show that the witness once had knowledge about the subject, that the witness does not have adequate recollection of the subject to testify "fully and accurately," and that the witness made the record (or adopted a record made by someone else) when the witness had a fresh memory of the information. The record will be read to the jury so the jury will be able to make use of the information it contains in exactly the way the jury would have made use of that information if the witness had remembered it and testified about it. The exception does allow the document to be treated as an exhibit at the opponent's option. If the document does become an exhibit, the jury may be allowed to have it with them while they deliberate and may pay more attention to it than they might pay to their memory of the witness's oral testimony.

Past recollection recorded is sometimes confused with a technique for assisting a witness's memory known as present recollection refreshed. Present recollection refreshed is a testimonial process that has no connection with the hearsay doctrine. A party questioning a witness is permitted to try to stimulate the witness's memory in a wide variety of ways. For example, the questioner can show objects to the witness and ask if seeing them helps the witness recall things that the witness once knew. The questioner can also show the witness a document and ask whether it helps the witness come up with a current memory of some topic. If showing the witness a document revives the witness's memory, there is no hearsay issue because the document (which is a written out-of-court statement) is not introduced into evidence. If showing the witness the statement does not enable the witness to say truthfully that his or her memory about some relevant subject has been refreshed, then the witness will not be able to testify about that subject. The document that refreshes the witness's memory does not have to meet the requirements of the hearsay exception for recorded recollection since the proponent is not allowed to have it read to the jury or introduced as an exhibit.

If the document used for refreshing past recollection happens to satisfy the requirements of a hearsay exception, it can, of course, be admitted under that other rationale. It should also be noted that the party against whom the "refreshed memory" witness has testified is entitled to introduce the document the witness used. Rule 612 establishes that right and provides additional safe-guards against misleading use of the past recollection refreshed procedure:

> Except as otherwise provided in criminal proceedings by sec-
> tion 3500 of title 18, United States Code, if a witness uses a writing
> to refresh memory for the purpose of testifying, either —
>> (1) while testifying, or
>> (2) before testifying, if the court in its discretion deter-
>> mines it is necessary in the interests of justice,
> an adverse party is entitled to have the writing produced at the hear-
> ing, to inspect it, to cross-examine the witness thereon, and to intro-
> duce in evidence those portions which relate to the testimony of the
> witness. If it is claimed that the writing contains matters not related
> to the subject matter of the testimony the court shall examine the
> writing in camera, excise any portions not so related, and order de-
> livery of the remainder to the party entitled thereto. Any portion
> withheld over objections shall be preserved and made available to the
> appellate court in the event of an appeal. If a writing is not produced
> or delivered pursuant to order under this rule, the court shall make
> any order justice requires, except that in criminal cases when the
> prosecution elects not to comply, the order shall be one striking the
> testimony or, if the court in its discretion determines that the inter-
> ests of justice so require, declaring a mistrial.

Business and Public Agency Records

Protecting business records from exclusion on hearsay grounds was a major reform trend in evidence law in the 1930s. The desirability of making it eas-ier to introduce evidence from typical documents made in the course of busi-ness was persuasive in many jurisdictions then, and it is now a universal policy. In the Federal Rules, what have often been called "business records" are ti-tled "records of regularly conducted activity." The exception is defined in Rule 803(6):

> Records of regularly conducted activity. A memorandum, report,
> record, or data compilation, in any form, of acts, events, conditions,
> opinions, or diagnoses, made at or near the time by, or from infor-
> mation transmitted by, a person with knowledge, if kept in the
> course of regularly conducted business activity, and if it was the reg-

ular practice of that business activity to make the memorandum, report, record, or data compilation, all as shown by the testimony of the custodian or other qualified witness, unless the source of information or the method or circumstances of preparation indicate lack of trustworthiness. The term "business" as used in this paragraph includes business, institution, association, profession, occupation, and calling of every kind, whether or not conducted for profit.

The policy justification for treating these records as exceptions to the hearsay exclusion is that they are likely to be accurate since they are made for the purpose of running an enterprise rather than for some purpose in litigation. For example, a store has a strong incentive to keep accurate credit records. If they have errors, the store will either lose money or alienate its customers.

To qualify a document for treatment under this exception, the proponent must show that it was made as part of the usual activities of the organization, that a person with knowledge of what the record says made the record or reported the information to the person who made the record, and that the record was made near the time of the occurrence of what it describes. A witness must testify about how the record meets these requirements. A record that meets these explicit requirements may be excluded from the scope of the exception (and thus remain subject to treatment as hearsay) if the circumstances of its preparation indicate a lack of trustworthiness or if the source of the information similarly seems unreliable.

Business records often involve multiple hearsay or hearsay within hearsay. The general issue of statements that themselves contain or are based on other statements is treated in Rule 805:

> Hearsay included within hearsay is not excluded under the hearsay rule if each part of the combined statements conforms with an exception to the hearsay rule provided in these rules.

In order for a business record to be admitted as substantive evidence of all its assertions, each statement it contains must fit the requirements of the business record exception or must avoid the hearsay barrier in some other way. For example, the counter clerk at a tool rental store might make a record stating that a customer had rented a certain tool. The store's manager might use records like those to make a report to the company's top management about what types of tools had been the most popular in a particular month. If monthly variation in the popularity of tools became an issue in a trial, the manager's report would be hearsay. It would involve two levels of hearsay: out-of-court statements by many clerks; and the out-of-court statement by the manager.

Note that in this example all the statements satisfy the business records exception since the clerks' statements involved the regular course of business, were made by them about things they knew, and were made at the time they knew the information. The manager's statement was made from information transmitted by others in the enterprise and would also qualify as a business record if it could be shown that reports such as the monthly tool usage report were typically made by managers. Sometimes these problems are treated in a shorthand way by using the concept "duty to report." If all the declarants in a multiple chain of hearsay had a business duty to report the contents of their statements, then the requirements of the business records exception are satisfied. It is also possible to combine various types of hearsay exceptions. For example, a business record might contain an excited utterance by someone who did not have a duty to report.

Related to the business records exception is an explicit provision in the Federal Rules that lack of an entry in a business record is admissible evidence, if relevant, of something's nonoccurrence or nonexistence if its occurrence or existence would normally have been recorded. While it is possible to argue that the absence of an entry is not hearsay because "no statement" is not a "statement," the Federal Rules moot the controversy about whether to call gaps in records hearsay by providing a specific exception. Rule 803(7) provides:

> Absence of entry in records kept in accordance with the provisions of paragraph (6). Evidence that a matter is not included in the memoranda, reports, records, or data compilations, in any form, kept in accordance with the provisions of paragraph (6), to prove the nonoccurrence or nonexistence of the matter, if the matter was of a kind of which a memorandum, report, or data compilation was regularly made and preserved, unless the sources of information or other circumstances indicate lack of trustworthiness.

Government entities, like other enterprises, keep records. The Federal Rules include a complex set of hearsay exceptions that apply only to "public records and reports." Rule 803(8) describes three types of reports and varies the power of the hearsay exception according to whether they are sought to be introduced in a civil or criminal case, and according to which party seeks to introduce them:

> Public records and reports. Records, reports, statements, or data compilations, in any form, of public offices or agencies, setting forth (A) the activities of the office or agency, or (B) matters observed pursuant to duty imposed by law as to which matters there was a duty to report, excluding, however, in criminal cases matters observed by police officers and other law enforcement personnel, or (C) in civil actions and proceedings and against the Government in criminal cases, factual findings resulting from an investigation made pursuant to authority granted by law, unless the sources of information or other circumstances indicate lack of trustworthiness.

The rule's categories are reports about: the activities of the government entity; matters observed and reported under legal duty by police and law enforcement personnel; matters observed and reported under legal duty by public employees other than police and law enforcement personnel; and factual findings resulting from legally authorized investigations. The theory supporting a hearsay exception for documents of this type is that they are exactly like ordinary business records when their topic is the internal workings of a part of the government and are therefore likely to be reliable because the organization that makes them also uses them in its day-to-day work.

Reports about an agency's own activities, in contrast to the other types of documents covered by the Rule, would be, for example, employment and personnel records. The fact that the office that has maintained them is a government office does not suggest that their accuracy would be any different from the accuracy of similar records in a nongovernmental organization. The Rule provides for their admission in civil and criminal cases. Reports of factual findings from government investigations may not have so exact a parallel in the work of private entities. The Rule allows their admission by any party in civil cases and by the defendant in criminal cases.

Another category of data specified in the Rule is government reports based on observations by workers, including law enforcement personnel, or conclusions based on investigations. It is hard to say for such reports that their routine nature is a strong guarantee of their accuracy. Nevertheless, Rule 803(8) exempts them from the hearsay exclusion in civil cases. This exemption does not apply in criminal cases. Observations by law enforcement personnel are excluded from the scope of the exception because the interest those personnel have in obtaining convictions might give them an incentive to falsify records. Even though this reasoning should not logically apply when a defendant seeks to introduce reports of this type, the rule is written to withdraw the exception in criminal cases whether the prosecutor *or* the defense seeks to introduce the evidence.

Courts have given some varied interpretations to the rule's reference to "law enforcement personnel." If the worker is a police officer, all courts would rule that the literal meaning of the exception governs the case, so that Rule 803(8)(B) cannot be used as a basis for admitting the evidence. If the worker is someone like a clerk in a police department property office, the risk of unreliability that is the basis for this subpart of Rule 803(8) might not be as great, and some courts would allow the exception to be used, refusing to define workers like clerks as "law enforcement personnel."

The admissibility of the types of material described in Rule 803(8)(A), (B), and (C) is shown in the following chart. Admissibility is the result under the Federal Rules in 13 of the 16 situations described.

Close attention should be paid to the instances in which a government report is defined as outside the coverage of this exception. In criminal trials, the defendant, but not the prosecution, may introduce findings from official investigations. The Rule treats reports of what law enforcement personnel have observed differently. Neither the prosecution nor the defendant may in-

CHART FOURTEEN
Admissibility of Public Records

Can it be Introduced By:

Type of Report	Civil Plaintiff	Civil Defendant	Criminal Prosecutor	Criminal Defendant
Activities of public office	Yes	Yes	Yes	Yes
Matters observed and reported pursuant to legal duty by public employees except law enforcement personnel	Yes	Yes	Yes	Yes
Findings from official investigations	Yes	Yes	No	Yes
Matters observed and reported pursuant to legal duty by law enforcement personnel	Yes	Yes	No	No*

*This is the Rule's provision, but some decisions allow such evidence, influenced by the criminal defendant's constitutional right to introduce relevant evidence, reinforced by an analogy to the Rules' treatment of admissions.

troduce material of this type. While the rationale for preventing the prosecution from use of this material is obvious, it is highly questionable whether keeping that material out of the defendant's case is supportable on grounds of policy, and whether it is constitutionally sound.[7]

Parallel to the Rules' provision on the absence of an entry in business records, there is a provision covering proof that a government report does not say something. This exception is set out in Rule 803(10):

> Absence of public record or entry. To prove the absence of a record, report, statement, or data compilation, in any form, or the nonoccurrence or nonexistence of a matter of which a record, report, statement, or data compilation, in any form, was regularly made and preserved by a public office or agency, evidence in the form of a certification in accordance with rule 902, or testimony, that diligent search failed to disclose the record, report, statement, or data compilation, or entry.

Ancient Documents

An exception with broad reach is the "ancient documents" doctrine. Rule 803(16) defines this exception:

---

7. See discussion of constitutional controls over evidence admissibility at pages 50-51.

> Statements in ancient documents. Statements in a document in existence twenty years or more the authenticity of which is established.

For ancient documents the policy justification for removing the hearsay bar is that it is very unlikely that the declarant would have been lying in a way intended to influence the outcome of a trial that occurs 20 years or more after the declarant's statement. The ancient documents rule is a good context for remembering that evidence must satisfy a wide variety of requirements to be admissible. Protection from the prohibition of the hearsay rule does not guarantee admissibility. And admissibility does not guarantee that the trier of fact will believe an item of evidence. So even though some "ancient" documents may seem limited in reliability, such as a teenager's diary found in an attic 20 years after it was written, the common law and the Federal Rules take the position that so far as the hearsay dangers are concerned, they do not present risks significant enough to require that they be denied admission.

Miscellaneous and Residual Exceptions

A number of other exceptions cover records that are usually highly reliable. They include records of religious organizations (for issues of personal or family history), marriage and baptismal certificates, family records such as tombstones or engravings on urns, market quotations and other information from generally used published material, and learned treatises. There is also a residual or "catch-all" exception, Rule 803(24), to permit the admission of hearsay evidence not covered by other exceptions:

> Other exceptions. A statement not specifically covered by any of the foregoing exceptions but having equivalent circumstantial guarantees of trustworthiness, if the court determines that (A) the statement is offered as evidence of a material fact; (B) the statement is more probative on the point for which it is offered than any other evidence which the proponent can procure through reasonable efforts; and (C) the general purposes of these rules and the interests of justice will best be served by admission of the statement into evidence. However, a statement may not be admitted under this exception unless the proponent of it makes known to the adverse party sufficiently in advance of the trial or hearing to provide the adverse party with a fair opportunity to prepare to meet it, the proponent's intention to offer the statement and the particulars of it, including the name and address of the declarant.

To comply with the rule's requirements, the proponent of evidence under this exception must compare the reliability of the offered evidence with the typical reliability of evidence covered by the specific exceptions.

EXAMPLES (availability of declarant immaterial)

1. Alan Williams was found strangled to death in his apartment. The building's janitor, who was well-known to Williams, is accused of the murder on

the theory that he had easy access to Williams' apartment. On the day that Williams was killed he had a phone conversation with a friend of his, Bruce Bender. Williams said to Bender, "I've got to hang up now. Somebody's just come in and he looks really upset. I don't know who he is, but he's got a crazy look on his face." Can the janitor have Bender give testimony quoting Williams?

2.   Carl Cashman was injured by a hit-and-run driver. While he was being treated in a hospital emergency room, he saw Edward Evers walk in. He started to tremble, and he shouted, "That's the guy who nearly killed me!" Can a nurse who heard Cashman's statement quote it at a trial in which Evers is accused of having driven into Cashman?

3.   A shopping center owner sought damages from a department store corporation, claiming that the store had failed to honor its obligation to operate a store at the center for five years. In defense, the store sought to show that the center had failed in its obligation to manage the shopping center under terms of an agreement describing it as a "first class facility" to be operated with "adequate security provisions." May the store introduce the agreement? May the store introduce a survey of shoppers at the center, showing that many stated that they felt nervous and unsafe at the center?

4.   Chris Lender is accused of attacking George Borrower. To show that Lender had a motive, the prosecution seeks to show that Borrower had borrowed money from Lender and had refused to repay it.

a.   The prosecution seeks to have a friend of Borrower's sister testify that two days before the assault, Borrower's sister said to the friend, "Borrower owes Lender a lot of money, but he just keeps stringing her along about it." Is the testimony admissible?

b.   The prosecution seeks to have a friend of Lender's testify that before the assault, Lender said to the friend, "Borrower owes me a lot of money, and he just keeps stringing me along." Is the testimony admissible?

5.   Harry Holmby was injured while using a product manufactured by the defendant. In his products liability suit, one issue concerned the seriousness and duration of Holmby's pain from the injury. A few years after the accident, Holmby was treated by Doctor Ina Iliff. May Dr. Iliff testify that Holmby told her he had been suffering from severe back pains since the incident with the product?

6.   In a medical malpractice suit, the plaintiff introduces testimony by a doctor who has never treated him but who has examined him as part of preparation for the trial. In her testimony, she states that in her opinion the defendant doctor failed to conform to typical standards of treatment. She states that her opinion is based on what the plaintiff has told her about his symptoms before and after the defendant doctor treated him. Is her testimony based on inadmissible hearsay?

7.   A child who could not swim was rescued from a deep swimming pool. The person who pulled him out rode with him in an ambulance and told the receptionist at a hospital emergency room, "This kid just jumped into a pool and he couldn't swim." The child's parents seek damages from the operator of the pool, claiming that their child slipped on a slick walkway near the pool and that this slip made him fall into the water. They contend that more frequent mopping would have prevented the walkway from being so slick. Can the emergency room receptionist testify about what the rescuer said had happened?

8.   Louise Levin sought damages for a nuisance inflicted against her property by a neighbor, Marvin Miller. Levin claimed that Miller had a furnace that emitted vast quantities of thick dark smoke and that the smoke drifted into Levin's house. Levin kept a diary, recording her daily observations of the smoke for a two-year period. The diary states hours and weather conditions on each day that the smoke was noticeable at Levin's house. How might Levin's lawyer make use of that diary at trial?

9.   A Buick driven by Mrs. Prince crashed at an intersection into a BMW driven by Mrs. King. In Mrs. King's civil suit, to establish that traffic signals at an intersection were probably working properly at the time of the accident, a witness testifies that she is an office manager at the city's traffic signals department and that she has with her a document that was in the department's regular files. The document was written by Zane Foreman, foreman of one of the department's maintenance crews. It states the following information: On the day of the accident Foreman and William Worker, another traffic signals department employee, went to the intersection to check the lights; while Foreman talked to police officers who were on the scene, Worker examined all the light bulbs and timing devices and found that they were all in good condition. Is the document admissible?

10.   Assume that the document from Example 9 also contained this sentence: "Worker said that while he was checking the timing units, the driver of the crashed Buick, Mrs. Prince, came up to him and said that driving is so hard to do nowadays that she knew she really shouldn't do it any more." Could that information be used at trial against Mrs. Prince, to show that she had driven carelessly?

11.   Assume that the document from Example 9 also contained this sentence: "Worker said that someone came up to him and said that last week she had seen the traffic lights all go off for about five minutes and that it nearly caused a crash." Could that information be used at trial to support a party's contention that the traffic signals had malfunctioned?

12.   Richard Rover was injured in an automobile accident. He seeks damages from the manufacturer of the car, claiming that it had design flaws that intensified his injuries. As a defense, the manufacturer asserts that Rover was speeding at the time of the injury. Rover's hospital record contains the fol-

lowing note made at the time of his admission to the hospital: "Patient says car crash, hit telephone pole at 90 m.p.h." What problems are there with admitting this document to prove that Rover (the patient) was speeding when he was injured?

13.   The Libertyville City Library seeks damages in a contract action from the supplier of a checkout and book inventory system. The Library states that the defendant's system was marketed as being capable of cutting down thefts and other losses from the Library's collection. The Library asserts that the number of books unaccounted for during typical months in which it has used the new system has exceeded the number for comparable months in years prior to purchase of the system. May the Library introduce its own records of books checked out, books found on shelves, and other inventory measures to show that losses have been worse since installation of the defendant's system?

14.   To prove that the defendant sold drugs, can the prosecution introduce a videotape which shows the defendant saying, "I've got the stuff, give me the money," and shows her exchanging drugs for money?

15.   In another trial, to prove that the defendant sold drugs, can the prosecution introduce a police officer's notebook with a description in the officer's handwriting stating that he observed the defendant exchanging drugs for money?

16.   To prove that a substance a defendant sold was an illegal drug, can the prosecution introduce a document prepared by a police chemist, stating the results of a test performed on a substance obtained from the defendant?

17.   An issue in a products liability suit is whether a car manufacturer used adequately strong material for the straps of a seatbelt. A federal agency has conducted research on materials that can be used for those straps and has issued a report. The report describes many different tests on various materials and shows that materials usually did well on some tests and less well on others. It also states that certain materials, on the basis of all the test results, will be able to withstand typical crash impacts. Should this report be admissible to show that what it concludes about the material used by the manufacturer is true?

EXPLANATIONS (availability of declarant immaterial)

1.   The out-of-court statement is hearsay since it would be introduced to show that a stranger had entered Williams' apartment. The present sense impression exception covers this statement because the declarant was apparently describing something while he was perceiving it. He saw someone come into his apartment, and he described it to Bender. One of the main justifications for this exception is that a false statement will be discovered and corrected. In this problem, Bender would not have had a way to determine the accuracy of

Williams' statement, and the stranger would probably not have had any interest in correcting it if it had been false. Usually, hearsay exceptions are given pro-admissibility interpretations. Here, although the underlying policy for the exception is not well-served by admitting the hearsay, the terms of the rule are so clearly met that admissibility would be certain.

2.   Yes. Cashman's statement is an excited utterance. It is hearsay since it is being introduced to show that Evers is the one who drove a vehicle into him, but the exception covers it. The statement relates to a startling event or condition — either the injury that had happened shortly before the statement or the shock produced by the sight of Evers. The statement explains either of those two possible stimuli.

3.   The agreement does not involve any hearsay problems. It is a legal document, which will be given meaning by the legal system, applying doctrines, precedents, and principles of interpretation that do not necessarily depend on the literal meaning of the words in the document. The survey is a method of introducing out-of-court statements by shoppers about how they felt at the time they were interviewed by the survey interviewers. Therefore, since the statements are being introduced to show what the speakers felt and since those statements do describe what the speakers were feeling, the definition of hearsay is satisfied. An exception allows the survey to be admitted: The words are descriptions of the declarants' then existing mental condition or state of mind.

4.   a. The out-of-court words are relevant only if the information they contain is true. That is, they would shed light on Lender's possible motive only if the proposition they assert — Borrower owed Lender money — is true. Therefore, they are hearsay. No exception applies to allow their admission. It is important to recall that evidence can be relevant *and* inadmissible, as in this example, where the evidence is relevant but is kept out by the hearsay rule.

     The mental state exception does not cover the mental state of memory if the declarant's memory would be relevant only to show that the event happened. Here, the recollection by Borrower's sister that Borrower owed Lender money is relevant not because she possessed that memory but only because what she remembered was true. The admissions rationale would not support admission of the statement by Borrower's sister since she is not a party to the suit.

b. Lender's out-of-court statement is admissible under the state of mind exception. Whether or not it was true that Borrower owed Lender money, Lender's statement that she believed Borrower owed her money shows a mental state consistent with a motive to attack Borrower. Even if her memory about a debt owed to her by Borrower was false, the fact that she possessed that memory is relevant to her having had a motive to harm Borrower. Statements of belief are outside the scope of the mental state exception if their relevance depends on their use to prove that the fact believed is true. That situation is illustrated in part "a" of this problem. Statements of belief are covered by the mental state exception if a speaker's possessing that belief is relevant independent of whether the belief is accurate. Part b of this problem illustrates this latter situation.

5.   Holmby's out-of-court words to Dr. Iliff are hearsay since they are sought to be introduced to show that since the time of the product-related injury, he has had severe pain. The statement is admissible, however, under the exception for statements for the purpose of medical diagnosis or treatment.

6.   The testimony includes hearsay, but it is admissible because the out-of-court words were spoken by the declarant to the doctor for the purpose of medical diagnosis. An expert physician's evaluation of a person is considered to be a diagnosis even if no treatment is expected. This points out the pro-admissibility orientation of the Federal Rules. A person has strong incentives to tell the truth to a doctor who will be performing or prescribing treatment to improve the chances that the treatment will be effective. On the other hand, if a person is speaking to a doctor who will only be giving an opinion in connection with a lawsuit, the incentive is only to say things that will help shape the doctor's opinion in a way that is legally favorable. The Federal Rules do not distinguish, as common law jurisdictions sometimes do, between treating and testifying physicians. Statements to both types of doctors are admissible. It is likely that opposing counsel will be able to alert jurors to the risk of untruthfulness inherent in the situation where a litigant talks to a doctor for the purpose of preparing testimony.

7.   The rescuer's out-of-court words are sought to be introduced to prove that their content is true — that the child jumped, rather than fell, into the pool. Used for this reason, they are hearsay. The exceptions for excited utterances and present sense impressions might or might not apply, depending on how soon after the incident the rescuer spoke to the receptionist and on how excited the rescuer was when speaking.

    If the excited utterance and present sense impression exceptions did not cover the statement, would the exception for statements for medical diagnosis or treatment apply? Statements under that exception do not have to be made to doctors. Any person involved in the providing of health care can be the person to whom the statement is addressed. The receptionist at an emergency room is closely enough connected to the delivery of health services for such statements to be defined as connected with obtaining medical services. It is difficult, however, to extend the reach of this exception to cover the actual out-of-court words that are important to the swimming pool operator's defense. The "jumped into a pool" part of the statement is not easily characterized as intended to facilitate treatment or diagnosis. Certainly a statement that the child had been underwater is fully within the coverage of the exception. But the fact that he got into the water by jumping is hardly something a physician would need to know to treat drowning. Details about causation of a person's health problem are covered by the exception only if they are reasonably pertinent to the medical worker's task.

8. The information in the diary would be relevant on the issue of the extent of the nuisance. It is hearsay since the written statements are relevant at trial only if what they assert is true. Assuming that Levin does not have the ability to remember the details it contains for many days of a two-year period, Levin's lawyer would attempt to use the hearsay exception for recorded recollection. The exception would apply if testimony by Levin showed that she made entries in the diary at the time she observed the smoke and weather or soon after those times, and that she did not have a good memory of those details at the time of the trial. The diary entries could be read to the jury, but the diary itself would not be admissible as an exhibit unless Miller (the neighbor) offered it.

The present sense impression exception might also apply. Its usual rationale for reliability, that the declarant's statements were subject to a contemporaneous check on accuracy, does not exist in this case. Some courts would refuse to apply the exception for that reason.

The diary cannot be a business record, because it was not made in the course of a regularly conducted enterprise. Allowing a personal diary to be admitted under the business records exception would ignore the policy behind the doctrine, that a business's own needs for accuracy and its employees' own needs for job security provide fairly strong guarantees that truth, not fiction, will be found in the records of the organization.

9. The document has two levels of hearsay. It is Foreman's written out-of-court statement containing a report of Worker's spoken out-of-court statements about the bulbs and timing devices. Unless Worker's information is true, the document has no relevance to the trial. Further, to establish relevance Foreman's statement must also be true (his statement is that Worker said certain things). The public records exception will cover the document. Worker obtained the information in the document as part of the usual operations of the department for which he works. It can also be said that Foreman wrote his report as part of the department's typical work. There was testimony in court that the document was found in a place where it was supposed to be kept, supporting a finding of reliability. When people are in the workplace, the fact that they want to avoid being fired and want their organizations to work well serves as some guarantee of reliability. Worker's spoken words to Foreman and Foreman's written statement about Worker's spoken words are all admissible under the public records exception, assuming that they related to topics that workers from the traffic signals department were supposed to observe and report.

10. This sentence adds a third level of hearsay to the problem. The document written out of court quotes Worker's statement that quotes Prince's

statement. If employees of the traffic signals department are supposed to observe and record information about traffic accidents, then *Worker's* repeating of Prince's statement, and *Foreman's* written statement recording what Worker said he had heard Prince say are covered by the public records exception. This treats Foreman's record of what Worker said he heard the same way Example 9 treated Foreman's record of what Worker said he saw.

Note, though, that the proponent of the document wants the jury to have more than a basis to believe that Worker said what Prince said. The proponent wants Prince's words to be available to the jury as proof of what they assert. That use would be hearsay, so the portion of the report that sets out Prince's words will be admissible, for the truth of what Prince's words assert, only if it has its own protection from the hearsay exclusion rule. In this case, Prince's statement will be treated as an admission. It is something she said, offered against her at a trial. Therefore, all three out-of-court statements are admissible.

11.   The first two levels of hearsay are taken care of by the public records exception. Because the information reported by the stranger is important to the operations of the traffic signal department, Foreman and Worker were probably acting within their duties of employment by listening to it and recording it. The stranger's words fit the definition of hearsay because they are introduced to show that the lights worked badly on a particular occasion (rather than just to show that the stranger said the words, which would avoid the hearsay problem but deprive them of relevance). No exception covers the words. They are not, for example, an excited utterance or a present sense impression. And while the public records exception allows proof of the fact that they were said, it does not allow the words to be introduced to prove the truth of what they assert.

12.   There are two out-of-court statements: the hospital worker's written statement; and Rover's words about speeding. Rover's words would be an admission if there was acceptable proof that he ever said them. The offered proof that Rover said those words is the hospital document. Is its written assertion that Rover said the words about speeding admissible to show that Rover said the words? The document is hearsay since its relevance depends on the truth of its statement that Rover said he had been speeding. The business records exception should not defeat the hearsay exclusion on these facts unless hospitals treat car crash victims differently depending on whether they were speeding, driving within the speed limit, or parked in a car that another vehicle crashed into. This shows that the mention of speeding in the hospital record was not necessary for the conduct of the hospital's business. Because it was not important to the hospital, there is an increased chance that it might not have been recorded carefully. If the business records rule were used as a means for introducing written material containing information that was not useful for the businesses that made the records, that would contra-

dict the general rationale for the exception: the idea that business documents are usually accurate because the workers have an incentive to be careful about what they record.

13.   Yes. These records are the public agency equivalent of business records in the private context. They are hearsay if introduced to show that what they state about the presence or absence of books is true. However, they are admissible because of the exception, under the Federal Rules, for records setting forth the activities of a public agency.

14.   There is only one level of hearsay in this problem: the out-of-court statement by the defendant about having "stuff." It would be admissible under the Federal Rules, defined as a non-hearsay admission. The videotape is not an out-of-court statement because it is made by a machine not a person.

15.   The notebook is hearsay since it is relevant only to prove that what it asserts — that the defendant sold drugs — is true. To be admitted, its statements must fit within an exception to the hearsay exclusion. They are not admissions since they are not sought to be introduced against the person who made them. They cannot be admitted under the exception for public records and reports because that provision of the Federal Rules cannot be used to admit records of police observations against a criminal defendant. The past recollection recorded exception might apply if the police officer who wrote the notes cannot remember the events at the trial.

16.   The document sought to be admitted is hearsay since its claimed relevance depends on the truth of what it asserts. This problem poses an issue that has been controversial in interpreting the Federal Rules. The public records exception states that it does not apply to documents about matters observed by law enforcement personnel. Taken literally, that limitation would prevent applying the public records exception to the report of the laboratory test. Many courts interpret this provision more narrowly so that "law enforcement personnel" are those individuals whose contact with a defendant is the most immediate and adversarial. They would apply Rule 803(8) to allow admission of the evidence.

A related issue is whether the business records exception can apply to a document like the police laboratory report or whether consideration of the admissibility of such a report must be limited to evaluating it in the context of the public records exception. There is some authority that recourse to the general business records exception is appropriate.

17.   The report is hearsay. Its admissibility depends on how narrowly part of the Federal Rules provision for public records and reports should be read. Rule 801(C) covers only "factual findings" from investigations. The findings in the report described in this problem are factual, but they are based on interpretations of how performance on various tests can be evaluated in reaching a single conclusion on suitability of materials for typical crashes. The Supreme Court has decided that material of this type is covered by the Fed-

eral Rules exception for public records, Rule 803(8).[8] The decision recognizes that defining a difference between fact and opinion is often impossible. It also may reflect the Federal Rules' general preference for a wide scope for expert testimony and opinion.

Statements Defined as Hearsay but Admissible if the Declarant Is "Unavailable"

Some hearsay exceptions apply only when the declarant is unavailable. This suggests that they must be thought to be less reliable, generally, than the out-of-court statements covered by exceptions that can be used even if the declarant is available to testify. The exceptions are tolerated, however, because they involve situations where the out-of-court statements have some claim to reliability and there is a strong need for the information they contain. Imposing the requirement of unavailability in connection with certain hearsay exceptions is partly a result of tradition. As will be seen, some of the material covered by the exceptions for which unavailability is required is probably as reliable as some of the material covered by the exceptions that apply regardless of the declarant's availability.

Definition of Unavailable

There are a variety of ways in which a party attempting to use one of the unavailability-required exceptions can establish the necessary unavailability of the hearsay declarant. Rule 804(a) establishes the meaning of unavailability:

> Definition of unavailability. "Unavailability as a witness" includes situations in which the declarant —
>
> (1) is exempted by ruling of the court on the ground of privilege from testifying concerning the subject matter of the declarant's statement; or
>
> (2) persists in refusing to testify concerning the subject matter of the declarant's statement despite an order of the court to do so; or
>
> (3) testifies to a lack of memory of the subject matter of the declarant's testimony, or
>
> (4) is unable to be present or to testify at the hearing because of death or then existing physical or mental illness or infirmity; or
>
> (5) is absent from the hearing and the proponent of a statement has been unable to procure the declarant's attendance (or in the case of a hearsay exception under subdivision (b)(2), (3), or (4), the declarant's attendance or testimony) by process or other reasonable means.
>
> A declarant is not unavailable as a witness if exemption, refusal, claim of lack of memory, inability, or absence is due to the procurement or

---

8. See *Beech Aircraft Corp. v. Rainey*, 488 U.S. 153 (1988).

> wrong-doing of the proponent of a statement for the purpose of pre-
> venting the witness from attending or testifying.

Under this rule, a declarant of an out-of-court statement is shown to be unavailable if the declarant: has a privilege that permits the declarant to refuse
to reveal a communication; refuses to testify about the subject matter of the
statement; or cannot remember the subject matter. A declarant is also unavailable if his or her presence is prevented by death or illness. These methods of showing unavailability apply to all the exceptions for which the Federal
Rules require unavailability.

Additional options for showing unavailability apply to particular exceptions within the group of unavailability-required exceptions. A showing that
the declarant is absent from the proceeding and the proponent of the declarant's out-of-court statement cannot obtain the declarant's presence allows
use of the exception for former testimony (discussed later in this chapter) or
the "catch-all" exception. That showing *and* a showing that the proponent of
the hearsay could not obtain the declarant's testimony by deposition is an adequate foundation for the other unavailability required exceptions, which are
dying declarations, statements against interest, and family history statements.

Although it is treated in the Federal Rules as a hearsay exception that can
be used whether or not the declarant is available, statements of "recorded
recollection," defined in Rule 803(5), can be analyzed as statements that can
be admitted only if the proponent establishes the declarant's unavailability.
For these statements to be admitted, the court must believe that the declarant-
witness has either no memory or just a slight memory of the previously
recorded information.

The wide variety of methods of proving unavailability reflects a pro-
admissibility stance by the drafters of the Federal Rules. At common law, requirements for the showing of unavailability may vary from exception to
exception. As a counterweight to the general acceptance of many reasons for
treating a declarant as unavailable, the Federal Rules also provide that a declarant will not be treated as unavailable if it is shown that the proponent of
the hearsay statement is responsible for creating the condition that would
otherwise meet one of Rule 804's definitions of unavailability.

Former Testimony

Since the importance of cross-examination is one of the underlying policy
groundings for the hearsay rule, it is understandable that there is an exception for testimony given under oath and subject to cross-examination at a
proceeding previous to the one at which the past testimony is sought to be
introduced. In fact, some consider it odd that this exception is grouped
among those for which unavailability of the declarant must be shown, since
the reliability of the statements will be virtually identical to the reliability of
statements made by a witness in a current trial. Rule 804(b)(1) defines this
exception to the hearsay exclusion:

Former testimony. Testimony given as a witness at another hearing of the same or a different proceeding, or in a deposition taken in compliance with law in the course of the same or another proceeding, if the party against whom the testimony is now offered, or, in a civil action or proceeding, a predecessor in interest, had an opportunity and similar motive to develop the testimony by direct, cross, or redirect examination.

In civil and criminal cases, testimony at an earlier proceeding or deposition is admissible to prove the truth of what its statements assert if the party against whom the testimony is offered had an opportunity to cross-examine the declarant. It is also admissible if that party's motive to cross-examine at the earlier proceeding was similar to the motive the party would have if the witness testified at the current trial. For civil cases there is an additional liberalization: The requirement of opportunity and motive to cross-examine can be satisfied by the presence in the earlier proceeding of a predecessor in interest to the party against whom the testimony is offered in the current trial.

Application of this rule is generally straightforward. One possible complication involves the concept of similar motive to cross-examine. If circumstances at the prior trial were such that the witness's testimony was unimportant or that the whole suit was unimportant to the party, then it would be unfair to permit use of the former testimony by that witness against the party in a new case where the topic of the testimony is important or where the consequences of losing the case are far more costly than in the prior case.

The provision that in civil cases former testimony may be admitted against a party if that party *or* a predecessor in interest of that party had the required opportunity and motive for cross-examination has been interpreted by federal courts with varied liberality. Some courts have taken a functional approach to interpreting "predecessor in interest" and have not required strict privity so long as the interests of the party opposed to the testimony in the prior case were similar to the interests of the party against whom the testimony is sought to be used in the current case. Other courts have required clear-cut contractual privity or some other type of recognized successor relationship.

Dying Declarations

The common law has recognized a hearsay exception for statements made by a person who believes that his or her death is imminent. The exception is based on the idea that people's religious beliefs make them highly reluctant to lie at the moment of death. A secular argument supporting the exception would be that a person who believes death is near has no motive to make false statements since there is nothing to be gained from them. Contrary to that idea is the possibility that a person might feel particularly free to lie at the

time of death because there is no risk of having to suffer worldly consequences for the untruth. The Federal Rules recognize dying declarations as a
hearsay exception. The exception is defined in Rule 804(b)(2):

> Statement under belief of impending death. In a prosecution for
> homicide or in a civil action or proceeding, a statement made by a de-
> clarant while believing that the declarant's death was imminent, con-
> cerning the cause or circumstances of what the declarant believed to
> be impending death.

Dying declarations are protected from the hearsay exclusion only for use on
one topic: the declarant's belief about the cause of what the declarant believed to be his or her impending death. The exception applies in all civil cases
and in homicide prosecutions. While most examples of dying declarations involve a speaker who dies after making the statement, a speaker can have a reasonable expectation of death but still survive. The words of a speaker who
believed death was imminent count as dying declarations even if the speaker
recovers. In that event, the proponent will have to establish the speaker's unavailability in any of the variety of methods permitted under Rule 804(a).

Statements against Interest

Under common law and the Federal Rules, there is a hearsay exception for
some statements that were contrary to the declarant's interests when the declarant made them. At common law, the affected interest had to involve monetary or property rights. Under the Federal Rules, the affected interests are
monetary or property rights and freedom from criminal liability. The details
of the exception are specified in Rule 804(b)(3):

> Statement against Interest. A statement which was at the time of its
> making so far contrary to the declarant's pecuniary or proprietary in-
> terest, or so far tended to subject the declarant to civil or criminal lia-
> bility, or to render invalid a claim by the declarant against another,
> that a reasonable person in the declarant's position would not have
> made the statement unless believing it to be true. A statement tending
> to expose the declarant to criminal liability and offered to exculpate
> the accused is not admissible unless corroborating circumstances
> clearly indicate the trustworthiness of the statement.

Note that this is different from the treatment of admissions. An admission is anything a party to a lawsuit has ever said, if it is relevant against him
or her at a trial. The important factors for admissions are whether: 1) the declarant was someone who is a party to the current suit; and 2) the statement
is sought to be introduced as relevant against the party in the current suit.
The declarant's unavailability is *not* a requirement for use of admissions. For
statements against interest, the declarant need not be a party nor does it matter in whose favor the statement is sought to be introduced. The proponent
must show that the declarant is unavailable and must show also that when the

declarant made the statement, it had the potential to harm an important interest of the declarant. The rationale for the exception is that when a person says something that is detrimental to a very important interest, it is likely to be true because people rarely say something carelessly or falsely that involves a subject that could be personally harmful.

In applying this exception, a judge must consider what a statement would typically mean to a "reasonable" person, in terms of having an effect

CHART FIFTEEN
Admissions and Statements against Interest, Compared

Points of Comparison	Admission	Statement against Interest
Declarant	Party in current case	Anyone
Declarant's availability	Available or unavailable	Must be unavailable
Subject of statement	Anything adverse to party's interest at trial	Creates financial or criminal risk to declarant when declarant makes statement
Admissible against	Declarant, coconspirator, declarant's employer	Any party

on that person's monetary, property, or criminal liability interests. The policy behind the rule could perhaps be served better by a subjective test. In that analysis, a statement would be thought of as trustworthy if, in the mind of the declarant, it had the potential to harm the declarant even if the vast majority of people would not have considered that type of statement to be one that could harm the specified interests. The problem with a subjective test is that it is hard to administer. Although the language of the Federal Rule is slightly ambiguous, because it refers to a "reasonable person" but also to someone "in the declarant's position," courts use an objective test and ask whether a statement would have seemed risky to a reasonable person rather than specifically to the declarant.

Deciding which interests are important enough to support the inference that a person's statements opposed to them are likely to be true has been controversial. While the Federal Rules add to the common law list of proprietary and pecuniary interests by recognizing "penal interest," — the interest a person has in being free from criminal liability — they limit that expansion by a detailed provision for one recurring situation: If a statement that would expose the declarant to criminal liability is offered to exculpate another person, the statement will be admissible only if corroborating circumstances clearly indicate that it is trustworthy. An example of maximum expansiveness in defining relevant interests is California's Evidence Code, where statements against social interests are treated as admissible hearsay.

Social interests are broader but harder to define than penal, pecuniary, or proprietary interests.

Residual Exception

The Federal Rules section on hearsay exceptions for which the declarant must be unavailable includes a residual (or "catch-all") exception, Rule 804(b)(5). It is identical to Rule 803(24), the residual provision in the group of exceptions for which the declarant may be available or unavailable. Since there is a residual exception that may be used if the declarant is either available or unavailable, the question arises: Why did the drafters of the Federal Rules include an identical residual exception that can be used only if the declarant is unavailable? This second residual exception is basically redundant. However, its inclusion does make it clear that with regard to the required showing of equivalent trustworthiness, a proponent may compare an unusual item of hearsay to the four types of hearsay for which unavailability is required as well as to any of the 23 types of hearsay for which a showing of unavailability is not required.

EXAMPLES

1. Horace Homer has sued Delta Pharmaceutical Corporation, claiming that it failed to provide an adequate warning that one of its drugs was habit-forming. Delta's defense, in part, is that Homer was extraordinarily predisposed to abuse drugs. Two years prior to instituting his suit against Delta, Homer sought Workers' Compensation benefits, claiming that hazardous conditions at his workplace had harmed him. At the Workers' Compensation hearing, Homer's employer introduced testimony by a psychiatrist who had treated Homer. The psychiatrist testified that Homer was addicted to a number of drugs. Under applicable substantive law, this testimony, if believed, would have led to drastic reduction of Homer's compensation benefits. If the psychiatrist is now deceased, can Delta introduce a transcript of his testimony?

2. Seeking damages for asbestos-related disease, John James sued Giant Asbestos Corporation, claiming that it had made some of the asbestos-containing products that James had worked with in a career as a pipefitter. May James introduce testimony given by a witness at another plaintiff's trial against Giant if that witness is now unavailable and the testimony concerned a general issue of the degree to which Giant's products did or did not contain asbestos?

3. What if the testimony sought to be introduced in Example 2 against Giant Asbestos Corporation had been given in a trial involving similar products produced by Medium-Sized Asbestos Corporation, a company that merged with Giant a week before Homer sued Giant?

4. What if the testimony sought to be introduced in Example 2 against Giant Asbestos Corporation had been given in a trial involving similar products produced by Enormous Asbestos Corporation, Giant's main competitor?

5.   An insurance company seeks to avoid paying the beneficiary of a life insurance policy, Paula Pillgiver, claiming that Pillgiver caused the insured's death by intentionally giving him an overdose of a prescription drug. Pillgiver concedes that the decedent took an overdose but contends that it was by mistake. A doctor from the hospital emergency room at which the decedent died heard him say, "I know I'm dying, and it must be the pills. I told Pillgiver not to make me take so many of them." Can the doctor quote that statement in testimony in a lawsuit between the insurance company and Pillgiver?

6.   Quentin Quire worked for 30 years as a billboard painter. He became ill with cancer and suspected that the disease had been caused by some of the paint products he used at work. One year before he died, he told his son that he thought one product in particular, "Super Smooth Brush Cleaner," had been the most harmful, and that he had used that brand of brush cleaner exclusively for the past 20 years. In a wrongful death suit against the maker of "Super Smooth Brush Cleaner," if there is a dispute about whether Quire ever used that brand of brush cleaner, may the son testify that his late father had told him "Super Smooth" was the brand he had used for 20 years?

7.   Rex Riley was on trial for selling drugs to high school students. When a witness testified that he had seen Riley sell drugs in the school gym, Riley shouted out in the courtroom, "You liar, it was the lunchroom." If the school board fired the lunchroom supervisor, could Riley's words be introduced in a suit challenging the firing?

8.   The state has condemned Lucy Lowin's small shopping center to obtain land for a highway project. In a suit contesting the amount the state must pay Lowin, the state contends that the center's value is $1.5 million. Lowin argues that its value is $4 million. The state seeks to introduce evidence that one year prior to the condemnation, a county real estate assessor had valued a very similar shopping center one block away at $1.5 million. Its owner, Max Miller, testified in a hearing that in his opinion the center was worth no more than $1 million. If Miller is now unavailable to testify, can Miller's words be used against Lowin in the current case?

9.   Nancy Neville sues a former friend, Oscar Ordway, claiming that she contracted a sexually transmitted disease from him, and that he negligently failed to inform her that he was infected at the time she and he had sexual relations. Ordway claims that Neville probably contracted the disease from a third person, Steve Stoner, with whom she had a sexual relationship prior to meeting Ordway. Stoner is unavailable to testify at the time of trial of the Neville-Ordway suit. However, at the time Neville and Stoner's relationship was ongoing, Stoner said at a party, "I've got a sexually transmitted disease, but I don't let it get me upset." Can someone who was at the party and heard Stoner admit that he was infected testify to Stoner's statements at the Neville-Ordway trial?

10.   A newspaper reporter wrote a series of articles exposing unsanitary

practices at various restaurants. The articles gave hypothetical names for the restaurants, but they were based on observations the writer made after having been hired as a dishwasher under an assumed name at the restaurants. A food poisoning victim seeks damages against a particular restaurant at which she claims she was given unwholesome food. To bolster her case, she seeks to introduce one of the newspaper articles, along with notes the reporter made that give the real names of the restaurants. Putting the notes and the article together, the plaintiff claims, provides a basis for allowing the jury to consider the reporter's observations about sanitary practices at the defendant restaurant. Assume the following facts: the reporter has died since writing the articles; and the articles were written only two years prior to the suit. Does the hearsay rule bar admission of the article and the reporter's notes?

EXPLANATIONS

1. The transcript is hearsay because it represents a method of bringing the out-of-court statements of the psychiatrist into the current trial to support the proponent's case by having the jury believe the conclusions the psychiatrist asserted in the Workers' Compensation proceeding. The former testimony exception will permit the hearsay to be admitted. To use it, the proponent must first establish that the declarant is unavailable. Death is the ultimate unavailability. Next, the rule's requirement that the testimony had been under oath must be satisfied. Finally, the proponent must establish that the party against whom the former testimony is sought to be introduced (or a predecessor in interest to that party) had a motive and opportunity to cross-examine that were similar to the motive that would be present in the current case if the declarant were to testify. To do that, Delta would have to show that under the circumstances of the Workers' Compensation case, resisting the import of the psychiatrist's testimony was important to Homer. Since the testimony, if believed, would have severely limited Homer's recovery, Homer would have had a strong motive to discredit it. This makes admission of the former testimony correct in the current tort case.

2. Yes. The testimony is hearsay, but it is sought to be introduced against the same party who opposed it at the earlier trial. Giant had an opportunity to cross-examine the witness at the earlier trial and had the same motive there that it would have had at the current trial if the witness had appeared in person.

3. Medium-Sized Asbestos Corporation would be a predecessor in interest to Giant Asbestos Corporation so these facts fit the Federal Rules description of testimony that was exposed to cross-examination by a predecessor in interest of the party against which the former testimony is sought to be introduced. Medium-Sized's motives in the case would have been similar to the motives Giant would have had if Giant had been the defendant so the testimony would be admissible.

4.   Enormous Asbestos Corporation would have had a strong motive to cross-examine the expert, and it presumably would have been the same motive that Giant would have had if Giant had been the defendant in the former suit. For a minority of courts interpreting the Federal Rules, this similarity of motive is adequate to permit use of the former testimony exception. Most courts continue to pay separate attention to the requirements of "similar motive" and "predecessor in interest" and would refuse to treat a party's competitor as a predecessor in interest to the party.

5.   Yes. The out-of-court words are hearsay because they are sought to be introduced to show that what they assert is true — that Pillgiver intentionally gave the decedent a drug overdose. The statement fits the definition of dying declaration, however, and could therefore be admitted. The speaker was aware of his impending death, the subject of the statement was the cause of his death, and the case in which the statement is sought to be used is a civil case. Recall that dying declarations are permitted in homicide cases and all civil cases.

6.   Identifying the out-of-court statement as hearsay is simple. The point to be proved is that Quire used "Super Smooth," and Quire's out-of-court statement was exactly to that effect. The only hearsay exception that might cover the statement is the dying declarations exception. However, the doctrine requires that the declarant have the belief that death is imminent. How broadly defined should this "imminentness" requirement be? Since it relates to the notion that people will be likely to tell the truth when they anticipate prompt consequences in the afterlife, applying a definition of "imminent" that would let Quire's statement in would be too great a stretch. In a sense, everyone knows that death will occur in the future and might be motivated by that knowledge to speak truthfully and act morally. The dying declarations doctrine, however, is based on the idea that those motivations are particularly strong when a declarant expects to die soon after making a statement.

7.   Riley's words would certainly meet the definition of a statement that exposes the declarant to criminal liability. For that reason, they would be admissible as a statement against interest in the suit between the school board and the lunchroom supervisor.

8.   Offered for the truth of its meaning that the nearby shopping center was worth only $1 million, Miller's statement is hearsay. The former testimony exception will not apply because there was no opportunity for Lowin or a predecessor of Lowin's to cross-examine Miller in the real estate assessment hearing. For the statement against interest exception to apply, the proponent of Miller's statement must show that the statement was contrary to Miller's pecuniary interest at the time he made it. Did it hurt Miller to state that his property was worth less than the real estate assessor said it was worth? A superficial response would be that it always harms an owner's interests to minimize the value of an asset. However, it is well-known that owners seek to

have their real estate assessments reduced to improve their financial status. Thus, it cannot fairly be said that Miller's claims at the assessment hearing were contrary to his financial interests. The words, therefore, do not qualify for admission under the statements against interest exception.

9. The out-of-court words by Stoner are relevant only if their content is true. Therefore, they are hearsay. Their admissibility would be governed by the jurisdiction's position on statements against interest. Under the Federal Rules, the words would be kept out since they did not expose Stoner to monetary or criminal liability (assuming there was no statute prohibiting sexual conduct by one who was infected with a sexually transmitted disease). In a jurisdiction that recognizes social interests as among those that can be a basis for invoking the statements against interest exception, an admission that the declarant has a sexually transmitted disease would be a statement against interest.

10. The article and notes are relevant only if their contents are taken as true, so the proponent must find a way around the hearsay bar. The ancient documents exception will not work because the material is too new. Calling the article and the notes business records has some superficial appeal, but there may not be any evidence about how much time elapsed between the observations and the reporter's recording of them in his diary. Also, the business records exception cannot apply if circumstances indicate a lack of trustworthiness. Many courts might hold that allowing a reporter's notes to be treated as business records would avoid most of the protections that are the basis for special treatment of those records: No one in the enterprise but the reporter relies on the notes, and there is no way of knowing whether the reporter even considered all of them accurate.

The residual exception might work here. The proponent would have to give notice of the intention to introduce the notes and article and would have to establish that their circumstantial guarantees of trustworthiness are equivalent to those of the specific exceptions. Reporters have an incentive to be accurate because their careers may depend on their reputations for accuracy and honesty. Their notes are likely to be accurate for the same reason. These items come so close to the descriptions of business records that their reliability might be equal to that of some business records. Another requirement would be harder for the proponent to meet. The evidence must be more probative on its point than other evidence that could be procured through reasonable efforts. Depending on what the article and notes taken together seem to say about the defendant restaurant, and depending on the availability of information from current and former employees of the restaurant, the article and notes might or might not satisfy that requirement.

5

Examination and Impeachment

Introduction

Under the Federal Rules almost anyone can be a witness. This is a change from common law doctrines that placed a variety of limits on competency to testify. The proponent of a witness shows that the witness has personal or expert knowledge about a disputed issue and asks that person questions about it in "direct examination." The main constraints on direct examination are the general requirement of relevance, the exclusionary rules, and the prohibition against "leading questions." When a witness testifies, parties are entitled to counteract the force of the testimony through cross-examination and by introducing other evidence that might make the witness seem less credible. These efforts are known as *impeachment*.

Impeachment generally involves showing that the witness lied intentionally, had questionable perception or memory of the subject of the testimony, or made statements that are factually incorrect. To use the method of impeachment that relies on suggesting that the witness has purposely told lies, the opponent usually introduces evidence of the witness's propensity to lie or evidence of a bias that could lead the witness to testify in a particular way regardless of the truth. Impeachment that focuses on faulty memory or perception involves evidence showing how the witness saw or learned what the witness thinks he or she knows. Either intentional lying or poor memory can be shown with evidence of statements made by the witness before the trial that are inconsistent with the witness's testimony during the trial. A witness may also be impeached by contradiction, with evidence showing that the witness has made incorrect statements.

General Competency Rules

At common law, a potential witness had to be characterized as "competent" in order to testify. In a number of recurring situations, potential witnesses were defined as *not* competent. Parties to a dispute were not competent to testify. Similarly, people who had been convicted of crimes were barred, as were people who did not believe in God. Young children were often treated as not competent.

Under the Rules, the competency of witnesses is controlled by state law when they testify in connection with substantive issues that are controlled by state law. In all other situations, the Rules reject the common law approach and define all people as competent to testify, subject to a few exceptions. Rule 601 makes this explicit:

> Every person is competent to be a witness except as otherwise provided in these rules. However, in civil actions and proceedings, with respect to an element of a claim or defense as to which State law supplies the rule of decision, the competency of a witness shall be determined in accordance with State law.

The pro-competency position of Rule 601 does not extend to permitting a judge to testify in a trial the judge is conducting. Rule 605 states:

> The judge presiding at the trial may not testify in that trial as a witness. No objection need be made in order to preserve the point.

Note that the prohibition related to judges is absolute and can be enforced even if a party prejudiced by a violation of the rule chooses not to object to the violation (the objection would have to be made, obviously, to the judge who was in the process of violating the rule by testifying while presiding).

The possibility that jurors might testify occurs in two different contexts: a juror might have information about the facts in dispute in a case for which the person is a juror; and a losing party might hope to have a result reversed by having a juror testify about improper conduct by the jury. These two possibilities are dealt with in Rule 606:

> (a) *At the trial.* A member of the jury may not testify as a witness before that jury in the trial of the case in which the juror is sitting. If the juror is called so to testify, the opposing party shall be afforded an opportunity to object out of the presence of the jury.
>
> (b) *Inquiry into validity of verdict or indictment.* Upon an inquiry into the validity of a verdict or indictment, a juror may not testify as to any matter or statement occurring during the course of the jury's deliberations or to the effect of anything upon that or any other juror's mind or emotions as influencing the juror to assent to or dissent from the verdict or indictment or concerning the juror's mental processes in connection therewith, except that a juror may testify on the question whether extraneous prejudicial information was improperly brought to the jury's attention or

whether any outside influence was improperly brought to bear upon any juror. Nor may a juror's affidavit or evidence of any statement by the juror concerning a matter about which the juror would be precluded from testifying be received for these purposes.

A person may not serve as both a witness and a juror in a trial. With regard to testimony about a jury's conduct, the Rule attempts to limit the instances in which such testimony will be allowed. No testimony may relate to "mental processes," to protect the freedom of jurors to speak freely in their private deliberations. Testimony is permitted only about "extraneous" information or "outside influence" on the theory that the events that would be described in this type of testimony will be clear and easy to establish and will not require an inquiry into how a juror evaluated various arguments during deliberations.

For witnesses whose competency is not treated specifically in the rules, the trial judge can apply Rules 401, 402, and 403 to control whether or not they will be permitted to testify. In addition to competency, a person must satisfy an oath or affirmation requirement to be permitted to testify. Rule 603 states:

> Before testifying, every witness shall be required to declare that the witness will testify truthfully, by oath or affirmation administered in a form calculated to awaken the witness' conscience and impress the witness' mind with the duty to do so.

If a witness chooses not to swear an oath but rather uses the secular "affirmation," that witness may not be impeached with references to his or her lack of religious belief. Rule 610, discussed later in this chapter, prohibits that type of impeachment.

Personal Knowledge

Analytically related to the concept of competency to testify is a requirement that a witness must have personal knowledge of the subject of his or her testimony (unless the witness is an expert allowed to base testimony on information obtained in other ways). Rule 602 states:

> A witness may not testify to a matter unless evidence is introduced sufficient to support a finding that the witness has personal knowledge of the matter. Evidence to prove personal knowledge may, but need not, consist of the witness' own testimony. This rule is subject to the provisions of rule 703, relating to opinion testimony by expert witnesses.

To satisfy the personal knowledge requirement, the proponent of the witness must introduce evidence that provides a basis on which a jury or a judge sitting as trier-of-fact could reasonably conclude that the witness has personal knowledge of the subject matter of his or her testimony. This evidence can be incorporated in the witness's own testimony or can be provided in other forms. For example, a witness has personal knowledge that a street was slippery on a certain day if the witness saw the street or experienced its slipperiness in any way. In contrast, a witness who thinks a street was slippery because someone else saw it and told him or her about it does *not* have personal knowledge of the condition of the street. All that witness has is personal knowledge of the fact that someone else thought the street was slippery.

Children

At common law, testimony by children was closely controlled and was barred if the judge thought the child did not understand the concept of truthfulness. The Federal Rules do not include any express provision allowing this inquiry and seem to reject it, given the explicit provision that all people are competent to testify. A statute[1] separate from the Federal Rules applies to children who are witnesses to crimes or who are alleged to be victims of physical abuse, sexual abuse, or exploitation. It provides that the judge, in response to an offer of compelling proof that a prospective child witness is incompetent, may have a competency examination on the record focussed on questioning the child to determine whether the child can understand and answer simple questions. The statute states that a child's age alone is not a compelling reason to have such a competency examination.

Even under the Federal Rules and parallel state codes, where a proposed witness is a child, courts can exclude the testimony under the general authority of FRE 403 if it seems that the probative value of the testimony will be very weak because of the child's inability to tell truth from falsehood. This treatment of children's testimony is supported by the oath and personal knowledge requirements as well. A judge might rule that a child does not have the ability to understand and give the required oath or affirmation related to truthtelling. The judge might also rule that the child's ability to recall events or to distinguish between reality and fantasy is so slight that no reasonable juror could find that the child has "personal knowledge" of the topics of the testimony. These rulings would keep the child off the stand, a result identical to that reached under the explicit federal statute and under common law doctrines that allowed the judge to determine competency of a child witness.

Hypnosis

A witness who has been hypnotized after experiencing something he or she will testify about presents special problems. Will the witness testify about his or her own personal knowledge of the event, or will the witness bring to the trial ideas and information implanted by the hypnotist? Will the effect of the

---

1. 18 U.S.C. §3509.

hypnosis on the witness detract from the jury's ability to use the witness's demeanor as a guide to the witness's certainty about the testimony? The witness may seem highly certain that his or her memory is accurate because it has been reinforced by the process of hypnosis. That extra confidence may or may not be correct, but it would be difficult for a jury to estimate how much confidence the witness would have shown in the absence of hypnosis.

No provision of the Federal Rules refers specifically to hypnosis, and the rule stating that all people are competent to testify would seem to preclude a general prohibition against testimony from previously hypnotized witnesses. Nevertheless, many federal courts have imposed restrictions on this type of testimony using the authority of FRE 403 to balance probative value against the risk of improper prejudice. In criminal cases restrictions on this type of testimony can be based additionally on constitutional prohibitions against the state's use of impermissibly suggestive processes to identify the perpetrator of a crime. Where it is the defendant who seeks to introduce such testimony, another constitutional principle (the defendant's right to introduce relevant defense evidence) has led to a holding that the state may not rely on the fact that a witness has been hypnotized to exclude that witness from testifying.

The majority view prohibits the admission of hypnotically enhanced testimony either on the theory (at common law) that a witness who has been hypnotized is not competent or on the theory (under the Federal Rules) that the risk of the jury giving improper weight to the testimony is too great since the jury will not have a basis for evaluating credibility. However, it is also part of the majority position that a witness who has been hypnotized may still give testimony that is limited to the witness's pre-hypnosis knowledge. Effecting this limitation requires significant procedural safeguards so that a record will exist showing the extent of the person's knowledge prior to the hypnosis. Some courts also require that the proponent of the testimony establish that the hypnosis itself was not suggestive.

Spousal Testimony in Criminal Cases

A vestige of the special common law competency rules continues to be important in criminal law. Under federal practice, a defendant's spouse has a privilege to refuse to testify at the trial of his or her spouse. At common law and under federal practice prior to 1980, this "spousal incompetency" doctrine allowed *either spouse* to prevent the testimony of a spouse so that in a husband's criminal trial, for example, the wife could not testify if either she or her husband chose to invoke spousal incompetency. The modern reform incorporated in federal practice allows only the *prospective witness spouse* to exercise the incompetency right.[2]

---

2. A decision by the United States Supreme Court effected this change in competency doctrine for federal courts. See *Trammel v. United States,* 445 U.S. 40 (1980).

Claims Involving Decedents ("Dead Man's Statutes")

In some states, a "dead man's statute" prevents witnesses from testifying about transactions with a person involved in the litigated claim if the person has died prior to the trial. The origin of the dead man's rule is an older and now completely rejected competency rule that prohibited testimony by plaintiffs in their own behalf and gave defendants a privilege to refrain from testifying. These older doctrines were based on the assumption that people with a strong interest in a case could not be trusted to tell the truth. The dead man's statutes are typically the product of reform efforts that abolished the general rule of parties' incompetency but retained it in the small category of cases involving claims by or against an estate.

The general reason for abolishing the broad incompetency doctrine is a belief that juries are likely to recognize and consider a witness's self-interest, so that bringing in a party's testimony can add to the available information without creating an opportunity for successful perjury. In line with this analysis, the Federal Rules completely reject the position represented by the dead man's statutes. Many states have also abrogated or restricted their dead man's statutes. Where they apply, it is usually said that the witness is not competent to testify about statements or events covered by the statute.

There are many variations in the language of state dead man's statutes and in judicial interpretations of them. Most courts seek to construe the statutes narrowly to favor the admission of testimony. Depending on the statute, a party may be prohibited only from testifying about his or her own statements to a decedent or may be prohibited from giving any testimony at all concerning a transaction. Courts also differ on how they define "transaction." For example, in some states an automobile collision is a transaction for the purpose of the dead man's statute, and a surviving participant may not testify in a suit against the estate of a driver killed in the accident. A position adopted in some states allows a witness to testify about his or her own statements to a decedent, but simultaneously eliminates any possible hearsay objection that might otherwise have prevented the quotation of the decedent's words.

Scope and Style of Examination

Rule 611 makes explicit that the trial judge controls the mode and order of presentation of each party's case:

> (a) Control by court. The court shall exercise reasonable control over the mode and order of interrogating witnesses and presenting evidence so as to (1) make the interrogation and presentation effective for the ascertainment of the truth, (2) avoid needless consumption of time, and (3) protect witnesses from harassment or undue embarrassment.

In direct examination, a party asks its witness questions about relevant issues, and the witness answers the questions. Cross-examination is the questioning of an opponent's witnesses after direct examination. In addition, the trial judge may question witnesses. While judges have considerable discretion in controlling the style and order of examination, some additional rules apply.

Leading Questions

The primary consideration of form for direct examination is that the Federal Rules restrict the use of leading questions. A leading question is one that suggests its answer. Rule 611(c) provides:

> (c) Leading questions. Leading questions should not be used on the direct examination of a witness except as may be necessary to develop the witness' testimony. Ordinarily leading questions should be permitted on cross-examination. When a party calls a hostile witness, an adverse party, or a witness identified with an adverse party, interrogation may be by leading questions.

The question, "Is it true that you locked the door when you left the house?" would be defined as leading, while "What did you do, if anything, when you left the house?" would be totally immune from an objection on grounds that it was a leading question. This doctrine is based on the belief that a witness is more likely to testify truthfully if the witness does not know what answer the questioner wants the witness to give. Obviously, characterizing a question as leading or not leading may be a matter of degree, subject to differences in judgment. Typically, judges permit leading questions freely when they involve topics that are not controversial or are really only preliminary to the main points of a witness's testimony.

Scope of Cross-Examination

After a witness has testified on direct examination, the opposing party is entitled to cross-examine the witness. Cross-examination is limited to two areas of inquiry: 1) topics involved in the witness's direct examination; and 2) topics concerning the witness's credibility. This is the "scope of direct" rule for controlling the coverage of cross-examination, adopted by FRE 611(b). The Federal Rules reject an opposite idea, the "wide-open" rule. Under the wide-open rule, a cross-examiner would be entitled to ask a witness anything that is relevant to an issue at trial. Under the scope-of-direct rule, the cross-examiner may only ask questions related to the scope of direct examination. If a witness has information on a topic outside the scope of the witness's direct examination, a party who would like the trier of fact to learn that information must use that witness as part of his or her own direct case and question the witness about that topic on direct examination.

The "scope of direct" rule thus allows a party a great deal of control over the order in which the trier of fact learns relevant information. Even if a witness has information on a variety of relevant topics, the rule allows a party to organize the presentation of his or her case by using that witness just to supply information on topics the party chooses to develop through that witness. The opposing party cannot use cross-examination of the witness to direct the jury's attention to other aspects of the case that might be within that witness's knowledge if the party presenting that witness has chosen to ignore them. The rule is flexible, however, and grants discretion to the trial judge to allow a cross-examiner to expand the scope of examination beyond the topics covered in direct examination.

Form for Cross-Examination Questions

Leading questions are permitted on cross-examination in contrast to direct examination. Additionally, a cross-examiner is permitted to make repeated efforts to obtain an answer by asking questions more than once, or by rephrasing questions to get at a single idea in more than one way. Balanced against this traditional freedom is the trial court's ability to protect witnesses from, in the words of FRE 611(a), "harassment or undue embarrassment."

Questions by the Judge

Judges may question witnesses, but they are supposed to be very sparing in using this right. Parties have primary responsibility for their own cases and should not be helped or hurt by the court. Additionally, questions from the bench may assume more significance to jurors than their substance would justify merely because the person asking the questions is the trial judge. While appellate courts are highly deferential to trial courts on an issue like the timing and extent of judicial questioning of witnesses, occasional remands for new trial are ordered where judicial questioning is excessive. The most acceptable occasions for questions from the bench are instances when a witness has accidentally used a word improperly and the judge, noticing it, can give the witness a chance to make the testimony clearer. In general, the judge's motive for questioning should always be to increase the clarity of the testimony rather than to influence the result in the case.

Statements of Opinion

Rule 701 limits the expression of opinions by witnesses. It provides:

> If the witness is not testifying as an expert, the witness' testimony in the form of opinions or inferences is limited to those opinions or inferences which are (a) rationally based on the perception of the witness and (b) helpful to a clear understanding of the witness' testimony or the determination of a fact in issue.

The theory behind the rule is that juries can find facts better if witnesses report concrete information and allow the juries' members to analyze the information. The rule provides that unless a witness is testifying as an expert, statements of opinion or inferences are allowed only if they help provide a clear understanding of the testimony or of a fact in issue. It must also be shown that the opinion or inference is based on some perception by the witness. This rule rejects a controversial common law position that attempted to distinguish clearly between factual and opinion statements and was supposed to exclude statements of opinion by any witnesses other than expert witnesses. A witness may state, for example, that a person seemed drunk, or that a driver seemed to be in control of a vehicle so long as those statements (which could be characterized as reporting conclusions, inferences, or opinions) have some support in actual perceptions of the witness.

Physical Location of Witnesses and Parties

A judge ordinarily controls the locations of witnesses and attorneys in the courtroom. An issue of current importance is whether a judge, in a case involving alleged assault against a child, may prevent a complaining witness and a defendant from seeing each other in the courtroom. Decisions of the United States Supreme Court suggest that the confrontation clause does not prohibit arrangements such as a physical barrier or the use of television for testimony from a location other than the courtroom so long as an individualized finding is made in each case that standard arrangements could traumatize the child due to the child's awareness of the defendant's presence.

The statute[3] providing detailed procedures for considering the competency of a child witness also sets up procedures for allowing a child to testify in a room separate from the defendant in a criminal case. If the trial judge believes that style of testimony is needed, the statute requires that television equipment be used to allow the child and defendant to see each other's faces.

At the request of any party, a witness may be sequestered, that is, barred from presence in the courtroom except during that witness's testimony. Rule 615 states:

> At the request of a party the court shall order witnesses excluded so that they cannot hear the testimony of other witnesses, and it may make the order of its own motion. This rule does not authorize exclusion of (1) a party who is a natural person, or (2) an officer or employee of a party which is not a natural person designated as its representative by its attorney, or (3) a person whose presence is shown by a party to be essential to the presentation of the party's cause.

Note that a person may not be sequestered if his or her presence when not testifying is shown to be necessary to a party's representation. For example, a

---

3. 18 U.S.C. §3509.

person who is expected to testify as an expert may be essential as an assistant to a lawyer for a party so that the lawyer can understand and counter testimony by experts for the opposing side. There is also a general limitation on the right of parties to require sequestration: A party cannot personally be required to be absent from the trial even if that party will be a witness. Where a party is an entity rather than a person, a representative of that entity is treated as equivalent to a person who is a party and is protected from sequestration as well.

General Right to Impeach

Any party may impeach any witness. Rule 607 states, "The credibility of a witness may be attacked by any party, including the party calling the witness." This rejects a common law doctrine that required a party who presented a witness to "vouch" for the witness's credibility and prohibited the party from showing that the witness might have testified untruthfully. In modern practice, where parties may have to rely on testimony from individuals whose reliability they may question, allowing any party the freedom to use impeachment techniques has seemed reasonable.

Various provisions of evidence law allow the admission of "impeachment-only" information; that is, information about a witness that can be considered by the trier of fact only for the light it may shed on whether the witness has testified truthfully. Material of this type may not be used by the trier of fact to prove any substantive part of a party's case. This distinction between information that is admissible only for impeachment and information that can be relied upon for substantive purposes leads to a limitation on parties' general ability to impeach all witnesses. Some courts have prohibited a party from impeaching its own witness when it seems that the party has used the witness only as part of a plan to impeach that witness with material that would be inadmissible for other purposes. In that setting, what purported to be a defensive use of impeachment material would really be an effort to bring that material into the trial so that the fact finder might improperly use it as a substantive basis for judgment rather than just as information that reflects on the witness's truthfulness.

Impeachment by Showing the Witness Lied Intentionally

Convictions of Crimes

If a witness has been convicted of a crime, evidence of the conviction is often admissible to support the following linked inferences: 1) the witness does not respect our society's rules of conduct; 2) the witness is a person who has a propensity to lie; and 3) because of that propensity, the witness may have lied while testifying. This general rule permits jurors to base a conclusion about the witness's conduct in court (the witness lied or spoke truthfully) on information about the witness's past conduct out of court. It is an exception to the general prohibition against propensity evidence. Under that general rule, for example, evidence of a person's past bad driving would be kept out if offered to support an inference about the person's driving on a later occasion. In connection with the conduct of testifying in court, however, evidence of a witness's past lying or other past conduct in disrespect of law is admitted to support an inference about the person's later conduct as a testifying witness.

There are a number of reasons why the standard bar against propensity inferences is modified for the issue of impeachment. Some think that there is a particularly strong logical link between past lying and current lying. Others justify allowing jurors to make propensity-based inferences about a witness's truthfulness because the veracity of witnesses is a highly important issue, or because they believe the types of data on which these propensity inferences are allowed to be based are likely to be accurate and subject to quick and clear proof. Finally, it may have seemed anomalous at common law and to the drafters of the Federal Rules for a person who had been convicted of serious crimes in the past to appear before a jury and benefit from the jury's likely assumption that the person did not have a criminal record. Obviously, the fact that a jury may learn about a witness's past wrongdoing will deter many defendants from testifying in their own defense since if they refrain from testifying, evidence of their past convictions will be admissible only on other rationales that are harder for the opponent to establish.

Admissibility of evidence of prior convictions is often determined in pretrial proceedings. If the court rules that this type of impeachment will be allowed, the defendant will only be allowed to challenge that ruling if he or she decides to testify and is then impeached with the controversial evidence. This means, in practice, that defendants are deterred from testifying in cases where a proper application of the rule would expose them to impeachment based on proof of past convictions *and* are also deterred in cases where a ruling allowing that type of impeachment might well be wrong. The deterrence occurs in the latter type of case because a defendant will only be able to challenge the ruling allowing that impeachment by testifying and allowing the jury to hear it. The gamble this presents may lead many defendants to refrain from testifying.

The arguments against allowing past convictions to be the basis for inferences about the credibility of witnesses are the same arguments that have led to strict limitations on this type of propensity evidence in other contexts. This may explain why common law judges and the Federal Rules have imposed detailed and complicated restrictions on the process even though they take the general position that the propensity inference can properly have some role in determining witness's credibility. Rules 609(a) and (b) set out the main controls on this process:

(a) General rule. For the purpose of attacking the credibility of a witness,

(1) evidence that a witness other than an accused has been convicted of a crime shall be admitted, subject to Rule 403, if the crime was punishable by death or imprisonment in excess of one year under the law under which the witness was convicted, and evidence that an accused has been convicted of such a crime shall be admitted if the court determines that the probative value of admitting this evidence outweighs its prejudicial effect to the accused; and

(2) evidence that any witness has been convicted of a crime shall be admitted if it involved dishonesty or false statement, regardless of the punishment.

(b) Time limit. Evidence of a conviction under this rule is not admissible if a period of more than ten years has elapsed since the date of the conviction or of the release of the witness from the confinement imposed for that conviction, whichever is the later date, unless the court determines, in the interests of justice, that the probative value of the conviction supported by specific facts and circumstances substantially outweighs its prejudicial effect. However, evidence of a conviction more than 10 years old as calculated herein, is not admissible unless the proponent gives to the adverse party sufficient advance written notice of intent to use such evidence to provide the adverse party with a fair opportunity to contest the use of such evidence.

The Rule varies the availability of proof of past convictions for impeaching the credibility of a witness in accordance with factors such as: whether the witness sought to be impeached is a criminal defendant; the type of crime committed (its seriousness and its connection with false statements); and the likely balance between probative value and prejudice, including the effect of the length of time between the trial and the conviction.

Crimes of "Dishonesty or False Statement" If a crime involved "dishonesty or false statement," evidence that any witness (whether or not a criminal defendant) was convicted of it is usually admissible to impeach that witness's credibility in the current trial. For these convictions, there is ordinarily no comparison of probative and possible prejudicial effects, and even the usual Rule 403 balancing test is withdrawn for this particular question of admissibility. The only time admission of this evidence is not automatic is when a ten-year period has elapsed since the date of conviction or the witness's release from confinement related to the conviction (whichever date is later). In that circumstance, the evidence is subject to a balancing test under Rule 609(b).

What crimes involve dishonesty or false statement?   Defining crimes that involve dishonesty or false statement is sometimes difficult. Forgery and embezzlement are classic examples that all would characterize as within the definition because they always involve circumstances in which truth-telling is required and the wrongdoer chooses to lie. Bank robbery has been treated by some courts as involving "dishonesty or false statement," although most courts reject that approach because the statements used by bank robbers are probably true as in "give me the money or I'll shoot you." Smuggling is another crime that has been given varied treatment by courts; where a smuggler makes an explicit false statement to a law enforcement official, the crime clearly involves "dishonesty or false statement," but where it is carried out with complete secrecy, some courts hold that it does not fit that definition. Similarly, filing a false tax return fits the category of offense that involves "dishonesty or false statement," but the offense of failing to file a tax return does not.

Crimes that do not involve "dishonesty or false statement" Proof of conviction of crimes that do not involve "dishonesty or false statement" is also admissible, subject to two important qualifications. First, the crime must have been punishable by death or imprisonment in excess of one year. Misdemeanors are thus not bad enough to be relevant for impeachment. Second, the evidence must pass a balancing test comparing its probative value to certain risks of misuse. If the witness is a criminal defendant, the evidence must be excluded if the court determines that its probative value is outweighed by its prejudicial effect to that person, the criminal defendant who testifies in his or her own trial. If the witness is anyone other than the defendant in a criminal trial, the evidence is excluded only if its probative value is *substantially* outweighed by its prejudicial effects. The balancing test for criminal defendants is unique to this issue; the balancing test for witnesses other than criminal defendants is the test set out in the general "unfair prejudice" rule, Rule 403. Trial court decisions on admissibility of this type of evidence are usually affirmed as within the court's discretion. It is considered good practice, however, for a trial court to make explicit findings about the balancing of probative force and possible prejudice.

The probative value of past convictions of crimes that do not involve "dishonesty or false statement."   If a person who is a witness in a current trial was once convicted of a crime that did not involve dishonesty or false statement, how does that fact relate to the likelihood that the witness gave truthful testimony in the current trial? The rationale for relevancy of a conviction such as assault, for example, must be that a person who breaks any law (in circumstances that make the conduct punishable by at least a year's imprisonment) has so little respect for propriety and the legal system that he or she is more likely to lie in court than an otherwise similar person who had not committed that type of crime. It is important to identify the probative value of past convictions because trial courts are required to balance that probative value against risks of prejudice or misuse of the evidence. Also, that balancing must involve an evaluation of the probative force of the evidence. Rule 609 explicitly treats nontruth-telling offenses as related to a witness's likely truthfulness while testifying. Therefore in evaluating the probative value of that type of conviction, courts usually focus on whether the witness's credibility is particularly important in the trial and on whether there are other means to give the jury a basis for assessing that credibility.

The risk of prejudice or jury misuse will depend on the nature of the past crime. If the witness is not a party, the only risk of jury misuse of the past crimes information will be that jurors may assume that the party on whose behalf the witness testified is to be disfavored because that party is associated with a witness who has previously committed a serious crime. While this "birds of a feather flock together" analysis may reflect reality in some instances, it is a fairly attenuated theory. In most cases, there is only a small risk that a jury will misuse information about the past of a non-party witness. This is why Rule 609 applies the balancing test of FRE 403 to past convictions of a non-defendant witness: They can be admitted even if the risk of prejudice outweighs their probative force (so long as that risk does not *substantially* outweigh their probative value).

Where the witness is a criminal defendant, Rule 609 uses a balancing test that tips slightly more in the direction of excluding this type of evidence. It requires exclusion if the probative value is outweighed in any degree by the risks of prejudice. In the situation of a criminal defendant who testifies, the strongest likelihood of prejudicial misuse of information about the defendant's past convictions arises where they involve an offense that is the same as or similar to the offense being adjudicated in the current trial. For example, evidence that an alleged bank robber has robbed a bank in the past would be barred by the propensity rule if offered to show that because the defendant robbed a bank once he or she is more likely to have robbed a bank another time. If an alleged bank robber testified at trial and was then impeached with evidence that he or she had robbed a bank in the past, the explicit theory of admissibility would be that information about the past robbery would help jurors decide whether the defendant acted truthfully on the witness stand.

There is a significant risk, however, that the jury would use the information about the past bank robbery to decide how the defendant acted on the day of the bank robbery. Jurors might ignore the permitted use of the evidence as a basis for evaluating the witness's credibility and might use it as a basis for deciding that having robbed a bank in the past, he or she probably committed the bank robbery that is the subject of the current prosecution. The risk of prejudice is extremely high in this situation. However, if credibility is a crucial issue, and other evidence about credibility is not available, courts will sometimes permit this type of information about a defendant's past to be used under the impeachment rationale. This strongly deters a criminal defendant who has been convicted in the past of any crime from testifying in his or her own defense.

Staleness, pardons, juvenile adjudications, appeals. The ten-year staleness provision of Rule 609(b), discussed above in the context of crimes involving dishonesty or false statement, also applies to other crimes covered by
the impeachment rules. Where a conviction has been the subject of a pardon
or was the result of a juvenile adjudication, the Rules restrict introduction of
evidence about it. Those limitations are in Rule 609(c) and (d):

> (c) Effect of pardon, annulment, or certificate of rehabilita-
> tion. Evidence of a conviction is not admissible under this rule if
> (1) the conviction has been the subject of a pardon, annulment,
> certificate of rehabilitation, or other equivalent procedure based on
> a finding of the rehabilitation of the person convicted, and that
> person has not been convicted of a subsequent crime which was
> punishable by death or imprisonment in excess of one year, or (2)
> the conviction has been the subject of a pardon, annulment, or
> other equivalent procedure based on a finding of innocence.
> (d) Juvenile adjudications. Evidence of juvenile adjudications
> is generally not admissible under this rule. The court may, how-
> ever, in a criminal case allow evidence of a juvenile adjudication of
> a witness other than the accused if conviction of the offense would
> be admissible to attack the credibility of an adult and the court is
> satisfied that admission in evidence is necessary for a fair determi-
> nation of the issue of guilt or innocence.

If a pardon was based on a finding of innocence, evidence of the conviction
for which the pardon was granted is inadmissible. If a pardon was based on
factors such as rehabilitation, evidence of the conviction is similarly inadmissible unless the person has subsequently been convicted of a serious crime.
Juvenile adjudications are ordinarily excluded from evidence, but trial courts
have discretion to admit them if necessary for fair evaluation of a witness's
testimony with regard to guilt or innocence of a criminal defendant.

Impeachment uses of past convictions involve four different possible descriptions of the relationship between the probative value of the information
and the risks of prejudice. Rule 609 relates admissibility to the type of past
conviction and the identity of the individual witness against whom the information is sought to be used. Chart Fifteen illustrates the choices incorporated in Rule 609. Notice that for evidence of past convictions to be
admitted, the Rule sets the required balance between probativeness and prejudicial potential increasingly towards probativeness as the likelihood of fair
and accurate use of the information decreases either because the conviction is
old or because it involved the current criminal defendant.

Past Bad Acts That Did Not Lead to Criminal Convictions

The same theory of logical relevance that supports admission of evidence of
a witness's conviction of crimes also applies to the relevance of information
that a witness committed bad acts that did not lead to criminal convictions.

CHART SIXTEEN
Is Evidence of a Witness's Past Conviction Admissible?

Type of Conviction and Type of Witness	*Balance between Probative Value and Risk of Prejudice*			
	Substantially More Probative than Prejudicial	*More Probative than Prejudicial*	*More Prejudicial than Probative*	*Substantially More Prejudicial than Probative*
Crime involved truth-telling; any witness	YES	YES	YES	YES
Crime did not involve truth-telling; any witness *except* a criminal defendant	YES	YES	YES	NO
Crime did not involve truth-telling; criminal defendant witness	YES	YES	NO	NO
Any crime more than ten years old; any witness	YES	NO	NO	NO

A person who has been seriously disrespectful of law may likely be a person who would not testify truthfully in a judicial proceeding. However, because proving that a person committed any particular act in the past is so much more difficult than proving he or she was convicted of a crime, extrinsic evidence of past bad acts is not permitted when their only relevance is to impeach a witness's credibility. Rule 608(b) states:

> Specific instances of conduct. Specific instances of the conduct of a witness, for the purpose of attacking or supporting the witness' credibility, other than conviction of crime as provided in rule 609, may not be proved by extrinsic evidence. They may, however, in the discretion of the court, if probative of truthfulness or untruthfulness, be inquired into on cross-examination of the witness (1) concerning the witness' character for truthfulness or untruthfulness, or (2) concerning the character for truthfulness or untruthfulness of another witness as to which character the witness being cross-examined has testified.
>
> The giving of testimony, whether by an accused or by any other witness, does not operate as a waiver of the accused's or the witness' privilege against self-incrimination when examined with respect to matters which relate only to credibility.

Thus, a witness may be questioned about past acts that did not lead to a conviction if they are relevant to the witness's character for truthfulness, but proof other than this testimony is prohibited.

There are two important controls on the use of information about a witness's past acts that did not lead to a criminal conviction. The questioner must have a good faith belief that the events actually occurred or else may not ask questions about it. Also, the questioner may not introduce other proof about the alleged past act by testimony from other witnesses or by any other method. This is why it is sometimes said that the examiner must "take the witness's answer." The examiner is allowed to ask about the past acts, but all the examiner can do if witness denies having committed the acts is to ask about them again (subject to limits on harassment of a witness).

The rationale for allowing inquiry but not extrinsic proof is that proving the occurrence of past acts by particular witnesses would be time-consuming since it might entail the equivalent of a trial within the current trial. Of course, the fact that a process is costly is significant only in comparison to the results it can be expected to accomplish. In this case the benefit from establishing the truth about a witness's past conduct would be that the jury could use the information to make an inference about the witness's character for truthfulness and then make an inference from its opinion about that character to a belief about how the witness acted while testifying (in conformity with that character or not in conformity with that character). Since character inferences are generally disfavored, it is sensible to give up the chance to let juries make them on the basis of information about the past bad acts of witnesses if it would be difficult to provide juries with clear information about those acts. In contrast, where the past acts have become the subject of a criminal conviction, it is easy to give juries clear information about them. It is also true that a conviction means that guilt was established under the beyond a reasonable doubt standard. These are the primary reasons for treating past convictions differently from past acts of witnesses. Convictions, subject to Rule 609's detailed provisions, may be proved with extrinsic evidence. Past acts of a witness, if relevant only to credibility, are treated only with the process in which an examiner asks about them and the witness gives a reply.

Proof of Bias

If a witness is biased either against or in favor of a party at a trial, proof of that bias is permitted on the theory that the witness may have shaded his or her testimony in line with it. A cross-examiner is entitled to ask questions that will show possible sources of bias. Other types of evidence of bias may also be introduced.

Common sources of bias involve family ties, financial ties, and membership in organizations. Information about links of this sort may suggest that a witness has slanted testimony in favor of a party with whom he or she is related. This type of proof may also support an inference that the witness has distorted his or her testimony to be unfavorable to an opponent of the party with whom the witness is related. Similarly, if a witness has been paid by a party, proof of that fact may help a jury evaluate the likely honesty of the witness's statements. In criminal cases, prosecution witnesses sometimes have made deals with the prosecution. If the prosecution is in a position to reduce the degree of a charged crime or to make a sentencing recommendation in a pending case involving a witness, that witness may be influenced to testify favorably to the prosecution in that case or some other case. Information concerning this type of relationship is usually admissible, although some courts will exclude it if the witness's arrangement with the prosecutor did not involve an obligation to testify.

Inquiry Into Religious Beliefs Prohibited

While learning about a witness's religious beliefs might influence some jurors to form an opinion about whether the witness has testified truthfully, just how that influence would work would probably vary among jurors and according to the type of religious beliefs the witness did or did not have. There is an explicit rule prohibiting this type of reference to religious beliefs. Rule 610 provides:

> Evidence of the beliefs or opinions of a witness on matters of religion is not admissible for the purpose of showing that by reason of their nature the witness' credibility is impaired or enhanced.

If a witness's religious beliefs or membership in a religious organization could be a basis for bias towards or against a party, then proof related to religion would be proper because kinship or antipathy would be the basis for the claim of relevance. In such a bias theory the nature of the witness's religious beliefs is not offered as a basis for believing or disbelieving the witness. Rather, the evidence is offered to show a motive that could affect the truthfulness of the witness. This use would not be prohibited by Rule 610.

Evidence of Character for Truth-Telling: A Permitted Propensity Inference

After a witness testifies, evidence may be introduced about that witness's character traits related to truth-telling. A party seeking to impeach the credibility of a witness may introduce evidence showing that the witness is the type of person who is likely to lie. Rule 608(a) allows this type of evidence and specifies the form in which it must be introduced:

> Opinion and reputation evidence of character. The credibility of a witness may be attacked or supported by evidence in the form of opinion or reputation, but subject to these limitations: (1) the evidence may refer only to character for truthfulness or untruthfulness, and (2) evidence of truthful character is admissible only after the character of the witness for truthfulness has been attacked by opinion or reputation evidence or otherwise.

Evidence attacking a witness's character for truth-telling is introduced by testimony from other witnesses. For clarity, they can be called "testifying witnesses" and "impeaching witnesses," although both testifying and impeaching witnesses, of course, give testimony. An impeaching witness is allowed to provide the fact finder with negative information about the testifying witness's untruthful nature in either of two ways: by describing the testifying witness's reputation for truth-telling or by giving an opinion about the testifying witness's typical truthfulness. This is another instance in which the usual rule against propensity evidence is modified where the issue at stake is whether a witness has given truthful testimony.

After a witness's character for truthfulness has been attacked with evidence in the form of reputation or opinion evidence, it can be rehabilitated. Other witnesses may testify about the testifying witness's positive character traits for truthfulness. These rehabilitating witnesses are limited to reporting the reputation of the testifying witness or to stating their own opinions about the testifying witness's character for speaking the truth. It is important to remember that no witness is allowed to give reputation or opinion evidence showing that another witness has probably testified truthfully unless character evidence has already been introduced to show that that witness probably gave false testimony. In criminal cases there may be an exception to the usual requirement that evidence about truthfulness is not permitted until there has been an attack on a witness's credibility: A defendant may comment on his or her own truthfulness if truthfulness is a trait pertinent to the charged crime, whether or not there has been a character-based attack on the defendant's truthfulness.

Impeachment by Proof of Poor Perception or Memory

Because a person's ability to perceive things is so strongly related to the likelihood that what a person says about those things is accurate, cross-examiners are permitted to ask witnesses questions about how well they can see or hear and about the circumstances in which they observed or heard things that are the subjects of their testimony. Independent evidence on these topics is also admissible.

Impeachment by Contradiction

If some of a witness's testimony is factually incorrect, proof that those portions were wrong could support a conclusion that the other parts of the testimony were also false. It is logical that a person who remembers or describes some things incorrectly might give incorrect testimony about other things also. Regardless of whether the falsehoods are intentional or accidental, the fact that the witness claimed to believe things that are actually false could decrease a juror's belief in the credibility of the witness. Evidence law recognizes the logical relevance of factual errors to general credibility. However, a party may not introduce extrinsic proof that particular details of a witness's testimony are false unless those details involve a topic that could be subject to proof even if the witness had not referred to them. In other words, the topic on which a party seeks to introduce evidence in contradiction to a witness's testimony must be a topic that would be relevant in the trial whether or not a witness had earlier given testimony about it. If it has no independent significance, the topic is called "collateral." Evidence that will only show a mistake or false statement in something a witness has said about a collateral topic is prohibited from being introduced extrinsically.

This limitation is based on the belief that allowing impeachment by contradiction would cost our litigation system too much for benefits that would probably be slight. A party seeking to impeach a witness by contradiction would introduce lots of evidence that was unrelated to the main issues at trial but did relate to the alleged error in the witness's testimony. A jury would have to deliberate not only about the factual issues related to the parties' claims and defenses but also about factual issues that would show whether minor portions of a witness's testimony were accurate. Of necessity, parties would spend large amounts of time and resources pursuing these factual questions. In contrast, the benefit a jury would derive from a full-fledged scrutiny of the factual accuracy of every part of a witness's testimony might be very slight. It might be worth far less than the expenditures of time and attention it would require.

For example, a witness might testify, "I was at the corner of Main and Broadway, and I saw the defendant run out of the National Bank carrying a gun and a bag of money." If the bank at that corner is really "Continental Bank," how much value would there be to having the jury find out that the witness had been mistaken in what he called the bank? It does not show very much about the witness's accuracy on the topics of identity, the gun, and the money that the witness remembered the name of the bank incorrectly. If a witness makes an error on some aspect of his testimony that has relevance to the disputed issues at trial, contrary evidence may always be introduced. For example, a defense witness in a bank robbery trial might testify, "I saw the defendant the afternoon of the robbery and he had a full beard." If eyewitnesses had testified that the robber was clean-shaven, this defense witness's testimony would help the defendant. A witness for the prosecution would be allowed to testify that he had seen the defendant on the same day and that the defendant did not have a beard. The prosecution's witness would be contradicting a point in the defense witness's testimony, but the testimony would be admissible. The physical appearance of the defendant on the day of the robbery would be relevant to an issue at trial (identity of the robber) and would not be called a collateral part of the defense witness's testimony. In contrast, suppose the defense witness stated, "I saw the defendant at a Burger King on the afternoon of the robbery and he had a beard," and suppose the prosecution knew that the restaurant was McDonald's, not a

Burger King. Proof that the witness had used the wrong name for the restaurant would not be permitted.

The limitation on impeachment by contradiction only prevents the introduction of extrinsic evidence (proof is proof in any style other than statements by the witness being questioned). During cross-examination a witness can be asked about any part of his or her direct examination. The defense witness could be asked, for example, "Wasn't it a McDonald's, not a Burger King?" but no matter what answer the witness gave to that inquiry, additional evidence from a source other than the witness would be prohibited.

Prior Statements by a Witness

When a witness says something in testimony but has also written or said something earlier that conflicts with that testimony, what the witness said or wrote at the earlier time is called a "prior inconsistent statement." On the theory that a person who says one thing one time and another thing another time has probably lied or has suffered from memory deficiencies on one of the two occasions, proof of prior inconsistent statements is permitted as a type of impeachment. Rule 613(a) states:

> Examining witness concerning prior statement. In examining a witness concerning a prior statement made by the witness, whether written or not, the statement need not be shown nor its contents disclosed to the witness at that time, but on request the same shall be shown or disclosed to opposing counsel.

Except in limited circumstances, the jury or judge may not rely on the past statement as proof of what it asserts (because of the hearsay bar), but the fact finder may rely on it to disbelieve what the witness has said in court.

A cross-examiner may ask a witness about a prior statement without showing it to the witness, if the statement was written, and without saying in advance what the details of that prior statement might have been. However, the Rules require that the contents of the prior statement be disclosed to opposing counsel on request. The cross-examiner may accept the witness's denial or explanation of the prior statement but is also given the right to introduce extrinsic evidence of the prior statement. Extrinsic evidence of the statement could be a document or testimony by another person who knows about the statement. If extrinsic evidence of a past statement is introduced, the witness who made the current and past statements must be given an opportunity to explain the past statement. That opportunity may come either before or after extrinsic evidence of the statement is introduced. Use of extrinsic evidence is controlled by Rule 613(b):

> Extrinsic evidence of prior inconsistent statement of witness. Extrinsic evidence of a prior inconsistent statement by a witness is not admissible unless the witness is afforded an opportunity to explain or

deny the same and the opposite party is afforded an opportunity to interrogate the witness thereon, or the interests of justice otherwise require. This provision does not apply to admissions of a party-opponent as defined in rule 801(d)(2).

There are a few situations in which prior statements, in addition to their use to influence a juror's opinion about credibility, may be used substantively. This substantive use is allowed when the prior statement was made under oath in some proceeding or when the prior statement was one that identifies someone and was made "after" having seen that person. Also, a prior *consistent* statement by a witness may be introduced substantively (that is, not only for its impact on the credibility issue) if impeachment efforts have suggested that the witness's testimony was a recently created lie or was influenced by improper motives. Showing that the witness had made statements consistent with the in-court testimony at a time previous to the trial before the alleged recent decision to lie would contradict the claim that the testimony was shaped by a recent plan to lie. Also, it can contradict a claim that a witness has slanted his or her testimony in response to pressure from prosecutors or family members or in response to other improper motives if it can be shown that the witness made statements before those influences were operative that were similar to the statements made in testimony. These special types of prior statements by a witness are defined in Rule 801(d)(1).

Impeaching a Hearsay Declarant

When hearsay evidence is admitted, any party is permitted to impeach the credibility of the hearsay declarant. This process is controlled by Rule 806:

> When a hearsay statement, or a statement defined in Rule 801(d)(2), (c), (D), or (E), has been admitted in evidence, the credibility of the declarant may be attacked, and if attacked may be supported, by any evidence which would be admissible for those purposes if declarant had testified as a witness. Evidence of a statement or conduct by the declarant at any time, inconsistent with the declarant's hearsay statement, is not subject to any requirement that the declarant may have been afforded an opportunity to deny or explain. If the party against whom a hearsay statement has been admitted calls the declarant as a witness, the party is entitled to examine the declarant on the statement as if under cross-examination.

The methods allowed for this impeachment are parallel to those permitted when a witness testifies in person during a trial. Evidence is admissible that the declarant was convicted of a crime, with the same restrictions that apply to an in-court witness's impeachment. Similarly, evidence is admissible showing that the declarant had a bias that could have affected the statement as well as evidence relating to the declarant's ability to have perceived what he spoke about. Evidence can be introduced showing the character of the declarant for untruthfulness, and also for truthfulness in instances where evidence of character for untruthfulness is first introduced.

When a witness testifies in person, inquiry is permitted during cross-examination about past bad acts that did not lead to criminal conviction but that might still reflect on the witness's truthfulness. No parallel procedure is possible for hearsay declarant since they are not present in court and cannot be asked about their past conduct. If, however, the declarant is available and can be a witness, then impeachment with inquiries about past bad acts would be possible.

Rule 806 also covers the use of inconsistent statements. Usually, they may be introduced only if the witness is given an opportunity at some time in the trial to explain or deny them. In the case of a hearsay declarant who had made a statement out of court that was inconsistent with the hearsay statement that was introduced, evidence of the inconsistent statement is admissible without regard to the usual rule that requires an opportunity for the speaker to explain the earlier statement. According to the literal words of the rule, there is no requirement that the additional statement have been made earlier than the time of the already introduced hearsay statement.

EXAMPLES

1. The losing party in a civil case seeks to have a new trial ordered on the ground of jury misconduct. He has found out that at the start of deliberations, the jurors agreed to have a brief period of silent prayer. A juror would be willing to testify that the foreman had recommended that the jurors "seek Divine guidance" in their work. Should the trial judge permit this testimony?

2. In a suit seeking damages for personal injury, the plaintiff testified that he was hurt in the lobby of a bank when someone entering the bank pushed a door open, towards the inside of the lobby, and banged it into her. At the close of direct examination, the judge said to the witness, "I use that bank all the time, and it's got revolving doors into the lobby, no regular doors that you push open. Are you sure you're remembering this right?" What evidentiary problems are raised by the judge's conduct?

3. The defendant, accused of embezzling money from a church at which he worked, testified in his own defense. Prior to testifying, he affirmed his intention to tell the truth but did not swear an oath of truthfulness. Is "Tell us why you wouldn't swear on the Bible to tell the truth" a permissible inquiry on cross-examination?

4. A defendant is accused of attacking a victim with a baseball bat. A prosecution witness testifies, "The defendant beat up the victim with a baseball bat. I know that because everyone in the neighborhood has heard about it." Is there a reasonable objection to this testimony?

5. In an assault and battery trial, a prosecution witness testifies, "I know

the defendant beat up the victim. I saw them go into a small storeroom to-gether, and then I saw the defendant run out. Then I went in and found the victim all bruised and bloody." Is this testimony admissible?

6.   A janitor is accused of thefts from a nursery school. The prosecution seeks to introduce testimony by a five-year-old child. If permitted to testify, the child will say that about a year ago he saw the janitor take a VCR machine from a classroom. If the defense was aware that the child has a vivid imagina-tion and has told numerous lies to playmates, how might it attempt to keep the child from testifying?

7.   Assume that someone who has seen a crime committed is going to be hyp-notized by the police in an effort to help the person remember more details. Why would it help that person's potential availability as a witness at a trial involving the crime if a tape recordings were made of his or her answers to ques-tions about the event prior to the hypnosis and of the hypnosis session itself?

8.   Allan Anders and Ellen Anders are husband and wife. Allan is on trial for robbery. The prosecution seeks to compel testimony by Ellen about vehicles she might have seen parked outside her and Allan's house on the day of the robbery. Can Allan prevent her from testifying on the grounds of spousal in-competency? Can Ellen refuse to testify on that theory? Could the prosecu-tion refute a claim of spousal incompetency with evidence showing that the Allan and Ellen's marriage was unstable and that they had been separated from time to time during recent years?

9.   In another bank robbery trial, a defense witness testifies about the de-fendant's whereabouts on the date of the crime. On cross-examination, the prosecution asks whether the defendant had experienced a sudden need for a large sum of money on the day prior to the robbery. Is that question permis-sible on cross-examination?

10.   In a prosecution involving a tax return with false statements, the gov-ernment is seeking to convict the tax preparer, claiming that he listed chari-table contributions on his client's return even though the client never told him he had made any. If a witness for the prosecution was the defendant tax preparer's client, could the prosecutor ask: "Did you tell the defendant you had made no charitable contributions?"

11.   Prosecutors believe that a defendant committed a sexual assault on a young child on a certain date in a certain locàtion. They have evidence that the child and the defendant were seen on that date in that location. A few days after that date, the child told law enforcement officials that there had been a sexual assault. A year later the child recanted and said that there had never been an assault. What issues are raised if the prosecution has the child testify in its case against the defendant, knowing that the child will say no sex-ual assault took place and planning to then impeach the child with evidence of the earlier report of an assault?

12.   In a rape trial, the alleged victim testifies that on the night of the al-leged attack:

a.   she spent some time with the defendant at a bar;

b.   the bar was very crowded and had a band playing loud music;

c.   she was wearing a dress she had bought at K Mart two years earlier; and

d.   the defendant surprised her by attacking her in the bar's parking lot and forcing her to have sexual intercourse.

The defendant testifies that the plaintiff's recollection is incorrect, and that they had consensual sexual intercourse in the parking lot. The defendant has other witnesses available who would testify that:

a.   there was no band at the bar that night; and

b.   K Mart had stopped selling dresses of the type worn by the alleged victim at least four years before the night of the alleged attack.

Should testimony by these other defense witnesses be admitted?

13.   Vilma Vane is a criminal defendant charged with the crime of extortion (threatening an alleged victim with violence to obtain something of value).

   a.   If she does not testify in her defense, can she put on a witness to testify that she has a reputation for being respectful of other people's property?

   b.   If she does not testify in her defense, can she put on a witness to testify that she has a reputation for truthfulness?

   c.   If Vane does testify, can she then put on a witness to testify that she has a reputation for truthfulness?

   d.   If Vane testifies and the prosecution cross-examines her, showing that she has been convicted in the past of perjury, can Vane then put on a witness to testify that she has a reputation for truthfulness?

14.   William Worsted is on trial for car theft. He testifies that he did not commit the crime. The prosecution has evidence that he was convicted in the past of car theft and was released from a prison sentence for that crime nine years before the trial. Can the prosecution introduce this evidence?

15.   How would it affect the analysis in Example 14 if the trial court thought Worsted's testimony was crucial to the defense and also knew that the prosecution had no means to discredit it other than the evidence of the past car theft conviction?

16.   In a breach of contract case, the plaintiff testifies that machinery supplied by the defendant failed to operate as well as the defendant had claimed it would.

   a.   If the defendant knows that the plaintiff was once fired from work as a security guard because he was caught stealing merchandise from a warehouse, would questions about that past theft be proper on cross-examination?

   b.   To impeach the plaintiff's credibility, can the defendant introduce testimony by the plaintiff's former employers stating that he had stolen merchandise from them?

17.   Frank First testifies at a trial. During cross-examination, he is impeached with evidence that he has been convicted of perjury. Another witness, Sandra

Second, then testifies that in recent years First has had a reputation in his community as a truthful person.

a. In cross-examining Second, can the cross-examiner ask whether she has heard about conduct by First, such as cheating on his income taxes, that is inconsistent with truth-telling?

b. In cross-examining Second, can the cross-examiner ask whether she knows that First was convicted 20 years ago of embezzlement?

18.   A witness who testifies about another witness's character for truthfulness is permitted to use two different bases for testimony: what the witness knows about the first witness's reputation for truthfulness; and what the witness thinks personally about the first witness's character for truthfulness. If a cross-examiner of a character witness knew that the witness about whom the character witness had testified once was seen stealing money from a church collection box, could the cross-examiner ask a question about that conduct no matter what type of character evidence the witness had given, or would the choice of reputation or opinion testimony affect the availability of cross-examination about the stealing?

19.   In a shoplifting prosecution, the state produces two witnesses. One says she thinks she saw the defendant stealing something from a store but that she's not sure whether it was the defendant or someone else. Another witness testifies that he is sure the shoplifter was *not* the defendant. May the prosecution impeach that second witness with evidence of a written statement by him saying that he had figured out that the defendant had been shoplifting?

20.   If the only evidence introduced by the state in Example 19 (shoplifting) is the testimony by the two witnesses and whatever use is allowed for the prior statement, should the judge let the case go to the jury?

21.   Alice Anders sought damages from the seller of a condominium apartment, contending that the apartment was smaller than the seller had represented it to be and that it had a terrible odor. She testified that she had bought the apartment without inspecting it, and that the defendant had concealed its true size and smell. The defendant has a copy of a letter Anders wrote to a friend a few months after buying the apartment: It says, "I'm living in my new apartment now. It's smaller than I thought it would be, but I like it anyhow." Might the defendant want to introduce that letter, and if so, should it be admitted?

EXPLANATIONS

1.   Testimony by jurors about their deliberations is forbidden unless it relates to "extraneous" or "outside" influences brought to bear on their work. No inquiry is permitted into the mental processes of a juror, and no testimony about those thoughts is allowed. In this problem, the jurors themselves might consider the divine guidance to originate outside the jury room. However,

because it only involves individual thoughts and feelings of jurors, it would not be the type of outside information or influence allowed to be a subject of testimony by a juror.

2.   The judge should not ask this type of question since the opposing party will have an opportunity to bring in a variety of evidence about what kinds of doors the bank has in its lobby. The justification for judicial questioning that is the strongest, a need to clarify the record or make a witness's testimony as clear as possible, does not apply here because since the judge's effort was to contradict, not to clarify. Additionally, the judge's remarks are equivalent to testifying. He has brought factual information to the jury's attention, but the rules prohibit the judge from being a witness in a case over which he is presiding.

3.   No. First of all, witnesses are allowed, under the federal rules, to swear *or* affirm that they will testify truthfully. To allow a negative implication from the choice of one of the two explicitly provided options would functionally eliminate the availability of the option to affirm rather than to give an oath. Secondly, FRE 610 precludes references to a witness's religious beliefs with respect to credibility.

4.   The testimony should be stricken. The witness does not have personal knowledge of the defendant's conduct. The witness only has personal knowledge of what people in the neighborhood think happened. Additionally, if offered to prove that what the neighborhood people say happened actually is what happened, the testimony would be inadmissible on hearsay grounds as well.

5.   This testimony is acceptable. With regard to the requirement of personal knowledge, all the Federal Rules require is that there be evidence adequate to support a jury finding that the witness has personal knowledge of the subject of his or her testimony. In this problem, even though the witness did not see the beating, the witness did personally see everything that the testimony states about who was present, where they went, and what happened. The statement, "I know the defendant beat up the victim," is arguably an opinion rather than a report of clear-cut information. It would, however, probably be allowed as a natural summary of what the witness really did observe.

6.   The defense could argue that the child's testimony will fail to fulfill the personal knowledge requirement on the ground that because of the child's past inability to separate fact from fiction, it cannot provide a basis for a belief that she has knowledge about the subject of her testimony. It is possible that the defense could also be persuasive in arguing that the child cannot satisfy the obligation of affirming or swearing to tell the truth if it appears that the child does not know what truth is. The past lies would not be particularly helpful to the defense because there is no general bar to testimony from frequent liars. Rather, the defense would have to rely on the child's proven imagination and difficulty (if any) in separating truth from fantasy to

suggest that the requirements of personal knowledge and a promise to tell the truth are not satisfied.

7.   Most courts reject testimony by a witness who has been hypnotized on the theory that the hypnosis creates a risk that the witness will think he or she knows something that was really only suggested during the hypnosis. For this reason the testimony can be rejected on grounds of lack of personal knowledge or on the ground in criminal cases, related to the constitution, that the prosecution has impermissibly facilitated the witness's identification of an individual. It is common, however, for courts to allow testimony by a person who had been hypnotized if the proponent of the witness can show that the testimony only repeats information the witness believed prior to the hypnosis and that the hypnosis session was not itself suggestive with regard to the topic of the witness's testimony. For these reasons, the tape recordings of what the witness knew in advance of the hypnosis and what went on during the hypnosis session would be valuable as a means of showing the court that the requirements for limited use of testimony by a formerly hypnotized witness had been met.

8.   Under federal practice Allan has no power to keep his wife off the witness stand. In some states spousal incompetency may be invoked by either spouse. Under federal practice the witness-spouse is in control of whether or not to testify. Thus, in this problem, Ellen's assertion of spousal incompetency would be binding on the court. The prosecution's attempt to avoid the spousal incompetency would fail because the underlying policy of the doctrine is to avoid putting stress on marriages. Presumably a weak marriage is as deserving of state-sponsored assistance as is a strong marriage.

9.   Questions on cross-examination are generally limited to topics covered in a witness's direct testimony. Since this defense witness only gave information about where the defendant was on a particular day, a question about the defendant's financial status would likely be treated as beyond the scope of cross-examination. The "scope-of-direct" rule is subject to the judge's discretion, so the prosecutor would have to argue for relaxing the rule on these facts. If showing a motive was an important part of the prosecution case, the prosecutor should have located witnesses who could provide information relevant to that theory and should have included them in the state's direct case. If the court is persuaded that the prosecutor has acted in good faith, seeking witnesses on this issue, it might allow the question.

10.   This is an improper leading question. The legitimate form for bringing out this information is a question like, "What did you tell the defendant, if anything, about charitable contributions?"

11.   The Federal Rules allow any party to impeach any witness, rejecting the common law doctrine that a party must support its own witness's testimony. In this case, it is clear that the only reason the prosecution has for

using the child as a witness is its plan to impeach the child's testimony with the child's earlier out-of-court statement. If that statement would otherwise be inadmissible (because of the bar against hearsay evidence), most courts would refuse to permit the prosecution to use the statement as impeachment material. Despite the literal requirements of the Federal Rule, most courts would hold that the prosecution in this case is only using the witness as part of a plan to avoid the restrictions of the hearsay doctrine. The freedom to impeach a party's own witness, courts usually hold, is meant to allow parties to use witnesses of unreliable truthfulness who have information on many topics; they can use those witnesses as sources for their information but can also try to control how the jury deals with the information. Where it is clear to the prosecution that the totality of a witness's testimony will be false, most courts prefer to rule in a way that leads the prosecution to keep the witness off the stand.

12. This problem requires an analysis of impeachment by contradiction, collateral matters, and impeachment by evidence related to the witness's ability to have perceived the things about which the witness has testified. The witness has testified that there was a band playing loudly at the bar and that the dress she had been wearing had been bought two years earlier at K Mart. Testimony by other witnesses that there was no band and that K Mart had sold those dresses four years earlier would contradict the complainant witness's testimony. A first step in analyzing the admissibility of the testimony is to apply the rule that prohibits extrinsic evidence of contradictory material if it is collateral. Would evidence about a band or about the date of a dress purchase be admissible in this trial, even if the complainant witness had not brought up those topics? Answering that question determines whether the inquiries are "collateral." In this case, presence of a band and age of a dress are not relevant to prosecution for the crime of rape so they would properly be classified as collateral matters. This analysis provides a complete treatment of the offered testimony about the age of the dress. There is another aspect to the testimony about the presence or absence of a band, however. If a witness's mistakes of fact involve collateral matters, extrinsic evidence about them is not admissible unless a theory of relevance other than impeachment by contradiction is available. The witness's possible mistake about whether a band was playing might be relevant to show that her ability to perceive events that night was weak or impaired in some way. That would be a theory different from showing contradiction to imply bad memory or intentional lying. Proof of error about the band could also support a finding that the witness was unable to comprehend reality well at the time. For this reason, it would probably be admissible through the extrinsic evidence of the witness who would testify that no band was playing.

13. a. Yes. Under FRE 404(a)(1), a criminal defendant is permitted to introduce character evidence of a trait that is relevant to the charged offense.

That rule would authorize her use of a witness to testify that she has a reputation for being respectful of people's property since that attitude towards property would be a trait "pertinent" to the charged offense.

b. No. Evidence showing that she is likely to tell the truth would be relevant to her credibility in her role as a witness. Since Vane has not taken the stand, her credibility is not in issue, and a witness's testimony that Vane has a reputation for truthfulness would not be admissible. Her truthfulness is not pertinent to a crime of violence.

c. No. A witness to bolster the credibility of another witness may not testify unless that other witness's credibility has been attacked.

d. Yes. Once Vane has been impeached, as in this case by evidence of her past criminal conviction of a crime related to truth-telling, rehabilitating testimony in the form of reputation or opinion may be introduced to show that she has a character consistent with giving truthful testimony.

14.   The prosecution's effort must be analyzed under the terms of Rule 609. The past crime is not one involving truth-telling. This means that its admissibility involves a balancing test. Under the rule, where the person sought to be impeached is a criminal defendant, evidence of the past conviction is only allowable if it will be more probative than prejudicial. If the conviction or date of release from confinement related to the conviction was ten years ago or more, then evidence about it can be introduced only if it is substantially more probative than prejudicial. Would a judge find that evidence of car theft is more probative than prejudicial on the issue of truth-telling as a witness in court? The fact that the conviction's timing approaches the ten-year period that triggers the "substantially more probative" requirement would also be an element in the judge's thinking. Because the past offense is identical to the charged offense, the risk of prejudice is extremely high; a juror might well use the information about the prior conviction not to test the credibility of the defendant's particular testimony but rather to decide that since he's committed car theft before, he likely did it on the occasion involved in the current trial, too. Rule 609 clearly adopts the position that past felonies are related to current truth-telling, so it must be acknowledged that the car theft conviction has relevance to truth-telling at trial. However, the risk of prejudice is quite high and the conviction was a relatively long time prior to the current trial. These reasons suggest that the stronger argument favors rejecting the evidence.

15.   Except for past convictions of crimes involving truth-telling, all treatment of a witness's past convictions in connection with the witness's credibility involves balancing tests relating the probative value and the risks of prejudice. If the witness's testimony is crucial, then discrediting it becomes highly important. Thus, the probative value of impeachment material increases. Similarly, if a challenged item of evidence is the only type of evidence its proponent has that speaks to a particular issue at trial, the probative value of that item is thought to be high. In this version of the car theft example,

the probative value of impeaching the witness with evidence of his past car theft conviction would be quite high, and the evidence might properly be admitted. The trial judge can require that some of the details of the past crime be "sanitized" so that a limited description of the conviction is all that the jury hears.

16.   a. Yes. Past bad acts, if they are relevant to a witness's truthfulness, can be inquired into on cross-examination. Stealing merchandise while in a position of trust such as security guard seems relevant to character for truthfulness, so questions about it would be proper.

   b. No. Extrinsic evidence of past bad acts is not permitted if their relevance is only to support an implication about the witness's character for truthfulness.

17.   a. Yes. A witness who supports the credibility of another witness can be asked about knowledge of past conduct by the first witness if there is good faith basis for believing that the past conduct did occur and if that past conduct would contradict or modify the witness's description of the first witness's reputation for honesty.

   b. If Second's testimony was clearly limited to recent reputation, then the question would be improper. Events 20 years prior to the trial cannot be logically related to Second's reports of First's current reputation. If Second's testimony was not clearly limited to a recent time period, then the question about the old conviction would be allowable. Note that extrinsic evidence of this conviction would probably not be permitted since it is much more than ten years old and may not be substantially more probative than prejudicial. However, there is no time limit in the rules concerning inquiries about past bad conduct.

18.   Most courts would allow the question in both situations. It can be argued, though, that if the character witness used reputation as the basis for testimony, a question about the stealing from a church collection box might not be proper. The most legitimate probings on cross-examination of a witness who reports someone's reputation are questions that confront the witness with contrary descriptions of the primary witness's reputation. Referring to particular conduct by the primary witness might not be allowed unless there was a good faith basis for the questioner to believe that knowledge of the conduct had become part of the person's reputation in the community. If, on the other hand, the character witness has used his or her own opinion about the primary witness as a basis for stating a belief about the primary witness's likely truth-telling, then questions about specific conduct of the primary witness would be proper. They show either that the witness does not really have a thorough basis for forming an opinion, or that the witness knows about the past conduct but has not reacted to it in a way that diminished his estimation of the likely truth-telling of the primary witness.

19.   The prosecution may ask the witness about his prior contradictory statement, under the rules for prior inconsistent statements. If the prosecu-

tion wants to introduce the document, it must give the witness an opportunity to explain it at some time during the trial.

20.   The judge should dismiss the case. The prior statement is admissible only as impeachment evidence; this means it is not an allowable basis for a substantive conclusion but can only be used to discredit the witness's statements. If the second witness's testimony is completely wiped out — the strongest allowable benefit to the prosecution from the impeachment evidence — the case for the prosecution would be too weak to support a conviction since it would consist only of a self-criticized eyewitness identification.

21.   The theory for admissibility would be that it is a prior inconsistent statement. Its explicit content supports part of Anders' testimony. On the other hand, its silence on the subject of the apartment's odor might be deemed equivalent to a statement that size, not odor, was the problem with the apartment. Proof that a person said nothing about a topic on an occasion when a comment would naturally have been expected can be treated identically to proof of a statement. In this case, the lack of a mention of a bad smell in the letter is contradictory to Anders' statement in court that the apartment had a bad smell. It could be inquired about in cross-examination, and the letter could be admitted without any hearsay problem because it is a statement by a party offered against that party.

6

Expert Testimony

Introduction

When resolving a disputed issue involves information or analysis beyond the knowledge or capabilities of a typical juror, parties are allowed to present testimony by expert witnesses. Unlike eyewitnesses or participants in events that are the subject of litigation, expert witnesses give testimony based on their own general experience and knowledge and are allowed to apply their expertise to the facts of the case.

The important issues connected with expert testimony involve determining: 1) what *topics* are appropriate for this type of testimony; 2) *who* should be permitted to testify as an expert; 3) what types of *data* an expert may rely on to form an opinion; and 4) whether the *style* or form of the testimony should be restricted. As this chapter will discuss in detail, the Rules cover all these issues. They provide that a subject is appropriate for expert testimony if an expert's opinion would assist the trier of fact, that a person can qualify as an expert witness by a showing of knowledge or experience, and that an expert's opinion can be based on any data that experts in the field ordinarily use. An expert may state an opinion or conclusion based on the facts the expert believes to be true or may answer a hypothetical question that asks the expert to make assumptions. In criminal cases, an expert's freedom to state conclusions is narrowed: An expert may not testify specifically that a defendant did or did not have a mental state that is an element of a crime.

Topics for Expert Testimony

Using an expert witness involves costs and risks. For example, the testimony will take time, and jurors may give great deference to the observations of someone with significant professional qualifications. For these reasons, parties are permitted to introduce expert testimony only when the trial court is persuaded that jurors (or the court personally in a non-jury trial) will benefit from help on the topic for which the expert testimony is proposed. Rule 702 states:

> If scientific, technical, or other specialized knowledge will assist the trier of fact to understand the evidence or to determine a fact in issue, a witness qualified as an expert by knowledge, skill, experience, training, or education, may testify thereto in the form of an opinion or otherwise.

Sometimes the substantive law underlying a dispute makes it clear that expert testimony will be required, as in medical malpractice suits where a plaintiff must establish that the defendant's treatment fell below a professional standard of care. In other instances, reasonable assumptions about the common knowledge of jurors make it clear that without information from an expert jurors would be unable to reach conclusions. Experts' knowledge would be necessary to prove whether something found in a defendant's possession was an illegal drug, or to establish that a product's design was likely to facilitate misuse.

There are some topics on which there is a dispute about whether expert testimony should be admissible. Some social scientists have conducted research on the reliability of eyewitness observations. They believe that crime victims or witnesses to crimes are likely to overestimate their certainty when they think they have identified an individual as a person who committed the crime. Where the identification is of a person whose race is different from the race of the person who does the identifying, some social scientists believe that the rate of incorrect identification is high. Defense lawyers in cases where identification of an individual is crucial often seek to introduce testimony by experts familiar with this research. A court faced with this issue must decide whether jurors can evaluate the risks of incorrect identification by eyewitnesses on the basis of their own knowledge and experience, or whether information from experts would help them reach a better conclusion about the reliability of an identification. Trial courts have been affirmed for either admitting or rejecting offered testimony of this type.

Courts uniformly reject offers of expert testimony on the issue of whether a witness in a case has testified truthfully. Deciding the credibility of witnesses is usually described as the "province of the jury," and that province is typically protected from being "invaded." Nonetheless, there is a trend to admit expert testimony about various syndromes in ways that may be close to the traditionally forbidden expert commentary on truthfulness. For example, "rape trauma syndrome" is widely considered to be a subject on which expert testimony may be admitted. An expert may testify that the statements or behavior of the alleged victim of rape are consistent with those of other rape victims. A common position courts take on this type of testimony is to admit it to provide an explanation for delayed reporting of the rape, where delayed reporting is suggested by the defense to indicate that the claimed sexual intercourse did not occur. Courts have stated that jurors can benefit from scientific explanations of the significance or prevalence of delayed reports of sex crimes, and that without such expert information jurors might be less able to evaluate what they learn about the alleged victim's delay in reporting the crime. This type of expert testimony may come close to being a statement by the expert that the expert believes the complainant. However, if it were characterized that way, virtually all courts would exclude it.

Cases involving alleged assaults against children also involve syndrome testimony. Experts may testify that a child's statements are consistent with those of children who have been abused. This testimony would be kept out if the rationale for its admission was that it supports the credibility of the alleged victim's testimony. However, it often is admitted on the theory that it provides a scientific assessment of the likelihood that an assault took place, based in part on the victim's own words and their believability and in part on the comparison of those words with the patterns of past cases involving other children.

Qualification as an Expert

The Federal Rules are extremely broad in their definition of how a person may qualify as an expert witness. Rule 702 refers to education, experience, and other attributes that can justify treating a witness as an expert. At one extreme, in a case where a crucial issue was whether a particular sample of marijuana had been grown inside or outside of the United States, an "expert" was permitted to testify that it was foreign-grown, based on his frequent experience in smoking Colombian marijuana and in selling that and other types of marijuana.[1] More conventionally, witnesses qualify as expert witnesses on the basis of their education and legitimate work experience.

Just how specifically a person's experience and training must relate to the topic of testimony is an issue on which trial courts have great discretion. In products liability cases, for example, a manufacturer will often contend that the only truly appropriate witness to testify about safety aspects of its product is someone who has designed that particular type of product. A plaintiff in such a case will often seek to qualify a person with general experience in product design as an expert. Obviously, if courts held that an expert must be someone who has worked on the specific type of product that allegedly harmed the plaintiff, the supply of experts would be reduced. On the other hand, if courts are extremely permissive in allowing generalists to testify as experts, or in allowing witnesses with expertise in one field to generalize and apply it to other fields, the value of the expert testimony will be considerably weakened. Courts usually favor the admissibility of expert

---

1. *United States v. Johnson,* 575 F.2d 1347 (5th Cir. 1979).

testimony, particularly because the opponent of a party who uses that type of testimony is free to counter it with opinions from rival experts.

Type of Data

When a court has decided that a case does involve a topic on which expert testimony will be helpful, and that a particular person is a suitable witness for giving expert testimony, the witness must comply with requirements about the basis for the testimony. These requirements are set out in Rule 703:

> The facts or data in the particular case upon which an expert bases an opinion or inference may be those perceived by or made known to the expert at or before the hearing. If of a type reasonably relied upon by experts in the particular field in forming opinions or inferences upon the subject, the facts or data need not be admissible in evidence.

The expert is entitled to state an opinion based on facts he or she believes to be true because of what the expert has seen or heard at the current trial, or based on facts the expert believes to be true because of observations outside the trial. Rule 705 allows the court to require disclosure of the data relied on by the expert.

With regard to testimony that is based on information the expert obtains other than by observing the trial, the rule makes it clear that there is no requirement that this information be admissible in evidence so long as it is the type of data that experts in the field reasonably rely on in forming opinions. A medical expert, for example, could base testimony on X-rays that the expert had seen outside of court even if technical rules would preclude admission of the X-ray films as evidence, if the trial court had a basis for believing that experts typically consider that type of X-ray reliable. An assessor of real estate could testify about the value of a house even if the testimony was based in part on hearsay statements by people who lived in the neighborhood where the house is located, if relying on statements of that kind is reasonable conduct in the field of real estate appraising.

Testimony Based on Scientific Experiments

When an expert's testimony is based on data from scientific experiments or procedures, common law courts since the 1920s have applied a famous rule known as the *Frye*[2] test, requiring that the proponent of the evidence show that the experiments or procedures are generally accepted in their field. The Federal Rules do not incorporate that test, although its use under the rules

---

2. The test was originated in *Frye v. United States*, 293 F. 1013 (D.C. Cir. 1923).

was debated until the Supreme Court resolved the issue in 1993.[3] The Federal Rules approach involves scrutiny by the trial judge of the scientific reliability of the evidence. General acceptance in a field of science would be one factor in the judge's analysis, but it is not controlling under the Rules.

Understanding *Frye* is important because the decision's doctrine is accepted in some states, and it continues to be a permissible portion of the analysis required under the Rules. In the *Frye* analysis, the consensus of scientists in the expert's field controls the admissibility of the testimony. Testimony based on scientific theories or processes that are on the cutting edge of knowledge will be rejected. This imposes a lag on the availability of current technical knowledge in the trial process, but it protects the process against using material that will later be discredited. The *Frye* standard also assures that opponents of scientific testimony will have a relatively easy chance to obtain rival experts to interpret and critique any scientific testimony that is admitted.

Under the Rules, a court must determine the admissibility of scientific evidence by evaluating the underlying validity of two separate aspects of the evidence: 1) its scientific method; and 2) the application of that method to the factual inquiry under consideration. Experimental or scientific testimony must be based on a principle that supports what the testimony purports to show, and there must also be a showing of another type of validity, the production of consistent results from repeated applications of the principle. The Supreme Court has ruled that this type of scrutiny is inherent in the language of Rule 702 that requires a science expert's testimony to be based on scientific knowledge.

Judges are permitted to take into account whether the theory can be tested, whether it has been tested in the past, whether it has general acceptance as was required by the *Frye* test, whether the expert's evidence has been submitted to peer review in a scientific community, and whether its error rate is too high. These inquiries under Rule 702 have also been justified as part of a relevancy analysis to see whether the offered testimony is "sufficiently tied to the facts of the case that it will aid the jury in resolving a factual dispute."[4]

The tension between the *Frye* test and the Rule 702 standard is illustrated in treatment of scientific testimony about epidemiology in drug injury cases. Scientists seeking to produce reliable research results ordinarily consider correlations between drug use and injury to be meaningless unless they are statistically reliable at the 95 percent confidence level. That statistical test is a convention widely supported by scientists and other users of statistical analysis. However, some scientists believe that data showing correlations at

---

3. *Daubert v. Merrell Dow Pharmaceuticals, Inc.*, 113 S. Ct. 2786 (1993).
4. *United States v. Downing*, 753 F.2d 1224, 1242 (3d Cir. 1985).

lower confidence levels are still suggestive of underlying reality. A scientist who bases an opinion on data with a statistical reliability of less than the 95 percent confidence level cannot be said to be using a method that has general acceptance in most scientific research fields. Testimony by that scientist would be kept out under the *Frye* test. A trial judge could apply the varied approaches determined by the Supreme Court to be part of Rule 702 to admit the testimony and would probably be affirmed in that decision.

Opponents of the use of unconventional scientific testimony have favored the *Frye* test. Under the current understanding of Rule 702, they may be able to argue forcefully for exclusion of "fringe" scientific testimony. In addition, they can sometimes argue against admissibility on grounds additional to the contention that the expert's basis is inadequate. They may seek to exclude it by making arguments that involve all three aspects of expertise: the topic, the training of the expert and the materials on which the expert will rely. If an accused bank robber sought to introduce testimony by a psychic that a person with an appearance different than his committed the crime, courts would reject that testimony. They might say that the topic of this proposed witness's testimony is not one on which specialized knowledge (in the words of Rule 702) can assist the trier of fact in determining whether the defendant committed the crime; the basis for this would be a belief that psychics are frauds. The court might also say that the proposed psychic does not have expertise since there is no legitimate field in which people can obtain training or recognition as psychics. Finally, the court might say that the proposed expert's basis for having an opinion — psychic feelings — is not reliable enough. Under Rule 703, the basis for an opinion must be a type "reasonably relied upon by experts" in a field. The testimony would be rejected on three bases: Psychic evaluation of robbers' identities is not a field of knowledge that can help the jury decide who robbed the bank; the proposed witness is not a qualified psychic because there can be no such thing as a qualified psychic; and even if the witness were qualified as an expert, the basis of the witness's testimony would be improper because psychic phenomena cannot be relied upon "reasonably" by anyone.

Style of Testimony

Expert witnesses may state their opinions and conclusions in any way they choose, subject only to a limitation in criminal cases that prevents them from saying explicitly whether a defendant possessed a specific mental state that is an element of a charged crime. Rule 704 provides:

> (a) Except as provided in subdivision (b), testimony in the form of an opinion or inference otherwise admissible is not objectionable because it embraces an ultimate issue to be decided by the trier of fact.
> (b) No expert witness testifying with respect to the mental state or condition of a defendant in a criminal case may state an

opinion or inference as to whether the defendant did or did not have the mental state or condition constituting an element of the crime charged or of a defense thereto. Such ultimate issues are matters for the trier of fact alone.

The basis of the expert's opinion does not have to be stated when the expert gives it, but when the expert is cross-examined, he or she must reveal the underlying data if asked about it. In prior practice, experts were sometimes required to give testimony in the form of answers to hypothetical questions. The questioner would state a long series of hypothetical conditions and then ask the expert for an opinion about the consequences of those conditions. If it later turned out that supporting evidence was deficient for any element of the hypothetical question, the jury would be prohibited from relying on the expert's opinion.

Hypothetical questions were used to prevent the jury from believing that the facts treated by the expert as true were really true just because the expert believed them. However, appellate courts were sometimes required to order new trials because a careful analysis of a long hypothetical question and the whole trial record showed that some minor premise in the question had not been supported by evidence. Also, use of these long questions may have made it hard for the jury to understand fully what the expert really believed. The drafters of the Federal Rules chose to reject the requirement of hypothetical questions to avoid unnecessary appellate reversals, and because they believed jurors could themselves decide whether an expert's opinion was well enough related to established facts to be persuasive.

An expert is permitted to state an opinion on an ultimate issue in a case with the exception of issues of mental state in criminal cases. Some common law jurisdictions prohibit statements on ultimate issues, but it is difficult to define "ultimate issues." The Rules generally avoid the complications that a limitation can present. The criminal case exception in Rule 704(b) was added in 1984 following John Hinckley's acquittal on the charge of attempted assassination of the President. It apparently is an effort to reduce the potential impact of psychiatric testimony in criminal cases. An expert on mental health can testify about definitions of mental states, symptoms, and methodologies for making diagnoses and can describe "facts." However, the testimony is improper if it crosses a vague line to make a specific statement about the crucial mental state of the defendant that is at issue in the criminal prosecution.

EXAMPLES

1.   The seller of a house is sued for fraud on the claim that she intentionally failed to disclose that the house had suffered severe termite damage a few years before the sale. The seller is 75 years old. Should the trial judge allow the seller to introduce testimony from a psychologist to show that as people get older, their memories become weaker?

2.   A plaintiff seeks damages for personal injury from the owner of an

amusement park ride that stopped suddenly and threw him out of his seat. The plaintiff's theory is that a part of the ride's drive motor suddenly broke, causing the motor to stop. The plaintiff seeks to introduce testimony about the motor from a person who has worked as an elevator mechanic for 20 years, but never graduated from college or from any technical training program. How should the court analyze an objection to this testimony, made on the ground that the person is not qualified to testify as an expert?

3.   In a tort action, the plaintiff accuses the defendant of having punched him and kicked him in the parking lot of a bar. The defendant denies that any contact occurred. On cross-examination of the plaintiff, the defendant's lawyer establishes that the plaintiff told no one about being harmed until several weeks after the attack allegedly had taken place. The plaintiff seeks to have a psychologist who has studied war veterans testify that the plaintiff, a war veteran, suffers from posttraumatic shock syndrome. The psychologist would also testify that a consequence of posttraumatic stress is a reluctance to talk about violence and a fear that reporting violence will lead to additional harm. Should the testimony be admitted?

4.   A passenger in a private plane was injured when the plane crashed during an attempted landing, and later files suit against the manufacturer of the plane. To establish the cause of the crash, the passenger offers testimony by a former Federal Aviation Administration crash investigator who studied the crash using the methods he had used in his prior work for the government. The witness will testify that the pilot flew the plane properly and that the crash must have therefore been due to a mechanical malfunction. The witness will base that conclusion on interviews he conducted with airport personnel who saw the crash and on his general experience in aviation. Statements by the airline personnel who saw the crash would be hearsay if they were quoted at trial by a witness. Is it permissible for the expert to base conclusions on those same statements?

5.   Can a medical expert witness state an opinion that a defendant doctor's conduct fell below the standard of care typically exercised by practitioners in the defendant's specialty, or must the expert describe the typical standard of care, describe what the defendant did, and leave it to the jury to analyze those facts to reach a conclusion?

6.   Can a medical expert state an opinion that a criminal defendant who admits the conduct for which he or she is charged lacked the capacity to intend the conduct and its consequences and therefore did not have the intentionality required by the relevant statute as an element of the charged crime?

7.   A disputed issue at a trial is whether paint applied to the exterior of a building 20 years ago caused deterioration in the building's brick walls. All parties agree that the walls are deteriorated, but they dispute the cause of the problem. What issues are raised by efforts to introduce each of the following types of testimony?

a. A professor of materials science who has worked in the field of building materials and their durability for 20 years seeks to testify that the type of damage found in the building is caused by internal flaws in the bricks and not by coatings applied to bricks.

b. An artist who makes ceramic sculptures and has experience in painting them and applying other coatings to them seeks to testify that paint does not harm surfaces in the way that the building has been damaged.

c. An expert in public opinion polling who conducted a survey of people who work near the damaged building seeks to testify that the majority of them believe that the paint caused the damage.

d. A chemist who specializes in analyzing bricks and paint seeks to testify that she performed widely used standard tests on the bricks. The witness seeks to testify that the tests show that the paint had no effect on the bricks.

e. A physicist is an expert in the use of high energy particle accelerators to conduct biochemical medical research. He has examined a brick from the building in the accelerator and is prepared to testify that although no other physicist has ever conducted such an experiment, the response of the brick in the accelerator can reasonably be evaluated in comparison to the results of biochemistry experiments. The physicist will state that the results show that the brick itself was flawed regardless of any effect the paint may have had.

f. An anthropologist who has studied witchcraft seeks to testify that she brought a live chicken to the building site, spoke to it about the problem, and then saw the chicken turn away from the building repeatedly. In the cultures the anthropologist has studied, this type of conduct by the chicken indicates that the bricks, not the paint, were bad.

EXPLANATIONS

1.   Probably not. Jurors can understand themselves that people suffer from weakened memories as they age. The offer of an expert witness must involve a subject on which expertise will be helpful to the jurors. If the defendant in this case claimed that a disease had impaired her memory, that claim would be different from reliance on the general effects of aging. Jurors could properly be given help from an expert witness about a specific disease even though information about what happens to people when they get old would likely be thought of as too well-known to be a permissible subject of expert testimony.

2.   The witness's lack of technical training or a college degree is not dispositive since the Federal Rules recognize that a person can obtain expertise through "experience" and "skill" as well as by education. The court should focus on how closely the witness's knowledge relates to the type of issue on which he is being offered as a witness. For example, the court would need to know whether elevator motors are the same type, generally, as the motor

on the amusement ride. Also, the court would need to know whether control devices and electrical components are similar in rides and elevators. If there are substantial similarities, the court should qualify the witness as an expert. If a court held that a person must have experience on amusement park rides specifically to be allowed to testify about them, this would impose a severe limitation on the number of potential witnesses. There is no reason to impose that significant a bar so long as knowledge about elevators, in this example, is related to the type of malfunction alleged in the case.

3.   Yes. Jurors might ordinarily assume that someone who had been beaten up in a bar's parking lot would complain about it to friends or others immediately. If there is a reason for silence, such as the effects of armed forces experience, that a typical juror would now know about in the absence of information from an expert, testimony by the expert should be admitted. Note that the expert's testimony will contradict the implication that because the victim did not complain promptly, no attack was committed against the victim. This supports the victim's testimony but is different from an expert's statement that the victim is a truthful person in general.

4.   Yes. An expert is allowed to rely on information in his or her testimony whether or not that information would ordinarily be admissible in evidence. The information must, however, be a type of information usually relied on by people in the expert's field. In this case, if the expert could persuade the court that air crash investigators reasonably rely on statements from people who work at airports, the testimony would be admissible. Ordinary eyewitness statements are not permitted to be used as a basis for expert testimony, according to the legislative history of the rule, but airport personnel would probably be treated differently from casual observers.

5.   An expert may state a conclusion even if it is an "ultimate issue" in the case. This allows the expert to speak more naturally and to give a description of his or her opinion in a manner that might closely resemble a lecture or a discussion. If the expert were prohibited from stating a conclusion on whatever were defined as ultimate issues, the testimony might be interrupted more frequently by objections and would likely be artificially constrained in how its ideas were expressed.

6.   No. Unlike the medical expert referred to in Example 5, the expert witness in a criminal case is prohibited from stating conclusions about the defendant's mental state in connection with any required element of the charged crime. Recall that this limitation is explicit in Rule 704(b).

7.   a. Because of his or her experience, the professor is qualified to form and state an opinion about the source of the damage.

    b. Admissibility of testimony by the artist is a closer question than admissibility of the professor's testimony. The judge would need to consider evidence, perhaps from the artist personally or from other witnesses, about the similarities between bricks and the ceramics with which the artist is experienced. If the field of sculpture was related enough to the topic of brick degradation so that information from the first field could make conclusions about the second field more likely than they would have been without the information based on experience with sculptures, a relevancy test would be satisfied, and the artist's expert opinion would be admissible.

c. This evidence must be kept out. No matter how accurate the poll is, it still reflects only the opinions of nonexperts about the bricks and the paint. Ideas possessed by people in the neighborhood about the cause of the problem have no relevance to determining the cause of the problem. Therefore, even if the ideas are collected and organized with good social science techniques, they must be kept out of the trial.

d. All courts would admit this testimony. A person whose expertise is squarely consistent with the subject matter at trial seeks to testify on the basis of a generally accepted test. This satisfies the multidimensional test in Rule 702 as well as the *Frye* requirements and poses no other problems.

e. The physicist seeks to use a scientific technique that has been established in biochemistry in a field to which it has not previously been applied — brick and paint interactions. A court could likely admit the testimony under Rule 702. The case for admissibility would be strongest if the witness could show that the tests had been repeated a number of times and had produced consistent results.

The fact that only the proffered expert has done this work makes it highly difficult for the opponent of the testimony to obtain a consultant or a witness who can identify possible weak points in the physicist's testimony. Depending on how unique the physicist's testimony seems to be, the trial court might be motivated to exclude it. The theory behind this would be that it carries too strong a risk of misleading jurors if the trial court believes that the opposing side has no reasonable opportunity to evaluate or refute it.

f. The methodology employed by the anthropologist is too far outside the current culture of the United States, both in terms of popular culture and scientific culture, to be acceptable. It illustrates the difference between a "far-out" adaptation of recognized techniques, on the one hand, and techniques that are themselves "far-out" on the other.

Privileges

Introduction

Privileges give special treatment — a cloak of secrecy — to a variety of confidential communications such as those made in the relationships of lawyer and client, husband and wife, or priest and penitent. The Federal Rules include only a general rule on this subject. Rule 501 states:

> Except as otherwise required by the Constitution of the United States or provided by Act of Congress or in rules prescribed by the Supreme Court pursuant to statutory authority, the privilege of a witness, person, government, State, or political subdivision thereof shall be governed by the principles of the common law as they may be interpreted by the courts of the United States in the light of reason and experience. However, in civil actions and proceedings, with respect to an element of a claim or defense as to which State law supplies the rule of decision, the privilege of a witness, person, government, State, or political subdivision thereof shall be determined in accordance with State law.

As originally drafted, the Rules contained detailed privilege provisions. Congress rejected that approach in part because of controversy that had arisen over executive privilege in the context of the then recent Watergate crisis.

Information conveyed in a privileged communication cannot be brought into a trial and cannot be a subject for discovery even though the statement may be relevant to a disputed issue. In the lawyer-client context, for example, a client can refuse to answer a question like, "What did you tell your lawyer?" The client is also entitled to prevent the lawyer from revealing what the client said. Similarly, a letter written by the client to the lawyer will not be admissible.

Only the actual statements made in confidential relationships are kept secret by privileges. Suppose that a client had said to his lawyer, "I knocked down a telephone pole while I was driving my red car." The client could not be asked (at a trial), "What did you tell your lawyer about the telephone pole and your car?" However, the lawyer-client privilege would not block questions like, "Did you knock down a telephone pole?" or "What color is your car?" The privilege protects against revealing the *statements* that a person makes privately to his or her lawyer. It does not protect against revealing the *information* a client knows whether or not the client may have communicated that information in privileged conversations. The privilege prohibits questions that would call for answers like, "My client told me his car is red," or "I told my lawyer my car is red." The privilege permits a question that calls for the answer, "My car is red." If information can be developed in ways that do not involve reliance on a communication made in a confidential relationship, privilege doctrines have no effect. They keep secret the fact that the information was discussed, but they do not make the information itself a secret.

Like the special relevance rules for character or subsequent remedial measures, privileges represent a social choice that particular goals should overcome the general premise that relevant evidence is admissible. The most widely accepted rationale for evidentiary privileges is a utilitarian analysis, that the communications are socially desirable, and that people would be less likely to make them if they were not privileged. In the lawyer-client case, the utilitarian argument would be that the society as a whole benefits when the frequency of people's consultation with lawyers increases. Also, people who need advice about complicated transactions or other events might decline to seek it if they thought that the words they spoke to lawyers could be used against them sometime later at trials. Besides the utilitarian point of view, two other explanations are sometimes given. One is that privileges reflect a recognition that the state should not intrude in certain personal relationships. In contrast, another theory argues that rather than showing government's sensitivity to privacy, privileges show government's interest in corrupting the search for truth to benefit powerful social groups such as lawyers.

Although there are many different privileges, they all involve certain basic issues. Did the communication take place within the relationship required for the privilege? Was it confidential? Who is entitled to claim the privilege? Has the proponent of the privilege waived its benefit by acting in ways that destroyed the confidentiality it is meant to provide? Does the communication involve a topic for which the protection of the privilege is removed to serve other social interests? This chapter discusses the general issues in connection with the details of the lawyer-client privilege. The chapter then covers significant aspects of other privileges such as those for communications between husband and wife, doctor and patient, psychotherapist and patient, priest and penitent, and informer and the government.

Attorney-Client Privilege

When a client talks or writes to a lawyer, the client's communications are protected by the lawyer-client privilege, provided that certain conditions related to the basic utilitarian justifications for the privilege are met. There must be a genuine lawyer-client relationship, the client must have a reasonable expectation of privacy in the communication, the client must have preserved the confidentiality of the communication after making it, the topic of the communication must be connected with obtaining legal counsel, and the topic must not involve planning a crime.

Defining "Communication"

An initial question in some privilege claims is whether the client actually made a communication to the lawyer. Easy cases involve words spoken in person or by telephone or letters written to the lawyer. More complex are instances where a lawyer might be asked to describe whether a client seemed drunk or sober on a particular occasion or whether the client has a scar or other physical attribute. Courts faced with these problems have not reached uniform results, although the majority support requiring disclosure of aspects of the client's appearance that were visible to the lawyer and would have been visible to others who saw the client.

Testimony is sometimes sought from lawyers on the questions of the identity of their clients or of the source of payment for services on behalf of a particular client. Courts generally allow such inquiries on the theory that the identity of a client or the source of payment is not so closely related to the actual providing of legal services that requiring these disclosures would counter the overall goals of the lawyer client privilege. However, where there are public policy reasons for keeping a client's identity secret, or where information on the client's identity or the source of funds for representation would provide a "last link" in an evidentiary chain that could incriminate the individual named, many courts retreat from the usual identity exception and allow the privilege to shield the information.

When clients give documents to their lawyers, another problem of defining communications arises. A letter from a client to a lawyer would clearly be treated as a communication for the purpose of obtaining legal services. It could not, therefore, be discovered in pretrial procedures, and neither the client nor the lawyer could be required to answer questions about it. On the other hand, clients sometimes give their lawyers documents that were created outside of the lawyer-client relationship so that their lawyers can read them and use them in providing legal advice. When this happens, the fact that the client gave a document to his or her lawyer would be privileged.

Despite the lawyer-client privilege, if a document would have been discoverable in the client's possession, it would not be shielded from discovery because the client had given it to his or her lawyer. Since the document cannot be kept secret, it might be supposed that the privilege should not prevent questioning a lawyer about the document's contents — for example, if there is suspicion that the document was altered at some time after it had been returned to the client. A court has nonetheless applied the privilege in circumstances like these, reasoning that to require a lawyer to disclose the identity of records he or she had looked at could inhibit some clients from seeking legal counsel.[1] If responses to questions regarding the contents of a document a client had given a lawyer might lead to inferences concerning the issues the client had sought advice about, the overall policy basis for the lawyer-client privilege supports applying the privilege to allow the lawyer to refuse to answer the questions.

Existence of the Lawyer-Client Relationship

Doubt about the existence of a lawyer-client relationship arises in a number of recurring circumstances. Sometimes a person has a conversation with a lawyer to explore the possibility of hiring the lawyer. While it could be argued that the statements made in such a conversation do not meet the definitional requirement of having been made during the lawyer-client relationship, courts will ordinarily apply the privilege, bearing in mind that one purpose of the privilege is to facilitate individuals' search for legal advice. Another occasional problem involves communications by a would-be client with someone who seems to be, but is not in fact, a lawyer. As long as the "client" has a reasonable basis for believing that he or she is speaking with a lawyer, the policies supporting the privilege suggest that it should cover the client's communications. Finally, clients sometimes employ lawyers for work that does not involve legal representation or legal counseling. A lawyer might study investment opportunities for a client and evaluate them in terms of economics or might collect rent for a landlord. Communications by the "client" to the lawyer in connection with these types of non-legal work are outside the protection of the privilege.

There has been considerable controversy over identifying the "client" and shaping the lawyer-client privilege where a lawyer provides legal services to a corporation. Since a corporation is not a human being, some of the ideas that support the privilege cannot logically apply: It has no sense of propriety and indeed cannot even possess "personal" information. The profit motive might be strong enough to establish links between corporations and lawyers whether or not there was a guarantee of privacy for communications made in that relationship.

Although a number of factors cut against applying a privilege where a client is a corporation, all jurisdictions extend some form of privilege, with variations as to which corporate employees are covered. Some jurisdictions grant the privilege for communications made by those in the "control group." They define those individuals as the people who are able to direct the company's acquisition of legal advice and are able to take actions in response to

---

1. *United States v. Hankins*, 631 F.2d 360 (1980).

legal advice. In *Upjohn Company v. United States*,[2] the Supreme Court ruled against limiting the privilege this way. Thus, in cases in which federal law applies, and in cases governed by the law of states that have adopted the *Upjohn* position, communications between a corporate employee and the corporation's lawyer are privileged if their topic relates to the employee's work, if the purpose of the communication is to facilitate the providing of legal services to the corporation, and if the communications are confidential. Under *Upjohn* the privilege determination does not depend on the employee's ability to direct litigation.

Required Confidentiality

If a client acts without caring whether communications to the lawyer are private or not, the utilitarian justification for the privilege is weakened. This has two consequences. If the client takes inadequate precautions to insure privacy when he or she makes a communication, there will be no privilege. In earlier days, an eavesdropper to a conversation between a client and a lawyer would be permitted to testify about the conversation on the theory that a client who did not protect against eavesdropping had not done enough to insure the confidentiality of the communications. Modern courts will apply a reasonableness analysis to preserve the privilege in situations where it would be unrealistic to believe that a client could have avoided being overheard.

The presence of a *known* third party when a client communicates to a lawyer will sometimes destroy the confidentiality required for the privilege. For example, if a client's friend is present while the client talks to a lawyer, the client's communications to the lawyer will not be considered confidential enough to be covered by the privilege. On the other hand, if an interpreter, a secretary, or someone else necessary to the providing of legal advice is present along with the client and the lawyer, the privilege will still protect the client's words.

Also, if a client who makes a private communication later reveals it to others, the client will no longer be able to rely on the privilege to refuse to disclose the communication in other circumstances. For example, a company charged with bringing baseless lawsuits against a competitor might use an "advice of counsel" defense by showing that it decided to sue after consultation with counsel. To do this, the defendant would have to reveal some of its communications with its lawyer. The competitor would then be entitled to ask questions about the whole range of communications between the defendant company and its lawyer on the theory that the company's own disclosure of some of its communications had breached the confidentiality required for application of the privilege.

---

2. 449 U.S. 383 (1981).

Defining confidentiality in the context of corporate clients can involve complications. If a corporate employee sends a memo to the corporation's lawyer, no special problem arises. However, if a corporate employee sends a memo to another corporate employee and also sends a copy of it to the lawyer, the fact that another person besides the memo writer and the lawyer has seen the memo might be thought to eliminate the type of confidentiality required for the lawyer-client privilege. Lawyer-client privilege is not defined so broadly that corporate employees can shield all their memos from discovery just by including their lawyers among the people to whom they circulate their memos. There would be no privilege if it were apparent that sending the memo to the lawyer was not reasonably related to obtaining legal advice or keeping the lawyer well enough informed so that the lawyer could give legal advice.

One response to this situation is to look at the dominant purpose of the memo and to examine the exact breadth of its distribution. If the primary purpose of the memo was to facilitate legal work, and if the people other than the writer and the lawyer who receive copies of the memo need to have its information to carry out their ordinary work for the corporation, privilege will probably apply. However, if the "extra" people who receive copies of the memorandum do not have a strong need for it, or if its functions could have been satisfied with some other kind of document, then their having received the memo will probably destroy the possibility of protecting it with the privilege.

Besides letting other people know that he or she had communicated certain information *to a lawyer*, a client might just disclose the *information* to others. This would indicate that secrecy about the information was not vital to the client. Yet the fact that the client had communicated with a lawyer about the information might still be something the client wished to conceal. Courts have not clearly resolved whether telling additional people about facts already communicated to a lawyer should waive the lawyer-client privilege and legitimize questions to the lawyer about the information. However, since courts are often antagonistic to the information-concealing consequences of privileges, it is sometimes said that any disclosure of the substance of a lawyer-client communication waives the privilege.

Purpose of the Communication

To be covered by the privilege, the client's communication with the lawyer must be for the purpose of obtaining legal advice about past lawful or unlawful conduct or about future conduct that the client wants to carry out lawfully. When a person seeks legal advice about any past events, no matter what their lawfulness, evidence law places the privilege shield over the communications in line with the social policy of facilitating access to legal representation. Since the conduct has already taken place, denying the privilege to discussions about it could not keep it from happening. There is a doctrinal shift, however, for communications made for the purpose of planning future events. If the client intends to obey the law, the consultation is privileged. If the client intends to break the law, then the privilege does not apply because there is no social benefit to facilitating the planning of illegal acts. Also, denying the privilege might have the socially desirable result of hampering the intended misconduct. This distinction between the treatment of planning consultations for the purpose of obeying the law and consultations for the purpose of breaking the law is theoretically sound but difficult to apply in practice. In some cases it depends on information about the subjective intent of the client. A judge may hold an *in camera* hearing (a hearing kept secret from the jury and the public) to determine whether future illegal acts were the subject of a client's conversation with his or her lawyer. As a practical matter, the fact that a client was in touch with a lawyer to plan a crime is not likely to be known to prosecutors or civil plaintiffs, so the issue of applying the privilege is not likely to arise.

Allowable Privilege Claimants

The privilege prevents disclosure of confidential communications in all parts of the trial process, including pretrial discovery. It can be claimed by the client, the client's lawyer (acting on behalf of the client), or by others who represent the client (such as a guardian or conservator). In the case of corporate clients, the claim must be made by the business's current lawyer, the lawyer with whom the privileged communication was made, or by other representatives of the business.

If the client is deceased, the privilege can be claimed by the decedent's executor or other personal representative. However, if there is a dispute in which rival parties each make a claim based on actions of a deceased client, then no privilege will be permitted, and the attorney will be required to reveal the substance of his or her communications with the client.

Issues Unique to Lawyer-Client Communications

For the lawyer-client privilege there are some particularized doctrines about loss of the privilege that reflect recurring aspects of legal practice. When there is a dispute between a lawyer and a client over the payment of fees or the quality of representation, for example, the lawyer-client privilege does not apply. Also, where two or more individuals have consulted a lawyer for advice on a matter that concerned all of the individuals, they will be characterized as joint clients. If the joint clients later sue each other, their communications to their lawyer will not be privileged if relevant to the dispute.

Work Product

A doctrine separate from attorney-client privilege also provides confidentiality to some material attorneys may possess in connection with their representation of clients. Announced by the Supreme Court in *Hickman v. Taylor*,[3] the work product doctrine protects from discovery any records of interviews and statements, for example, or tangible items collected in connection with serving a client to further the same principles that underly the attorney-client privilege (facilitation of the use of legal services). The doctrine is conditional in most cases: A party who seeks material from an opponent's lawyer can obtain it (if it is not subject to the attorney-client privilege) by demonstrating a strong need for the material. A lawyer might interview someone who saw an incident and might take a statement from that person or might write down a summary of the person's information. Those documents are not covered by the attorney-client privilege because they do not involve communications between the attorney and the client. The work product doctrine, however, does shield them unless the opponent makes a showing that it would be very difficult to obtain the information in any other way than from the lawyer. An example of strong need might be the death or disappearance of the person who talked with the lawyer about the incident. The portions of a lawyer's work product that reflect the lawyer's own thinking are given almost total protection under the doctrine, and courts order their production only when there is an extremely compelling showing of need.

EXAMPLES

1.   Defendant is accused of fraud in the sale of a business, and the plaintiff seeks damages. The plaintiff claims that at the time defendant sold the business, defendant knew that it was in very weak shape financially. At the trial, could the plaintiff's lawyer ask the defendant the following question: "At the time you and the plaintiff were negotiating for the sale of the business, did you consult Alan Able [a lawyer who specializes in bankruptcy] to find out how your business might use the bankruptcy laws?"

2.   In the case described in Example 1, could the plaintiff's lawyer ask the defendant this question: "At the time you and the plaintiff were negotiating, did you buy a book Fundamentals of Bankruptcy Law and charge its cost to your business?"

3.   Lawyer James Fielding wrote a letter to a regulatory agency urging it to investigate bribe-soliciting by some of its inspectors. The letter stated that one of Fielding's clients had been a victim of the inspectors' illegal conduct. The agency sought to compel testimony by Fielding on the issue of the identity of his client. Should the client's identity be privileged?

4.   A restaurant is sued by an alleged victim of food poisoning who claims that her illness was caused by some of the restaurant's food. The restaurant denies that the plaintiff's illness was related to its food. At trial, can the restaurant's lawyer be required to respond to any of these questions:

---

3. 329 U.S. 495 (1947).

a. Did the restaurant owner tell you that he fired a cook the day after the incident because he found that the cook did not follow proper sanitary practices in his work?

b. Did the restaurant owner write to you about this case and enclose a document reporting on a food safety inspection carried out at the restaurant by a private consulting firm *two weeks before* the plaintiff's alleged injury? If the owner did, what did the report say?

c. Did the restaurant owner write to you about this case and quote from a report of a food safety inspection that had been conducted at the restaurant two weeks before the plaintiff's alleged injury? If the owner did, what did his letter say the report said?

5. John Wilson, an accountant employed by a company that operates a group of movie theaters, was at one of his company's theaters one night to see a movie. While he was waiting to buy a ticket, he saw another customer slip and fall. He later sent the company's lawyer a memo describing what he had seen. If the person who fell sues the company, can the lawyer be required to give the plaintiff a copy of the accountant's memo?

6. While Harry Lang was talking with his lawyer in her office, painters were working there, preparing the walls before applying new paint. In a lawsuit filed by Lang against a business competitor, can the competitor seek to have Lang or Lang's lawyer state what Lang said to the lawyer during that consultation?

7. Rex Riley was on trial for selling drugs in a high school. When a witness testified that she had seen Riley selling the drugs in the gym, the client turned to his lawyer at the defendant's table in the courtroom and shouted, "It was in the cafeteria, not the gym." He sought a mistrial on the ground that his shouted statement was probably heard by the jury and that their use of its information would violate attorney-client privilege. Does Riley have a valid claim of privilege?

8. A car manufactured by ABC Automobile Company was involved in an accident. The company's lawyer asked its vice president for product safety to investigate the accident, and the vice president wrote a memo describing her conclusions. She addressed it to the company's lawyer and sent copies to the company's president and about 50 members of the company's engineering staff. Would lawyer-client privilege prevent someone who was injured in the accident from getting a copy of the memo from the vice president or the lawyer?

EXPLANATIONS

1. The question seeks to develop information that would be relevant to the disputed issues. If the defendant did try to get information on how the bankruptcy laws would have affected his business, it suggests that the business was in weak shape financially at that time. However, establishing relevance

does not guarantee the admissibility of evidence. In this problem, lawyer-client privilege would prohibit a response to the question. As long as the consultation with the lawyer was private, and a lawyer-client relationship did exist when it took place, the lawyer-client privilege provides secrecy for the communications for the purpose of encouraging people to obtain legal advice free from the fear that their statements or questions to their lawyers might someday be used against them.

2.   The defendant's purchase of a book, "Fundamentals of Bankruptcy Law," would be relevant because it tends to show that he was concerned about the financial strength of his business at the time he bought it. Even though the topic of the book relates to law, the lawyer-client privilege would not prevent the asking and answering of this question. The privilege does not cover everything a person does with respect to law, but covers only communications between a client and a lawyer. A book on bankruptcy is not, obviously, a lawyer.

3.   Traditionally, the identity of a client has not been protected by the lawyer-client privilege. However, if public policy reasons suggest that confidentiality would be valuable, some courts are now willing to extend the privilege to cover the issue of the client's name. On the facts of this problem, there are policy arguments both for and against revealing the client's name. If the agency learns the name of the client who complained about the inspectors' solicitation of bribes, it may be able to do a better investigation than if it only has an anonymous tip. On the other hand, if the client's name is revealed, there is a risk that it will become known to the allegedly corrupt inspectors. That could lead to retaliation by the inspectors. It would certainly be contrary to public policy to expose a "whistleblower" to the risk of harm at the hands of those whose conduct the whistleblower has exposed. Finally, even if this particular client was not harmed by the people he or she named, there is a risk that a practice of obtaining the names of those who give investigatory leads to law enforcement agencies could have a general effect of making people less likely to give those leads to agencies than they otherwise would be. In a famous case involving facts similar to those of the problem, the court struck this balance in favor of confidentiality.[4]

4.   a. The lawyer cannot be asked to state what the restaurant owner told him about firing a cook the day after the incident. This is an example of the kind of information a client would reasonably give a lawyer while trying to obtain legal advice about a past problem. It should be remembered that lawyer-client privilege does not apply if a lawyer is consulted for advice in nonlegal matters such as general business management. This kind of conversation, though, is clearly relevant to anticipated legal problems and could not reasonably be treated as merely a business consultation.

---

4. See *In re Kaplan*, 8 N.Y. 2d 214, 203 N.Y.S.2d 836, 168 N.E.2d 660 (1960).

b. The lawyer is being asked a two-part question about a document that had nothing to do with the current litigation when it was created since it was created two weeks before the food poisoning incident. The first part asks if the client gave the lawyer a document. The second part asks what the document said. Because giving a lawyer a document does not protect it from being disclosed in future litigation, the plaintiff in this example could have obtained a copy of the document in discovery. If the document had not been obtained before trial, a balance would have to be drawn between protecting the confidentiality of the lawyer-client consultation and protecting the right of litigants to have access to relevant documents possessed by their opponents.

If the lawyer had to state whether the client gave him or her a safety inspection report, this could reveal to the fact finder something regarding the nature of the topics about which the lawyer and client communicated. A careful judge would press the parties to resolve the question of the document and its contents before the trial. If the client no longer has a copy of the document, and the lawyer does have a copy of it, production from the lawyer would be compelled. If the client has lost it, and the lawyer has lost it, then testimony from either of them about its contents would be proper, and the question in the example, "what did it say," would be proper.

If sought to be introduced to show that the information about the restaurant was true, the documents would be hearsay; they might be admissible as government reports under Rule 803(8) or might be treated as non-hearsay adoptive admissions under Rule 801(d)(2).

c. This part of the Example is identical to Part b, except that in Part b the client enclosed an actual copy of the inspection report to the lawyer as part of a letter seeking legal advice, and in this part the client quotes the inspection report in a letter seeking legal advice. Should it make a difference that in one case the document was enclosed and in another case the document was quoted? The privacy of the lawyer-client communications would be easier to maintain if the actual inspection report was given to the plaintiff. The report could be divulged without revealing anything about the lawyer-client communication. Where the lawyer received the defendant's letter quoting the report, revealing the entire letter would totally conflict with the usual operation of the lawyer-client privilege. If the client's letter included a direct quotation of the report, and that quotation could be extracted from the letter without revealing the rest of the letter's contents, a strong argument could be made that the quotes from the safety inspection report should not be privileged. It would be logical to treat them as equivalent to the attached copy of the report discussed in Part b.

5.   Wilson, the accountant, has no responsibilities in the theater company concerning safety and maintenance to prevent patrons' injuries. He also is not employed in a function that requires him to direct litigation or obtain legal advice on matters such as the plaintiff's injury. For these reasons, no

attorney-client privilege would attach to the report he gave the company's lawyer. The company's lawyer would be required to produce a copy of the memo. For the purposes of privilege, Wilson is identical to a bystander who was not a company employee who might nonetheless have given a written report to the company's lawyer.

6.   The privilege for *confidential* lawyer-client communications will be lost if nonessential individuals are allowed to overhear the client's or the lawyer's words. The painter cannot be classified rationally as someone whose presence was required for the providing of legal services (as the presence of secretaries and interpreters sometimes may be). In contrast, statements by a client to a doctor during an examination arranged by the client's lawyer are usually covered by the lawyer-client privilege on the theory that the doctor is serving as a necessary intermediary between the client and lawyer.

7.   There can be no privilege on these facts because the client could not reasonably have considered his communication confidential. He said it in a room where other people were present and said it loudly enough so that they were able to hear it. (This problem was also used in connection with the former testimony hearsay exception in Chapter 2.)

8.   The vice president's memo was circulated widely within ABC Automobile Company. Since the lawyer-client privilege will only be applied in situations where there is a *confidential* communication between the lawyer and the client, having lots of people see the memo makes this problem harder than it would be if the vice president had written the memo just for the lawyer and had sent it only to the lawyer. In *Upjohn*, the company's employees made communications directly to the company's lawyer, and although he made a report to corporate officers about the information contained in those communications, he did not disclose their precise substance to others. The Supreme Court characterized the communications as having been kept confidential.

The Supreme Court's *Upjohn* decision was meant to expand the application of privilege to more cases than the "control group" test would permit. Therefore it is reasonable to assume that the lawyer-client privilege would not be lost if a company's lawyer shared memos from employees with the company's officers who are in a position to direct litigation or respond to legal advice. On the other hand, if the vice president had sent her memo to a newspaper as well as to the company's officers and engineers, no one would make a claim that it could be treated as a privileged communication. In this example, the hard issue is deciding whether there was adequate confidentiality to support lawyer-client privilege when the document in question was shared with 50 members of the engineering department. Since learning about the cause of a vehicle's bad performance would clearly be within the scope of the engineers' responsibilities, giving the memo to those people would probably not vitiate the privilege. This area of the law is unsettled. Certainly the argument for keeping the privilege intact would be stronger if the engineering department employees needed the information for a law-related purpose.

Notice the broad scope of privilege under *Upjohn*. In this problem, the accident study would probably be unobtainable by parties suing ABC Company. If the vice president had decided to do the study without having had a request from the lawyer and had addressed the study to the engineers, even sending a copy to the lawyer would probably not entitle the company to claim lawyer-client privilege and avoid disclosing the study.

Spousal Communications

One of the most revered and widely accepted privileges is the spousal communications privilege protecting communications between spouses. This privilege keeps information about statements made in confidence between spouses secret when a spouse or anyone else testifies. This is distinct from spousal disqualification, which prevents a spouse from being a witness (discussed in the section on competency of witnesses at p. 133). When a spouse is prohibited from being a witness, none of his or her knowledge is available to the trial in the form of testimony from the spouse. Other people who know the same things as the spouse are allowed to testify about them. When the spousal communications privilege is invoked, the occurrence or the contents of confidential communications between a husband and wife may not be the subject of testimony by the husband, wife, or anyone else. The following chart shows the main comparisons between the two concepts.

CHART SEVENTEEN
Spousal Communication Privilege and
Disqualification, Compared

Points of Comparison	Spousal Communication Privilege	Spousal Disqualification
Topics covered	Confidential communications	Everything spouse knows
Proceedings covered	All	Proceedings brought against other spouse
May someone other than the spouse testify about the covered topics?	No	Yes
Duration	Forever	During marriage

It is usually stated that our society respects the institution of marriage and helps make marriages happier and more enduring by providing a privilege to keep confidential marital communications out of trials. The empirical accuracy of this rationale might be questioned by asking whether those who know the most about the existence of the privilege — lawyers — have happier marriages than those others in society who meet, fall in love, marry, and live their lives without knowledge of how evidence law shields their private statements. Nevertheless, the privilege is deeply entrenched.

For the privilege to apply, the spouses must have been married when the communication was made. This is a question of state law. For example, there is great variation among states on the issue of common law marriage. People living together in identical arrangements might be treated as married in some states and as not married in others. That issue of family law would control application of the spousal communications privilege.

The privilege is ordinarily described as shielding marital communications. This can lead to problem cases where a husband, for example, learns something about his wife from her conduct at home, but where she did not have any intent to convey the information. If the privilege is strictly limited to communications and meant to foster communications between husbands and wives, then no protection should apply and the husband should be allowed to testify about what he learned. An illustration would be a wife hiding stolen property at home, her husband seeing it, and an effort by the wife to prevent the husband's testimony about the stolen property by stating that she kept it at home relying on the confidential relationship that inheres in marriage. Deciding whether to sustain the wife's objection would depend on whether a jurisdiction characterizes the privilege as meant to protect marriages through fostering communications or as meant to protect marriages through fostering a zone of privacy and freedom from fear of disclosures. The zone of privacy idea would protect far more information than would be covered by the communications theory. Since many courts are hostile to privileges and seek to curtail the circumstances in which they deprive the legal system of relevant information, there may be a trend towards limiting the definition of "communication" to verbal and non-verbal acts meant to convey information.

The topic of the communication must have some relationship to the spouses' marriage. Meeting this requirement in attempting to claim application of the privilege is ordinarily easy since virtually all things that husbands and wives may say or indicate to each other may have some significance for their marital relationship. However, there may be instances where spouses have a business relationship as well as a marital relationship, and their communications about how their business operates might be characterized as outside the range of coverage of the marital communications privilege.

Even after a marriage has ended by death of a spouse or by divorce, the privilege applies to prevent testimony about confidential communications between the spouses during the marriage. Clearly this approach cannot be justified as being intended to increase the future happiness of the married couple who communicated with each other. The common law belief that privacy is essential to the relationship between a husband and wife supports the idea of extending the privilege beyond the life of the marriage. Spouses might not feel the freedom and intimacy the privacy is supposed to encourage if they knew that after death or dissolution of the marriage their statements and communicative conduct could be revealed in court.

The marital communications privilege is subject to important exceptions. Spouses' communications are no longer shielded when they litigate against each other. The privilege is also removed in criminal proceedings that involve a charge of intrafamilial wrongdoing such as assault on a spouse or a child. It is straightforward to justify removal of the privilege for criminal cases because society's need to deter and punish criminal conduct in marriages exceeds the need to foster privacy in a relationship that is marked by violence.

Physician-Patient

Out of respect for the intimacy of the typical relationships between doctors and patients, common law treats statements made by patients to their doctors as privileged. On utilitarian grounds, however, this is hard to support since people who are sick have a strong motivation to speak to doctors regardless of whether evidence law will shield their words with a privilege. The fact that its practical underpinnings are weak may explain why the privilege, though widely recognized, has a great number of exceptions. The exceptions are so broad that some have argued that no physician-patient privilege should be recognized at all.

The most significant exception to application of the privilege is for cases where the holder of the privilege has put his or her own physical condition into dispute in litigation. Statements by a litigant-patient to a doctor are not protected from being revealed. Also, in most jurisdictions, the privilege does not apply in criminal cases.

Therapist-Patient

Related to the physician-patient privilege is the psychotherapist-patient privilege, recognized in all states and under the Federal Rules. This privilege has broader application than the physician-patient privilege because it covers statements made to therapists who are not physicians as well as to physician-therapists. The privilege has been adopted by judicial decision and by legislation because of beliefs that psychotherapy is valuable to individuals and society, and that it cannot be performed effectively unless a patient is assured that statements to the therapist will be confidential.

A small number of states limit the privilege to statements made to psychiatrists and psychologists. In most states, the privilege also covers communications to social workers. In *Jaffee v. Redmond*,[5] the United States Supreme Court adopted this privilege for federal courts, holding that it should extend to licensed social workers performing psychotherapy, and that it should be an absolute privilege applied without any balancing of the public's need for information against the social value of encouraging psychotherapy.

Priest-Penitent

All jurisdictions recognize a privilege for confessional statements to Catholic priests. Additionally, this privilege extends in many jurisdictions to statements made to ministers, rabbis, and practitioners of other religions to whom similar communications might be made. In the narrowest form, the privilege is limited to statements made: in confidence; due to the requirements of a religion; to a person authorized within the applicable religion to receive such statements. It is often extended to cover statements made to members of the clergy for purposes of counseling (even including draft counseling, in a case[6] that provided a notably broad application of the "priest-penitent" notion).

Governmental Executives and Informers

Privileges protect certain types of governmental communications thought to have high societal value. One privilege allows the government, in the criminal justice process, to keep secret the identity of informers in many circumstances. This "informer's privilege" is intended to encourage people to give information to police about criminal conduct without fear that they will be identified and thus put at risk of injury by the person about whom they give information. The possessor of the privilege is the government. The claim of privilege will be rejected if the criminal defendant makes a showing that revealing the contents of an informer's communications will not reveal the identity of the informer, or shows clearly that knowledge of the informer's identity is critical for his or her defense.

There are also privileges for "state secrets" and "executive communications." These privileges prevent disclosure of communications that could impair national security and of communications made by those in the executive branch of government as part of their decision-making process. This "executive privilege" is based on the idea that people in high office require frank advice from their governmental associates, and that their conversations would not be free and open if there was a risk that what they said could be disclosed in judicial proceedings. Where executive privilege is claimed, courts usually

---

5. — S. Ct. — (1996).
6. *In re Verplank,* 329 F. Supp. 433 (Cal. Ct. App. 1971).

require a statement from the head of the relevant agency that disclosure would be harmful, and courts often conduct an *in camera* examination of the material sought to be protected. If a claim is made involving military secrets or national security information, courts are likely to uphold the privilege even without examining the material if the surrounding circumstances make the claim plausible.

EXAMPLES

1.   The wife of a defendant accused of bank robbery is willing to testify for the prosecution. One evening, after the robbery and before the trial, she said to her husband at home, "You never make any money, and you waste all your time." Hearing that, her husband then silently opened a desk drawer so that she could see lots of large denomination bills wrapped in bands with the name of the bank that had been robbed. Can the defendant prevent his wife from testifying about what she saw?

2.   Someone accused of a crime discussed it with her spouse and then had a discussion with her lawyer in which she revealed that she had discussed it with her spouse. Should her multiple revelations destroy her claim of privilege with respect to either of the conversations? How would it affect your analysis if the spouse and lawyer were both present with the accused and had a group conversation?

3.   A theater owner sues a musician for fraud, alleging that at the time the musician agreed to appear in a series of performances at the theater, the musician knew he was very ill and was unlikely to fulfill the contract. The day the musician signed the contract, he had been examined by his doctor. Can the theater owner have the doctor testify concerning: a) what the musician said to the doctor about his physical condition; or b) what the doctor believed the musician's condition was, based on the doctor's physical examination of the musician?

4.   An actor sues a theater owner for negligence, claiming that he was scratched by a sharp piece of metal backstage and suffered a serious infection as a consequence of the injury. May the theater owner question the actor's doctor about: 1) things the actor said and things the doctor observed during a check-up prior to the alleged injury; or 2) the actor's statements and the doctor's observations during an examination conducted by the doctor after the alleged injury?

5.   A defendant in a tax evasion case is charged with making false statements in connection with claims of charitable deductions for contributions to a foundation she had established to benefit musical groups. The defendant claims that she had no intent to make false claims of charitable deductions. May the prosecution introduce testimony by the defendant's minister that the defendant had talked privately with the minister about setting up a char-

itable foundation to benefit the church, and that the defendant had said the foundation could receive money from the defendant and then secretly repay a portion of that money to the defendant to reduce the defendant's tax liability?

6.   Edward Elbert sues the United States claiming that he is owed back pay for work in foreign countries on behalf of the C.I.A. Can the plaintiff be barred from introducing evidence about the agency's methods of operation in foreign countries and about the identity of those individuals whom it employs?

7.   A police department obtained a copy of a prisoner's diary and address book. When she sought an injunction barring allegedly unconstitutional surveillance, the police department claimed that it had obtained the copy from an informant but that it had not asked the informant to make the copy and was therefore not responsible for any misconduct that might have been involved in the informant's actions. The prisoner sought the name of the informant. How should the court rule?

EXPLANATIONS

1.   The defendant-husband will base his claim on the marital communications privilege. He must show a valid marriage and a communication made in confidence during that marriage. Assuming that the marriage was legitimate and that no one else was present when he opened the drawer, the remaining issue is whether the conduct involved in showing the bank's money should be characterized as a communication. Since the husband acted as he did in response to a verbal statement by the wife, there is a strong argument that the conduct was the equivalent of a verbal reply to the wife's accusation. Seen that way, it ought to be considered a statement and ought, therefore, to be covered by the privilege.

2.   If a person voluntarily reveals details of a communication that is ordinarily privileged, the privilege is abolished. This Example poses the situation in which the possessor of the marital communications privilege disclosed her privileged marital communications in a conversation that is itself subject to the lawyer-client privilege. It would not make sense to have disclosure of one privileged communication in another privileged communication work to eliminate the privilege for the first communication. The overriding policy behind the privileges is to encourage the conversations so long as they are kept secret.

When the wife told her lawyer about what she had earlier told her husband in confidence, she did expand the number of people who knew the information. But the expansion included only one person, the lawyer, and posed no risk of further communication of the information because the lawyer was obligated to keep it confidential. Since sharing the information with the lawyer is so different from sharing it with a person who would be permitted to repeat it, mentioning the spousal communication in the attorney-client communication should not be treated as waiving the confidentiality ordinarily applied to marital communications.

The fact that part of the conversation with the attorney involved revealing something that had been said before would not in any way impair the client's ability to invoke attorney-client privilege to prevent testimony that she had actually told the attorney what she had said to her husband.

If the husband and lawyer were both present, the better view is that both privileges are intact. Communications by the wife to the "extra" people present (the husband in the context of the attorney-client privilege, and the attorney in the context of the marital communications privilege) are themselves privileged, so it makes sense to treat the simultaneous disclosure of information to the husband and lawyer equivalently to sequential individual disclosures to them.

3.   Communications from the musician to the doctor are covered by the physician-patient privilege. None of the many exceptions to the privilege are operative here, mainly because the musician is not the party who has raised an issue about his physical condition. Clearly, words spoken by the musician to the doctor are protected from disclosure by the privilege.

Things the doctor observed about the musician during the examination are also protected by the privilege. One of the ways people communicate with their doctors about their symptoms and physical condition is by allowing doctors to look at them and touch them. For this reason, "communication" is usually defined broadly for purposes of applying the physician-patient privilege.

4.   The defendant is entitled to both types of testimony: descriptions by the doctor of what the actor said and of what the doctor observed. The reason the physician-patient privilege does not apply is that the plaintiff-actor has put his own physical condition into issue by alleging that the defendant had caused him harm. Depriving the defendant of information about the plaintiff's physical condition before and after the alleged injury would place too heavy a burden on the defendant's ability to present a defense. If the plaintiff values privacy, he can preserve it by declining to sue for damages.

5.   The evidence would be relevant because it shows the defendant's knowledge of charitable contribution law and shows that the alleged improprieties in the musical foundation were probably not due to inadvertence. The conversation with the minister would not be privileged because it was not for the purpose of confession or religious counseling.

6.   Information about C.I.A. activities would clearly be protected by the state secrets privilege. If the plaintiff is unable to establish a prima facie case on his contract claim without disclosing details of how the agency operates, his claim must be dismissed.

7.   In applying the informant's privilege, a court must balance the need for secrecy against the need described by the party seeking the informant's identity. In this case, without knowing the identity of the informant, the prisoner will be unable to verify the police department's claim that the informant supplied the material acting on his own and that the police department had not asked him to make the copy. On these facts, the court should reject the claim of privilege.

8

Authentication and the Original Writing Rule

Introduction

This chapter covers two related topics: authentication and the original writing rule. Authentication is a requirement that the proponent of evidence provide a basis for the fact finder to believe that the evidence is what the proponent claims it is. The rule applies to documents, records, or other physical things described in testimony or offered into evidence. It also applies to references to human beings as having been seen by a witness or as having spoken to a witness.

The original writing rule, also known as the best evidence rule, applies to documents, photographs, and recordings. If their contents is the subject of testimony, the party offering the testimony must provide the original of the writing, document, or recording. This rule is applied far less strictly under the Federal Rules than it was at common law, so that the requirement of an original can usually be satisfied by introducing a copy or by providing an excuse for failure to have the original. Issues in these areas do not arise frequently at modern trials because pretrial discovery and the use of stipulations usually sort out the problems and avoid the dangers the rules are meant to avert.

Authentication

The requirement of authentication is ordinarily very easy to satisfy under the Federal Rules. Rule 901(a) sets out the general rule:

193

> The requirement of authentication or identification as a condition precedent to admissibility is satisfied by evidence sufficient to support a finding that the matter in question is what its proponent claims.

The proponent must introduce evidence adequate to support a jury finding (or a finding by the court if there is no jury) that the matter is what its proponent claims it is. The rule offers as examples a group of frequently used methods for authentication, but a party is not limited to the methods used in the examples. The authentication requirement is essentially a refinement of the requirement of relevancy because testimony about objects or conversations can be relevant only if it refers to objects or conversations that really did involve the people or things the witness claims were involved. Authentication is an example of conditional relevance, discussed in Chapter 1. Testimony that satisfies the authentication requirements is often called "foundation testimony."

Witness with Knowledge

The first example in Rule 901(b) makes it plain that parties are entitled to use a wide variety of methods to supply the information the authentication rule requires. It states:

> By way of illustration only, and not by way of limitation, the following are examples of authentication or identification conforming with the requirements of this rule: (1) Testimony of witness with knowledge. Testimony that a matter is what it is claimed to be.

This type of testimony could be as simple as a witness saying that he knows the person he talked to on a certain day was the defendant because he has known the defendant for many years and is always able to recognize him. It could be more complex "chain of custody" testimony in which various witnesses state that some object was the same object obtained from another person by stating how, at what time, and from whom each one obtained the item.

In criminal cases involving a claim that a substance possessed by the defendant was an illegal drug, a witness (usually a police officer) will testify about taking the substance from the defendant, sealing it in a container, and marking it. That witness will state what he or she did next with the substance. Then, another witness will describe having obtained the marked container from the first witness and will say what he or she did with it. In this way, a number of witnesses will provide a basis for a jury conclusion that testimony the last witness in the chain may give, such as a report of a chemical analysis of the substance, is really testimony about the actual substance that was taken from the defendant.

Handwriting

The rule provides examples concerning the identification of handwriting. If a party claims that a document was written by a particular person, the authentication rule requires that evidence be introduced adequate to support a finding that the document really was written by that individual. Laypersons who are familiar with someone's handwriting may testify that handwriting on a document offered into evidence is by that person. An example of this would be someone identifying her or her spouse's handwriting. An expert on handwriting analysis may testify that a document was written by a particular person if the expert can base that opinion on samples of the person's handwriting that are themselves authenticated. Those examples would have to have been authenticated in some way other than by the handwriting expert who uses them for comparison. Where authenticated examples of someone's handwriting are available, they can also be used by the trier of fact to decide whether a challenged writing was made by the person who wrote the authenticated examples.

Distinctive Characteristics

The uniqueness of an object or an object's appearance, along with the circumstances of how it was found, can provide adequate evidence to satisfy the authentication requirement. For example, under a doctrine known as the "reply doctrine," if a party introduces evidence that a communication was made to another party, that evidence is treated as adequate authentication of another communication that seems to have been a reply to the first communication.

Voices and Telephone Conversations

A witness may authenticate a voice by testifying about familiarity with it if the witness has a reasonable basis for recognizing and identifying the speaker. That type of familiarity may be obtained in circumstances that provided a connection between that voice and the identity of the person whose voice the witness testifies that it was. That method of authentication is allowed for voices heard in telephone calls or in other ways. For telephone calls, other methods of authentication are also outlined in the rule when there is testimony that a call was made to a number assigned by the telephone company to a person or a business. If a call was made to a business, it can be authenticated with testimony that the conversation was about business reasonably transacted by phone. For other phone calls, authentication is permitted by testimony that the person who answered the call was the person who was called. This testimony can describe the circumstances of the call, including self-identification by the person who was called.

Public Records

For documents required or authorized to be recorded or filed in a public office, or any other records or "data compilation" from a public office, one of the rule's examples states that authentication can be provided by evidence that the writing or data compilation came from the office where items of that type are kept. The proponent of the evidence may have to produce a witness who knows and can testify about the source of the exhibit. This is a kind of chain of custody method of establishing that a document is what it is claimed to be. The reference to data compilations extends the example to computerized records and various forms of computer output.

Ancient Documents

Another of the rule's examples relates to "ancient" documents, defined as documents or data compilations 20 years old or older at the time they are offered, that are found in a place where they would likely be if they were authentic and in a condition that does not create suspicion about their authenticity. Satisfying the criteria in the example is adequate compliance with the authentication rule. Recall that there is a hearsay exception covering the statements made in these documents.

Process or System

Where an item of evidence has been produced with a process or system, such as a computer system or a scientific device, testimony describing the process or system can serve to authenticate the evidence. For example, a computer-generated listing of information could be authenticated with testimony about the way in which data were assembled and the program used to organize and extract the data.

Self-Authentication

The fairly straightforward methods of authentication sometimes burden litigants. For a specific class of documents called self-authenticating, litigants may satisfy the authentication requirement simply by presenting the documents themselves. These documents are described in Rule 902 as exceptions to the ordinary requirement of "[e]xtrinsic evidence of authenticity as a condition precedent to admissibility." They include certain certified documents, where the certification takes the place of a witness who could state where the document had been found and establish that it is legitimate, and other items such as newspapers and "trade inscriptions" where the chance of forgery or mistake is remote.

Self-Authentication Categories. Self-authentication is controlled by Rule 902. That rule withdraws the requirement of extrinsic authenticating evidence for certain specific types of documents, defined in subparts of the rule. This differs from the structure of Rule 901, which sets up the general requirement of authentication and provides examples illustrating possible ways of satisfying it. The examples in Rule 901 are not exclusive, but are merely suggestive. The categories established in Rule 902 are limiting definitions of the types of documents that qualify for self-authentication. They are: a domestic public document bearing a seal of a governmental entity; a domestic public document not bearing a seal but containing a signature of an official and accompanied by a document under seal attesting to the official's signature; certain foreign public documents bearing certified signatures; certified copies of public records, official publications, newspapers and periodicals, trade inscriptions, acknowledged documents, and commercial paper and related documents. Also within the rule's definitions are documents or other items declared by federal statutes to be prima facie genuine or authentic.

The significance of self-authentication can be illustrated with respect to one of its categories: trade inscriptions. If a party wished to introduce a package allegedly marketed by a defendant for the purpose of establishing what types of directions for use the defendant had provided in the product's labeling, the package would be self-authenticating.[1] If self-authentication were not allowed, the proponent would be required to introduce testimony from a witness with knowledge about the way in which the label's words got on the package and about how the manufacturer and the package were linked. Self-authentication saves the proponent those steps on the theory that items in the specified classes are virtually never forgeries. Protection against phony exhibits is still available since the party against which a self-authenticating item is introduced is free to introduce evidence casting doubt on its legitimacy.

EXAMPLES

1.   The plaintiff in a products liability case was injured when a screwdriver slipped out of his hand and cut him. Claiming that the product's design was defective, he seeks to introduce a screwdriver as an exhibit, asserting it is the actual screwdriver that hurt him. If the plaintiff testifies that the screwdriver has been in his control since the accident and that the screwdriver offered in evidence is the actual one that was involved in his injury, would the plaintiff's testimony be adequate to satisfy the authentication requirement?

---

1. It is important to remember that evidence must satisfy more requirements than merely authentication to gain admission. For example, depending on the purpose for which this package was sought to be introduced, hearsay problems might arise. Also, the original writing rule could apply.

2.   In the same case as Example 1, the plaintiff seeks to introduce a screwdriver into evidence, testifying that:

a)   after the accident he threw the screwdriver down into a pile of hammers, screwdrivers, and other tools on his workbench;

b)   several weeks later, the plaintiff picked up the screwdriver sought to be introduced into evidence from that pile of tools;

c)   the plaintiff saw a number of screwdrivers in that pile and does not know if this screwdriver is the one that he was using at the time of his injury: and

d)   this screwdriver looks like it probably is the one that hurt him.

Is this testimony adequate to authenticate the screwdriver sought to be introduced into evidence?

3.   To authenticate a surveillance videotape showing that there was no activity at a certain door to a building during certain hours, the prosecution introduces testimony of a technician who states the location of the camera and the time at which the videotape was made. Would that be an adequate basis for a finding that the videotape was in fact made as the technician claimed?

4.   To support a claim that a neighbor made harassing phone calls, the plaintiff states that she received several calls from someone who identified herself as the neighbor late at night. If this was all the plaintiff stated, would there be adequate authentication of the calls?

5.   In a suit about adverse possession of real property, a party claims that a letter written 25 years ago granted permission for use of a portion of a driveway and that because permission had been granted, no adverse possession was possible. The letter was found in a real estate company's files in a folder marked "driveway permissions" in a group of similar letters. With respect only to authentication, what ruling should the judge make if the judge believes that the letter is not 20 years old or more but also believes that a jury could reasonably conclude that in fact the letter is 25 years old?

6.   Has the proponent provided adequate authentication that a can of a soft drink was manufactured by the "CBE Bottling Group" if the proponent introduces a can with that statement printed on it?

7.   A cigarette company seeks to establish that the health risks of smoking were commonly known in the 1950s. What would the company need to do to authenticate copies of *Life* magazine and the *Readers' Digest* published during that decade, containing articles about smoking and health?

EXPLANATIONS

1.   Yes. All that the authentication rules require is that the proponent of evidence supply an adequate basis for a finding that the evidence is what the proponent claims it to be. Here, the offered evidence is a screwdriver that

the proponent claims is the screwdriver that hurt him. His own testimony is an adequate basis for a finding that the screwdriver is the tool he claims it to be.

2.   No. In this version of the screwdriver Example, the proponent claims that the screwdriver he is seeking to introduce is the same one that was involved in his injury. The plaintiff's statements are too weak to support a finding that this screwdriver really is the particular one he was using when he was hurt. Therefore, the screwdriver would not be properly authenticated. It would be excluded from evidence. However, on another theory, the screwdriver could be admitted. If it were helpful to his case, the plaintiff could describe the screwdriver as very similar to the one with which he got hurt. It could then be admitted for the limited purpose of serving as an illustrative example for purposes of clarifying the plaintiff's testimony.

3.   Yes. The technician has knowledge that the tape was made in the way she stated. Additional evidence might be required to rule out possible tampering. It could be supplied by witnesses who testify as to the chain of custody so that opportunities for tampering could be explored, or it could be supplied by internal evidence from the videotape itself such as superimposed time and date markings.

4.   No. To authenticate these calls, the plaintiff could testify that she recognized the voice. If she did not recognize the voice, all she can say is that an unknown person claimed to be the neighbor. This example shows a distinction in Rule 901 between incoming and outgoing telephone calls: Outgoing calls can be authenticated by testimony that a witness called a certain number and that a person at that number to whom the number was assigned either identified herself or seemed through other circumstances to be that person. Incoming calls require more because the witness received the call and did not make it, and there is no way to know from what number the call was made. The witness can still testify about the calls but would be precluded from identifying the speaker as her neighbor.

5.   The judge should rule that the letter is adequately authenticated. The proponent need only introduce evidence adequate to support a finding that the item is what the proponent claims it to be. Here, the judge personally believes that the document is less than 20 years old, but that is not a valid reason for ruling that it has not been authenticated. Because the judge believes that the opposite finding would be supportable, and because the rule requires only that the proponent introduce evidence adequate to support such a finding, the correct ruling would be that the document was authenticated. Recall that authentication is only one aspect of admissibility. In the example, there might be issues of hearsay and the original writing rule as well.

6.   Yes. Printing on a commercially produced can would qualify as a self-authenticating "trade inscription" under Rule 902. Because it is self-

authenticating, extrinsic evidence that could provide additional authentication is not required.

7.   The company would need only to introduce the magazines themselves. Periodicals and newspapers are treated as self-authenticating. Note that relevancy, original writing rule, and hearsay issues might also need to be considered.

Original Writing Rule

The original writing rule applies only to documents, writings and recordings. Rule 1002 states its basic requirement:

> To prove the content of a writing, recording, or photograph, the original writing, recording, or photograph is required, except as otherwise provided in these rules or by Act of Congress.

If a party seeks to introduce testimony specifically about what such an item says, the party must produce the original of the item or satisfy the requirement with a method authorized by other rules related to this issue. Rule 1003 provides an easy way to avoid introducing the original:

> A duplicate is admissible to the same extent as an original unless (1) a genuine question is raised as to the authenticity of the original or (2) in the circumstances it would be unfair to admit the duplicate in lieu of the original.

If a duplicate is not available, a party can offer an excuse, instead, under Rule 1004:

> The original is not required, and other evidence of the contents of a writing, recording, or photograph is admissible if —
>
> (1) Originals lost or destroyed. All originals are lost or have been destroyed, unless the proponent lost or destroyed them in bad faith; or
> (2) Original not obtainable. No original can be obtained by any available judicial process or procedure; or
> (3) Original in possession of opponent. At a time when an original was under the control of the party against whom offered, that party was put on notice, by the pleadings or otherwise, that the contents would be a subject of proof at the hearing, and that party does not produce the original at the hearing; or
> (4) Collateral matters. The writing, recording, or photograph is not closely related to a controlling issue.

The rule derives from the "best evidence rule" that once, in abstract theory, prohibited testimony about the contents of any document unless the original of the document was itself introduced. The policy basis for the rule is that having a document physically present at trial will increase the chances of discovering any forgery or tampering. Also, details in documents are sometimes hard to remember so that it is unfair to allow testimony about a document without having the actual document available as a check on memory lapses. At present, pretrial discovery gives parties ample opportunity to judge the accuracy of copies. As ways of transacting business have changed, the concept of an "original" document has reflected actual business practices less and less.

The original writing rule does not necessarily affect testimony about every aspect of a past event or condition that was a subject of a writing, recording, or photograph. If the witness has a means of knowing about that past reality that does not depend on having obtained the knowledge from the writing, recording, or photograph, he or she is allowed to testify from personal knowledge, and the fact that a tangible record of the event or condition exists has no bearing on the testimony.

Illustratively, whether the plaintiff had given a dress to a tailor for alterations might be an issue at a trial. The original writing rule would not prevent the plaintiff from testifying that she did leave the dress with the tailor even if the tailor had given her a receipt that said she had left the dress. Her statement about leaving the dress would not be testimony about the contents of a writing (the receipt) even though the existence of the receipt is consistent with her testimony. If the plaintiff sought to testify that the receipt had specific words written on it, then her testimony would properly be characterized as within the scope of the original writing rule, and its requirement of an original, a copy, or an excuse would have to be met.

The rule's text and history make it clear that its main targets are documents and things like computer tapes that are equivalent to documents. In this sense, a document is a medium meant primarily for containing data and making it accessible. When an object has writing on it but is not really like a document, the rule's role is less clear. There might, for example, be a serial number on a huge piece of industrial equipment or a sign painted on the wall of a building. Dealing with "inscribed chattels" such as the machine or the building, courts will assess the benefit to be obtained from applying the rule (in terms of protection from fraud or mistake). They will also consider the inconvenience or impossibility of producing the "original." One solution is to require introduction of a photograph of the item. Another solution is to define the item as something other than a "writing, recording or photograph" covered by Rule 1002.

Definition of "Original"

According to Rule 1001, an original of a document or recording is the document or recording itself or any "counterpart" meant to be an original by the parties who created the first version of the document or recording. For example, if parties to a contract prepare two copies of the agreement and sign each copy, each of the signed contracts is an "original." The rule defines the original of a photograph as the negative and any print made from the negative. Any output from a computer that is readable by sight is defined as an original.

Definition and Use of "Duplicate" Writings and Recordings

Rule 1001 defines a duplicate as a "counterpart" produced at the same time as the original or produced through other processes such as photocopying. The word counterpart is apparently synonymous with "copy" for the purpose of this rule. The original writing rule is technically a rule requiring the production of originals where it applies. Under Rule 1003 duplicates are admissible to the same extent as originals unless there is a genuine question about the authenticity of the original or there are circumstances that would make the use of a duplicate unfair. If a reasonable claim of forgery were made, for example, a court would require production of the original document so that experts could evaluate it.

Excuses for Non-production of Original or Duplicate

The fairly weak requirements of the original writing rule are revoked entirely by Rule 1004 in a variety of circumstances so that a witness is allowed to testify about the contents of documents without the production of an original or a duplicate. These circumstances are: when the original has been lost or destroyed by someone other than the proponent of the testimony; when the original cannot be obtained through judicial procedures; when the opponent has control of the original and has failed to produce it despite notice that there would be testimony about it; and when the writing, recording, or photograph is "not closely related to a controlling issue."

Summaries

Sometimes materials covered by the original writing rule are so voluminous that it would be inconvenient to use them in court. Rule 1006 authorizes the use of summaries:

> The contents of voluminous writings, recordings, or photographs which cannot conveniently be examined in court may be presented in the form of a chart, summary, or calculation. The originals, or duplicates, shall be made available for examination or copying, or both, by other parties at reasonable time and place. The court may order that they be produced in court.

With respect to the risks that justify the original writing rule, Rule 1006 reflects those concerns by its provisions that the originals or duplicates must be made available for the opposing party, and that the court can order their product at trial.

EXAMPLES

1.   An undercover police officer secretly tape-recorded a conversation with Alice Andrews. Andrews is now on trial, charged with selling illegal drugs to the officer. The officer seeks to testify about what Andrews said to her during the alleged sale. Does the original writing rule require that the prosecution introduce the tape recording in order for the officer to testify about what Andrews said?

2.   After being arrested and given the *Miranda* warnings, Bruce Blair told a police officer that he had stolen a car. He then wrote down his confession and signed it. May a police officer testify: "Blair told me he stole it, and then we wrote out a confession that gave all the details," if the prosecution fails to introduce the written confession?

3.   To prove that Carl Classen was knowledgeable about Corvettes, a party seeks to introduce testimony by the publisher of a newsletter for Corvette owners that Classen had written to him describing an unusual problem with a particular Corvette and suggesting some ways to solve it. Would the proponent of testimony by the publisher need to satisfy the original writing rule? Are there issues of authentication and hearsay as well?

4.   For a witness to testify that an application for an insurance policy contained no statement by the applicant that she had been hospitalized for a particular disease, must the proponent satisfy the original writing rule?

5.   Can a witness testify that a defendant hit a victim on the head with a "Louisville Slugger" baseball bat without introducing the bat?

EXPLANATIONS

1.   The officer may testify without the prosecution being required to introduce the tape recording. The original writing rule would require introduction of the tape only if the officer's testimony stated that the tape contained certain words by Andrews. Since the officer knows herself what she and Andrews said, the officer is permitted to testify about those statements. The existence of the tape provides an additional means of proof, but its introduction is not required.

2.   Yes and no. The existence of the writing is independent of the information that the police officer learned in some way other than by reading the written confession, so the officer is entitled to testify what Blair "confessed" without the prosecution introducing the written confession. Proof of what Blair said is *not* proof of the contents of the written confession even if — coincidentally — the written document's contents are equivalent to what Blair said. On the other hand, the testimony that Blair wrote a confession with "all the details" should be characterized as testimony about the contents of a document; that part of the officer's testimony is inadmissible unless the prosecution complies with the original writing rule.

3.   Since the publisher's testimony is that a letter written by Classen contained certain statements, the only fair way to characterize the testimony is that its subject is the contents of the writing by Classen. For that reason, the original writing rule applies. The proponent would need to introduce the original of the letter, a duplicate, or would have to explain that one of the excuses for non-production applied. It might be, for example, that the letter had been lost or destroyed in good faith. Additionally, the Rule 901 authentication requirement would have to be met with regard to testimony about the letter or introduction of the letter or a copy of the letter. The proponent might have testimony that the signature was known to a witness, that the stationery was printed with Classen's name, that the letter was a reply to a communication from the publisher, or there might be an admission by Classen that he had written it.

With regard to hearsay, if Classen is a party and the letter was sought to be introduced or testified about by an opposing party, it would be a party admission under Rule 801(d)(1). If Classen is not a party, his statements about the Corvette could be treated as non-hearsay because they would be introduced not to show their primary meaning (that a particular problem with Corvettes could be solved in a certain way) but rather for their implication that Classen knew about Corvettes.

4.   This testimony could be analyzed as literally outside the scope of the original writing rule since it is about a lack of information in a document rather than about the "contents" of a document. The policy reasons for the original writing rule, however, would support applying it because introduction of the document would assist the trier of fact in knowing how accurately its contents were being described by the witness.

5.   Yes. The bat is not a writing, recording, or photograph. The policy justifications for the original writing rule are that mistakes and forgeries will be easier to discover if the actual writing or its equivalent is introduced. On these facts, the likelihood of forgery or confusion is miniscule. This would support a court's refusal to apply the original writing rule. Even if a court felt that the inscription on the bat did qualify the bat as a writing, the brand name is a collateral matter, so Rule 1004(4) would excuse compliance with the rule.

9

Presumptions

Introduction

Parties ordinarily introduce testimony or exhibits to support conclusions about the facts they seek to prove. Evidence law also offers two shortcut techniques for establishing facts. These are presumptions and judicial notice. With a presumption, a party is allowed to establish its position about a disputed fact by introducing evidence on some other fact. The party does not have to introduce evidence that is explicitly about the disputed issue. Judicial notice, discussed in Chapter 10, is another technique for quick and efficient proof of some types of facts. Where it applies, the court will treat certain facts as true without any requirement that they be supported by admissible evidence.

Presumptions

A presumption is a procedural device that relates two factual propositions, so that proof of the first fact (called the basic fact) is sometimes treated as equal to proof of the second fact (the presumed fact). Rule 301 defines the function of presumptions:

> In all civil actions and proceedings not otherwise provided for by Act of Congress or by these rules, a presumption imposes on the party against whom it is directed the burden of going forward with evidence to rebut or meet the presumption, but does not shift to such party the burden of proof in the sense of the risk of nonpersuasion, which remains throughout the trial upon the party on whom it was originally cast.

Additionally, Rule 302 states:

> In civil actions and proceedings, the effect of a presumption respect-
> ing a fact which is an element of a claim or defense as to which State
> law supplies the rule of decision is determined in accordance with
> State law.

Presumptions have developed for a variety of reasons. Many of them reflect common experience, such as a presumption that a person driving a car is
driving it with the authorization of the owner, or that a letter properly mailed
will be received by its addressee. Some presumptions are established by
statute to further social policies such as a presumption that a child born to a
married woman is the child of that woman and her husband.

Using the mailed letter presumption as an example, the basic fact is the
proper mailing of a letter, and the presumed fact is the addressee's having
received the letter. Under the Rules, a presumption shifts the "burden of
going forward with evidence to rebut or meet the presumption." Assume
that in the mailed letter example, a party wanted to establish that the addressee
of a letter had received it. That party could introduce evidence of the basic
fact — that he or she had mailed the letter. If the evidence of the basic fact
was adequate to support a finding that the basic fact was true, then unless
the addressee presented evidence about not having received the letter, the
judge would instruct the jury to find that the addressee had received the
letter.

The Federal Rules Choice

This represents a choice by the drafters with respect to a crucial and controversial issue about presumptions: how much benefit the proponent of a presumption should receive for introducing evidence that could support a
finding that the basic fact is true. The Rules incorporate a shift only in the
production burden and do not affect the persuasion burden. Understanding
the rule involves analyzing the differences between the burdens of production and persuasion.

Production and Persuasion Burdens Defined and Compared

The burdens of production and persuasion are procedural concepts. A party
who bears the burden of production on an issue loses if the party does not
produce some evidence on it. When a party bearing the production burden
does not produce some evidence on the issue, the party's opponent will be
entitled to a directed verdict. The burden of persuasion (sometimes called
the risk of non-persuasion) works differently. A party who bears the burden
of persuasion on an issue loses on that issue if the party does not persuade

the finder of fact that the proposition has been established by the preponderance of evidence or some other applicable standard. If the party bearing the persuasion burden fails to produce evidence that could support a jury verdict on the issue, the opponent will be entitled to a directed verdict. More importantly, the jury will be instructed that it feels that the evidence on an issue is evenly balanced, it must decide against the party who bore the burden of persuasion.

In many states and under Rule 301, presumptions affect only the production burden. This means that the proponent of a presumption is entitled to a directed verdict on the presumed fact if: 1) the proponent introduces evidence adequate to support a finding that the basic fact is true; and 2) the opponent fails to produce evidence showing that the presumed fact is not true. On the other hand, if the opponent of the presumption does introduce some evidence about the existence of the presumed fact, that evidence (whether or not believed by the jury) stops the presumption from having any effect in the case. The jury will decide about the existence of the fact the proponent of the presumption wanted to establish by thinking about it in the same way the jury considers any other disputed fact. The jury will weigh all the evidence in the case to see if the proponent has established the fact's existence by a preponderance of the evidence, or by whatever other standard of proof applies to the case.

A presumption affects the persuasion burden under some state procedures. In those situations, there are stronger benefits to the proponent of the presumption. First, the proponent must prove the basic fact or introduce evidence adequate to support a finding that the basic fact is true. Then, even if the opponent of the presumed fact introduces evidence about the presumed fact, the presumption continues to affect the case. The court will instruct the jury to find that the presumed fact is true unless the jury is persuaded by the opponent of the presumed fact that the presumed fact does not exist. This represents a shift in the burden of persuasion, taking it away from the party who would ordinarily have borne it and placing it instead on the party who opposed the operation of the presumption.

Using the mailed letter presumption as an example, if a plaintiff had the burden of persuasion on the issue of whether the addressee of a letter had actually received the letter, the plaintiff might seek to satisfy that burden without using a presumption at all. The plaintiff could introduce direct evidence of the proposition such as testimony of an eyewitness who saw the defendant read the letter. If the plaintiff did want to use the presumption, the plaintiff would have to introduce evidence that could support a finding of the basic fact, that the plaintiff mailed the letter. In a jurisdiction that follows Rule 301, the plaintiff would then be entitled to a directed verdict on that issue unless the defendant introduced some evidence related to nonreceipt of the letter. If the defendant did introduce some evidence contradicting the existence of the presumed fact, that the defendant had received the letter, then the presumption would no longer have any power in the case. The judge would instruct the jury to decide the letter issue in the plaintiff's favor only if the jury was persuaded under the applicable standard that the letter was received.

In a jurisdiction that allows presumptions to shift the persuasion burden, once the plaintiff introduces evidence establishing the basic fact or providing a basis on which a jury could decide that the basic fact exists, the plaintiff would then be entitled to a directed verdict on that issue unless the defendant introduced some evidence related to non-receipt of the letter. This is the same as in a Rule 301 jurisdiction. The difference between Rule 301's production burden shift and the other approach that shifts the persuasion burden shows up if the defendant introduces some evidence contradicting the existence of the presumed fact. In that circumstance, Rule 301 requires that the presumption be ignored as a matter of procedure. In contrast, in jurisdictions where the persuasion burden is shifted, the judge would instruct the jury to decide the letter issue in the plaintiff's favor unless the jury was persuaded under the applicable standard that the letter was not received. If the jury is in doubt, the party who originally has the production burden (usually the plaintiff) wins in a persuasion-shift jurisdiction, while the party who originally has the production burden loses in a Rule 301 jurisdiction since the burden of persuasion stays where it was originally located.

The two positions on the possible effects of presumptions are identified by the names of evidence scholars who advocated them. Thayer's position, also known as the bursting bubble theory, advocated shifting only the production burden. For Thayer (and the Rules), when the opponent of a presumption introduces evidence that contradicts the existence of the presumed fact, the bubble of the presumption bursts and the presumption disappears.

The point of view that would shift the persuasion burden is identified with the scholar Morgan. This view is more complex. Morgan emphasized that many presumptions reflect common experience about the likely link between the basic fact and the presumed fact. Because of this, Morgan argued that once a party introduced evidence adequate to support a finding that the basic fact was true, the burden of persuasion should be placed on the opponent of the presumption. This point of view was rejected in the Rules.

When a presumption related to a particular issue has no effect in a case as a matter of procedure, the party who sought its benefit may still win on that issue. Referring again to the mailed letter presumption, a jury that hears testimony that a plaintiff had mailed a letter and also hears testimony that the defendant did not receive the letter could well be entitled to decide that the defendant did, in fact, receive it. In reaching that conclusion, the jury members would be relying on their own experience of life, even though they might never know that a presumption about mailed letters (based on similar conclusions about typical consequences of events) is part of our legal system's doctrines.

The following chart illustrates the consequences under Rule 301 for various combinations of proof by proponents and opponents with regard to basic and presumed facts.

CHART EIGHTEEN
Consequences of Opponent's Responses When Proponent Introduces Evidence that Could Support a Finding that a Presumption's Basic Fact Exists
(Rule 301 and Morgan Theory Compared)

Opponent's Response	Rule 301	Morgan Theory
No evidence on basic or presumed fact	Proponent entitled to directed verdict on the presumed fact	Same as Rule 301
Evidence that could support a finding that the basic fact does not exist	Jury instructed to find the presumed fact if it finds the basic fact	Same as Rule 301
Evidence that contradicts the existence of the presumed fact	No jury instruction requiring a finding; possible instruction on allowable inference from the plaintiff's evidence	Jury instructed to find the presumed fact unless it is persuaded that the presumed fact does not exist.

Criminal Cases

Presumptions can cause constitutional problems in criminal cases if they are seen as foreclosing the jury's factfinding function too much. Instructions about permitted inferences pose no difficulty because they leave a jury free to disregard the possible conclusion suggested by the inference. If using a presumption, however, would require a jury to treat proof of a basic fact as equivalent to proof of a presumed fact, then the constitutional guarantee of a jury trial may be impaired.

EXAMPLES

1. A common presumption is that a death that appears to be from unnatural causes was the result of an accident rather than of suicide. This presumption may be important in claims against insurance companies where policies may exclude recovery for suicide and may provide double recovery for accidental death. Assume that a plaintiff's decedent died as a result of a fall from a high window. No one knows if he jumped intentionally or fell by accident. The

decedent's estate seeks double benefits under an insurance policy, and the defendant insurance company claims that no benefits are due because the insured committed suicide. Neither party introduces any evidence about the cause of death other than evidence that would support a finding of the facts stated in this Example. If the jurisdiction recognizes the accidental death presumption and treats presumptions as Rule 301 provides, how should the court rule if the plaintiff seeks a directed verdict on the insurance company's liability?

2.   Another common presumption is that a person who has been absent from home without explanation for at least seven years prior to the time of trial is dead. Assume that a plaintiff seeks life insurance proceeds claiming that the insured is dead and offers evidence that the insured left home one evening eight years ago, saying he would return, and has never been seen again. The defendant insurance company introduces evidence that the insured was hospitalized and treated successfully for an illness only four years prior to the trial. The jurisdiction recognizes the seven years unexplained absence presumption and treats presumptions as Rule 301 provides. If the plaintiff presents only the evidence set out in this Example, is the defendant entitled to a directed verdict?

3.   In a jurisdiction that follows Rule 301, there is a presumption that if goods are given to a bailee in good condition but are returned by the bailee to the owner in damaged condition, the damage was caused by the bailee's negligence. A plaintiff owned a valuable antique automobile in excellent condition. The defendant company agreed to store the car outdoors for two years. When the defendant returned the car after that time to the plaintiff, the car showed signs of body damage. The plaintiff seeks damages from the storage company on a negligence theory, with no evidence other than testimony about the condition of the car when he dropped it off and when he picked it up. If the defendant shows that an unprecedented hail storm had occurred, causing body damage to many cars on the defendant's property, what effect would the presumption have in the case? Would a Morgan jurisdiction treat the case differently?

EXPLANATIONS

1.   The plaintiff has introduced evidence adequate to support a finding of the basic fact, an unnatural death. This places the burden of producing evidence related to the nature of the death to the defendant under Rule 301. Since the defendant has failed to produce any evidence on the subject, the plaintiff is entitled to a directed verdict.

2.   The plaintiff has introduced evidence adequate to support a finding of the basic fact, absence from usual whereabouts without explanation for at least seven years. The defendant has introduced evidence contradicting the

existence of the basic fact. This means that there is a jury question as to the existence of the basic fact. The judge should charge the jury that if it believes that the plaintiff has established the basic fact, it must find that the insured is dead. This result is required because in a circumstance where the jury believes the basic fact has been established, Rule 301 states that the presumed fact will be taken as true unless the opponent of the presumption produces some evidence about the presumed fact. In this case, the defendant has failed to produce any evidence about whether the insured is dead or alive at the time of trial. The defendant's only evidence relates to the insured's being alive at an earlier date. That evidence might be adequate to prevent a finding of the basic fact, but it does not counter the fact sought to be presumed (that the insured is dead at the time of trial).

3.   Under Rule 301, this is a case in which the plaintiff has gained the benefit of the presumption by providing evidence on which it could be concluded that the basic facts were true. There was credible evidence that the car was bailed in good condition and was returned with damage. The effect of the presumption was to require the defendant to produce evidence related to the presumed fact. The defendant has done that, by showing that the harm to the car could have been caused non-negligently (by an unpredictable hail storm). Under Rule 301, the jury instructions would make no reference to the presumption, and it would have no effect on the outcome of the case. In a Morgan jurisdiction, the jury would be instructed to decide whether the plaintiff had established the basic facts. If the jury believed that the basic facts were established, it would be required to find negligence *unless* the defendant proved it had exercised reasonable care. This is in contrast to the standard approach in negligence cases, which requires the plaintiff to show that the defendant was unreasonable. Morgan's view would shift the persuasion burden in a case like this, while the Federal Rules treat it as one in which the "bubble" of the presumption has burst.

10

Judicial Notice

Introduction

The Federal Rules regulate judicial notice of "adjudicative" facts. Those are facts that are unique to the parties in the litigation in contrast to other facts, called "legislative" facts, that are related to background ideas about reality or law. These legislative facts are so unavoidably a part of the judicial process that they operate without any controls from the law of evidence. For this reason, the judicial notice provisions of the Rules apply only to adjudicative facts. The necessary definitions and procedures are set out in Rule 201:

> (a) Scope of rule. This rule governs only judicial notice of adjudicative facts.
>
> (b) Kinds of facts. A judicially noticed fact must be one not subject to reasonable dispute in that it is either (1) generally known within the territorial jurisdiction of the trial court or (2) capable of accurate and ready determination by resort to sources whose accuracy cannot reasonably be questioned.
>
> (c) When discretionary. A court may take judicial notice, whether requested or not.
>
> (d) When mandatory. A court shall take judicial notice if requested by a party and supplied with the necessary information.
>
> (e) Opportunity to be heard. A party is entitled upon timely request to an opportunity to be heard as to the propriety of taking judicial notice and the tenor of the matter noticed. In the absence of prior notification, the request may be made after judicial notice has been taken.
>
> (f) Time of taking notice. Judicial notice may be taken at any stage of the proceeding.
>
> (g) Instructing jury. In a civil action or proceeding, the court shall instruct the jury to accept as conclusive any fact judicially no-

ticed. In a criminal case, the court shall instruct the jury that it may, but is not required to, accept as conclusive any fact judicially noticed.

Adjudicative and Legislative Facts Distinguished

When a witness uses a word like "chair," no one requires that it be defined because we assume that everyone knows what the witness means. If a case involves bad driving and a witness wants to testify that the driver seemed extremely tired just before he started to drive, a judge will decide the relevancy of that testimony on the basis of the judge's own knowledge about driving and tiredness. Judges will not require a witness to define "chair" because they assume we all know what it is. They base that assumption not on evidence introduced by any party but on what they know of our society and culture. Similarly, when a judge uses his or her perceptions of how our civilization works to decide whether tiredness is relevant to poor driving, the judge is permitted to decide the relevancy question without any evidence being admitted on just how tiredness and driving may really be related.

Adjudicative facts are usually more specific than legislative facts. They include such matters as the identity of people or companies involved in a dispute, what they might have done, where they did it, when they did it, and why and how they have acted. Parties usually seek to establish this type of fact through witnesses and physical evidence. With judicial notice, however, a party can be excused from presenting any proof at all. The doctrine applies only to facts that are generally known in the trial court's jurisdiction or that can be determined easily from sources whose accuracy cannot reasonably be questioned. The location of a large hotel, the residential character of a neighborhood, typical fees charged by attorneys, typical costs of staying in a hotel and buying meals in local restaurants, and frequent occurrences of icy driving conditions in an area would all be types of facts that could be subject to judicial notice as well-known in the court's jurisdiction. The other basis for judicial notice, that a fact can be ascertained from a standard trustworthy source, supports judicial notice, for example, of times of sunrise and sunset found in an almanac, the incubation period for measles found in a medical text, and a person's past conviction of a crime found in court records.

Procedures for Judicial Notice

Any party may request the court to take judicial notice of a fact, and argument is permitted on that motion. A court may also take judicial notice on its own motion. It is significant that the party opposed to the use of judicial notice is entitled to argue that the process should not be used, because once judicial notice is taken of a fact, the jury will be instructed in a civil case that it must take that fact as true. In criminal cases, the instruction will be that the jury may treat the judicially noticed fact as true because a mandatory instruction might impinge on the constitutionally protected right to jury consideration. Since judicial notice may completely or partially foreclose the jury's decision on an issue, the ability to argue against it is important. Evidence that would be relevant in an effort to persuade a jury about the issue will be presented instead to the judge in the effort to keep the decision as one for the jury and to prevent it from being made personally by the judge.

EXAMPLES

1.   Masterful Detergent Corporation has sued a competitor, Kenmore Cleansers Corporation, claiming that its advertisements falsely represent that Kenmore's detergent is better for the environment than brands sold by Masterful. Assuming that an advertisement is actionable only if its claims involve a topic that is important to buyers, could Masterful successfully seek to have a court judicially notice the fact that concern about the environment is common among consumers of household products?

2.   In Example 1, if the defendant claimed that the main ingredient in the plaintiff's detergents is poisonous to fish, how should a court respond to a request that it take judicial notice of that fact?

3.   In a negligence suit, the plaintiff sought to establish that the defendant was on notice that some consumers had problems with its products because it had been the defendant in several suits alleging injuries from the products. Could the court take judicial notice of the judgments in those suits?

4.   In a suit involving alleged negligent driving, the plaintiff sought judicial notice of the fact that a street where an accident occurred is in a residential neighborhood. Since that fact was well-known in the jurisdiction, the court ruled that it would take judicial notice of it. If a defense witness stated in testimony that the neighborhood has a lot of stores and gas stations, is the defendant entitled to a jury instruction that leaves to the jury the question of whether the street is in a residential neighborhood?

EXPLANATIONS

1.   Judicial notice would be wrong for this claimed fact. A court would probably consider this fact to be "legislative" since it is a general fact about the society, rather than a specific fact about one of the party's products. The idea that people generally care about health or the environment is something that a court could assume itself in its own interpretation of legal standards. On the other hand, if the *degree* to which consumers care about the environment is at issue in the current trial, the court would not consider it suitable for judicial notice since it is not ascertainable from well-regarded reference books and it might be hard to describe it as generally known in the court's jurisdiction.

2.   If the poisonous nature of the chemical in the plaintiff's detergent is described in standard reference books, the court could properly take judicial notice of that fact.

3.   Because court records of judgments are likely to be highly reliable, the requested judicial notice should be taken. Note that the plaintiff's theory of relevancy does not require that hearsay issues be considered because whether the claims were true or not, they would support a showing of the defendant's awareness of consumers' dissatisfaction with the products.

4.   Once judicial notice has been taken, the fact noticed is properly made the subject of a conclusive jury instruction. In this case the jury would be told that as a factual matter, it must hold that the street is in a residential neighborhood. Despite the contrary statement made by one of the defendant's witnesses, if the court has decided to judicially notice a fact, the jury must treat that fact as conclusively established.

Appendix

Federal Rules of Evidence

This Appendix provides the full text of the Federal Rules of Evidence. Explanations are provided for most of the rules, clarifying their meaning and providing reminders of important issues in their application. The paragraphs bordered by vertical lines that begin with the word "Explanation" are *not* part of the text of the Rules.

Article I. General Provisions

Rule 101. Scope

These rules govern proceedings in the courts of the United States and before United States bankruptcy judges and United States magistrate judges, to the extent and with the exceptions stated in Rule 1101.

> **Explanation:** The Federal Rules of Evidence apply in the federal proceedings described in the rule. They also have been copied in a large majority of states, with some variation among states in specific provisions.

Rule 102. Purpose and Construction

These rules shall be construed to secure fairness in administration, elimination of unjustifiable expense and delay, and promotion of growth and development of the law of evidence to the end that the truth may be ascertained and proceedings justly determined.

> **Explanation:** In cases requiring interpretation of these Rules, the United States Supreme Court has generally adopted a "plain meaning" approach and applied a literal analysis.

Rule 103. Rulings on Evidence

(a) **Effect of erroneous ruling.** Error may not be predicated upon a ruling which admits or excludes evidence unless a substantial right of the party is affected, and

(1) Objection. In case the ruling is one admitting evidence, a timely objection or motion to strike appears of record, stating the specific ground of objection, if the specific ground was not apparent from the context; or

(2) Offer of proof. In case the ruling is one excluding evidence, the substance of the evidence was made known to the court by offer or was apparent from the context within which questions were asked.

> **Explanation:** To preserve an evidentiary issue for appeal, a party must object to the court's ruling. This protects the system against wasteful circumstances in which a party might tolerate an incorrect ruling in the hope of obtaining a favorable trial result, but then seek reversal on the evidentiary ground if the result was unfavorable. The offer of proof requirement is intended to assist trial courts in making evidentiary rulings, since it guarantees that the trial court will have a clear idea of the offered evidence.

(b) **Record of offer and ruling.** The court may add any other or further statement which shows the character of the evidence, the form in which it was offered, the objection made, and the ruling thereon. It may direct the making of an offer in question and answer form.

(c) **Hearing of jury.** In jury cases, proceedings shall be conducted, to the extent practicable, so as to prevent inadmissible evidence from being suggested to the jury by any means, such as making statements or offers of proof or asking questions in the hearing of the jury.

(d) **Plain error.** Nothing in this rule precludes taking notice of plain errors affecting substantial rights although they were not brought to the attention of the court.

Rule 104. Preliminary Questions

(a) **Questions of admissibility generally.** Preliminary questions concerning the qualification of a person to be a witness, the existence of a privilege, or the admissibility of evidence shall be determined by the court, subject to the provisions of subdivision (b). In making its determination it is not bound by the rules of evidence except those with respect to privileges.

> **Explanation:** The trial judge, not the jury, decides whether evidence is admissible. For almost every possible objection to admission, the judge rules. There is only one specific type of objection that is left for the jury to rule on, "conditional relevance," described in the next part of this rule. See pages 2-4.

(b) Relevancy conditioned on fact. When the relevancy of evidence depends upon the fulfillment of a condition of fact, the court shall admit it upon, or subject to, the introduction of evidence sufficient to support a finding of the fulfillment of the condition.

> **Explanation:** This is the one type of objection to admissibility that the jury decides itself (and is not, therefore, something ruled on by the judge). If the party seeking to introduce an item of evidence agrees that it is not relevant by itself but states that it will be relevant when some other fact is established that provides a context for it, the situation is defined as "relevancy conditioned on fact." In this situation, the evidence is required to be admitted. The jury will hear it. If the proponent then fails to produce information about the supporting context that is required to make the challenged evidence relevant, the jury can be depended on to notice that the challenged evidence has no relevancy to the case. The jury will thus disregard it easily, since there will be no temptation to use a non-relevant item of evidence in deliberations. See pages 8-9.

(c) Hearing of jury. Hearings on the admissibility of confessions shall in all cases be conducted out of the hearing of the jury. Hearings on other preliminary matters shall be so conducted when the interests of justice require, or when an accused is a witness and so requests.

(d) Testimony by accused. The accused does not, by testifying upon a preliminary matter, become subject to cross-examination as to other issues in the case.

(e) Weight and credibility. This rule does not limit the right of a party to introduce before the jury evidence relevant to weight or credibility.

> **Explanation:** When evidence is admitted because of a ruling by the judge that it is relevant or otherwise suitable for admission, that finding by the judge does not

prevent the opponent of the evidence from attempting to show that it is not relevant or that in some other way its admission was based on an incorrect finding. For example, a confession may be introduced after a finding by the judge that it was given voluntarily, but the opponent of that evidence is still entitled to introduce evidence and argue to the jury that the confession was coerced.

Rule 105. Limited Admissibility

When evidence which is admissible as to one party or for one purpose but not admissible as to another party or for another purpose is admitted, the court, upon request, shall restrict the evidence to its proper scope and instruct the jury accordingly.

Explanation: Sometimes there is a legitimate basis for bringing evidence into a trial even though the same evidence would have to be excluded if its proponent sought to have it admitted on another basis. In this situation, a rule could state that the evidence must stay out, but the drafters of the Federal Rules decided that it was better to bring the worthwhile information into the trial, and take the chance that a jury would be able to obey an instruction telling it that certain evidence could influence their deliberations only with respect to a certain party or with respect to a certain issue. See page 8.

Rule 106. Remainder of or Related Writings or Recorded Statements

When a writing or recorded statement or part thereof is introduced by a party, an adverse party may require the introduction at that time of any other part or any other writing or recorded statement which ought in fairness to be considered contemporaneously with it.

Explanation: When a writing or recording is introduced, any other parts of it or any related statements selected by the opposing party must be admitted if the judge thinks they provide a fair context for understanding the portions already admitted.

Article II. Judicial Notice

Rule 201. Judicial Notice of Adjudicative Facts

(a) **Scope of rule.** This rule governs only judicial notice of adjudicative facts.

> **Explanation:** "Adjudicative facts" are facts that are specific to a particular litigation, such as whether a certain street is in a business or residential district. A related term, "legislative facts" refers to more general facts about society and human nature that are not available for judicial notice, such as whether business districts usually have more pedestrian traffic than residential districts do. See pages 213-216.

(b) **Kinds of facts.** A judicially noticed fact must be one not subject to reasonable dispute in that it is either (1) generally known within the territorial jurisdiction of the trial court or (2) capable of accurate and ready determination by resort to sources whose accuracy cannot reasonably be questioned.

> **Explanation:** Examples of facts suitable for judicial notice are the time of sunset on a particular day, found in an almanac, or the location of a well-known building in a city. See pages 213-216.

(c) **When discretionary.** A court may take judicial notice, whether requested or not.

(d) **When mandatory.** A court shall take judicial notice if requested by a party and supplied with the necessary information.

(e) **Opportunity to be heard.** A party is entitled upon timely request to an opportunity to be heard as to the propriety of taking judicial notice and the tenor of the matter noticed. In the absence of prior notification, the request may be made after judicial notice has been taken.

> **Explanation:** A party seeking to have a court judicially notice a fact is entitled to present arguments in favor of judicial notice, and the opponent may counter those arguments. If a court announces it is taking judicial notice of a fact and there has been no argument in advance about it, an opposed party is entitled to present arguments to show that the fact is not appropriate for judicial notice. See pages 213-216.

(f) Time of taking notice. Judicial notice may be taken at any stage of the proceeding.

(g) Instructing jury. In a civil action or proceeding, the court shall instruct the jury to accept as conclusive any fact judicially noticed. In a criminal case, the court shall instruct the jury that it may, but is not required to, accept as conclusive any fact judicially noticed.

> **Explanation:** The special provision for criminal cases reflects the constitutional right to a jury trial and a belief that requiring the jury to accept as true a fact that the judge had accepted as true would be an unconstitutional invasion of that right. See pages 213-216.

Article III. Presumptions in Civil Actions and Proceedings

Rule 301. Presumptions in General in Civil Actions and Proceedings

In all civil actions and proceedings not otherwise provided for by Act of Congress or by these rules, a presumption imposes on the party against whom it is directed the burden of going forward with evidence to rebut or meet the presumption, but does not shift to such party the burden of proof in the sense of the risk of nonpersuasion, which remains throughout the trial upon the party on whom it was originally cast.

> **Explanation:** A presumption is a procedural device involving a relationship between a specific "basic" fact and a "presumed" fact. Under the federal rules, when a party introduces evidence that could support a finding that a basic fact is true, the consequences vary according to how the opponent responds. If the opponent introduces no evidence about the presumed fact, the jury will be instructed to treat the presumed fact as true if it believes that the basic fact is true. If the opponent introduces evidence about the presumed fact that is too weak to support a conclusion that the presumed fact is not true, the result will be the same as if the opponent had introduced no evidence about the presumed fact. If the opponent introduces evidence strong enough to support a finding that the presumed fact is not true, then the trier of fact will decide about the existence of the presumed fact in the same way it decides about the existence of any

other fact without regard to presumptions. See pages 205-209.

Rule 302. Applicability of State Law in Civil Actions and Proceedings

In civil actions and proceedings, the effect of a presumption respecting a fact which is an element of a claim or defense as to which State law supplies the rule of decision is determined in accordance with State law.

> **Explanation:** State law may grant the proponent of a presumption greater benefits than the standard treatment set out in Rule 301 for presumptions that are not a matter of state law; in those situations, state law controls. See pages 205-209.

Article IV. Relevancy and Its Limits

Rule 401. Definition of "Relevant Evidence"

"Relevant evidence" means evidence having any tendency to make the existence of any fact that is of consequence to the determination of the action more probable or less probable than it would be without the evidence.

> **Explanation:** This crucial definition of relevancy sets up a pro-admissibility standard: evidence is relevant if it has any effect on the likelihood that a disputed fact is true. Relevant evidence can make it more likely or less likely that a disputed fact is true, but no piece of evidence will make a fact more *and* less likely to be true. See pages 2-4.

Rule 402. Relevant Evidence Generally Admissible; Irrelevant Evidence Inadmissible

All relevant evidence is admissible, except as otherwise provided by the Constitution of the United States, by Act of Congress, by these rules, or by other rules prescribed by the Supreme Court pursuant to statutory authority. Evidence which is not relevant is not admissible.

> **Explanation:** In order to be admitted, evidence must satisfy Rule 401's definition of relevancy. However, some

evidence that would satisfy that definition is still excluded, for various reasons of policy. For example, privileges and the rules about character evidence exclude material that meets the definition of relevance.

Rule 403. Exclusion of Relevant Evidence on Grounds of Prejudice, Confusion, or Waste of Time

Although relevant, evidence may be excluded if its probative value is substantially outweighed by the danger of unfair prejudice, confusion of the issues, or misleading the jury, or by considerations of undue delay, waste of time, or needless presentation of cumulative evidence.

> **Explanation:** This balancing test allows trial courts to exclude relevant evidence where its admission would harm the judicial process through delay, confusion or unfair prejudice. All evidence is intended to be prejudicial to the party against which it is introduced (a party ordinarily avoids introducing evidence that is favorable to the opposing side). For prejudicial effect to be significant under this rule, the effect must be one of *unfair* prejudice. See pages 4-6.

Rule 404. Character Evidence Not Admissible to Prove Conduct; Exceptions; Other Crimes

(a) **Character evidence generally.** Evidence of a person's character or a trait of character is not admissible for the purpose of proving action in conformity therewith on a particular occasion, except:

> **Explanation:** Evidence may not be admitted, generally, if its only relevance is to support an inference that because a person has a certain type of character the person acted in a way typical of that character at a particular time. This is the rule against "propensity" evidence. See pages 30-31.

(1) Character of accused. Evidence of a pertinent trait of character offered by an accused, or by the prosecution to rebut the same;

> **Explanation:** Despite the general rule against the propensity inference, a criminal defendant may introduce evidence of "good" character related to the type of of-

fense for which the defendant is being tried. Once the defendant takes advantage of this opportunity, the prosecution is entitled to introduce opposing character evidence. See pages 45-47.

(2) Character of victim. Evidence of a pertinent trait of character of the victim of the crime offered by an accused, or by the prosecution to rebut the same, or evidence of a character trait of peacefulness of the victim offered by the prosecution in a homicide case to rebut evidence that the victim was the first aggressor;

> **Explanation:** To establish the defense of self-defense in criminal cases involving an attack by the defendant on another person, the defendant is entitled to introduce evidence that the victim had a violent character. In some situations, the prosecution may also use character evidence about a victim. See pages 47-48.

(3) Character of witness. Evidence of the character of a witness, as provided in Rules 607, 608, and 609.

> **Explanation:** Character evidence that would otherwise be prohibited due to the general bar against propensity evidence is admissible for impeachment purposes under Rules 607, 608 and 609. See pages 138-145.

(b) Other crimes, wrongs, or acts. Evidence of other crimes, wrongs, or acts is not admissible to prove the character of a person in order to show action in conformity therewith. It may, however, be admissible for other purposes, such as proof of motive, opportunity, intent, preparation, plan, knowledge, identity, or absence of mistake or accident, provided that upon request by the accused, the prosecution in a criminal case shall provide reasonable notice in advance of trial, or during trial if the court excuses pretrial notice on good cause shown, of the general nature of any such evidence it intends to introduce at trial.

> **Explanation:** The general bar against propensity evidence excludes evidence when the *only* rationale for admission is to support inferences about a person's character and the person's having acted in conformity with that character. This rule confirms that information about a person's past conduct that would naturally lead to inferences about the person's character may be introduced for different, and therefore allowable, purposes. It provides examples of typical allowable rationales such as proving that the person had special knowledge or a particular motive. See pages 33-36.

Rule 405. Methods of Proving Character

(a) **Reputation or opinion.** In all cases in which evidence of character or a trait of character of a person is admissible, proof may be made by testimony as to reputation or by testimony in the form of an opinion. On cross-examination, inquiry is allowable into relevant specific instances of conduct.

> **Explanation:** Character evidence requires a two-step analysis. The first step, treated in Rule 404, is determining *whether* any information related to character is allowed to be introduced. The second step, treated in this rule, is determining *how* that character information may be proved. In every situation where character information is admissible, it may be shown with opinion or reputation testimony. Information about specific past acts relevant to establishing a person's character may be asked about on cross-examination. See pages 39-41.

(b) **Specific instances of conduct.** In cases in which character or a trait of character of a person is an essential element of a charge, claim, or defense, proof may also be made of specific instances of that person's conduct.

> **Explanation:** Information about specific things a person has done can support conclusions about that person's character. Proof of this type of information about character is permitted only when character itself is an issue required to be resolved in a case, as it may be in defamation or negligent entrustment cases or cases where a criminal defendant seeks to establish entrapment. See page 40.

Rule 406. Habit; Routine Practice

Evidence of the habit of a person or of the routine practice of an organization, whether corroborated or not and regardless of the presence of eyewitnesses, is relevant to prove that the conduct of the person or organization on a particular occasion was in conformity with the habit or routine practice.

> **Explanation:** A habit or custom is a routine way of doing something that a person or organization accomplishes in a uniform way, free from individual thought or judgment about how to do it. Proof that a person has a habit is admissible, since it is different from proof that a person has

> a particular character trait. For example, always parking in a certain space in an office building's parking lot would be treated as a habit, while always driving carefully would be treated as a character trait. See pages 20-21.

Rule 407. Subsequent Remedial Measures

When, after an event, measures are taken which, if taken previously, would have made the event less likely to occur, evidence of the subsequent measures is not admissible to prove negligence or culpable conduct in connection with the event. This rule does not require the exclusion of evidence of subsequent measures when offered for another purpose, such as proving ownership, control, or feasibility of precautionary measures, if controverted, or impeachment.

> **Explanation:** Evidence that a defendant repaired something after an injury is not admissible to establish that the defendant was negligent before the injury. If there is a rationale for proving the subsequent repair to establish something other than negligence, proof of the repair may be admitted. The rule lists examples of such other uses, such as to prove ownership or control. Courts are split as to whether this rule applies in strict liability cases. See pages 18-20.

Rule 408. Compromise and Offers to Compromise

Evidence of (1) furnishing or offering or promising to furnish, or (2) accepting or offering or promising to accept, a valuable consideration in compromising or attempting to compromise a claim which was disputed as to either validity or amount, is not admissible to prove liability for or invalidity of the claim or its amount. Evidence of conduct or statements made in compromise negotiations is likewise not admissible. This rule does not require the exclusion of any evidence otherwise discoverable merely because it is presented in the course of compromise negotiations. This rule also does not require exclusion when the evidence is offered for another purpose, such as proving bias or prejudice of a witness, negativing a contention of undue delay, or proving an effort to obstruct a criminal investigation or prosecution.

> **Explanation:** Evidence about a settlement or statements made in settlement negotiations may not be admitted with respect to the validity of the claim involved in the settlement or settlement negotiations. The evidence may,

however, be admitted on any other rationale such as those the rule lists as examples. See pages 20-21.

Rule 409. Payment of Medical and Similar Expenses

Evidence of furnishing or offering or promising to pay medical, hospital, or similar expenses occasioned by an injury is not admissible to prove liability for the injury.

> **Explanation:** Information about medical payments and promises of medical payments is not admissible to show liability for the injury. Statements made while paying or promising can be admitted, in contrast to the Rule 408 treatment of statements made in settlement negotiations. See page 22.

Rule 410. Inadmissibility of Pleas, Plea Discussions, and Related Statements

Except as otherwise provided in this rule, evidence of the following is not, in any civil or criminal proceeding; admissible against the defendant who made the plea or was a participant in the plea discussions:

(1)   a plea of guilty which was later withdrawn;

(2)   a plea of nolo contendere;

(3)   any statement made in the course of any proceedings under Rule 11 of the Federal Rules of Criminal Procedure or comparable state procedure regarding either of the foregoing pleas; or

(4)   any statement made in the course of plea discussions with an attorney for the prosecuting authority which do not result in a plea of guilty or which result in a plea of guilty later withdrawn

However, such a statement is admissible (i) in any proceeding wherein another statement made in the course of the same plea or plea discussions has been introduced and the statement ought in fairness be considered contemporaneously with it, or (ii) in a criminal proceeding for perjury or false statement if the statement was made by the defendant under oath, on the record and in the presence of counsel.

> **Explanation:** Certain pleas and plea bargaining statements are inadmissible except to provide a full context for partial revelation of plea bargaining statements or where a case involves perjury. See pages 22-24.

Rule 411. Liability Insurance

Evidence that a person was or was not insured against liability is not admissible upon the issue whether the person acted negligently or otherwise wrongfully. This rule does not require the exclusion of evidence of insurance against liability when offered for another purpose, such as proof of agency, ownership, or control, or bias or prejudice of a witness.

> **Explanation:** Evidence of insurance may not be admitted to show liability for negligence or other wrongful action, but if other rationales, such as those given as examples, can provide a basis for admission. See pages 17-18.

Rule 412. Sex Offense Cases; Relevance of Alleged Victim's Past Sexual Behavior or Alleged Sexual Predisposition

(a) Evidence generally inadmissible. The following evidence is not admissible in any civil or criminal proceeding involving alleged sexual misconduct except as provided in subdivisions (b) and (c):

(1) Evidence offered to prove that any alleged victim engaged in other sexual behavior.

(2) Evidence offered to prove any alleged victim's sexual predisposition.

> **Explanation:** This rule is sometimes called the "rape shield" provision, but it applies to all types of sexual misconduct cases. Evidence about a person's past sexual conduct and sexual traits may not be admitted to show how he or she acted in a situation that is the basis for a sex offense charge. See pages 48-50.

(b) Exceptions.

(1) In a criminal case, the following evidence is admissible, if otherwise admissible under these rules:

(A) evidence of specific instances of sexual behavior by the alleged victim offered to prove that a person other than the accused was the source of semen, injury, or other physical evidence;

(B) evidence of specific instances of sexual behavior by the alleged victim with respect to the person accused of the sexual misconduct offered by the accused to prove consent or by the prosecution; and

(C) evidence the exclusion of which would violate the constitutional rights of the defendant.

> **Explanation:** In criminal cases, the rule's general prohibition does not apply to evidence of the alleged victim's sexual behavior that: a) supports a claim that someone other than the defendant was the source of semen or other physical evidence; b) occurred with the defendant and supports a claim of consent; or c) is so crucial that exclusion would be unconstitutional.

(2) In a civil case, evidence offered to prove the sexual behavior or sexual predisposition of any alleged victim is admissible if it is otherwise admissible under these rules and its probative value substantially outweighs the danger of harm to any victim and of unfair prejudice to any party. Evidence of an alleged victim's reputation is admissible only if it has been placed in controversy by the alleged victim.

> **Explanation:** In civil cases, this rule's general prohibition does not apply if evidence of the alleged victim's sexual behavior or sexual traits passes a balancing test. Where the balance between probative value and risk of unfair prejudice is very close, the evidence will be excluded, even though under Rule 403 evidence will be admitted when the balance between that rule's factors is very close. Note that harm to a victim is included in this rule's list of factors to be balanced.

(c) Procedure to determine admissibility.
(1) A party intending to offer evidence under subdivision (b) must:
(A) file a written motion at least 14 days before trial specifically describing the evidence and stating the purpose for which it is offered unless the court, for good cause requires a different time for filing or permits filing during trial; and
(B) serve the motion on all parties and notify the alleged victim or, when appropriate, the alleged victim's guardian or representative.
(2) Before admitting evidence under this rule the court must conduct a hearing in camera and afford the victim and parties a right to attend and be heard. The motion, related papers, and the record of the hearing must be sealed and remain under seal unless the court orders otherwise.

> **Explanation:** Evidence covered by this rule must be the subject of an in camera hearing on its admissibility. This protects an alleged victim from emotional trauma and in-

vasion of privacy that otherwise might occur if implications about his or her sexual behavior were made in open court. If a judge believes that information about an instance of an alleged victim's past sexual conduct would be admissible if the past event really did occur, this would be treated as a question of conditional relevancy to be resolved by the jury on the basis of evidence and testimony presented in open court.

Rule 413. Evidence of Similar Crimes in Sexual Assault Cases

(a) In a criminal case in which the defendant is accused of an offense of sexual assault, evidence of the defendant's commission of another offense or offenses of sexual assault is admissible, and may be considered for its bearing on any matter to which it is relevant.

> **Explanation:** Evidence of a defendant's past sexual offense is admissible to support an inference that his or her commission of such an act in the past increases the likelihood that he or she committed the charged offense. See page 48.

(b) In a case in which the Government intends to offer evidence under this rule, the attorney for the Government shall disclose the evidence to the defendant, including statements of witnesses or a summary of the substance of any testimony that is expected to be offered, at least fifteen days before the scheduled date of trial or at such later time as the court may allow for good cause.

> **Explanation:** Because evidence of past sexual offenses is so prejudicial, a notice provision requires that the defendant have warning prior to its introduction.

(c) This rule shall not be construed to limit the admission or consideration of evidence under any other rule.

(d) For purposes of this rule and Rule 415, "offense of sexual assault" means a crime under Federal law or the law of a State (as defined in section 513 of title 18, United States Code) that involved —

(1) any conduct proscribed by chapter 109A of title 18, United States Code;

(2) contact, without consent, between any part of the defendant's body or an object and the genitals or anus of another person;

(3) contact, without consent, between the genitals or anus of the defendant and any part of another person's body;

(4) deriving sexual pleasure or gratification from the infliction of death, bodily injury, or physical pain on another person; or

(5) an attempt or conspiracy to engage in conduct described in paragraphs (1)-(4).

Rule 414. Evidence of Similar Crimes in Child Molestation Cases

(a) In a criminal case in which the defendant is accused of an offense of child molestation, evidence of the defendant's commission of another offense or offenses of child molestation is admissible, and may be considered for its bearing on any matter to which it is relevant.

> **Explanation:** Evidence of a defendant's past sexual offense is admissible to support an inference that his or her commission of such an act in the past increases the likelihood that he or she committed the charged offense. This rule is parallel to Rule 413, except that it deals with child molestation cases rather than "sexual assault" cases. See page 48.

(b) In a case in which the Government intends to offer evidence under this rule, the attorney for the Government shall disclose the evidence to the defendant, including statements of witnesses or a summary of the substance of any testimony that is expected to be offered, at least fifteen days before the scheduled date of trial or at such later time as the court may allow for good cause.

(c) This rule shall not be construed to limit the admission or consideration of evidence under any other rule.

(d) For purposes of this rule and Rule 415, "child" means a person below the age of fourteen, and "offense of child molestation" means a crime under Federal law or the law of a State (as defined in section 513 of title 18, United States Code) that involved —

(1) any conduct proscribed by chapter 109A of title 18, United States Code, that was committed in relation to a child;

(2) any conduct proscribed by chapter 110 of title 18, United States Code;

(3) contact between any part of the defendant's body or an object and the genitals or anus of a child;

(4) contact between the genitals or anus of the defendant and any part of the body of a child;

(5) deriving sexual pleasure or gratification from the infliction of death, bodily injury, or physical pain on a child; or

(6) an attempt or conspiracy to engage in conduct described in paragraphs (1)-(5).

Rule 415. Evidence of Similar Acts in Civil Cases Concerning Sexual Assault or Child Molestation

(a) In a civil case in which a claim for damages or other relief is predicated on a party's alleged commission of conduct constituting an offense of sexual assault or child molestation, evidence of that party's commission of another offense or offenses of sexual assault or child molestation is admissible and may be considered as provided in Rule 413 and Rule 414 of these rules.

> **Explanation:** This is the only provision in the Federal Rules that allows character evidence to be introduced in a civil case as relevant to the issue of someone's out-of-court conduct. It allows introduction of evidence of a party's past sexual offense or child molestation to support an inference that his or her commission of such an act in the past increases the likelihood that he or she committed the conduct charged in the civil suit. See page 48

(b) A party who intends to offer evidence under this Rule shall disclose the evidence to the party against whom it will be offered, including statements of witnesses or a summary of the substance of any testimony that is expected to be offered, at least fifteen days before the scheduled date of trial or at such later time as the court may allow for good cause.

(c) This rule shall not be construed to limit the admission or consideration of evidence under any other rule.

Article V. Privileges

Rule 501. General Rule

Except as otherwise required by the Constitution of the United States or provided by Act of Congress or in rules prescribed by the Supreme Court pursuant to statutory authority, the privilege of a witness, person, government, State, or political subdivision thereof shall be governed by the principles of the common law as they may be interpreted by the courts of the United States in the light of reason and experience. However, in civil actions and proceedings, with respect to an element of a claim or defense as to which State law supplies the rule of decision, the privilege of a witness, person, government, State, or political subdivision thereof shall be determined in accordance with State law.

> **Explanation:** No specific privilege provisions have been adopted as part of the federal rules, although detailed provisions had been proposed by the drafters. Privilege law, therefore, under the federal rules, is open to traditional common law development. In civil cases, state privilege law governs where an issue is governed by state law. See pages 173-180, 185-190.

Article VI. Witnesses

Rule 601. General Rule of Competency

Every person is competent to be a witness except as otherwise provided in these rules. However, in civil actions and proceedings, with respect to an element of a claim or defense as to which State law supplies the rule of decision, the competency of a witness shall be determined in accordance with State law.

> **Explanation:** In contrast to the common law, virtually all people are competent as witnesses, under the federal rules. Where state law governs a claim, state competency law applies. See pages 130-134.

Rule 602. Lack of Personal Knowledge

A witness may not testify to a matter unless evidence is introduced sufficient to support a finding that the witness has personal knowledge of the matter. Evidence to prove personal knowledge may, but need not, consist of the witness' own testimony. This rule is subject to the provisions of Rule 703, relating to opinion testimony by expert witnesses.

> **Explanation:** If someone testifies as a lay, not an expert, witness, evidence must be introduced that could support a jury finding that the witness has direct knowledge of the subject of his or her testimony. That evidence may be introduced as part of the witness's own testimony. See pages 131-132.

Rule 603. Oath or Affirmation

Before testifying, every witness shall be required to declare that the witness will testify truthfully, by oath or affirmation administered in a form calculated to awaken the witness' conscience and impress the witness' mind with the duty to do so.

> **Explanation:** The requirement of an oath or affir-
> mation to tell the truth must be understood in the con-
> text of Rule 610 which prohibits references to religion if
> relevant only to attack or bolster a witness's credi-
> bility. See page 131.

Rule 604. Interpreters

An interpreter is subject to the provisions of these rules relating to qualification as an expert and the administration of an oath or affirmation to make a
true translation.

Rule 605. Competency of Judge as Witness

The judge presiding at the trial may not testify in that trial as a witness. No
objection need be made in order to preserve the point.

> **Explanation:** A judge may not testify at a trial over
> which he or she presides. The rule protects a litigant
> from the futile effort of asking a judge who violates this
> rule to sustain an objection to his or her testimony. See
> page 130.

Rule 606. Competency of Juror as Witness

(a) **At the trial.** A member of the jury may not testify as a witness before that jury in the trial of the case in which the juror is sitting. If the juror
is called so to testify, the opposing party shall be afforded an opportunity to
object out of the presence of the jury.

> **Explanation:** A juror cannot testify in a case he or she
> will be deciding. In contrast to the provision related to
> judges as witnesses (Rule 605), an objection is required
> to be made, but it can be made without the jury's knowl-
> edge. See pages 130-131.

(b) **Inquiry into validity of verdict or indictment.** Upon an inquiry
into the validity of a verdict or indictment, a juror may not testify as to any
matter or statement occurring during the course of the jury's deliberations or
to the effect of anything upon that or any other juror's mind or emotions as
influencing the juror to assent to or dissent from the verdict or indictment or
concerning the juror's mental processes in connection therewith, except that
a juror may testify on the question whether extraneous prejudicial information
was improperly brought to the jury's attention or whether any outside influence
was improperly brought to bear upon any juror. Nor may a juror's affidavit or

evidence of any statement by the juror concerning a matter about which the juror would be precluded from testifying be received for these purposes.

> **Explanation:** Jurors may not testify nor may affidavits from jurors be accepted on the subject of any juror's mental processes, statements, or anything else concerning how the jury reached its conclusion, except that testimony and affidavits are allowed on the subject of "extraneous prejudicial information." See pages 130-131.

Rule 607. Who May Impeach

The credibility of a witness may be attacked by any party, including the party calling the witness.

> **Explanation:** This rejects the common law requirement that an offering party vouch for the honesty of its witness. All parties may impeach all witnesses. See page 138.

Rule 608. Evidence of Character and Conduct of Witness

(a) **Opinion and reputation evidence of character.** The credibility of a witness may be attacked or supported by evidence in the form of opinion or reputation, but subject to these limitations: (1) the evidence may refer only to character for truthfulness or untruthfulness, and (2) evidence of truthful character is admissible only after the character of the witness for truthfulness has been attacked by opinion or reputation evidence or otherwise.

> **Explanation:** Opinion and reputation evidence may always be introduced to detract from the credibility of any witness. These types of evidence may also be introduced to support the credibility of any witness whose credibility has been attacked in any way. See pages 146-147.

(b) **Specific instances of conduct.** Specific instances of the conduct of a witness, for the purpose of attacking or supporting the witness' credibility, other than conviction of crime as provided in rule 609, may not be proved by extrinsic evidence. They may, however, in the discretion of the court, if probative of truthfulness or untruthfulness, be inquired into on cross-examination of the witness (1) concerning the witness' character for truthfulness or untruthfulness, or (2) concerning the character for truthfulness or untruthfulness of another witness as to which character the witness being cross-examined has testified.

The giving of testimony, whether by an accused or by any other witness, does not operate as a waiver of the accused's or the witness' privilege against self-incrimination when examined with respect to matters which relate only to credibility.

> **Explanation:** Past conduct of a witness, relevant to truthfulness, may be asked about in cross-examination of the witness or in cross-examination of another witness who has testified in support of the witness's credibility. The past conduct may not be the subject of extrinsic proof unless it was a crime for which the witness was convicted. See pages 143-145.

Rule 609. Impeachment by Evidence of Conviction of Crime

(a) General rule. For the purpose of attacking the credibility of a witness,

(1) evidence that a witness other than an accused has been convicted of a crime shall be admitted, subject to Rule 403, if the crime was punishable by death or imprisonment in excess of one year under the law under which the witness was convicted, and evidence that an accused has been convicted of such a crime shall be admitted if the court determines that the probative value of admitting this evidence outweighs its prejudicial effect to the accused; and

> **Explanation:** If a witness other than a criminal defendant has been convicted of a felony, evidence of the conviction shall be admitted unless its probative value on the topic of the witness's credibility is substantially outweighed by the risk of prejudicial effect on the defendant. If a witness is a criminal defendant, such evidence shall be admitted unless its probative value is outweighed in any degree by the risk of prejudice. See pages 138-143.

(2) evidence that any witness has been convicted of a crime shall be admitted if it involved dishonesty or false statement, regardless of the punishment.

> **Explanation:** If any witness has been convicted of a crime involving dishonesty or false statements, such as perjury, evidence of the conviction shall be admitted with no balancing of probative and prejudicial impact. See page 140.

(b) Time limit. Evidence of a conviction under this rule is not admissible if a period of more than ten years has elapsed since the date of the conviction or of the release of the witness from the confinement imposed for that conviction, whichever is the later date, unless the court determines, in the interests of justice, that the probative value of the conviction supported by specific facts and circumstances substantially outweighs its prejudicial effect. However, evidence of a conviction more than 10 years old as calculated herein, is not admissible unless the proponent gives to the adverse party sufficient advance written notice of intent to use such evidence to provide the adverse party with a fair opportunity to contest the use of such evidence.

> **Explanation:** If a conviction or a release from confinement related to a conviction (whichever occurred later) took place ten years or more before the trial, evidence of the conviction is admissible only if its probative value substantially outweighs its prejudicial effect. Advance notice is required. See pages 140-143.

(c) Effect of pardon, annulment, or certificate of rehabilitation. Evidence of a conviction is not admissible under this rule if (1) the conviction has been the subject of a pardon, annulment, certificate of rehabilitation, or other equivalent procedure based on a finding of the rehabilitation of the person convicted, and that person has not been convicted of a subsequent crime which was punishable by death or imprisonment in excess of one year, or (2) the conviction has been the subject of a pardon, annulment, or other equivalent procedure based on a finding of innocence.

(d) Juvenile adjudications. Evidence of juvenile adjudications is generally not admissible under this rule. The court may, however, in a criminal case allow evidence of a juvenile adjudication of a witness other than the accused if conviction of the offense would be admissible to attack the credibility of an adult and the court is satisfied that admission in evidence is necessary for a fair determination of the issue of guilt or innocence.

(e) Pendency of appeal. The pendency of an appeal therefrom does not render evidence of a conviction inadmissible. Evidence of the pendency of an appeal is admissible.

Rule 610. Religious Beliefs or Opinions

Evidence of the beliefs or opinions of a witness on matters of religion is not admissible for the purpose of showing that by reason of their nature the witness' credibility is impaired or enhanced.

> **Explanation:** A witness's religious beliefs or views may not be the subject of evidence introduced as relevant to credibility. This rule relates to Rule 603 that allows a witness to swear or affirm to tell the truth. See page 146.

Rule 611. Mode and Order of Interrogation and Presentation

(a) Control by court. The court shall exercise reasonable control over the mode and order of interrogating witnesses and presenting evidence so as to (1) make the interrogation and presentation effective for the ascertainment of the truth, (2) avoid needless consumption of time, and (3) protect witnesses from harassment or undue embarrassment.

> **Explanation** The judge controls the order and style of testimony. See pages 134-135.

(b) Scope of cross-examination. Cross-examination should be limited to the subject matter of the direct examination and matters affecting the credibility of the witness. The court may, in the exercise of discretion, permit inquiry into additional matters as if on direct examination.

> **Explanation** Cross-examination may cover only the topics raised in direct examination, unless the judge allows a broader scope. See pages 135-136.

(c) Leading questions. Leading questions should not be used on the direct examination of a witness except as may be necessary to develop the witness' testimony. Ordinarily leading questions should be permitted on cross-examination. When a party calls a hostile witness, an adverse party, or a witness identified with an adverse party, interrogation may be by leading questions.

> **Explanation** Leading questions are allowed on cross-examination and in examining an opposing party or a hostile witness. In direct examination of a party's own witness, they are only allowed "to develop" the testimony. See page 135.

Rule 612. Writing Used to Refresh Memory

Except as otherwise provided in criminal proceedings by section 3500 of title 18, United States Code, if a witness uses a writing to refresh memory for the purpose of testifying, either —
(1)   while testifying, or
(2)   before testifying, if the court in its discretion determines it is necessary in the interests of justice,
an adverse party is entitled to have the writing produced at the hearing, to inspect it, to cross-examine the witness thereon, and to introduce in evidence those portions which relate to the testimony of the witness. If it is claimed

that the writing contains matters not related to the subject matter of the testimony the court shall examine the writing in camera, excise any portions not so related, and order delivery of the remainder to the party entitled thereto. Any portion withheld over objections shall be preserved and made available to the appellate court in the event of an appeal. If a writing is not produced or delivered pursuant to order under this rule, the court shall make any order justice requires, except that in criminal cases when the prosecution elects not to comply, the order shall be one striking the testimony or, if the court in its discretion determines that the interests of justice so require, declaring a mistrial.

> **Explanation:** When a witness uses a document to refresh his or her recollection and then testifies from "present recollection refreshed," the opposing party is entitled to see the document, cross-examine the witness about it, and introduce parts of it that are relevant to the testimony. See pages 103-104.

Rule 613. Prior Statements of Witnesses

(a) **Examining witness concerning prior statement.** In examining a witness concerning a prior statement made by the witness, whether written or not, the statement need not be shown nor its contents disclosed to the witness at that time, but on request the same shall be shown or disclosed to opposing counsel.

> **Explanation:** A common impeachment technique is to show that something a witness said or wrote before the trial conflicted with the witness's testimony at trial. This rule allows a questioner to use this technique without being required to produce the document or describe the statement in advance. See pages 149-150.

(b) **Extrinsic evidence of prior inconsistent statement of witness.** Extrinsic evidence of a prior inconsistent statement by a witness is not admissible unless the witness is afforded an opportunity to explain or deny the same and the opposite party is afforded an opportunity to interrogate the witness thereon, or the interests of justice otherwise require. This provision does not apply to admissions of a party-opponent as defined in Rule 801(d)(2).

> **Explanation:** Ordinarily, if a party wants to introduce a witness's past statement, rather than just ask the witness about it, the witness must be given an opportunity to comment specifically on that past statement, and the op-

posing party must also have an opportunity to question the witness about it. See pages 149-150.

Rule 614. Calling and Interrogation of Witnesses by Court

(a) **Calling by court.** The court may, on its own motion or at the suggestion of a party, call witnesses, and all parties are entitled to cross-examine witnesses thus called.

(b) **Interrogation by court.** The court may interrogate witnesses, whether called by itself or by a party.

(c) **Objections.** Objections to the calling of witnesses by the court or to interrogation by it may be made at the time or at the next available opportunity when the jury is not present.

Rule 615. Exclusion of Witnesses

At the request of a party the court shall order witnesses excluded so that they cannot hear the testimony of other witnesses, and it may make the order of its own motion. This rule does not authorize exclusion of (1) a party who is a natural person, or (2) an officer or employee of a party which is not a natural person designated as its representative by its attorney, or (3) a person whose presence is shown by a party to be essential to the presentation of the party's cause.

> **Explanation:** Someone who is a witness may be excluded from the courtroom, so that he or she cannot hear the testimony of other witnesses. Witnesses who are exempt from this treatment are people who are parties themselves or are designated representatives of entities like corporations. Also exempt is anyone a lawyer in the case persuades the court is essential as an assistant to the lawyer. See pages 137-138.

Article VII. Opinions and Expert Testimony

Rule 701. Opinion Testimony by Lay Witnesses

If the witness is not testifying as an expert, the witness' testimony in the form of opinions or inferences is limited to those opinions or inferences which are (a) rationally based on the perception of the witness and (b) helpful to a clear understanding of the witness' testimony or the determination of a fact in issue.

> **Explanation:** A witness may speak in terms of opinions if that style of narration makes the testimony clearer. The opinions must be based on actual perceptions by the witness. See pages 136-137.

Rule 702. Testimony by Experts

If scientific, technical, or other specialized knowledge will assist the trier of fact to understand the evidence or to determine a fact in issue, a witness qualified as an expert by knowledge, skill, experience, training, or education, may testify thereto in the form of an opinion or otherwise.

> **Explanation:** Where expertise from an identifiable field will assist the finder of fact, opinion testimony by an expert in the field is permitted. The trial court must determine whether "scientific" evidence adheres well enough to standards of logic and scientific method to be admissible. See pages 161-163.

Rule 703. Bases of Opinion Testimony by Experts

The facts or data in the particular case upon which an expert bases an opinion or inference may be those perceived by or made known to the expert at or before the hearing. If of a type reasonably relied upon by experts in the particular field in forming opinions or inferences upon the subject, the facts or data need not be admissible in evidence.

> **Explanation:** An expert can base testimony on anything the expert has heard at the trial. The testimony can also be based on anything else experts in the field reasonably rely on, such as hearsay, whether or not that material is admissible. See page 164

Rule 704. Opinion on Ultimate Issue

(a) Except as provided in subdivision (b), testimony in the form of an opinion or inference otherwise admissible is not objectionable because it embraces an ultimate issue to be decided by the trier of fact.

> **Explanation:** Testimony may contain conclusions on issues that the trier of fact must decide. See pages 166-167.

(b) No expert witness testifying with respect to the mental state or condition of a defendant in a criminal case may state an opinion or inference as to whether the defendant did or did not have the mental state or condition constituting an element of the crime charged or of a defense thereto. Such ultimate issues are matters for the trier of fact alone.

> **Explanation:** Experts in criminal cases are prohibited from expressing an opinion on the specific issue of a defendant's possession of a mental state that is an element of a crime. See pages 166-167.

Rule 705. Disclosure of Facts or Data Underlying Expert Opinion

The expert may testify in terms of opinion or inference and give reasons therefor without first testifying to the underlying facts or data, unless the court requires otherwise. The expert may in any event be required to disclose the underlying facts or data on cross-examination.

> **Explanation:** An expert's testimony does not have to include the basis for the opinion it states, but that basis must be given on cross-examination if it is requested. See page 164.

Rule 706. Court Appointed Experts

(a) **Appointment.** The court may on its own motion or on the motion of any party enter an order to show cause why expert witnesses should not be appointed, and may request the parties to submit nominations. The court may appoint any expert witnesses agreed upon by the parties, and may appoint expert witnesses of its own selection. An expert witness shall not be appointed by the court unless the witness consents to act. A witness so appointed shall be informed of the witness' duties by the court in writing, a copy of which shall be filed with the clerk, or at a conference in which the parties shall have opportunity to participate. A witness so appointed shall advise the parties of the witness' findings, if any; the witness' deposition may be taken by any party; and the witness may be called to testify by the court or any party. The witness shall be subject to cross-examination by each party, including a party calling the witness.

> **Explanation:** Allowing the court to appoint an expert is a response to the "battle of the experts" problem in which rivals are hired by opposing sides; the provision is rarely used, however, and carries the risk that a jury will give improperly significant weight to the expert's opinion on the theory that because the judge has appointed the expert, the opinions must be respected.

(b) **Compensation.** Expert witnesses so appointed are entitled to reasonable compensation in whatever sum the court may allow. The compensation thus fixed is payable from funds which may be provided by law in criminal cases and civil actions and proceedings involving just compensation under the fifth amendment. In other civil actions and proceedings the compensation shall be paid by the parties in such proportion and at such time as the court directs, and thereafter charged in like manner as other costs.

(c) **Disclosure of appointment.** In the exercise of its discretion, the court may authorize disclosure to the jury of the fact that the court appointed the expert witness.

(d) **Parties' experts of own selection.** Nothing in this rule limits the parties in calling expert witnesses of their own selection.

Article VIII. Hearsay

Rule 801. Definitions

The following definitions apply under this article:

(a) **Statement.** A "statement" is (1) an oral or written assertion or (2) nonverbal conduct of a person, if it is intended by the person as an assertion.

> **Explanation:** A person's words in speech or writing and a person's conduct can all be statements under the hearsay rule, if the person intended them to convey an idea or information. See pages 67-70.

(b) **Declarant.** A "declarant" is a person who makes a statement.

> **Explanation:** Note that only people, not machines, can make "statements," so that a print-out from a measuring device, for example, does not involve any hearsay considerations. See page 75.

(c) **Hearsay.** "Hearsay" is a statement, other than one made by the declarant while testifying at the trial or hearing, offered in evidence to prove the truth of the matter asserted.

> **Explanation:** A statement made by anyone (including a person who testifies as a witness at a trial) out of court is "hearsay" if the proponent seeks to introduce it to support a conclusion that the idea or information it asserts is true. See pages 61-67.

(d) Statements which are not hearsay. A statement is not hearsay if —

(1) Prior statement by witness. The declarant testifies at the trial or hearing and is subject to cross-examination concerning the statement, and the statement is (A) inconsistent with the declarant's testimony, and was given under oath subject to the penalty of perjury at a trial, hearing, or other proceeding, or in a deposition, or (B) consistent with the declarant's testimony and is offered to rebut an express or implied charge against the declarant of recent fabrication or improper influence or motive, or (C) one of identification of a person made after perceiving the person; or

> **Explanation:** These specified situations are exceptions from the usual rule that a witness's own out-of-court words can be hearsay if introduced to support the conclusion that their assertions are true. Note that prior inconsistent statements must have been made under oath, but that prior consistent statements do not have that requirement. See pages 89-92.

(2) Admission by party-opponent. The statement is offered against a party and is (A) the party's own statement, in either an individual or a representative capacity or (B) a statement of which the party has manifested an adoption or belief in its truth, or (C) a statement by a person authorized by the party to make a statement concerning the subject, or (D) a statement by the party's agent or servant concerning a matter within the scope of the agency or employment, made during the existence of the relationship, or (E) a statement by a coconspirator of a party during the course and in furtherance of the conspiracy.

> **Explanation:** At common law, admissions are an exception to the general rule of excluding hearsay. Under the Federal Rules, admissions are treated as outside the definition of hearsay. An admission is any statement a party ever made out of court that is relevant for use against the party. The rule classifies a variety of types of admissions, ranging from a party's own statement to statements made by a party's agent, employee or coconspirator. See pages 87-89.

Rule 802. Hearsay Rule

Hearsay is not admissible except as provided by these rules or by other rules prescribed by the Supreme Court pursuant to statutory authority or by Act of Congress.

> **Explanation:** Evidence that fits the definition of hearsay may not be admitted. Although the rule is written in absolute terms, there may be circumstances where excluding evidence on grounds of hearsay would violate a criminal defendant's constitutional right to present evidence.

Rule 803. Hearsay Exceptions; Availability of Declarant Immaterial

The following are not excluded by the hearsay rule, even though the declarant is available as a witness:

> **Explanation:** This rule sets out a large group of hearsay exceptions, usable without regard to the availability or unavailability of the declarant.

(1) **Present sense impression.** A statement describing or explaining an event or condition made while the declarant was perceiving the event or condition, or immediately thereafter.

> **Explanation:** Note that the statement must describe or explain something while it is going on or immediately after it was going on. See pages 99-100.

(2) **Excited utterance.** A statement relating to a startling event or condition made while the declarant was under the stress of excitement caused by the event or condition.

> **Explanation:** The statement stimulated by something startling must relate to (but need not describe) the startling experience. It must be made when the stress is present, although that condition may be satisfied where a long period of time has passed if the circumstances (such as awakening from unconsciousness) support the idea that the stress could still be having an impact on the declarant. See pages 99-100.

(3) **Then existing mental, emotional, or physical condition.** A statement of the declarant's then existing state of mind, emotion, sensation, or physical condition (such as intent, plan, motive, design, mental feeling, pain, and bodily health), but not including a statement of memory or belief to prove the fact remembered or believed unless it relates to the execution, revocation, identification, or terms of declarant's will.

> **Explanation:** This exception lets in statements like "I am the King of Mars" when introduced to show that the declarant believed he was the King when he spoke. It does not let in statements of belief about past facts. The mental state of intent is covered by the exception, as in a declarant's statement, "I plan to go to the restaurant tomorrow," introduced to show that the declarant had that plan. See pages 100-101.

(4) Statements for purposes of medical diagnosis or treatment. Statements made for purposes of medical diagnosis or treatment and describing medical history, or past or present symptoms, pain, or sensations, or the inception or general character of the cause or external source thereof insofar as reasonably pertinent to diagnosis or treatment.

> **Explanation:** Statements about physical condition, medical history, and symptoms are covered. The declarant may make the statements to either treating or diagnosing medical personnel. Statements about the cause of a condition are within the coverage of this exception only if they involve topics that reasonably relate to diagnosis or treatment. See pages 102-103.

(5) Recorded recollection. A memorandum or record concerning a matter about which a witness once had knowledge but now has insufficient recollection to enable the witness to testify fully and accurately, shown to have been made or adopted by the witness when the matter was fresh in the witness' memory and to reflect that knowledge correctly. If admitted, the memorandum or record may be read into evidence but may not itself be received as an exhibit unless offered by an adverse party.

> **Explanation:** Note that the witness must be shown to have either slight or no memory of the information recorded in the document, but must have known it when he or she made the record or accepted the record as accurate. See pages 103-104.

(6) Records of regularly conducted activity. A memorandum, report, record, or data compilation, in any form, of acts, events, conditions, opinions, or diagnoses, made at or near the time by, or from information transmitted by, a person with knowledge, if kept in the course of regularly conducted business activity, and if it was the regular practice of that business activity to make the memorandum, report, record, or data compilation, all as shown by the testimony of the custodian or other qualified witness, unless the source of information or the method or circumstances of preparation indicate lack of trustworthiness. The term "business" as used in this paragraph includes business, institution, association, profession, occupation, and calling of every kind, whether or not conducted for profit.

> **Explanation:** This "business records" exception is widely used. The declarant who is the originating source of the information in the record has a duty within the organization to provide the information. The information must be of a type that the organization usually records. If someone with no duty to report provides information that is the type of information usually kept by the organization, the document will serve as proof that the words were communicated, but the words will be admissible for their truth only if some other exception applies to them. See pages 104-106.

(7) **Absence of entry in records kept in accordance with the provisions of paragraph (6).** Evidence that a matter is not included in the memoranda, reports, records, or data compilations, in any form, kept in accordance with the provisions of paragraph (6), to prove the nonoccurrence or nonexistence of the matter, if the matter was of a kind of which a memorandum, report, or data compilation was regularly made and preserved, unless the sources of information or other circumstances indicate lack of trustworthiness.

> **Explanation:** This is the mirror image of the business records exception, allowing evidence that information is lacking in a place where it would normally be recorded. An argument could be made that this type of omission is not hearsay, but the presence of this exception moots that controversy. See page 106.

(8) **Public records and reports.** Records, reports, statements, or data compilations, in any form, of public offices or agencies, setting forth (A) the activities of the office or agency, or (B) matters observed pursuant to duty imposed by law as to which matters there was a duty to report, excluding, however, in criminal cases matters observed by police officers and other law enforcement personnel, or (C) in civil actions and proceedings and against the Government in criminal cases, factual findings resulting from an investigation made pursuant to authority granted by law, unless the sources of information or other circumstances indicate lack of trustworthiness.

> **Explanation:** This exception applies the basic idea of business records to public entities. Note that it treats criminal and civil cases differently in some instances. The expression "factual findings resulting from an investigation" means both statements of observed facts and statements of conclusions developed from observed facts. See pages 106-108

(9) Records of vital statistics. Records or data compilations, in any form, of births, fetal deaths, or marriages, if the report thereof was made to a public office pursuant to requirements of law.

> **Explanation:** These documents are usually made by people with an obligation to report and with no motive to lie. Also, their information may be difficult to obtain from any other sources. Unlike the business records exception, this exception does not require testimony from a custodian of the records. The authentication provision of Rule 902(4) would require the proponent to offer a certified copy of the record.

(10) Absence of public record or entry. To prove the absence of a record, report, statement, or data compilation, in any form, or the nonoccurrence or nonexistence of a matter of which a record, report, statement, or data compilation, in any form, was regularly made and preserved by a public office or agency, evidence in the form of a certification in accordance with Rule 902, or testimony, that diligent search failed to disclose the record, report, statement, or data compilation, or entry.

> **Explanation:** This is the mirror image of the public record or entry exception, and is based on the same rationale. See page 108.

(11) Records of religious organizations. Statements of births, marriages, divorces, deaths, legitimacy, ancestry, relationship by blood or marriage, or other similar facts of personal or family history, contained in a regularly kept record of a religious organization.

> **Explanation:** The information treated in this exception does not need to have been provided to the religious organization by someone with a duty to report it. Nevertheless, the circumstances in which religious organizations usually make notes in their records provide fairly strong guarantees of accuracy.

(12) Marriage, baptismal, and similar certificates. Statements of fact contained in a certificate that the maker performed a marriage or other ceremony or administered a sacrament, made by a clergyman, public official, or other person authorized by the rules or practices of a religious organization or by law to perform the act certified, and purporting to have been issued at the time of the act or within a reasonable time thereafter.

> **Explanation:** This exception covers topics additional to those in the public records exception, Rule 803(9), with no requirement that a certified copy of the record be provided.

(13) Family records. Statements of fact concerning personal or family history contained in family Bibles, genealogies, charts, engravings on rings, inscriptions on family portraits, engravings on urns, crypts, or tombstones or the like.

> **Explanation:** Yes, even engravings on urns have their own hearsay exception. The theory behind this exception is that statements about family history are likely to be either accurate or corrected when they are made in places that are subject to inspection and are regarded as important.

(14) Records of documents affecting an interest in property. The record of a document purporting to establish or affect an interest in property, as proof of the content of the original recorded document and its execution and delivery by each person by whom it purports to have been executed, if the record is a record of a public office and an applicable statute authorizes the recording of documents of that kind in that office.

> **Explanation:** Under this exception a title document can serve as proof of the detailed information recorded in another document, only if local statutes set up a recording system that includes documents such as records of title documents.

(15) Statements in documents affecting an interest in property. A statement contained in a document purporting to establish or affect an interest in property if the matter stated was relevant to the purpose of the document, unless dealings with the property since the document was made have been inconsistent with the truth of the statement or the purport of the document.

> **Explanation:** This exception provides a means of proving information stated in documents involved in the transfer of property interests, such as descriptions of the grantors.

(16) Statements in ancient documents. Statements in a document in existence twenty years or more the authenticity of which is established.

> **Explanation:** At common law, an ancient document had to be thirty years old, but the Federal Rules drafters shortened the period to twenty years. A twenty-year-old document, found in a place where it would likely have been kept, is admissible to prove the truth of its assertions. See pages 108-109.

(17) Market reports, commercial publications. Market quotations, tabulations, lists, directories, or other published compilations, generally used and relied upon by the public or by persons in particular occupations.

> **Explanation:** Information like published weather reports, stock prices, commodity prices, or telephone directories is covered by this exception. They are compiled by people with no motive to lie, and because they are used by the public, errors are likely to be discouraged.

(18) Learned treatises. To the extent called to the attention of an expert witness upon cross-examination or relied upon by the expert witness in direct examination, statements contained in published treatises, periodicals, or pamphlets on a subject of history, medicine, or other science or art, established as a reliable authority by the testimony or admission of the witness or by other expert testimony or by judicial notice. If admitted, the statements may be read into evidence but may not be received as exhibits.

> **Explanation:** If the judge under Rule 104(a) concludes that published material is considered reliable by professionals in a field, statements in such material are admissible for their truth, if they are used in direct or cross-examination of an expert witness. To avoid the risk that the jury will rely too heavily on these items, the rule prohibits their use as exhibits.

(19) Reputation concerning personal or family history. Reputation among members of a person's family by blood, adoption, or marriage, or among a person's associates, or in the community, concerning a person's birth, adoption, marriage, divorce, death, legitimacy, relationship by blood, adoption, or marriage, ancestry, or other similar fact of personal or family history.

> **Explanation:** It is likely that the only way people will have knowledge of issues of kinship such as birth, marriage and the other specified family relationships is through hearsay statements by others. This rule allows testimony about such statements, on the basis that the need for this type of information is likely to be great, and that statements on these subjects are likely to be careful and therefore accurate. The rule does not limit its coverage to statements made prior to disputes or to statements made in any specified community.

(20) Reputation concerning boundaries or general history. Reputation in a community, arising before the controversy, as to boundaries of or customs affecting lands in the community, and reputation as to events of general history important to the community or State or nation in which located.

> **Explanation:** Note that for reputation in a community concerning land use must have arisen prior to the dispute in which the statements are sought to be introduced. No such requirement is imposed for statements connected with general history.

(21) Reputation as to character. Reputation of a person's character among associates or in the community.

> **Explanation:** This Rule is related to the provisions in Rule 405(a) and Rule 608(a) which detail how character may be proved when its admission is proper. This rule protects the uses of reputation allowed by those other rules from being barred by the hearsay doctrine.

(22) Judgment of previous conviction. Evidence of a final judgment, entered after a trial or upon a plea of guilty (but not upon a plea of nolo contendere), adjudging a person guilty of a crime punishable by death or imprisonment in excess of one year, to prove any fact essential to sustain the judgment, but not including, when offered by the Government in a criminal prosecution for purposes other than impeachment, judgments against persons other than the accused. The pendency of an appeal may be shown but does not affect admissibility.

> **Explanation:** Conviction of a serious crime may be used in other proceedings as proof of any fact that was essential support for the judgment. Note that in criminal cases, this exception may not be used against a person different from the person who was found guilty.

(23) Judgment as to personal, family, or general history, or boundaries. Judgments as proof of matters of personal, family or general history, or boundaries, essential to the judgment, if the same would be provable by evidence of reputation.

> **Explanation:** This exception is parallel to the exceptions for proof by reputation in property disputes. Judgments are at least as reliable as reputation, so this exception permits their substantive use.

(24) Other exceptions. A statement not specifically covered by any of the foregoing exceptions but having equivalent circumstantial guarantees of trustworthiness, if the court determines that (A) the statement is offered as evidence of a material fact; (B) the statement is more probative on the point for which it is offered than any other evidence which the proponent can procure through reasonable efforts; and (C) the general purposes of these rules and the interests of justice will best be served by admission of the statement into evidence. However, a statement may not be admitted under this exception unless the proponent of it makes known to the adverse party sufficiently in advance of the trial or hearing to provide the adverse party with a fair opportunity to prepare to meet it, the proponent's intention to offer the statement and the particulars of it, including the name and address of the declarant.

> **Explanation:** Note the five main requirements under this "catch-all" exception. The statement offered must have equivalent trustworthiness, in comparison to statements treated in the specific exceptions. Strong necessity must be shown. The topic on which the statement is relevant must be important. Justice and the purposes of the rules of evidence must be served by admission. The proponent must have given notice of intention to use the rule. This exception has been used to admit types of statements that have significant reliability but are not provided for in the detailed exceptions. A controversial example is the use of grand jury testimony, given under oath. See page 109.

Rule 804. Hearsay Exceptions; Declarant Unavailable

(a) **Definition of unavailability.** "Unavailability as a witness" includes situations in which the declarant —

> **Explanation:** Rule 804 provides additional exceptions to the hearsay exclusion, allowed only if the declarant meets any of its definitions of "unavailability." See page 118.

(1) is exempted by ruling of the court on the ground of privilege from testifying concerning the subject matter of the declarant's statement; or

> **Explanation:** A declarant is unavailable if an order of the court excuses him or her from testifying.

(2) persists in refusing to testify concerning the subject matter of the declarant's statement despite an order of the court to do so; or

> **Explanation:** A declarant who refuses to testify is unavailable.

(3) testifies to a lack of memory of the subject matter of the declarant's testimony, or

> **Explanation:** People state that they have no memory in many instances, sometimes truly and sometimes because they do not want to testify. In either circumstance, such a witness is unavailable.

(4) is unable to be present or to testify at the hearing because of death or then existing physical or mental illness or infirmity; or

> **Explanation:** Death is the ultimate unavailability to testify. Serious illness also receives treatment as establishing unavailability.

(5) is absent from the hearing and the proponent of a statement has been unable to procure the declarant's attendance (or in the case of a hearsay exception under subdivision (b)(2), (3), or (4), the declarant's attendance or testimony) by process or other reasonable means.

> **Explanation:** This alternative for showing unavailability states that unavailability for the purposes of Rules 804(b)(1) and 804(b)(5) is established by a showing that the presence of the declarant cannot be obtained. To establish unavailability under this alternative for Rules 804(b)2, 804(b)(3) and 804(b)(4), the proponent must show inability to obtain both the declarant's presence and the declarant's testimony (for example, by deposition). See page 119.

A declarant is not unavailable as a witness if exemption, refusal, claim of lack of memory, inability, or absence is due to the procurement or wrongdoing of the proponent of a statement for the purpose of preventing the witness from attending or testifying.

> **Explanation:** The hearsay exceptions in this rule may not be used by a party who intentionally prevents the declarant from being present.

(b) Hearsay exceptions. The following are not excluded by the hearsay rule if the declarant is unavailable as a witness:

(1) Former testimony. Testimony given as a witness at another hearing of the same or a different proceeding, or in a deposition taken in compliance with law in the course of the same or another proceeding, if the party against whom the testimony is now offered, or, in a civil action or proceeding, a predecessor in interest, had an opportunity and similar motive to develop the testimony by direct, cross, or redirect examination.

> **Explanation:** Testimony or deposition statements are admissible if at the time they were made the party against whom they are currently sought to be introduced had an opportunity to develop the testimony by questioning. In addition to the opportunity, that party's motivation at the time of the testimony must have been similar to its motivation in the current trial. In civil cases a predecessor in interest is treated as equivalent to the current party. See pages 119-120.

(2) Statement under belief of impending death. In a prosecution for homicide or in a civil action or proceeding, a statement made by a declarant while believing that the declarant's death was imminent, concerning the cause or circumstances of what the declarant believed to be impending death.

> **Explanation:** In murder cases (not all criminal cases) and in all civil cases, a statement made by a person who believed he or she was about to die that relates to the cause of the expected death is admissible. This is the classic dying declarations exception. See pages 120-121.

(3) Statement against interest. A statement which was at the time of its making so far contrary to the declarant's pecuniary or proprietary interest, or so far tended to subject the declarant to civil or criminal liability, or to render invalid a claim by the declarant against another, that a reasonable person in the declarant's position would not have made the statement unless believing it to be true. A statement tending to expose the declarant to criminal liability and offered to exculpate the accused is not admissible unless corroborating circumstances clearly indicate the trustworthiness of the statement.

> **Explanation:** Because people do not usually say things that could harm them, it is likely that when a person does say such a thing, it is true. Statements that could hurt a person in the contexts of money, property or criminal liability are covered by this exception, provided that a reasonable person would have understood the risks involved in making the statement. If the statement is made to exculpate an accused, it can qualify only if it is corroborated. See pages 121-123.

(4) Statement of personal or family history. (A) A statement concerning the declarant's own birth, adoption, marriage, divorce, legitimacy, relationship by blood, adoption, or marriage, ancestry, or other similar fact of personal or family history, even though declarant had no means of acquiring personal knowledge of the matter stated; or (B) a statement concerning the foregoing matters, and death also, of another person, if the declarant was related to the other by blood, adoption, or marriage or was so intimately associated with the other's family as to be likely to have accurate information concerning the matter declared.

> **Explanation:** Statements by the declarant about himself or herself, about the declarant's relatives or about people with whom the declarant had intimate associations are admissible to show kinship and similar family history.

(5) Other exceptions. A statement not specifically covered by any of the foregoing exceptions but having equivalent circumstantial guarantees of trustworthiness, if the court determines that (A) the statement is offered as evidence of a material fact; (B) the statement is more probative on the point for which it is offered than any other evidence which the proponent can procure through reasonable efforts; and (C) the general purposes of these rules and the interests of justice will best be served by admission of the statement into evidence. However, a statement may not be admitted under this exception unless the proponent of it makes known to the adverse party sufficiently in advance of the trial or hearing to provide the adverse party with a fair opportunity to prepare to meet it, the proponent's intention to offer the statement and the particulars of it, including the name and address of the declarant.

> **Explanation:** This provision is identical to Rule 803(24). The "catch-all" requirement of equivalent trustworthiness can be satisfied by a showing that the proposed hearsay statement has trustworthiness similar to that of the statements defined in any of the four exceptions for which unavailability is required. See page 123.

Rule 805. Hearsay Within Hearsay

Hearsay included within hearsay is not excluded under the hearsay rule if each part of the combined statements conforms with an exception to the hearsay rule provided in these rules.

> **Explanation:** Out-of-court statements that themselves contain additional statements may be admitted, so long as each statement can overcome a hearsay objection. A police officer's notebook might contain a quote from someone who claimed to have seen a vehicular accident. To introduce the eyewitness's statement, two levels of hearsay would have to be overcome. The first hearsay statement is the words of the eyewitness. The second is the written words of the police officer. The eyewitness's statement might have fit the present sense impression exception, and the police officer's notes might fit the public records exception. See pages 105-106.

Rule 806. Attacking and Supporting Credibility of Declarant

When a hearsay statement, or a statement defined in Rule 801(d)(2), (C), (D), or (E), has been admitted in evidence, the credibility of the declarant may be attacked, and if attacked may be supported, by any evidence which would be admissible for those purposes if declarant had testified as a witness.

Evidence of a statement or conduct by the declarant at any time, inconsistent with the declarant's hearsay statement, is not subject to any requirement that the declarant may have been afforded an opportunity to deny or explain. If the party against whom a hearsay statement has been admitted calls the declarant as a witness, the party is entitled to examine the declarant on the statement as if under cross-examination.

> **Explanation** Hearsay declarants and the people whose statements are admissible as admissions may be impeached with any technique that would have been available if they had made their statements in testimony. The provisions for allowing a declarant to deny or explain inconsistent statements do not apply, since the declarant may not be available at trial. See pages 150-151.

Article IX. Authentication and Identification

Rule 901. Requirement of Authentication or Identification

(a) **General provision.** The requirement of authentication or identification as a condition precedent to admissibility is satisfied by evidence sufficient to support a finding that the matter in question is what its proponent claims.

> **Explanation** When a party seeks to introduce a document or any object or thing, the party must also provide a basis for a finding that the document or object really is what the proponent claims it is. This requirement also applies to testimony about conversations. It is important to remember that authentication is only one requirement that must be satisfied for admission of an item of evidence. For example, an authenticated document may still need to satisfy the rules concerning hearsay and original writings. See pages 193-194.

(b) **Illustrations.** By way of illustration only, and not by way of limitation, the following are examples of authentication or identification conforming with the requirements of this rule:

> **Explanation** It is extremely easy to satisfy the authentication requirement. The examples provided in this part of the rule are typical methods litigants use, but any proof that could support the required finding is allowed. See page 194.

(1) **Testimony of witness with knowledge.** Testimony that a matter is what it is claimed to be.

(2) **Nonexpert opinion on handwriting.** Nonexpert opinion as to the genuineness of handwriting, based upon familiarity not acquired for purposes of the litigation.

(3) **Comparison by trier or expert witness.** Comparison by the trier of fact or by expert witnesses with specimens which have been authenticated.

> **Explanation:** The specimen with which the trier of fact compares the item sought to be authenticated must itself be authenticated. The specimen can satisfy that requirement in a variety of ways, such as circumstantial evidence or through testimony by a witness who can state that the specimen is what it is claimed to be. See pages 194-195.

(4) **Distinctive characteristics and the like.** Appearance, contents, substance, internal patterns, or other distinctive characteristics, taken in conjunction with circumstances.

> **Explanation:** A common authentication technique recognized by this example is the "reply" doctrine. If there is testimony about a telephone call or other communication to a particular person or business, a call or communication that seems to be a reply will be treated as authenticated as actually having been made by the person or business that was the recipient of the original call or communication. See page 195.

(5) **Voice identification.** Identification of a voice, whether heard firsthand or through mechanical or electronic transmission or recording, by opinion based upon hearing the voice at any time under circumstances connecting it with the alleged speaker.

(6) **Telephone conversations.** Telephone conversations, by evidence that a call was made to the number assigned at the time by the telephone company to a particular person or business, if (A) in the case of a person, circumstances, including self-identification, show the person answering to be the one called, or (B) in the case of a business, the call was made to a place of business and the conversation related to business reasonably transacted over the telephone.

(7) **Public records or reports.** Evidence that a writing authorized by law to be recorded or filed and in fact recorded or filed in a public office, or a purported public record, report, statement, or data compilation, in any form, is from the public office where items of this nature are kept.

(8) Ancient documents or data compilation. Evidence that a document or data compilation, in any form, (A) is in such condition as to create no suspicion concerning its authenticity, (B) was in a place where it, if authentic, would likely be, and (C) has been in existence 20 years or more at the time it is offered.

> **Explanation:** "Ancient" documents are those twenty years old or older. If circumstances suggest reliability, they are treated as authenticated. See page 196.

(9) Process or system. Evidence describing a process or system used to produce a result and showing that the process or system produces an accurate result.

(10) Methods provided by statute or rule. Any method of authentication or identification provided by Act of Congress or by other rules prescribed by the Supreme Court pursuant to statutory authority.

Rule 902. Self-Authentication

Extrinsic evidence of authenticity as a condition precedent to admissibility is not required with respect to the following:

> **Explanation:** The items described in this rule's examples are considered so likely to be what they seem to be that further proof is not required. See pages 196-197.

(1) Domestic public documents under seal. A document bearing a seal purporting to be that of the United States, or of any State, district, Commonwealth, territory, or insular possession thereof, or the Panama Canal Zone, or the Trust Territory of the Pacific Islands, or of a political subdivision, department, officer, or agency thereof, and a signature purporting to be an attestation or execution.

(2) Domestic public documents not under seal. A document purporting to bear the signature in the official capacity of an officer or employee of any entity included in paragraph (1) hereof, having no seal, if a public officer having a seal and having official duties in the district or political subdivision of the officer or employee certifies under seal that the signer has the official capacity and that the signature is genuine.

(3) Foreign public documents. A document purporting to be executed or attested in an official capacity by a person authorized by the laws of a foreign country to make the execution or attestation, and accompanied by a final certification as to the genuineness of the signature and official position (A) of the executing or attesting person, or (B) of any foreign official whose certificate of genuineness of signature and official position relates to the execution or attestation or is in a chain of certificates of genuineness of signature and official position relating to the execution or attestation. A final certification may be made by a secretary of an embassy or legation, consul general, consul, vice consul, or consular agent of the United States, or a diplomatic or consular official of the foreign country assigned or accredited to the United States. If reasonable opportunity has been given to all parties to investigate the authenticity and accuracy of official documents, the court may, for good cause shown, order that they be treated as presumptively authentic without final certification or permit them to be evidenced by an attested summary with or without final certification.

(4) **Certified copies of public records.** A copy of an official record or report or entry therein, or of a document authorized by law to be recorded or filed and actually recorded or filed in a public office, including data compilations in any form, certified as correct by the custodian or other person authorized to make the certification, by certificate complying with paragraph (1), (2), or (3) of this rule or complying with any Act of Congress or rule prescribed by the Supreme Court pursuant to statutory authority.

(5) **Official publications.** Books, pamphlets, or other publications purporting to be issued by public authority.

(6) **Newspapers and periodicals.** Printed materials purporting to be newspapers or periodicals.

(7) **Trade inscriptions and the like.** Inscriptions, signs, tags, or labels purporting to have been affixed in the course of business and indicating ownership, control, or origin.

(8) **Acknowledged documents.** Documents accompanied by a certificate of acknowledgment executed in the manner provided by law by a notary public or other officer authorized by law to take acknowledgments.

(9) **Commercial paper and related documents.** Commercial paper, signatures thereon, and documents relating thereto to the extent provided by general commercial law.

(10) **Presumptions under Acts of Congress.** Any signature, document, or other matter declared by Act of Congress to be presumptively or prima facie genuine or authentic.

Rule 903. Subscribing Witness' Testimony Unnecessary

The testimony of a subscribing witness is not necessary to authenticate a writing unless required by the laws of the jurisdiction whose laws govern the validity of the writing.

Article X. Contents of Writings, Recordings and Photographs

Rule 1001. Definitions

For purposes of this article the following definitions are applicable:

> **Explanation:** The definitions are used to establish the Federal Rules' version of the "best evidence" rule. It applies only to items defined as writings, recordings or photographs, and does not require "best" evidence of their contents, but rather sets up a specific requirement about production of originals rather than copies. See pages 201-202.

(1) **Writings and recordings.** "Writings" and "recordings" consist of letters, words, or numbers, or their equivalent, set down by handwriting, typewriting, printing, photostating, photographing, magnetic impulse, mechanical or electronic recording, or other form of data compilation.

(2) **Photographs.** "Photographs" include still photographs, X-ray films, video tapes, and motion pictures.

(3) **Original.** An "original" of a writing or recording is the writing or recording itself or any counterpart intended to have the same effect by a person executing or issuing it. An "original" of a photograph includes the negative or any print therefrom. If data are stored in a computer or similar device, any printout or other output readable by sight, shown to reflect the data accurately, is an "original".

(4) **Duplicate.** A "duplicate" is a counterpart produced by the same impression as the original, or from the same matrix, or by means of photography, including enlargements and miniatures, or by mechanical or electronic re-recording, or by chemical reproduction, or by other equivalent techniques which accurately reproduces the original.

Rule 1002. Requirement of Original

To prove the content of a writing, recording, or photograph, the original writing, recording, or photograph is required, except as otherwise provided in these rules or by Act of Congress.

> **Explanation:** The requirement of the original applies only when the proponent seeks to prove the contents of the writing, recording or photograph. A party may provide evidence of a fact without regard to the original

writing rule if the proof does not depend on a showing that a writing, recording or photograph shows that the fact is true. If a party's technique for establishing a fact is to demonstrate that a writing, recording or photograph contains evidence of the fact, then the rule applies. As the next portions of the rule show, the requirement of producing the original is essentially a requirement to produce the original, a copy, or an excuse for having neither the original nor a copy. See page 201.

Rule 1003. Admissibility of Duplicates

A duplicate is admissible to the same extent as an original unless (1) a genuine question is raised as to the authenticity of the original or (2) in the circumstances it would be unfair to admit the duplicate in lieu of the original.

> **Explanation:** Despite the existence of this original writing rule, a duplicate is almost always as acceptable as the ostensibly required original. See page 202.

Rule 1004. Admissibility of Other Evidence of Contents

The original is not required, and other evidence of the contents of a writing, recording, or photograph is admissible if —

> **Explanation:** In the situations described in the following portions of this rule, testimony about the contents of a writing, recording or photograph is permitted even without the introduction of either the original or a copy of the item. See page 202.

(1) Originals lost or destroyed. All originals are lost or have been destroyed, unless the proponent lost or destroyed them in bad faith; or

(2) Original not obtainable. No original can be obtained by any available judicial process or procedure; or

(3) Original in possession of opponent. At a time when an original was under the control of the party against whom offered, that party was put on notice, by the pleadings or otherwise, that the contents would be a subject of proof at the hearing, and that party does not produce the original at the hearing; or

(4) Collateral matters. The writing, recording, or photograph is not closely related to a controlling issue.

Rule 1005. Public Records

The contents of an official record, or of a document authorized to be recorded or filed and actually recorded or filed, including data compilations in any form, if otherwise admissible, may be proved by copy, certified as correct in accordance with Rule 902 or testified to be correct by a witness who has compared it with the original. If a copy which complies with the foregoing cannot be obtained by the exercise of reasonable diligence, then other evidence of the contents may be given.

Rule 1006. Summaries

The contents of voluminous writings, recordings, or photographs which cannot conveniently be examined in court may be presented in the form of a chart, summary, or calculation. The originals, or duplicates, shall be made available for examination or copying, or both, by other parties at reasonable time and place. The court may order that they be produced in court.

Rule 1007. Testimony or Written Admission of Party

Contents of writings, recordings, or photographs may be proved by the testimony or deposition of the party against whom offered or by that party's written admission, without accounting for the nonproduction of the original.

> **Explanation:** If a party against whom information about the contents of a writing, recording or photograph is sought to be introduced gives testimony about the contents, the original writing rule does not apply.

Rule 1008. Functions of Court and Jury

When the admissibility of other evidence of contents of writings, recordings, or photographs under these rules depends upon the fulfillment of a condition of fact, the question whether the condition has been fulfilled is ordinarily for the court to determine in accordance with the provisions of Rule 104. However, when an issue is raised (a) whether the asserted writing ever existed, or (b) whether another writing, recording, or photograph produced at the trial is the original, or (c) whether other evidence of contents correctly reflects the contents, the issue is for the trier of fact to determine as in the case of other issues of fact.

> **Explanation:** Where questions of fact are involved in deciding whether Rule 1004's provisions about other evidence of the contents of a writing, recording or photograph may be admitted, the trial judge decides most of those questions, as Rule 104(a) would require. Certain specified issues related to the rule are left to the jury, however. They are whether a particular writing ever existed, whether an item at trial is an original, and whether other evidence of contents is accurate.

Article XI. Miscellaneous Rules

Rule 1101. Applicability of Rules

(a) **Courts and magistrates.** These rules apply to the United States district courts, the District Court of Guam, the District Court of the Virgin Islands, the District Court for the Northern Mariana Islands, the United States courts of appeals, the United States Claims Court, and to United States bankruptcy judges and United States magistrates, in the actions, cases, and proceedings and to the extent hereinafter set forth. The terms "judge" and "court" in these rules include United States bankruptcy judges and United States magistrate judges.

(b) **Proceedings generally.** These rules apply generally to civil actions and proceedings, including admiralty and maritime cases, to criminal cases and proceedings, to contempt proceedings except those in which the court may act summarily, and to proceedings and cases under title 11, United States Code.

(c) **Rule of privilege.** The rule with respect to privileges applies at all stages of all actions, cases, and proceedings.

(d) **Rules inapplicable.** The rules (other than with respect to privileges) do not apply in the following situations:

(1) **Preliminary questions of fact.** The determination of questions of fact preliminary to admissibility of evidence when the issue is to be determined by the court under Rule 104.

(2) **Grand jury.** Proceedings before grand juries.

(3) **Miscellaneous proceedings.** Proceedings for extradition or rendition; preliminary examinations in criminal cases; sentencing, or granting or revoking probation; issuance of warrants for arrest, criminal summonses, and search warrants; and proceedings with respect to release on bail or otherwise.

(e) **Rules applicable in part.** In the following proceedings these rules apply to the extent that matters of evidence are not provided for in the statutes which govern procedure therein or in other rules prescribed by the Supreme Court pursuant to statutory authority: the trial of minor and petty offenses by United States magistrates; review of agency actions when the facts are subject to trial de novo under section 706(2)(F) of title 5, United States Code; review of orders of the Secretary of Agriculture under section 2 of the Act entitled "An Act to authorize association of producers of agricultural products" approved February 18, 1922 (7 U.S.C. 292), and under sections 6 and 7(c) of the Perishable Agricultural Commodities Act, 1930 (7 U.S.C. 499f, 499g(c)); naturalization and revocation of naturalization under sections 310-318 of the Immigration and Nationality Act (8 U.S.C. 1421-1429); prize proceedings in admiralty under sections 7651-7681 of title 10, United States Code; review of orders of the Secretary of the Interior under section 2 of the Act entitled "An Act authorizing associations of producers of aquatic products" approved June 25, 1934 (15 U.S.C. 522); review of orders of petroleum control boards under section 5 of the Act entitled "An Act to regulate interstate and foreign commerce in petroleum and its products by prohibiting the shipment in such commerce of petroleum and its products produced in violation of State law, and for other purposes", approved February 22, 1935 (15 U.S.C. 715d); actions for fines, penalties, or forfeitures under part V of title IV of the Tariff Act of 1930 (19 U.S.C. 1581-1624), or under the Anti-Smuggling Act (19 U.S.C. 1701-1711); criminal libel for condemnation, exclusion of imports, or other proceedings under the Federal Food, Drug, and Cosmetic Act (21 U.S.C. 301-392); disputes between seamen under sections 4079, 4080, and 4081 of the Revised Statutes (22 U.S.C. 256-258); habeas corpus under sections 2241-2254 of title 28, United States Code; motions to vacate, set aside or correct sentence under section 2255 of title 28, United States Code; actions for penalties for refusal to transport destitute seamen under section 4578 of the Revised Statutes (46 U.S.C. 679); actions against the United States under the Act entitled "An Act authorizing suits against the United States in admiralty for damage caused by and salvage service rendered to public vessels belonging to the United States, and for other purposes", approved March 3, 1925 (46 U.S.C. 781-790), as implemented by section 7730 of title 10, United States Code.

Rule 1102. Amendments

Amendments to the Federal Rules of Evidence may be made as provided in section 2076 of title 28 of the United States Code.

Rule 1103. Title

These rules may be known and cited as the Federal Rules of Evidence.

Table of Cases

Index

A GOWN
OF
SPANISH
LACE

Books by Janette Oke

Janette Oke's Reflections on the Christmas Story

SEASONS OF THE HEART

Once Upon a Summer	*Winter Is Not Forever*
The Winds of Autumn	*Spring's Gentle Promise*

LOVE COMES SOFTLY

Love Comes Softly	*Love's Unending Legacy*
Love's Enduring Promise	*Love's Unfolding Dream*
Love's Long Journey	*Love Takes Wing*
Love's Abiding Joy	*Love Finds a Home*

CANADIAN WEST

When Calls the Heart	*When Breaks the Dawn*
When Comes the Spring	*When Hope Springs New*

WOMEN OF THE WEST

The Calling of Emily Evans	*A Bride for Donnigan*
Julia's Last Hope	*Heart of the Wilderness*
Roses for Mama	*Too Long a Stranger*
A Woman Named Damaris	*The Bluebird and the Sparrow*
They Called Her Mrs. Doc	*A Gown of Spanish Lace*
The Measure of a Heart	

DEVOTIONALS

The Father Who Calls	*Father of My Heart*
The Father of Love	*Faithful Father*

Janette Oke: Heart for the Prairie
Biography of Janette Oke by Laurel Oke Logan

The Oke Family Cookbook
by Barbara Oke and Deborah Oke

JANETTE OKE

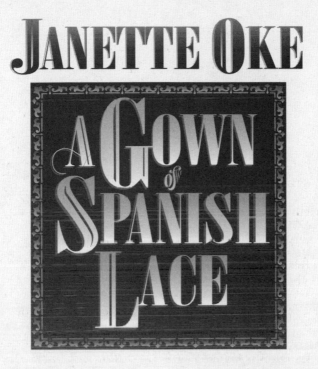

A GOWN of SPANISH LACE

BETHANY HOUSE PUBLISHERS
MINNEAPOLIS, MINNESOTA 55438

Published by Bethany House Publishers
A Ministry of Bethany Fellowship, Inc.
11300 Hampshire Avenue South
Minneapolis, Minnesota 55438

Printed in the United States of America.

Library of Congress Cataloging-in-Publication Data

Oke, Janette
   A Gown of Spanish lace / Janette Oke.
      p. cm. — (Women of the West)

    I. Title.
II. Series: Oke, Janette, 1935–   Women of the West.
PR9199.3.O38B57   1994
813'.54—dc20   94–49703
ISBN 1–55661–683–X Trade Paper   CIP
ISBN 1–55661–684–8 Large Print
ISBN 1–55661–690–2 Hardcover

In memory of my father.

A true gentleman, a special daddy,
a lover of nature, and an avid reader,
who good-naturedly humored
my "romance" with the West.

JANETTE OKE was born in Champion, Alberta, during the depression years, to a Canadian prairie farmer and his wife. She is a graduate of Mountain View Bible College in Didsbury, Alberta, where she met her husband, Edward. They were married in May of 1957, and went on to pastor churches in Indiana as well as Calgary and Edmonton, Canada.

The Okes have three sons and one daughter and are enjoying the addition to the family of grandchildren. Edward and Janette have both been active in their local church, serving in various capacities as Sunday-school teachers and board members. They make their home in Didsbury, Alberta.

A Word From the Author

In the WOMEN OF THE WEST fiction series, I have attempted to present several different facets of pioneer life. A rough, rugged element of the "new frontier" was also a significant part of the history of the West. With that in mind I have included this story, which takes a look at the coarser life of the new land—the lawless side. What happened when good and bad collided?

This story is not born of sudden inspiration. My fascination with the West began when I was a teenager, and because of my growing love for the land and the people, I read everything I could find that dealt with the subject. The fictional accounts I discovered were written in one genre— westerns. So it was natural that my very first idea for a story was also in that vein. In my mid-teens, I romanticized about a West far different than the one in which I had grown up.

When it came time for me to begin my own writing, I chose to deal with the settlers—those courageous people who carried with them far more than their walking plows and cooking pots. In many instances they also had a deep personal faith in a sovereign God. They built towns in sheltered valleys and shaped the rugged open plains into productive farmlands.

So I put aside this story plot—supposing I would never

have use for it. That was forty-plus years ago.

But over the years the idea continued to push itself forward. Each time I gently nudged it back into some hidden recess of my mind. Finally, I came to the conclusion that God might have some use for it. I began to pray for His direction.

I knew I would have to honestly present the ruthless mind-set of the outlaws to make the reader understand the real danger of my characters—the ones who were victims and the ones who struggled to free themselves from such a life. Could this be presented in such a way as to show the hopelessness and helplessness of those who choose to live without law—without compassion—without God? Was there a reader of westerns who could benefit from this approach? This story?

The answer seemed to be yes. If even one reader finds some encouragement or direction—or hope—then the story will have served a purpose.

If you happen to be that reader, may you know at the outset—I have prayed for you.

Janette Oke

Contents

Chapter One

A Girl and a Town

The schoolhouse was set in the ideal spot. The simple wood-slab walls blended in with the slate gray of the rocky hillside behind it. A wooden step led to a heavy, hewed oak door with its leather-strap pull and squeaky iron hinges. The building faced east and looked out over the downward slope. The blend of nearby trees was broken by the silver of the now-quiet stream that could at times become a tempestuous surge of flood waters. A simple wooden bridge that after every spring runoff had to be rebuilt, or at the least repaired, spanned the water. Farther down and beyond stood a cluster of more wood-frame buildings. The town's businesses melted together along one long, winding street, seeming to point the way to the town's single church marking the outskirts on the east. Rows of simple homes spilled out blue-gray smoke lifting lazily into the brightness of the morning sky. All seemed quite still except for an occasional stirring here or there announcing that one or another of the town's occupants was busy on some self-appointed mission.

The scent of autumn's fallen leaves hung delicately in the air to mix with the tang of the woodsmoke. Bright gold of aspen interchanged with the greenery of spruce and pine, filling the valley with color that continued on up the slopes of the hills enfolding the little town. Birds, wishing to remain long enough to feast on the last red berries from mountain ash or wild chokecherry before making their flight south, sprinkled the morning air with song, reminding the saucy squirrels that the summer's bounty had to be shared.

On the wooden steps of the school, a young woman stood, cast-iron bell in hand. Though she looked to be little more than a schoolgirl herself, her face held a look of serenity and her eyes reflected her sense of responsibility.

But for the moment she appeared to have forgotten the noisy little group of children who chased about the small yard that had been coaxed from the forested hillside. She seemed to have forgotten even the bell in her hand and what she had come out to do. Her eyes gazed out over the scene before her to drink in every aspect of the picture. It was a beautiful morning. A beautiful autumn. Yes, and a beautiful, sleepy little town. Smithton. She loved it. Everything about it.

She stirred and sighed deeply.

Finally her eyes turned to the frolicking youngsters. Her students. She loved them, too.

With a flick of her wrist the bell brought them to attention. The clear ringing lifted eyes in the streets below to the little schoolhouse on the hill. She could see the few pedestrians raise their heads, or stop midstride to glance upward before hurrying on their way. She knew that the contentment she felt, the love for the town she claimed as home, was shared by those who walked the morning streets below her.

The bell caused a change in the noise that came from the schoolyard. It didn't lessen—simply altered in tone as boys and girls of various ages and dispositions hastened to fall into line, eventually to be led with some measure of decorum into the classroom.

The young woman marched directly to the front of the room and turned to face the scurrying troop. After depositing lunch pails and outer wraps at their assigned spots, all students hurried to the simple wooden desks that were their centers for learning. The little crew stood at attention, hands fidgeting slightly or hanging limply at their sides.

The teacher's eyes scanned the group quickly. They were all there. No one missing because of colds or grippe. That would come with the winter months. She reminded herself to take full advantage of the days of good weather and good health.

"Good morning, class," she said evenly, trying to keep the joy she was feeling inside from spilling out too enthusiastically into the words.

"Good morning, Miss Benson," they replied in ragged unison.

"We will salute our flag," announced the teacher and turned her back to her class to face the faded cloth that had been proudly mounted on the wall above the blackboard.

The flag would have hung rather forlornly had it not been firmly supported and carefully secured by caring hands. Ariana Benson knew the local school officials were proud of that flag. Not all schools in the territories could boast a flag of their own. It might look worn and a bit scruffy to outside eyes, but this flag had done honorable duty. It had once led the way for a contingent of blue-coated soldiers who had fought to bring law and order to the West.

The voices of the fifteen students joined in with their teacher as the pledge to flag and country was solemnly repeated. Though Miss Benson could not see her students, she was confident that all fifteen stood rigidly at attention, hand held over heart as the words were spoken.

As soon as the salute ended, the teacher turned and lifted a Bible from the corner of her desk. She had already marked the passage for the day, Proverbs, chapter three, and she read it now in a clear voice, accentuating the words she particularly wanted the children to hear and understand.

When she reached the fifth verse, her eyes lifted slightly from the page to quickly scan her small audience. "Trust in the Lord with all thine heart," her tone encouraged, "and lean not unto thine own understanding. In all thy ways acknowledge him," she went on, "and he shall direct thy paths."

As she closed the Book and looked out over her class of students, willing them to hear and heed the words, she wondered just how fully she understood the verses herself. Silently she vowed to remind herself of them frequently in the days to come, to gain deeper insight into their meaning for her.

She could recite the verses by memory. Her father and mother had seen to that. Now she needed to get them from her head to her heart. To learn to do as the verses admonished.

"Let us pray together," she invited in a soft voice, and fifteen heads bowed as one, and fifteen young voices lifted together in the Lord's Prayer.

A general shuffling followed as students took their seats. The teacher's full attention was turned to the lessons of the day.

ᴪ   ᴪ   ᴪ

After the students had been dismissed at school day's end, Ariana remained behind, poring over lesson books as she corrected grammar and sums. When the last assignment had been properly marked, she turned her attention to preparations for the next day's lessons. It required hours of careful planning to make sure she had meaningful, productive studies for each of the students in the eight grades. And as it was Ariana's first year as a schoolteacher, and her sixteenth birthday had just passed, at times the task seemed almost overwhelming.

But she loved to teach. She was thankful her parents had sacrificed in order for her to get her teacher's certificate. Ariana could imagine doing nothing else with her life. The light in a child's eyes when a new discovery was made was worth all the long hours and every effort on her part to make learning fun and exciting.

The last glow of twilight was fading from the skies before Ariana finally closed the last book, picked up her wrap, and carefully fastened her hat in place with its two pins.

She was weary. Yet she had exciting news to tell when she reached home. Little Jeff Newcome had recited the entire alphabet on his own for the first time. She had worked and prompted and struggled and prayed. She had begun to fear that he would never master the letters. But today—today he had stood proudly and carefully worked his way through the alphabet. She had asked him to repeat, fearing that the one time might have been some fortunate accident. But he had made his way through the list again. Ariana felt nearly as triumphant as he did as she handed him the wrapped sweet from Barker's Store as his reward.

She carefully pulled the heavy door shut tightly behind her. The cumbersome door with its worn hinges did not cooperate well, and the leather pull tended to slip through one's hands in resistance. Ariana tugged again—just to be sure it was properly in place. She turned her eyes to the rocky path that wound its way down the hillside, over the footbridge, and into town.

It was darker than she had expected. The sun slipped quickly behind the hills, bringing night to the town before it was so evident on the surrounding prairies. Ariana quickened her step. She did not wish to be the cause of her mother's worrying.

❧   ❧   ❧

"It's Saturday," Mrs. Benson said, her tone gentle but firm.

Ariana lifted her head from the book opened on the table before her. Her eyes held a question, though she did not voice it.

"It's Saturday," repeated the woman. "Don't you think you can lay your books aside for one day?"

Ariana stirred restlessly. She did wish she could forsake

her reading. Her eyes were weary from perusing the printed pages. She lifted a hand to rub the ache from the back of her neck.

"I haven't enough knowledge of the Industrial Revolution to challenge my two eighth graders," she responded.

"I would think any knowledge of the Industrial Revolution would be more than what they know now," put in Mrs. Benson.

Ariana pushed the book aside. She straightened tired shoulders and reached up to tuck in a stray lock of hair. Inwardly she once again bemoaned the fact that the tresses were too soft and wayward to stay pinned. Outwardly she turned her attention to her mother.

"You've been at that book all morning," her mother continued.

"Was there something you wished me to do?" asked Ariana, who was careful to tend to her share of household chores.

"No. No—except give yourself a bit of rest. You can't keep studying all the time."

With a sigh Ariana closed the book and stood to her feet.

"You are right," she admitted reluctantly. "But it is so—so hard to keep up."

"You'll be getting sick if you don't get some fresh air and exercise," her mother went on.

Ariana let her gaze steal to the open window. Her mother was letting fresh air sweep into the home, spilling its fall fragrance into the room along with the breeze that rustled the curtains.

"It's not the same as walking in it—breathing it in," her mother said as though reading Ariana's thoughts.

Ariana's eyes stayed on the window. Another beautiful day called—it beckoned. She longed to forget her responsibility as the town's schoolteacher and follow her heart up the winding trail and into the woods. She knew the little creek would sing. The fallen leaves of aspen and birch would rustle beneath her feet. The sky would present just enough fleecy clouds to make one's imagination have full run. Ariana longed to be out in the sunshine—the freshness of the day. It would be so easy to feel like a kid again. She longed for that. Longed to lay aside her adult responsibilities for just a few hours.

She stretched and gave her shoulders a little shake. She had another hour's reading to do to be properly prepared for Monday morning.

"I really—" she began.

"You really need to get out," her mother encouraged. "Surely a break will make you fresher for finishing the studying later."

Ariana considered the comment, then nodded slowly. "You're right," she said, her voice trembling slightly with eagerness. "I'll just—take a little walk. I can finish up later."

She gave her book another little push as though to inform it that she was done with it for the present.

"Where's Papa?" she asked.

"At the church. Putting final preparations on his Sunday sermon."

"Can I take him a cup of tea?"

"He'd like that."

The older woman smiled and moved toward the kitchen to prepare the tea while Ariana went to her room to gather a shawl and change into something more suitable for walking. By the time she reappeared, her mother had a small tray with a teapot wrapped snugly in a cozy, a single cup, and a slice of toast smothered with wild blueberry jam.

"Remember it gets dark earlier than it did," her mother warned as she kissed Ariana's cheek.

Ariana nodded.

Once the door closed behind her, Ariana breathed deeply. Her eyes took on a new sparkle. Her step quickened and her chin lifted. Her mother was right. The fresh air and fall sunshine would do her a world of good.

Chapter Two

A Boy and a Camp

Tall trees shadowed the winding trail hidden from view of all eyes save the lone eagle drifting on soundless currents of morning air far above the crags and rocky slopes.

To those below, the hillside was unbroken from its wildness—uninhabited by humankind. Uninformed eyes would not have detected the slight indentation that resulted in a passageway, small and tucked securely away against the face of steep outcroppings of rough and ragged rock, leading into a secret valley.

It was the perfect setting for any who wished to keep their whereabouts concealed from an outside world. Outlaws. Bandits. Desperadoes. Blackguards. Brigands. Freebooters. Highwaymen. They had been called many things throughout the years—but always the names carried with them the same sense of hostility and hatred. They were seen as parasites—by terror and force living off the sweated brows and calloused hands of honest workers.

But the young man who removed his stained hat, who squinted his eyes against the harshness of the midday sun, cared little about any of those names. He paid no heed to the expressions of hatred. The words of contempt. He had been raised in the hidden camp, had known no other life, no other family—if one could call the band of rough, cursing, hard-riding, desperate men a *family*.

He had been sent to the rise by his father to survey the valley below. It was not unusual for a close eye to be kept on the valley floor. A sentry was always posted to be sure there was no chance of discovery. He took his shift like every other man in the outfit. But still—there was something different about the order this time. He had yet to sort it through, but he had this strange gut-feeling. . . .

He could see McDuff, already posted on the shelf of rock that overlooked the entire area—hills, streams, valley, and connecting valleys. There was only one way into the camp. If anyone was on the trail that paralleled the small creek below, McDuff would spot them. So why did his father feel this added vigilance was needed? Had his pa reason to think they had been followed? Or was his pa simply using this as an excuse to get him away from the camp for a while? But why? What could his pa be planning that he didn't want discovered?

The young man fanned his bronzed face slightly to get some coolness on his sweating brow. The day was unusually warm for fall. Indian Summer, they called it. Indian Summer that could get as hot as any mid-July day. He stepped back into the shade of a large pine before increasing the action of the Stetson. Even a small movement could be detected in an otherwise motionless setting.

As his eyes traveled over the slope before him, they took in everything—the flit of a bird, the stirring of tall grasses as some cautious, small creature moved about seeking food, the rollicking bounding of an energetic squirrel. He even saw the shift of hand from McDuff on his ledge perch as he brushed away a pestering fly. McDuff could be careless. His rifle was lying in plain sight on the ledge. Not that anyone from below could see the Winchester, but what if the shifting of the afternoon sun should reflect off the barrel? McDuff needed to be more cautious. The young man frowned as he thought about the danger carelessness could bring to the entire group. He wouldn't refer the matter to his pa—that might cause an unnecessary fuss. He'd speak to McDuff himself when they were both back in camp.

After another thorough study of the valley, he was content that they had no cause to be concerned about unwanted visitors.

Guests were not welcomed at the camp of the band. Not even those of similar stripe. Years of living on the edge had proved that no man was to be trusted. They had learned to guard their own backs even from those of their own company. And one never left a trail that was too easy to follow, or rode without checking frequently over a shoulder.

He moved slowly from the shadows and replaced the stained Stetson. His steps were lithe, deliberate, and smooth. His body fit and muscular. He intended to keep it that way. He abhorred the wasting away of manhood, of body and mind that he observed in those with whom he shared the simple log buildings of the small camp. He attributed their slovenliness, their softness, and their paunchy bellies to their lives of boozing and idleness. Except for the frequent night excursions that supplied the needs of the group, they did little but lounge around and take their occasional watch. He had no intention of becoming like them. Secretly he admired the strong bodies and straight backs of the braves in the local Indian tribe—but he knew better than to express that thought to his pa.

His pa had no love for the Indians. That was evident each time one was seen or talked about. His father, dark and swarthy and given to black moods, would spit in the dust, curse profusely, then spit again. "Only good Indian is a dead Indian," the boy had heard all through his growing years. He knew better. Yet he was smart enough not to argue with his pa.

"Well—nothin' goin' on down there," he murmured to his mount as he reached one hand to gather the reins. The horse tossed its head and snorted.

With one easy movement he was in the saddle. The horse danced in his impatience to get going, but the rider held him in check. For some reason he could not understand, he was reluctant to head back into camp, even though he had planned to spend a good share of the afternoon practicing his draw. With the raid of the night before, he was now supplied with ammunition. His pa allowed him no shells for target practice when their store was low.

He loved the feel of the cool, ivory-covered pistol butt in his hand. He loved the tension he felt in his own coiled body as he hit leather. The click of the hammer as the gun whipped upward—the feel of his finger being at one with the cold metal as he squeezed off a shot. He felt close to his gun. As though it really was an extension of himself. He felt closer to his gun than to any of the men down in the valley shacks below him. It had been his only "toy" as a child, his source of entertainment as a boy, his challenge of skill as a young man.

Now part of him itched to take full advantage of the new supply of ammunition. Yet part of him held back. Something strange was going on. He could almost taste it. He had to try to think it through. To see if he could work out the puzzle. Nothing had been said to him directly—but he could sense it. Could feel it. And it had something to do with him. His pa seemed unusually morose—black in his mood of the morning, even though the raid of the night before had been even more successful than any of them had dared hope. Not a single man—nor horse—had been lost or even hit. They had returned with supplies that would last them clear through the winter if necessary, and cash to add to the ample collection that each man guarded with his life.

It had been a good night's work. And no man even appeared to try to tail them. So why the tension? Why the scowls among the group? He just couldn't figure.

With a word to his horse he moved forward. He wasn't going back into the camp. Not yet. He'd give things a chance to cool off down there. Give his father time to be mellowed by whiskey.

He turned the buckskin back down the trail, but he knew he would take the left branch once he hit the bottom. He would head for the spot where the spring formed a deep crystal pool and take a leisurely dip in the frigid waters. Maybe it would clear his head and help him to think.

❧   ❧   ❧

"I don't know why yer growlin'."

The man named Sam was the only person in the small company of men who would have dared to speak to "The Boss" in such a fashion. Perhaps he dared because they had traveled together for so many years. Perhaps he knew that under the sweating, stomping, cursing exterior was a man who might—on occasion—be willing to listen to some reason. Perhaps Sam was just too hardened to care what the other man thought of his comments. His gun was faster, and both men knew it.

"He's a coward," spoke the prowling boss with a curse and a spit into the thick dust on the floor of the room. "Jest a yella-bellied coward."

"Ya know thet ain't so, so I'll not even favor thet comment with a re-ply," spoke the first man as he sliced a section from a wad of dark tobacco. He poked the tobacco back into a torn pocket and stuffed the chew into his mouth, tucking it firmly between his stained teeth and droopy lip.

"He covers it. He covers it well—but he's a coward all the same." The big, brooding man cursed again and kicked at the only chair in the room. It toppled, breaking once again the leg that had been patched over and over.

"Dawgone it, Boss," said the smaller man, irritated. "Don't know how many times ya think thet I can mend thet thing." It was his turn to curse. But his voice was softer, less menacing.

"Fergit the chair. It's the boy we're talkin' on." The big man stopped his pacing and turned to the man who sat on one of the log blocks that made up the other seats in the dark room. He leaned close to the tobacco chewer and his eyes shot sparks of fire.

"He covers it." He almost shouted the words into the face of the smaller man. "He—"

"Back off," said Sam, the smaller of the two, giving a push to the heavy chest leaning over him. "I ain't nohow wantin' to share yer whiskey. Not when you've already downed it."

The big man glowered but straightened and moved back slightly. His hand was trembling. He cursed again, this time more from habit than venom, and moved off to moodily peer out the one window with its broken, smoke-blackened glass.

"What'd he do wrong now?" inquired the smaller man, still seemingly undisturbed. He spit into the corner.

At first the big man just glared as though the other should understand. Then he spoke angrily. "He had a chance to finish thet no-good gunslinger yesterday. To finish 'im. What'd he do? Wing 'im. Jest winged 'im. He's a coward."

The smaller man didn't share the opinion. "Look, Boss— iffen the Kid is wrong—he's wrong. But he ain't a coward. I've known him 'long as you have. I've watched him grow. He ain't no coward—an' you know it well as I do."

The big man continued to stare out the window.

"He can shoot straighter and draw faster'n any man I know," Sam continued from his perch on the log stool. "He's strong as a bear an' springy as a wildcat an' he has eyes like an eagle—never misses the flutter of a wood moth. He hears the slightest rustle. Leaf can't fall in a tornado without he hears it, and besides all thet—he's got this uncanny sense— this feelin' in his bones when somethin's amiss. Why, you'd a walked right into an ambush over there in Widder's Pass hadn't been fer him. And you'd never got away from thet posse in—"

"Shet up," barked the man known as "The Boss."

"Jest remindin' ya," said the tobacco chewer mildly, spitting again into the corner.

"Well—ya needn't. I know all thet, Sam. Think I've been somewhere else whilst he's been growin' up? I know all thet."

"Then what's stickin' in yer craw? I don't figger."

Silence hung in the air while Sam worked his tobacco, and Will Russell, the boss, stared off into the distance. The latter ran a hand through thinning, dark greasy hair. "I dunno," he said at last. "Jest this—this sick feelin' in my innards. This—this funny fear—thet iffen it came to it—he'd back down."

"Back down?" Sam aimed a stream of tobacco into the corner. The big man whirled and moved toward him, his voice lowered, though one could not call it soft.

"Ya ever seed him shoot a man?" he hissed, the sound raspy and harsh.

"Well—shore. He's got the quickest hand—"

"Have ya seed him shoot a man?" the big man insisted.

"Shore. I told ya."

"Dead?"

There was silence. Sam stared at the scowling face before him. "Don't think dead. He jest—takes out their shootin' arm."

"Exactly. Exactly."

Sam shrugged his shoulders. The stiff leather vest lifted and fell with resistance. "So what's yer beef? They sure don't do no more shootin' fer a while."

"But he's never taken 'em *out*. Never."

"So—"

"So—don't ya think folks notice thet? Don't ya think word gets around? Here's a feller quick with a gun—but he never shoots to kill. Every gunslinger in the West is soon gonna be in on thet little secret."

The big man kicked at the sprawled chair, sending it careening across the room to smash into the log walls of the cabin.

He cursed and Sam joined him.

"Good thing this here shack is built sturdy or ya woulda kicked it down by now," Sam complained.

"Make some coffee," snarled the big man, and Sam stirred himself from his seat and moved toward the blackened stove near the cabin door.

The big man crossed to lift the chair and study the damage. "Fix this thing when ya get around to it," he told the smaller man. "I hate sittin' on a wood block. Most as bad as sittin' on a rock."

Sam shrugged, nodded, and shoved some wood into the firebox. He filled the blackened pot with water and slashed open a small bag holding coffee grounds and liberally dumped some into the pot.

Silence followed until Sam had finished his duties and returned to his log seat.

"We oughta get us a few more chairs," he said more to himself than to the big man.

"Hard to carry behind a saddle," the boss growled. He reached out a hand to drum his fingers in agitated fashion on the boards of the wooden table.

Silence again. At last Sam spoke.

"So yer worried about 'im?" he asked. His voice was lower now—his manner less defensive.

"I worry," admitted the big man in response.

"I still think he can handle hisself."

"Maybe," replied the big man. "But odds are agin' it."

"How so?"

The fingers beat more rapidly on the tabletop.

"Doublin' up. One man forces a draw—another comes in—gits his attention. First man has a chance for a slow, careful shot with his good hand. Takes 'im."

"Come on, Boss," scoffed Sam. "How often ya seed thet happen?"

"It could."

"Sun could come up in the west, too, I reckon—but I ain't seen it do it yet."

"Could happen," insisted Will.

Sam got up to check the coffee. It wasn't boiling yet.

"Sure gonna be good to have a decent cup of coffee," he muttered. "Thet stuff we been drinkin' tasted 'bout like slop."

He brought two chipped, stained cups to the table.

"Know what I think?" he asked softly.

There was no response, so after a few moments of silence he continued. "I think yer jest worryin' too much. The boy is doin' jest fine. Can't think me of a better tracker—smarter woodsman—more careful feller at watchin' his back—why— bet there ain't an Injun—"

He stopped. The big man had begun cursing and spitting. Sam quickly changed the course of the conversation.

"It's jest 'cause yer his pa thet yer frettin'," he hurried on. "Boys are gonna think yer a stewin' ole woman iffen—"

The big man stirred restlessly and his curses grew louder. Sam went for the coffee, hoping it was boiling. He may have pushed a bit too far. It was time to back off.

"I know he can take care of hisself," the big man growled. "Iffen he chooses to—thet's the rub. He's gotta learn thet ya have to take yer man. Dead men don't carry grudges. No smart man leaves him a trail of one-armed men carryin' a full pail of bitter with 'em. Sooner or later one of 'em var- mints is gonna turn up and he ain't gonna be lookin' to play fair."

It was a new thought for Sam and the first one he agreed with. He poured the coffee and moved to put the pot back on the stove.

"Too hot to be drinkin' coffee," he muttered to himself, even though he sniffed the deep aroma with appreciation.

He returned to his seat and took a drink of the scalding liquid. The coffee burned all the way down, causing his eyes to water. When he recovered he spoke again.

"So what ya plannin'?"

There was silence while the big man fingered his cup.

"Gotta force his hand," he said at last.

"Force his hand? You mean—make him take his man?"

The big man nodded, his eyes dark and smoldering.

"And how ya fixin' to do thet? You gonna call him out?"

Will Russell answered that ridiculous question with a dark stare.

"Okay, okay," hurried Sam. "So thet was dumb. I take it ya got a better idea."

The big man sipped his coffee slowly, smarter than to gulp it as Sam had done.

"Well—" prompted Sam.

"What's the one thing thet a man—almost any man—would kill fer?" asked the boss.

"Money?"

The big man cursed. "We got thet," he reminded Sam. "Stashed away. An' we can get more—anytime we take a notion."

"Then—?" Sam let the question hang between them.

"A woman," said Will simply.

"A what?"

Sam could not believe what he had just heard. The boss only nodded.

"Ain't no woman within miles of here," Sam reminded him.

"Thet means we gotta find one."

"Find one. How?"

"I ain't got it all figured out yet, but it'll come."

"An' if an' when ya do find one—how ya aim to get them together? An' what makes ya sure he'll—go fer her? He ain't got no idee what a woman's even about."

The big man gave the smaller one a withering look and then turned back to the table as though the absurd comment deserved no reply. He hiked his large frame a little closer to the table and returned to drumming his fingers in an irritating fashion, his brow furrowing with deep, dark thoughts.

At length he turned. "We've got a lot of figurin' to do, Sam," he said, then nodded his head toward the coffeepot to indicate he'd be needing his cup refilled.

Chapter Three

Ariana

Saturday walks became an anticipated part of Ariana's week. She no longer resisted her mother's counsel. She had learned that she was more productive after a stroll in the neighboring woods or along the local stream. Often she invited one or another of her students to accompany her. It became a time to build relationships and teach lessons that could not be learned in the schoolroom. Ariana prayed that she might be able to teach not only about life but also about the Giver of Life. Not just scientific facts of the world but about the One who established the Laws of Nature. Not just mathematics but about the One who made the consistency of mathematics a possibility.

"God has given us an ordered world," she said often, and she hoped her students would see and understand what she was trying to convey as they looked at the world around them.

If there were any whose children attended the little schoolhouse on the hill who thought that the preacher's daughter was bringing "too much religion" into the classroom, they never voiced it. Even the owner of the local saloon suggested that "a little law and order wouldn't hurt" his two offspring any. He thought the world was bound to quickly chip away any "excess goodness" they might obtain.

"We need us some high principles," said the school board chairman in a community meeting. "And I for one don't know where to find 'em 'ceptin' in the Good Book. Far as I'm concerned, thet little gal can pour in 'em all the Bible learnin' they can hold. Make upright citizens of 'em, the way I see it."

Others seemed to agree. Ariana thought of her teaching in the local school as an addition to her Sunday school class in her father's church. Not all the townsfolk felt Sunday services a necessity. So her Saturday walks were one more means of bringing valuable lessons to her students who might not be attending church.

There were those few who had little patience with the biblical teaching. But it could also be said that, by and large, those individuals had little use for any teaching at all.

"Can't 'magine a boy his age goin' off to school. When I was his age I drove a team of mules and put in sixty acres of crop each summer," huffed one elderly man.

"What do young gals need all thet book learnin' fer?" scoffed another. "Don't help none with makin' a pot of stew or hoein' a garden."

Ariana chose to ignore such remarks. But she often had to bite her tongue to keep from responding with a lecture.

"If the West is ever to be civilized and prosperous," she wanted to say, "we need people who are educated. Educated not just in book learning—but in moral living. That's the only hope for taming the West and making it a place of fulfilled promise for future generations."

Ariana determined to do all she could to prepare her students for the future, whether or not every townsperson approved.

🙲   🙲   🙲

"You have such pretty dresses."

The words were spoken with such wistfulness that Ariana almost felt like apologizing. She had chosen Chloe Travis, a seventh-grader, for her Saturday walk companion.

The girl was sallow skinned and frail and came from a poor home on the edge of the town. Ariana supposed that the girl's slight frame was due to the fact she never really had enough nutritious food. Her father seldom worked, and her mother sat in the shade of the front porch from sunup to sundown.

"The poor woman must be ill," Ariana's mother had said with honest concern. "No one who is well would be content to sit and let the family do without."

Ariana secretly wondered if her mother was being generous. Now and then a pot of stew or a roasted chicken was sent to the home from the parsonage. There was little verbal response from the adults in the family, but the looks on the faces of the hungry children were enough thanks for the preacher's wife.

Ariana turned to the girl in the patched, faded frock. "My mama sews," she said simply.

"Wish my ma could sew," the girl replied.

"Perhaps if—" But Ariana was not allowed to finish.

"Naw—she wouldn't. Not even iffen she had a machine, she wouldn't. She don't like to do nothin'."

Ariana was tempted to gently correct the grammar, but in order to do so she would have needed to restate the girl's comment. She couldn't do that.

"Yer really lucky," went on the girl.

"Yes," said Ariana with deep feeling. "I am . . . really lucky . . . only . . . only I don't see it as luck. I see it as—"

She stopped. She had been about to say that it was because God was good to her. How could she say that? How could she claim that God loved and cared for her—and left Chloe struggling along in a family that did not even function? Ariana bit her lip.

"Shall we sit down and rest for a little while?" she asked instead. "Mama sent along a little lunch."

The girl's eyes lit up, and Ariana could see her tongue pass quickly over her upper lip.

They found a place to sit, and Ariana brought out the cold beef sandwiches. She held one out to the young girl and watched as she hungrily devoured it. Ariana broke off a small piece of another sandwich and took a bite. She felt hungry too. The crisp fall air had a way of increasing one's appetite. But she held herself in check. There would be plenty of food waiting for her when she returned to her home. Who knew when Chloe might get another meal?

Ariana's thoughts were on the previous conversation. She wished to say more to the young girl. Something that would make sense. Something that might give her reason for hope. Ariana hardly knew where to start.

"You know, " she said at last as she passed the rest of the sandwiches to Chloe, "you said I'm lucky—and I am. I have been . . . blessed. My parents are wonderful. I love them dearly. I have been blessed. . . ."

She let the words fade away as she thought on them. Then she turned again to the young girl and spoke. "It wasn't—well, always so. Did you know that?"

Ariana took a deep breath before she went on. "My parents—my birth parents—were . . . were killed in an Indian raid . . . when I was a baby. The whole wagon train of people were . . . killed."

Ariana saw the eyes of the young girl open wide with surprise—then horror.

"What happened?" Chloe asked around the rest of the roast beef sandwich.

"We were traveling west. For a new life. A new beginning. I . . . I don't remember, of course. I was just . . . just a baby. But one night—for some reason—the Indians attacked. There had been trouble in the area. I don't know what had happened. Some Indians had been killed. They blamed it on the scouts from the train. So they . . . they decided to get revenge." She paused a moment.

"Anyway, the people were killed," she told the young girl. "All but me and Aunt Lucy."

"Who's Aunt Lucy?" asked the young girl, her voice little more than a whisper.

"Aunt Lucy was a . . . a dear old woman. Not really my

aunt. And not really old, I guess, though she seemed old. She was a friend of my mama's. I think of her as my second mama." Ariana's voice threatened to break. "She took care of me until I was five years old. I . . . I don't know how she managed. She was crippled—from a fall and—"

Ariana stopped again.

"When the Indians attacked," she was finally able to explain, "Aunt Lucy snatched me up and ran. There was a cliff—all rocks. Aunt Lucy bundled me close and jumped. Jumped right off the cliff. Both of her legs were broken. The Indians were so sure the fall would have killed us that they never even came down to check. Just looked over the edge, Aunt Lucy said, and pointed and shouted. Blood-curdling yells, Aunt Lucy said.

"Then they . . . they finished their . . . their raid and set fire to the wagons. A storm was approaching and soon it was pouring rain. Some of the wagons didn't even burn.

"Later, Aunt Lucy heard someone come to the train. Local ranchers or maybe soldiers from the nearby garrison. She didn't know. At first she was afraid it might be the Indians returning, but they spoke English. She heard them cursing as they looked at the . . . the carnage. She called and called until she was hoarse, but she was already weak and she couldn't make them hear her.

"For three days we lay there. It was hot. Aunt Lucy dipped water from a small puddle and gave me drinks from her cupped hand. She was sure I would die before help came.

"On the third day a band of soldiers did come by. Aunt Lucy was able to make herself heard, and they came to us. They checked the wagon train. There were no other survivors, but they . . . they saved a few things that had been my mother's. Aunt Lucy insisted that they bring them when they took us into town.

"Gradually Aunt Lucy's legs healed enough that she could struggle along with two canes. She never did regain her health—she had been hurt inside, too—but she cared for me for those five years. I don't know how she managed to make enough pennies to keep us fed—though I do know that she often went without.

"Aunt Lucy was getting weaker and weaker, and I often heard her praying—for me—that God would take care of me when she was gone. Then a miracle happened. At least, Aunt Lucy said it was a miracle. A preacher moved into the town. Aunt Lucy went to see him and he . . . he and his wife agreed to take me. They had no children of their own."

"The Bensons?" asked Chloe, her eyes large.

"The Bensons," nodded Ariana.

"I thought they were your folks."

"They are—now," smiled Ariana.

"Where's Aunt Lucy?"

Ariana's eyes filled with tears. "She died about two months after I went to the Bensons," she said softly.

The young girl shook her head. "That's pretty awful," she said.

"Yes," said Ariana. "Yes—it was. For my folks—for all of the people on the wagon train. For Aunt Lucy. I've been the one who has been blessed—and I . . . I really don't know why. Not yet. I hope to one day discover just why—why God chose to spare a baby. What does He have for me to do? I keep telling myself there must be a reason—and I think I've found it. I think it was so I could be a teacher. So I could help you—and others—to know—to really understand that God is real. That He cares about us—no matter what our circumstances."

Ariana laid her hand on the young girl's faded sleeve. "He really does care, you know."

Chloe stared into her face.

"He loves you, Chloe," Ariana said gently. "He knows all about you—and He loves you. Can you believe that?"

The girl hesitated. She looked down at the limp dress, the shoes with holes in the toes. Then she looked back into the solemn blue eyes and nodded slowly.

❧ ❧ ❧

"May I walk ya home?"

Ariana had just stepped out the church door. She looked up into the tense face of the tall young man who stood before her. It was not an attractive face. Willis Boyd was probably the last person she would have hoped to make such a request. His skin was blotchy with youthful acne, and his ears were much too big for the size of his head. Crooked teeth were stained from tobacco juice, and his hair looked like the only washing it ever received was when he was caught in the rain.

Yet something about his pathetically hopeful look made her smile softly and swallow hard. How could she refuse him—just because of his appearance? It would be cruel. Especially since he had just recently been showing up at her father's church.

She was about to reply when someone brushed his way between them. Bernard Dikerson stood before her. He smiled and pushed back smooth dark hair with a well-groomed hand. Ariana couldn't help noting the sharply creased trousers, the tailored suit jacket, and the natty cravat. Bernard Dikerson was the son of the local banker, newly arrived in the town. Every girl had her hat set for the banker's son.

Bernard said nothing—just gave the derby in his hand a slight tip with the flick of his wrist and jovially offered her his arm.

Ariana prayed a quick and beseeching prayer—*What should I do, Lord?*—then lifted her eyes to survey both young men. Inwardly she struggled. *I . . . I should befriend Willis. He'll be so shamed if . . . everyone is looking our way . . . he'll . . . he might not come to church again . . . yet . . . yet Bernard . . .*

Willis had stepped back, his face red with embarrassment. Bernard stood, arm still offered, a look of total confidence giving him a boyishly charming expression.

Trust in the Lord with all thine heart, came the soft inner voice to Ariana.

But I . . . I . . . this is an opportunity I've dreamed of, argued Ariana silently. *If I . . . yet . . .*

Ariana cast another quick glance at the flushed Willis, then gave Bernard the benefit of a full smile.

"I appreciate your kind offer, Mr. Dikerson," she said as sweetly as she could, "and under other circumstances I would be honored to accept. But Mr. Boyd had already asked to escort me home. Perhaps another Sunday."

Ariana smiled again and moved to take the limp arm of Willis Boyd. He flushed again, this time with pleasure.

O Lord, breathed Ariana as she walked away with her head held up in spite of her desire to lower it and cry, *Bernard likely will never speak to me again after this. . . .*

Trust . . . trust, came the silent words. *Trust in the Lord with all thine heart and lean not unto thine own understanding. . . .*

Ariana's head lifted higher. She swallowed back tears of disappointment and turned to the eager young man beside her.

"Have you had a good fall, Willis?" she inquired sociably, but she honestly found it hard to concentrate on his reply.

❧   ❧   ❧

Ariana and her students worked hard to prepare for the school Christmas program. It was a great success, and even some townspeople without any children in the school came and enjoyed the singing and recitations. The following week Ariana was heavily involved in another program held in the little church. She was relieved when both events were over. Now she would be able to relax and focus wholly on her family's celebration of Christmas.

That evening she was turning from the church door, supposing that all had gone on home except her father, who still lingered to care for last-minute cleanup, when a voice spoke softly from the shadows. "Would now be a convenient time for me to ask to accompany you home, Miss Benson?"

Bernard Dikerson stepped into the light of the winter's moon and looked up to where she stood on the step. Ariana's breath caught in her throat. Bernard Dikerson had made no further approach since the incident a full two months earlier.

Ariana swallowed and nodded her head slowly. Then fearing that he could not see her nonverbal agreement, she forced the words through trembling lips. "Yes . . . yes, I guess so."

"Splendid," he said with enthusiasm, and moved forward to offer his arm.

Still tongue-tied, Ariana stepped down to accept his invitation.

"I do hope you haven't judged my silence as disinterest," he began as they walked together.

"I . . . I really . . ." Ariana stammered, but she didn't know what to say. She had thought about it—she could not deny it. She had wondered. She had felt disappointment. How could she respond without admitting more than she wished to?

"I know how busy you've been with the two Christmas programs—which both were delightful, if I might express my humble opinion," Bernard said. He chuckled softly.

Ariana smiled to herself. Somehow she couldn't imagine him having a humble opinion—about any subject. But he did sound genuinely interested in spite of the formal words.

"So I thought I should try to be patient. But I have been watching you—with admiration."

Ariana tilted her head slightly so she might catch a glimpse of his face. He did sound sincere. It made the breath catch in her throat.

"Now that your busyness is over—I do hope you will have some time for . . . for . . . some pleasantness. Work with no play can—"

"Oh, but I love teaching," Ariana interrupted.

She felt his hand move to press her fingers that rested on

his arm. "Of that I am convinced," he said, smiling down at her easily. "But perhaps it is time for you to discover a . . . a few other loves."

Ariana was puzzled and had no idea what he might mean by such a remark.

They reached the walk leading to the door of the parsonage. He stopped and Ariana was forced to pause beside him since he still held her hand firmly.

"Will you—would you like to come in?" she asked, though she felt uncertain about her offer.

"Not tonight. It's late—and you must be very tired. But I will be in touch. Soon."

He emphasized the last word. Ariana's breath caught in her throat again. He released her hand and tipped his hat.

"Good-night, Miss Benson," he said, very properly.

"Good-night . . . Mr. Dikerson," replied Ariana.

As she mounted the steps of the front porch, she felt the whole world spinning at a delightful pace.

❦ ❦ ❦

"When?" asked Sam as he sat with his boss at the wooden table.

"Next big snowstorm," came the gruff reply.

"Storm? You outta yer mind? Ain't a body in his right mind thet'd ride out in a snowstorm. Ya know what storms can be like in these parts."

"I do. An' thet's why we're choosin' one. No way we're gonna be tracked nowhere in a snowstorm."

"Well, thet all depends. A light snow an' they can track ya right on in here like ya laid it out fer 'em."

"We won't pick a light snow."

"An' how ya gonna know 'head o' time whether it's gonna be heavy or light?" snorted Sam. But he knew it was almost uncanny how the boss could read storms.

"I kin tell."

Sam snorted again. "Sounds risky to me. Body can freeze to death in them storms."

"We've been in storms before and we ain't freezed yet."

"What ya mean, we? I ain't goin' out in no winter storm, I tell ya. Not me. Not fer—nobody."

The flickering light from the open fire cast eerie shadows across the dark face of the bigger man, making the scowl more pronounced, the dark eyes more menacing. "If I say ya ride—ya ride," he growled. "Nobody made you boss—yet."

Curses followed as each man expressed his anger in dark words.

"Who's goin'?" Sam finally asked, conceding the fact that he would ride if the boss said ride.

"Jest you and me."

"Jest. . . . Thet's plumb foolhardy. Two ain't enough to even—we'll die in the storm fer sure. Not to mention the girl. She'll never make it—an' she'll keep us from makin' it, too."

"Quit yer squawkin'," the big man barked. "You ain't gonna die before yer time. Iffen yer number's up—then it's up."

"But I sure don't plan on helpin' it out in a snowstorm," Sam argued once more.

"Better than a shot in the back."

"Maybe not. Least a shot in the back would be faster."

Sam moved to throw another log on the fire, sending sparks flying up the smokey chimney.

"Next storm," Will repeated. "You be ready to ride tomorrow. We're gonna move in closer and take thet ole trapper's cabin down by the river. We'll work out from there."

"Thet's Injun country," interjected Sam.

Will placed his whiskey bottle on the table while he spit and swore at the mention of the tribe that made their home in the valley. Then he took another long draught of the fiery liquid.

"Be ready to ride tomorrow," he barked. "I got it all worked out. Yer sure about the girl?"

Sam nodded. "She'll be there," he answered slowly.

Will lifted the whiskey bottle to his lips again. But when he discovered it was already empty, he flung the bottle angrily into the corner, scattering shards of broken glass about the cabin.

Chapter Four

The Snowstorm

Will turned to his son. "Not certain jest when we'll be back," the big man said to the tall young man before him.

Laramie made sure his face betrayed no emotion, but he was not pleased with the fact that his father and Sam were riding off with a winter storm imminent.

"Any orders?" he asked quietly. He would not openly question his father's decision, even though he felt it was downright foolhardy. He had a strong feeling Sam agreed with that assessment, though the man had not expressed such to him. Still, Sam stomped and cursed and looked particularly menacing as he saddled his own mount. The packs had been tied securely on the backs of the two other animals.

"No orders," said Will curtly. "You know the ropes."

The young man nodded. This was his father's way of saying that he was in charge.

His eyes turned back to the waiting horses. His father's horse pawed at the ground and blew, his nostrils flaring. He too seemed reluctant to leave the shelter of the buildings but was impatient to be off if a trip had to be made. Sam's horse stood head down, eyes nearly closed against the cold wind. He was getting old, but Sam refused to give him up in place of a younger mount.

The two pack animals crowded in against each other as

though seeking warmth. The young man's eyes narrowed slightly as he studied the two animals. Why two? The packs weren't that cumbersome. One horse could have easily carried the load. And there was something very odd about the one. A blanket covered the entire pack—as if something was being concealed. But hidden from whom? He was puzzled, but he knew better than to ask.

"Ya sure this rope is—" he began nonchalantly and stepped forward to check the rope that reached across the pack. He let his hand run over the contents beneath the blanket. Again his face gave nothing away, but he had discovered the mystery of the blanket. There was a saddle underneath it, camouflaged by small packs that rested on it. And it sure wasn't a pack saddle. It was a riding saddle. Why did his father need a third horse for a rider?

He stepped back and nodded to Sam, his way of casually acknowledging that the rope was secure. Sam cursed softly.

"Ya think I'm fergittin' how to pack a horse?" he grumbled.

The young man did not answer. He knew that none was expected. The rule of the gang was to keep quiet unless talk was required. He had already broken one of the rules. He had questioned a superior. Anyone but Sam would have been more than upset by the interference.

There were no goodbyes. No calls of "Safe trip," or "Be seein' you." The two men mounted their horses in silence; each picked up a lead for a pack horse and moved out onto the trail that wound away from the crude buildings. The few men left behind did not stand and watch them go or even wave a hand to send them on their way. They turned back to whatever their own activities had been, which in most cases was simply to be in where the fire would warm the frigid air.

"Skidder—best git up there and spell off Rawley," said the young man as they entered the cabin.

"He ain't been up there any four hours," protested the man called Skidder.

Laramie stopped. He looked straight into the eyes of the

man a few feet across the cabin. Something changed about the young man's stance. Not that his face—or even his body—gave much away, except that he was ready. Ready for whatever he might face.

They both knew there was some bad blood between them. The entire gang knew it. Had always felt it, though no one was quite sure what had started it. Now the whole cabin tensed.

"I don't think I asked how long he's been out there," Laramie said, and his words were coolly controlled. "I jest said thet it's time he was relieved."

He stopped and his eyes sent their own message. The others in the cabin shifted slightly. The young man appeared loose and easy—yet coiled like a snake about to strike. Everyone knew that the few words of question from Skidder had challenged the younger man's right of leadership.

Laramie spoke again, suggesting that he was not anxious to start a row—but he was in charge. "It's cold out there. We'll take shorter shifts," he said in explanation. He hesitated, and then drawled slowly, but with meaning, "Unless, of course, yer anxious to have yerself one extry long shift."

Skidder shuffled nervously but seemed to feel some relief. Had it been Will he had questioned, his dead body likely would have been cooling off out behind some barn by now. Will, as boss, had never been known to give a gang member a second chance. And Will never stopped to explain an order. "Only one boss in this here outfit," he said coldly to any new member that might be taken in. "An' you ain't it." The meaning was always clearly understood.

Skidder, who had been around gunmen for most of his life, had already figured out that the Kid, as all the camp called Laramie, would not shoot to kill. Still, he had no desire to have his shooting arm all messed up.

Without another look toward Laramie, Skidder reached for his heavy mackinaw and his rifle. The room stirred again. It seemed that bloodshed had been avoided. Shadow pulled out a deck of cards, and James pulled a log stool up to the table to let the man know that he wanted to be dealt in.

Laramie moved toward the fire and reached for another piece of wood. This one was over—but he'd have to watch his back even more closely in the future.

❧   ❧   ❧

In another cabin some distance away, Sam threw another log on the fire and shivered visibly in spite of sparks that shot upward.

"This here cabin's got enough cracks to run a bear through," he grumbled.

Will paid no attention to his complaining. He sat with a bottle of whiskey at his elbow and every now and then stopped to take a long, bored draught of the liquor.

"Fella gotta wear his hat to keep his ears from freezin'," Sam went on. He rubbed his hands together to keep the circulation going.

"Why don't ya sit down and quit yer grousin'?" Will said sourly.

"Gotta go git us some more firewood, thet's why," Sam threw back at him. "How many days we gotta keep this fire goin' anyway?"

" 'Til it storms."

"An' when ya bringin' in this here storm of yers?" Sam's sarcasm was more felt than heard.

Will scowled and shifted. Sam wondered if he had pushed too far and was relieved when Will's right hand reached for the whiskey bottle. The man couldn't hold a bottle and a gun in the same hand.

"Soon now," he answered, almost civil. "I can feel it. It'll be soon."

Sam said no more but picked up the hatchet and went out to look for more firewood.

❧   ❧   ❧

Ariana sighed and stacked the day's marked assignments into a neat little pile on the corner of her desk. She was glad to have the grading completed so she could get home. The sky had darkened and the temperature had dropped. Even though she had recently added more wood to the potbellied cast-iron stove, it was unable to keep the room warm. Her feet cold, she stomped them on the floor once more as she sat at her desk.

She had some assignments to get ready for the next day and a Scripture passage to choose for the morning reading, and then she could bank the fire and be off home. She pulled her sweater a bit closer about her body.

The heavy door creaked open and Ariana raised her head. Along with a few flakes of snow, two men in long, heavy buffalo coats and black hats pulled down over bearded faces stepped through the opening. Ariana knew she had not seen them before.

"Hello," she said pleasantly, thinking them to have lost their way. "Can I help you?"

There was no answer. The two men moved farther into the room. Ariana could sense that their dark eyes were sweeping quickly over the interior, taking in everything they saw. Something about them made her feel very uncomfortable. She stood.

"Can I help you?" she repeated. "If you are looking for the town—"

The smaller man looked longingly at the iron stove. Ariana saw one hand reach out toward it, as though to take full benefit of its heat if only for a moment.

"Please, feel free to warm yourselves before you go on," offered Ariana. In spite of herself, she felt a tremble of fear pass through her.

"Reckon we won't take time fer warmin'," said the bigger man gruffly. "Got some ridin' to do. Now iffen you'd jest git yer coat, miss—we'd welcome ya to join us."

Ariana stared in unbelief.

"What—?"

"Git yer coat, miss." The order was growled more loudly from the gravelly voice. Ariana froze to the spot.

"I think ya better do as told, miss," advised the smaller man. "It'll be easier on ya iffen ya co-operate."

"But I . . . I can't go with you. My family is expecting me—"

"Then yer family will jest have to wait a spell," said the big man. Ariana saw the end of a pistol peeking out from the furry sleeve of his heavy coat.

"But I—"

Ariana stiffened and pulled herself to her full height. She took a deep breath and told herself to hold steady. Not to panic. But at the same moment her whole body trembled. She was afraid she was going to faint.

She closed her eyes and grasped her desk with both hands. *Trust in the Lord*, she managed inwardly. That was as far as she got with her prayer.

"Git yer coat," barked the big man again. "An' I'd advise thet ya git any other wraps thet might keep out the weather. We got us some tough trails ahead."

"If you think I have any intention of riding off—" began Ariana, finding courage she did not know she possessed.

Her words were interrupted by a hoarse laugh. The big man turned to the smaller one. "Ya got us one with spunk, Sam." He laughed again. "I like thet. Should work in our favor—later." Then his eyes turned cruel again. "But not now. Now—ya git yer coat."

Ariana lifted her chin and tried to still its trembling. "I will go nowhere with you," she managed.

The big man reached out a hand that closed firmly on Ariana's wrist, making her wince with the pain. Roughly he jerked her toward the hook where her coat hung. She struggled against his iron grip, writhing this way and that in an effort to free herself. The grip on her wrist tightened, sending spasms of pain shooting up her arm.

With one last mighty effort, Ariana spun around and raked her fingernails down the face of her opponent. She saw the prickles of blood appear on the broken skin before he wrested her to the floor.

Dark curses filled the air. "Sam, gimme the rope," he shouted.

The other man stepped forward, an ugly frayed rope dangling from his hand. For a moment he stood looking down at her, chewing on his stained mustache. Ariana was fighting against tears. Her wrist felt as if it had been broken.

"We be needin' this, miss—or are ya gonna be reasonable?" asked the man named Sam.

Ariana nodded mutely. The big man pulled her roughly to her feet. "Then git yer coat—and I ain't sayin' it agin," he growled.

Ariana had no choice but to obey.

"Take everything thet ya be needin', miss," said the smaller man. "Ya won't be back fer a while."

Ariana felt there might be just a trace of sympathy in his voice. Instinct told her to respond quietly to his orders. Perhaps, if she did not resist, in time she would have an ally.

She quickly moved to get her coat, her eyes darting over the room to see just what she might take with her that could be of use in the uncertain future. With her wrist throbbing painfully, she managed to pull on her heavy coat and do up the buttons. Then she pushed a few items into her cloth carrying bag. She really had very little at the schoolhouse. Just as she was about to move off, she noticed her Bible and quickly slipped it into the bag as well. She had the impression that it might become more important than ever to her.

She felt as though she were in some horrid nightmare. Nothing seemed real. She prayed that it wasn't. That she would soon wake up to her usual life. But the pain in her wrist was a reminder of how real her present circumstance was. She had to do something. Had to protect herself someway. But what could she do?

Her hands trembled and she felt weak and faint. There was no point in screaming—no one was within hearing distance. There was no use trying to fight—she'd never be the winner. And there was no way she could break and run—at least not now.

She was being kidnapped. Cruelly, frighteningly *kid-napped*—by two desperadoes. She knew not why and she knew not where they were taking her, but her whole being trembled at the questions tumbling through her mind. What would they do with her—to her? Would she ever see home again? What would her parents think? Her poor mother! Her pupils? Bernard Dikerson? Her—

No. No, she must stop thinking. It would drive her insane. She had to pray. She had to trust God. She had to.

But it was hard to concentrate on Bible passages as she was roughly pushed out the door and toward waiting horses. It was hard to pray sensibly. It was even hard to think.

"Oh, God," was all she was able to whisper.

She was boosted up on one of the horses and given a blanket to cover her legs and feet.

"Wrap yerself in this. It's bitin' cold," said the smaller man.

Reluctantly Ariana obeyed.

"Ya ride?" snarled the bigger man.

"Some," replied Ariana in a trembling voice.

He nodded as though that was good enough. "Yer gonna ride now," he said in his rough voice, and he grabbed the lead rope attached to her horse and gave a jerk. They were moving out. One man in front of her, one behind.

It was snowing quite heavily now.

※   ※   ※

Mrs. Benson let the curtain fall back into place. Her eyes were dark with worry as she turned back to the kitchen stove, where the evening meal waited. She was troubled. Ariana was never this late. And it was snowing. Fairly hard now. She didn't like it. She moved toward the living room to speak again to her husband. Maybe he should go—

When she reached the door he was already pulling on a

heavy coat. "I think I'll just walk on out and meet her," he said, making the words sound reasonable.

Relieved, she smiled at him. "You'll take the lantern?" she asked simply.

He looked out the window at the falling snow. It was getting darker. He nodded slowly.

"Might be a good idea," he said. "I suppose she's been busy and just lost track of time. Doesn't realize that a storm has moved in so quickly."

Mrs. Benson knew he was trying to reassure her. She also knew he was aware that their Ariana was not one to lose track of time or the weather.

"She might have slipped and twisted her ankle—or something," she responded. "It's awfully—"

"Now, Mother," said her husband gently. "Let's not borrow trouble."

His words could not erase the worry from her face or the pang in her heart.

She quickly lit the lantern and brought it to him. "She might have stopped at the hardware store," she said, trying her own explanation. "She did say she needed another bottle of ink."

"Likely got talking with one of her students—or friends—and has—" He floundered to a stop.

Mrs. Benson could tell he was going to add "lost track of time."

"I'll check there first," he said instead.

She watched him go, anxiety making her body tense. Ariana had never worried them with tardiness before. It just wasn't like her.

Ariana's mother turned back to the kitchen. She would busy herself with finding a way to keep the evening meal palatable.

Chapter Five

Searching

All through the long night and into the next day they traveled. Ariana had lost all sense of direction or any clear knowledge of time. Once they stopped, and the man Sam dismounted and came up to Ariana.

"Best slip off those shoes and put on these," he informed her. Ariana was so cold she couldn't comply. It was the man who pulled the shoes from her feet and slipped on soft-furred moccasins. He tucked her shoes into one of the packs on the extra animal. Then he handed Ariana some heavy fur mittens. "Put these on," he ordered, and Ariana managed to obey.

At least they were protecting her—in some ways. But why? Why was she taken? What was their reason for picking up a simple schoolteacher? They must have confused her with someone else. Surely there would be no demand for ransom. Her father was simply a village parson—not a wealthy man. He had no money to pay for her release. But if a ransom was not the motive, then why was she taken?

The very question made Ariana's blood run cold. Was she to experience a fate worse than death?

"Oh, God—please not that," she breathed into the cold night air.

It was again dark when Ariana saw the dim outlines of a

cabin. She was helped to dismount by the man named Sam and led—almost carried—into the cold interior—no better than the outside as far as temperature went.

Sam busied himself with starting a fire and nodded his head toward the flame as he spoke to Ariana.

"Jest don't git too close, too quick. Might faint."

And he left her with the big, surly man while he went out to the horses.

The big man said nothing. He did not even remove his coat or hat. He crossed to a wooden frame in the corner that made some sort of crude sleeping platform.

"Gonna git me some shut-eye," he said, and even those words sounded threatening. "Don't go try nothin' foolish. I've shot more'n one man in my sleep."

Ariana shivered from more than just the cold. She bit her lip to keep from crying and huddled more closely to the fire in spite of Sam's warning.

When Sam returned he made a pot of coffee. Ariana was surprised at how good it smelled. She wondered how her stomach could even respond to it under the circumstances.

When the coffee had boiled he poured her a cup, then rummaged in a pack he had brought in and handed her something. It didn't look good—and it didn't smell good either. Ariana's stomach revolted, even though it ached for something to eat.

"Pemmican," the man informed her. "Boss ain't got much use for Injun ways—'ceptin' pemmican. Lets me make it the way I learned from—" He stopped, then shoved something else into her hand. "Hardtack. Eat it. It's all yer gonna git fer a while, an' yer gonna need yer strength."

Ariana cast a glance toward the corner. She could hear snoring coming from the big man. She took a tentative bite of the hardtack. It was tasteless and hard chewing, but it wasn't too bad. She took another and washed it down with the coffee.

She glanced toward the big man. Dared she—dared she ask Sam questions?

"I . . . I don't understand . . . what this is all about," she ventured in a quiet voice. "There must be some mistake. I . . . I'm not who you think I am."

Sam chewed off a big bite of the pemmican and spent some time trying to get his teeth to work up the piece before he even attempted a response.

"An' who do we think ya are?"

"I . . . I've no idea. I . . . I'm just a schoolteacher," she stumbled on.

"Got nothin' agin' schoolteachers," said the man, taking a swallow of the hot coffee to wash down the pemmican.

"But why—?"

"Now, miss—don't ya go frettin' yerself over it none."

He took another bite of the pemmican.

"Don't fret myself!" exclaimed Ariana, raising both her position and her voice.

Sam cast a quick glance toward the corner, reminding Ariana that she'd best watch her step.

She shrank back into her crouched position before the fire. In spite of her strong resolve, tears began to fill her eyes and trickle down her still-cold cheeks. She brushed them away with a trembling hand. Sam continued to eat his pemmican.

Ariana said nothing more. It was Sam who first broke the silence. He had finished munching on his trail provisions. He had even finished his third cup of coffee. Now he pulled the back of his hand across his unkempt mustache and sniffed.

"How's yer wrist?" he asked, as though it was an ordinary question.

Ariana's eyes showed her surprise, but she said nothing.

"Let's see it," he suggested.

She hesitated for one moment, and then held it out obediently.

He took the wrist in his two hands and ran his thumbs and fingers over the area, bending it forward, then back, nearly making Ariana cry out. He pushed it to one side, then the other, his fingers feeling each bone and muscle as he moved it. Ariana fought the tears.

"Don't think nothin's broke," he said at last, "but it's gonna pain fer a while."

There was no apology. No offer to give any assistance with the pain. He released her hand and went back for another cup of coffee.

As he poured out the thick, steamy liquid he spoke again. "Iffen I were you, I'd jest curl up there beside the fire and try to git some sleep. Once daylight comes I 'spect we'll be movin' on out—an' we got a mighty tough ride 'head of us."

Ariana nodded. The fire was making her feel drowsy.

"Here," said Sam, "use this," and he tossed his big buffalo-hide coat on the floor at her feet. Ariana reached for it and awkwardly spread it out before the fire.

❧   ❧   ❧

Mrs. Benson opened the door as soon as she heard her husband's steps. Her eyes quickly scanned the darkness, but to her dismay he stood there in the snow alone.

"What—?" she began, but he brushed past her and into the room.

She saw his face then and knew that he was just as concerned as she herself was.

"I . . . I didn't find her," he admitted.

"Did you try the store?"

He nodded. "I went to the store first."

"Did you go to the school?"

"Of course I went to the school." His anxiety made him a bit curt, which was most unusual. His words, spoken in sharpness, brought terror to her heart.

Tears formed in her eyes, and she began to wring her hands in agitation. He stepped forward and pulled her to him. "Now, my dear," he said, and she could tell that he was fighting to put down his own fears. "Let's not jump to any conclusions. I'm sure there's a reason—"

"What reason?" she cut in, her voice full of panic as she

pushed back from him. "What possible—?"

"I don't know yet, but—"

"She has never been late. This is not like her."

"Perhaps one of her students had an emergency."

It was something to grasp at. She prayed he might be right. But even as he spoke the words, her heart began to doubt again.

"But—she would have let us know—someway. She'd know we'd worry."

"Maybe she had no way to let us know. Maybe—there wasn't time," he continued.

"Come on to the table," she said, brushing at the snow on his coat. "I've got your supper." Her voice sounded weary—dead.

He resisted. "No . . . no, I just came to . . . to let you know . . ." His voice trailed off in an evasive manner. "We—I've spoken to the sheriff—some of the townfolks. We . . . we're going to keep looking. We . . . we'll check out the homes of all the students. Make sure—"

"But it's dark. And the storm—"

"We'll all carry lanterns."

Her next protest caught in her throat, between concern for her husband and worry over her daughter. Silently she nodded her head. "Travel in pairs," she said softly. "Are you dressed warmly enough?"

He nodded.

He reached for her again. Her worry had turned to alarm, and now she felt as though her heart were being squeezed. She allowed herself to be drawn up against him, and the tears spilled out and mixed with the melting snow on his shoulder.

She felt him bend his head and kiss her silvery hair.

"We'll find her," he promised, his voice full of emotion.

She lifted her head and fumbled for her pocket hanky. "You should eat," she tried once more through her sniffles.

"Later."

"Travel in pairs," she reminded him again.

He nodded.

"You should have your heavier mittens," she fussed.

He nodded. "Would you get them, please?" he asked her.

She knew he was trying to distract her, but she brought the mittens and watched as he removed the ones he was wearing and replaced them with the heavy pair.

"I'll be praying," she said and lifted her hanky to wipe tears again.

He again held out his arms to her and she quickly took refuge. He was her minister now as well as her husband, and together they bowed their heads while he led them in fervent prayer. Then with one final kiss on her forehead he released her and turned back into the night.

※   ※   ※

The search continued until it was impossible to carry on. Every home that had a student in the local school was called upon. The response was always the same. The children were shocked and bewildered. "She was still there when we left— same as always," came the reply to the question.

Little girls cried and young boys shuffled in agitation. It just wasn't like their teacher—to just disappear. Something awful must have happened.

At last the tired, hungry searchers returned to their homes, chilled by the cold winds and hampered by blowing snow. There simply was no logic in searching on through the darkness.

※   ※   ※

In spite of the continued blowing snow, the next morning the sheriff organized a posse of town citizens to fan out into the surrounding hills and even beyond to the plains. An intense search was made along the creek bank, in the fear that Ariana might have slipped and fallen while crossing the footbridge. No sign of her was found.

Bernard Dikerson asked his father to post reward money for her safe return, and the man responded. As the day wore on and the searchers drifted back with no news, the whole town was stricken.

Nothing—not a trace of the missing girl was found. The doors of the school were closed, and folks of the town huddled in whispering groups, shocked and saddened by the tragic and mysterious disappearance of the beloved schoolteacher.

In the parsonage, the fear and grief filled every room. The Bensons clung to each other. They prayed, they cried, they reminded themselves that they had a sovereign God, then they prayed and cried some more.

"Surely God . . . surely God knows where she is and . . . and can preserve her," insisted Pastor Benson. With her handkerchief clutched in her hand and tears on her cheeks, Mrs. Benson shakily nodded her head in agreement.

🙙 🙙 🙙

Ariana could not tell if it was day or night when she was roused from sleep by the nudge of a well-worn boot. The big man stood over her, staring down into her face.

"Time to ride," he ordered.

Ariana struggled to stand. She moved nearer the fireplace, brushing futilely at her wrinkled skirts. The door opened and Sam came in. He was shivering from the cold and muttering words of profanity.

"Fool weather fer anyone to be out," she heard him grumble.

"Where's yer coat, ya dumb ox?" demanded the big man, no sympathy in his tone.

"Didn't think I'd need it jest to get the horses ready," Sam replied, not looking up from the coffee he was pouring.

Ariana's eyes dropped to her feet. Sam's heavy coat had been her bed for the night. She felt her cheeks warming with the thought that he had chosen to face the bitter cold rather than awaken her. It both embarrassed her and gave her reason to hope. Perhaps the man was not all bad.

"How're the horses?" asked the big man between gulps of coffee.

Sam nodded. "Near froze to death, I'm thinkin'. Anxious to be movin' so's their blood'll flow agin."

"Then let's git movin'," said the big man, and he drained his cup of the last swallow of coffee.

"Girl ain't et yet," remarked Sam.

The big man turned to Ariana and scowled. "Best grab ya a biscuit or two. Won't be stoppin' fer no teatime."

Ariana moved forward. Every bone in her body protested. First the ride through the cold. Then the night on the crude bed on the floor. Her entire being hurt.

She reached for a biscuit, but the pain in her wrist brought a sharp intake of breath. For a moment she felt faint and fought to stay upright.

Sam made a motion as if to move toward her, but then stopped. Neither made comment.

As soon as the room came back into focus, Ariana reached out with her left hand and claimed one of the biscuits lying on the table. She switched it to her right hand so she could accept the cup of coffee Sam held out to her.

The biscuit was hard. The hardest thing Ariana had ever tried to chew. Hesitantly she dipped one edge into her coffee and chewed off the softened portion. It was not pleasant— but at least it was edible.

Ariana did not have to be encouraged to take full advantage of all of the warmth she was offered. She accepted the heavy mittens, the blanket, along with the moth-eaten beaver hat for her head. Even with this, she still shivered against the cold.

She could hardly tell if it was day or night. The snow continued to fall, obliterating the sun—if indeed it was somewhere up above. The swirling whiteness wiped out all landmarks. All sign of the world around them. Ariana wondered if the two men really knew where they were going or were simply wandering on through the storm. She dared not ask any questions.

After what seemed hours and hours of stumbling their way along the hidden trail, the big man pulled up his horse and the other horses stopped in line behind him.

"Snow's deep," he said when Sam pushed up beside him. "Think it might be wise to camp here tonight."

"I was sure hoping to git on home to my own bed," said Sam.

"It's been slow goin'. Don't think we'll make it home tonight. A bit too risky on thet ridge."

Sam nodded. He didn't seem about to argue on that score.

"There's a cave mouth in there somewhere," said the big man, motioning vaguely. "See iffen ya can find it."

Sam moved off cursing. "Jest hope no big bear found it first," Ariana heard him say.

The big man turned to her. "Git on down," he said, not offering her any assistance. Ariana wasn't sure if her legs would hold her, but she moved stiffly to obey.

It was as she had feared. Even though she clung to the horse for support, she could not stand upright. Her legs gave way and she found herself in a heap in the deep snow.

"Women," groused the big man to accompanying curses. "Don't got no more starch in their backbone then a snake."

Ariana quite expected to remain in the snow until she could find the strength to move—unless Sam took mercy on her. But to her surprise the big man reached down and roughly scooped her up. He carried her easily to the side of the trail and deposited her unceremoniously on a tree stump without bothering to brush off its cap of snow.

Ariana sat silently, willing herself to hold her tears at bay. They would only freeze on her frosted cheeks, making her even more miserable than she already was.

Sam returned after some moments and announced he had found the cave—and it was uninhabited.

Sam moved the horses toward it. Ariana managed to get one foot to proceed the other. With great difficulty she followed the trail broken by Sam and the mounts. The big man brought up the rear.

They gathered in the cave. Sam built a fire, and to Ariana's surprise it was warmer than the cabin had been. But soon swirling gray smoke filled the cave and made Ariana's eyes sting. She moved back into the farthest corner, even though she longed to take advantage of the heat that radiated from the beckoning flames. Sam made the coffee, and along with more hardtack and pemmican, they shared the simple supper. Ariana was only too willing to curl up on spruce boughs and Sam's buffalo robe. She was exhausted. Besides, it was only in sleep that she could shut out the horror of her present experience—even if only for a few hours of time.

Chapter Six

Arrival

As they traveled the next day, Ariana grieved as each hour took her farther and farther away from her family and home. She ached for her father and mother. If only she had some way to communicate with them. To let them know she had not been harmed—at least not yet. She worried about her students. What would they do? What would they think of her, failing to show up for classes?

She prayed and worried by turn. Frantic mental searching for ways of escape, followed by clinging to the one word, *trust.* "Surely God knows where I am, even if I don't," she would remind herself, and then turn right back to worrying again.

Stop it, she scolded herself. *I can't trust and worry at the same time—can I?*

It was so difficult to obey her own admonition.

The blinding snow still swirled around her. Her tired pony stumbled on and on. Her bones ached. Her flesh felt numb with cold. She sometimes wondered if she was more dead than alive—but they traveled on through the blank whiteness.

Guessing it to be afternoon, she had a strange sense that more than falling snow obliterated the pathway. She looked around but could make out little of the landscape. At times she knew she was very close to brushing up against something on one side or the other. She caught brief glimpses of solid rock. *Is it some sort of passageway?* she wondered. But she could not see well enough for her question to be answered.

She was slumped in her saddle, eyes half closed, when she felt the steps of her horse quicken. Then she heard a neigh from the big black that the man ahead was riding. Sam's horse pushed at hers from behind.

From the near distance came an answering whinny. Ariana felt a new stirring of the animals and the two men who guided her. Before her eyes buildings began to take shape. She could not see them clearly through the snow, nor could she count them. Was it a town? But no, they all looked poorly kept. Ramshackle. And then she heard the big man say "Whoa" in his loud raspy voice, and the four horses stopped as one.

Ariana did not move. She was aware that someone stood near her. She wondered if she would be lifted down or left to fall off her mount.

"Git her to the south shack. I'll have one of the boys take care of the horses," the big man's voice instructed, and she was moving off again, her horse being led away by Sam.

There was no way she could have made it into the building on her own. Sam half supported, half carried her. Once inside, he helped her to a wooden bunk in the corner.

"I'll git a fire goin'," he announced. "It'll soon be almost livable in here."

Ariana did not respond.

She heard the man moving about the cabin and sensed that the fire had been started. But she didn't care. Didn't care about any of it. She was cold clear through and weary beyond belief. Her swollen wrist did not hurt any more than the rest of her. She closed her eyes and almost immediately fell into a deep sleep.

☙ ☙ ☙

Ariana woke up stiff and sore and in a strange place with no idea how long she had slept.

Her first conscious thought was that the sun was now shining. She could see its faint light through the cracked, dirty window. She breathed a prayer of thanks for the sun. Now someone would be looking for her. Now there was some hope she would be found.

Her next awareness was that she was not alone. She felt a moment of panic and her eyes quickly scanned the room.

Sam sat on his log stool with his back against the cabin wall. He was tilted back so his feet could extend to be propped up on a rough table.

"Mornin'," he said lazily when their gaze met.

Ariana groaned in response. It brought a little chuckle.

"Little stiff?" he asked good-naturedly.

Ariana struggled to get her feet off the bed and under her. Every movement hurt.

"You'll git yer bones shook out—all in good time," Sam commented, cutting himself a chew of tobacco.

Ariana concentrated hard on standing to her feet.

"Brung ya the things ya be needin'," went on Sam, and he dropped his heavy-booted feet to the floor with a clunk.

Ariana looked about her. The room was small. It had a potbellied stove, the rough wood table, two log stools, and the bunk in the corner on which she had slept. Over by the door, a simple shelf held a dented basin and a sickly green, chipped enamel pitcher. On the floor stood a pail with water. A second pail stood near. Sam nodded at it now.

"Yer slops," he explained. "Winder is nailed shut so's ya'll jest have to wait 'til we come to dump 'em."

Ariana noticed her schoolbag on the table. She was comforted to see even that little bit of home.

Sam stood to his feet. "Reckon ya'd like to get washed up. Water's hot in the kettle."

Ariana had missed the kettle that sat near the back of the stove.

"I'll brung ya over some vittles."

Sam shuffled toward the door.

Ariana moved as though to follow. She wanted to call after the unshaven man. She had so many questions. Where were they? Is this where she would stay? For how long? Why? *Why?*

Before she could get her voice to work, he had gone. She heard the thunk of a heavy bar falling into place over the outside of the door. She was locked in.

❧   ❧   ❧

Ariana spent most of the first two days in her captive cabin in tears of fear and frustration. She was locked in. Solidly and securely. She didn't know where she was or why she was there. The most frightening thought was that she didn't know what her captors intended.

There was no way out. She had already pushed with all her might on the door and clawed at the window until the tips of her fingers bled. There was nothing she could do. Nothing but weep and pray.

On the third day, Ariana awakened from a troubled sleep and took a fresh look at her situation. So far, nothing too terrible had happened to her. She was a prisoner, yes, but other than that first encounter with the two men and her damaged wrist, she had not been hurt or mistreated, at least so far. Only Sam had been to the cabin—though she had heard other voices outside and other footsteps on the path. She should thank God for each day of safety. Her father—and the townsfolk—would be looking for her, led by the sheriff and his men. Maybe they were closing in even at the moment. She just had to be patient. Be calm. Trust. Really trust in her heavenly Father. Her fighting and agitation and tears were getting her nowhere. Ariana wiped her eyes and decided that those tears would be her last.

❧   ❧   ❧

"Well, ya got her here—now what?"

Sam spit at the fire and turned back to eye his boss. The big man said nothing. He seemed to be thinking.

At last he stirred and turned to Sam. "So far—plan's worked jest fine," he said with satisfaction. "Ya picked a good one. Pretty an'—well, she oughta race the blood of any man. Even one as cool and calculating as the Kid."

He stopped and laughed, not a pleasant sound. Sam shifted nervously on his wooden block.

"The storm did jest what we wanted it to," went on Will Russell, then stopped to curse and spit on the floor. "Not even an Injun could track us through all thet."

Sam shivered at the thought of the storm. There had been more than once when he'd thought they would all end up frozen in the saddle.

"So now—" prompted Sam.

The big man scowled. "What ya frettin' on now?" he growled.

"Ain't frettin'," responded Sam, unruffled. "Jest wonderin' how long I'm gonna be playin' nursemaid to the little schoolmarm."

Will stomped across the room and looked out the window at the sunny day. The snow lay in shimmering drifts across the floor of the canyon. The buildings all wore big fluffy caps of winter snow, and the trees bowed down with the weight of the whiteness. It was a pretty world.

But Sam could tell his thoughts were on other things. "'Bout time to have us a meetin'," Will said, and he grinned an ugly grin that showed his stained teeth and highlighted the jagged scar crossing his cheek.

He turned back to Sam. "Tell the fellas we want to have them all in here followin' supper. Who's on guard duty?"

Sam thought for a moment. "Right now—James. Then Curly. First night shift—McDuff."

"Good," said the big man. "I wanna be sure that Skidder is here fer this meetin'. And the Kid. Make sure the Kid's here."

❧   ❧   ❧

Will Russell began as usual, spitting on the floor, then clearing his throat. His son watched as the big man's eyes scanned the group of rough and rugged men, a motley crew, to be sure.

"Ya all know thet we got us a guest," was his opening statement. He paused. There was no response.

"Now this here guest is—special. I can't give ya none of the particulars—jest want to say thet the keepin' is important. Thet's all thet's necessary to say. Iffen anything should happen to—our guest—thet is anything thet would lend itself to—leavin'—well, I wouldn't take a bit kindly to thet."

He paused again and his eyes swept the room, stopping to bear down on each of the occupants in personal challenge.

"Ya git my meanin'?" he growled.

No one moved. Laramie knew that each man understood. The prisoner was not to escape.

"Thet means thet we gotta have extry guard duty."

He let the words hang heavy in the air, and then turned slightly to look at his son. Laramie forced himself not to flinch.

"Kid," he said, "thet's you."

The young man's face purposely showed no change of emotion. He did not even nod. There was no need to agree to the assignment. It was understood that he would.

"From now on, yer off the usual sentry duty. Yer full duty will be to guard thet cabin."

The father looked at the son. Their eyes locked for a moment. The Kid had never been shown favoritism by the big man. He expected none now. Yet it didn't seem fair that he was to be given the sole responsibility for guarding the man in the south shack. Who did his father have in there, anyway? Some bank president? A wealthy rancher? Some politician? Or was it an Indian chief? And what was the game? Some huge ransom? Laramie didn't like it. Didn't like it at all. He had sensed—had known—that something strange was going on. He just hoped the whole camp didn't live to regret it. If they lived at all.

"Like I said," continued his father, his dark beard and dark eyes making his scowling face appear even more menacing, "I won't be happy iffen anything should happen—no matter who allows it."

The meaning was clear to Laramie. He was guarding the prisoner at the risk of his own life.

❧   ❧   ❧

"Please," said Ariana as Sam opened the door a crack and handed her in a plate of unsavory food. "Please—can't . . . can't you wait a minute? I really need to . . . to talk."

Sam looked about the camp. No one was in sight. Uneasily he shifted his weight from one foot to the other. Then he pushed the door open farther and slipped into the room.

"I . . . I . . ." Ariana looked down at her rumpled garments. "I really do need to . . . to freshen up," she ventured. "I've been in these same clothes for . . . days." She had not counted the days. She truly had lost track of time.

For a moment Sam looked sympathetic, then he shrugged thin shoulders. "Missy," he said, "iffen ya didn't notice, there ain't 'xactly a ladies' shop nearby."

"But surely . . . surely there is some way for me to . . . to bathe. To wash my . . . my hair and my . . . garments," protested Ariana. "I . . . I'm filthy."

The man shrugged again. "I'll see what I can do," he promised as he turned to go, but he quickly added, "But don't ya go expectin' much. I've no notion where we gonna find any—bathtub."

"Thank you," breathed Ariana as he left.

She had been living one day at a time since arriving. She spent most of her hours reading her cherished Bible. It was the only way she could survive the uncertainty and tedium. Then Sam came. Only to bring her a supply of wood and fresh water. He emptied her slop pail and brought her a plate of food. Other than Sam, she saw no one.

Her one window faced away from the camp into the woods. There was a small window on the camp side—but it had been covered over on the outside, so Ariana still had no idea where she was. She prayed for release. She thanked the Lord for daily safety. But she felt as though something needed to happen—soon—or she would lose her sanity. How long had it been? Six days? A week? More? She wasn't sure. But each day seemed like an eternity.

She was pushing the food around on the plate—the fork had a broken tine—when she heard someone at the door again. It was Sam who poked in his head.

"You found one," she exclaimed, jumping to her feet.

He waved her words aside.

"Ain't even had time to look," he quickly informed her. "Jest thought of somethin' else."

Ariana sat back down.

Sam entered the room again and his voice lowered as though he feared someone might overhear their conversation.

"Jest thought ya oughta know," he said in a raspy whisper, "things have changed. I won't be comin' anymore. Boss has assigned—"

Terror gripped Ariana, and she stood shakily to her feet and reached out her hand to him.

"Please. Please," she pleaded. "Please don't let him change. I . . . I don't want anyone—"

"Now calm down some," Sam said with a measure of irritation. "It won't be all thet bad. The Kid will be takin' care of ya. Ya jest . . . jest mind yer manners an'—"

"Who's . . . the Kid?" asked Ariana, her eyes wide with fright.

"Aw, he ain't so bad. It's the boss's son."

Ariana's mind filled with an image of the man Sam called the Boss. She hadn't seen him well. There had always been the storm—or the darkness of the cabin or cave, lit only by the light from the open fire. But she knew enough to fear him. To feel terror at the very thought of his nearness. Unconsciously she reached her left hand to rub her right wrist. Though it was improving, Ariana well remembered the searing pain. Sam's boss was some kind of madman. And now— she was to be guarded by *his* son. Her whole body began to tremble.

Sam turned back to the door. "Jest thought ya oughta know," he said as he exited the room and pulled the door shut behind him. Ariana heard the bar fall into place.

❧   ❧   ❧

There was little sleep for Ariana that night. She forgot about her unkempt hair. Her rumpled clothes. She even forgot to throw more fuel into the heavy iron stove. Hour after hour she lay shivering in the darkness. Shivering with terror.

She tried to pray. Tried to trust, but every time she shut her eyes she saw the dark, brooding face of the man they called the Boss. What was to happen to her now? Ariana found herself wishing she had perished in the storm.

❧   ❧   ❧

Ariana stirred from her sleep to thumping on her door. Sam must be bringing her breakfast. But then she became fully conscious and remembered Sam had said he would not be coming anymore. That she would now be cared for by the boss's son.

Ariana frantically cast her eyes about the room, looking for a place to hide. Even as she acknowledged that there was none, the door pushed open.

A tall young man ducked his head to enter. She saw his hand on his pistol as his eyes swept the room quickly. When they lit on her, he froze. She saw the confused, shocked expression that momentarily transformed his face.

Chapter Seven

The Dilemma

He stood where he was, staring at her. The food in his left hand threatened to spill from the forgotten, tilting plate. His eyes quickly scanned the room again as though he must have missed something, then came back to her.

She stared back with eyes wide and frightened. She clasped the tattered blanket in both hands, holding it up against her like a protective shield. Her breath caught in her throat in a little gasp.

The sound seemed to jerk him back to reality. The gun hand lifted to push his Stetson up a little on his head. From the way his hand moved, she guessed it to be a nervous gesture on his part. Yet he looked so calm. So composed. She still had not risen to her feet but sat on the edge of the crude bunk, as though poised for flight.

He nodded silently and moved into the room.

Without a word he set the plate of food on the table. His eyes moved over the room once more. She could see a steeliness in his face and instinctively knew she would never wish to challenge this young man. She noticed the hard set of his jaw—as though something had deeply disturbed him. He looked almost angry—yet what had she done?

He cast a glance toward her iron stove and without a word proceeded to build a fire. Then he picked up her water pail, filled the kettle and set it on the stove, then poured the remainder of the water into the empty basin.

He still had not spoken, and Ariana had not moved toward the plate of food. He did not look her way again, but left, the water pail in his hand.

Ariana heard the thunk of the wooden bar across her door. She heard the steps crunching on the new snow of the path. And then he was gone—as quickly and as silently as he had come.

Ariana shivered anew. She felt all trembly inside, further frightened—but she knew not why.

Whoever had entered her cabin had not looked *vicious*. He had not looked at all like the man Sam called the Boss. While that man was dark and heavyset, this man was tall and lithe. He was much fairer, too. His eyes were blue rather than almost black.

But the memory of those piercing blue eyes made her shiver again. She longed for the return of Sam. It was frightening enough to be held captive, but to have to face a new guard. . . .

Ariana shook her shoulders slightly and wrapped her arms close to try to hold at bay the fear that had overtaken her being. This new guard had brought food. She must eat if she were to keep up her strength. Surely the day would come when she would find some way to escape from her prison. She must be ready.

In spite of her fear and her lack of interest in the bland plate of food, her stomach growled. She forced herself to her feet and moved toward the shelf with its basin.

She splashed the fresh water over her face and washed her hands as best as she could. Without soap, she always felt she hadn't really washed—simply rinsed. Still it felt refreshing, if nothing else.

She dumped the used water into the pail beside her feet. It was full.

He hadn't emptied the slop pail.

❧　　❧　　❧

Laramie had never felt so disturbed in all his life. First of all, the secrecy of his father's plans and mission had bothered him. Then the strict orders on the importance of guarding the prisoner, leading the whole camp to believe they had some—some armed desperado or high-ranking official in the south cabin. And now this. A girl. A mere girl. A girl did not belong in a camp of men. Any camp of men. And certainly not in their camp of men. He shook with anger. He had never questioned his father before—but he was going to demand some answers now.

He had to calm himself. He was in no condition for either a confrontation with his father or another visit with the prisoner. He took the path through the woods to the spring where they got their water, glad for the pail in his hand that gave him a good excuse.

Not calmed down by the time he reached his destination, Laramie stared at the spring. The small pool had frozen over again during the night, and he picked up the axe, relieved to be able to expend some of his anger in strenuous activity.

He made a hole large enough to dip in the pail and still kept chopping. The silver slivers of ice flew with each swing of the axe, sprinkling the new blanket of snow that lay on the surface.

Why had his father done it? Why? What was behind this fool scheme? Surely this bit of a girl was worth nothing to the gang. Or was she? Was she some wealthy rancher's daughter? Was there a large ransom on her head? If so, he hoped that it quickly would be paid so she could be returned to wherever she belonged.

He knew nothing of women, but he didn't like the thought of one in the camp. Instinctively he knew that this eventually would mean trouble.

He finally laid aside the axe and dipped the pail. But he was not prepared to see her again. Not yet. He was still shaking from the last encounter. She was so young. So—so delicate. And her hair hung about her shoulders like—

He shivered and pushed away the memory. He didn't want to even think about it. He emptied the pail back into the pool and hung it on a tree limb. He'd care for his horses first. Maybe by then he'd have himself back under control.

❧   ❧   ❧

"I'd like to talk."

Laramie stood before his father in the main cabin that the gang shared during the daylight hours. All the men were there except for Shadow, who was taking the morning watch. Seven pairs of eyes lifted at the simple words. There was something different in the voice.

"Alone," he added.

Will Russell did not look up from his game of solitaire, simply nodded. The men, without question or further orders, began to rise from wherever they sat and leave whatever they were doing, to file from the room, grabbing needed wraps from the pegs by the door.

At another nod from his boss, Sam took his log seat again. Laramie made no objection.

A few of the men dared to curse under their breath as they went. The day was not warm even though it was sunny, and some had been in the middle of a game of cards. McDuff was grumbling along with the curses. "Jest when I had me a good hand," Laramie heard him mutter. They could not take the game along with them like Curly was doing with his whiskey bottle.

The door closed and the room became silent. Will Russell continued his game. Sam shuffled uneasily, then pulled his plug of tobacco from his shirt pocket and began to cut off a large chew.

"What's on yer mind?" Will growled, still not lifting his eyes.

Laramie took a deep breath to control his emotions—his voice.

"I've got a feelin' thet ya know," he responded.

They had never played games with each other. The father looked up now and met the steely eyes of his son.

"The girl?" he asked simply.

Laramie nodded.

Silence hung heavy in the room. Will played a few cards.

"What's she doin' here?" asked Laramie, his voice controlled and hard.

Will looked up quickly. "You questionin' me, boy?" asked the man, his black eyes growing darker.

Sam shifted on his log seat again.

"Jest askin' fer a little information—man to man," Laramie replied coolly.

The father appeared to calm himself. He returned to his cards, laying a ten of diamonds on a jack of spades.

"Pa?" Laramie prompted.

Will shoved back from his card game and looked up at the tall young man. He nodded toward another log section that stood upright near the table, and Laramie knew he was to take a seat. Obediently he pulled the log forward and straddled it.

"We gotta git us some more chairs," growled the big man.

"The girl," reminded Laramie.

"Pretty little thing, ain't she?" said the father, and Laramie felt his cheeks grow hot. It was a new experience for him to flush with anger. His father misunderstood the reddened cheeks and haw-hawed heartily, slapping Laramie on the back and making ogling eyes at Sam.

Laramie's flush deepened. So this was how it would be with a girl in camp.

He fought for calm. He had to remain cool and levelheaded.

"She's pretty," he agreed so as to distract his father, but he tried hard not to think of the head of tumbling curls, the frightened eyes.

"How long she gonna be here?" asked Laramie.

Will looked up and exchanged glances with Sam. "Well,

now," he drawled in his raspy voice. "That there depends."

"What's she here for?" asked Laramie.

"Boy—you sure are full of questions, now ain't ya?" said the big man. He was beginning to sound irritated. Laramie knew better than to make his father angry.

"I jest figure—bein' part of the gang—"

"I don't need to talk things over with the gang," cut in his father.

Laramie paused. He was inclined to rise and walk out the door. His father was not being at all cooperative.

Yet he needed some answers. He took a deep breath to steady his nerves and decided on another approach.

"Well—bein' yer son—"

He had never done that before—never inferred that he should be treated differently from any other gang member simply because he was the boss's son.

His father did not take kindly to the words now. His dark eyes lifted, and a scowl deepened the creases on his cheeks above the line of his dark beard. "An' I say," he thundered, his fist coming down on the table and making his cards dance, "when the time comes fer you to be given privileges, it'll be because I give 'em to ya. Ya hear?"

"Yes sir," answered Laramie, and he touched his hat in unconscious subservience.

"Now git out there an' follow yer orders," barked the big man.

Laramie nodded and left the room, more troubled than ever.

᯽   ᯽   ᯽

"Ya really think this is gonna work?" asked Sam as he poured them both a cup of strong coffee after the boss had calmed down some.

The big man looked up and his eyes began to twinkle. "'Course it's gonna work," he growled pleasantly. "He's riled up already."

✿   ✿   ✿

It was midmorning before Laramie felt in control enough to take the fresh pail of water to the south cabin. He deliberately made plenty of noise with the bar on the door to give her lots of warning that he was coming.

She was at the table, sitting on the log stool that had been provided. An open book was spread out before her, and she nervously looked up from it as he pushed open the door.

Her hair was no longer spilling about her shoulders but had been pinned up behind her head. It made her face look even smaller, her eyes larger. They were dark blue and as open as her book. She looked both scared and confused. Laramie looked away quickly, feeling that he was looking into her very soul and thus invading her privacy.

"Brung yer water," he said for something to break the silence, even though he knew it was quite evident what he had brought.

The plate was on the table. Some of the food had been eaten—but not as much as should have been. He supposed that, under the circumstances, she found it hard to have much of an appetite.

He checked the fire but found that she had recently added wood. At least she could take care of herself, he thought.

He wanted to check to see if she had other needs, but he knew he had to get out of there quickly. He was most self-conscious in her presence. She sat there watching him, saying nothing—just looking alone and scared and out of place.

He was at the door before she spoke. Her voice was low and soft—and trembly.

"The slop pail," she reminded him.

He stopped in his tracks and looked at her. Her voice had surprised him. He was used to male voices that were little more than dark growls.

"The slop pail is almost full," she explained. "It is all I have for—"

She stopped and looked down in embarrassment. Her

cheeks flushed. "For . . . everything," she finished softly.

He nodded and lifted the pail.

His anger flamed again as he carried the pail down the path to the edge of the bush and dumped it. "What a way for sech a little bit of a thing to live," he exploded. "It's jest plumb crazy."

🌱   🌱   🌱

He had to renew her wood supply. He was glad for the chore—it gave him reason to swing the axe in his frustration. He cut far more than he needed. By the time he was done he was sweating in spite of the cold winter day. He put down the axe and pulled his sleeve across his brow, knocking his Stetson into the snow. He had forgotten it was up there. With soft curses he reached down and retrieved his hat, whipping it against his knee to shake off the snow.

He still hadn't figured anything out. He had gotten no answers from his father. Nor was he likely to. He didn't know why she was there or how long she was expected to stay. He only knew that they had a girl in camp and that he was expected to guard her. She was living in deplorable conditions. Even a man would hate the bareness, the crudeness of the cabin, the isolation.

Then an unfamiliar idea crossed his mind and caused him to flush slightly. Was that why he was riled? If it had been a man in there, he wouldn't have given him a thought—except to watch him carefully and guard his own back. But a girl. It wasn't a case of just guarding her; he had to somehow—care for her. And he had no idea how to go about it.

🌱   🌱   🌱

Ariana paced back and forth across the squeaky boards of the cabin, trying to sort through her troubled thoughts.

On the one hand she felt terror. On the other hand she dared hope. For what? She wasn't sure. But the young man, though hardly to be considered friendly, had not really been menacing.

But he was the boss's son. He was her prison guard.

He was strangely quiet. Hardly seeming to acknowledge her presence. She had the impression he did not care much for his assignment. Did not want her in the camp any more than she wanted to be there.

Ariana trembled slightly. No, it was not realistic. Sam might have been persuaded to be an ally, to help her—but not this cool, distracted young man with the steely blue eyes.

She shivered again at the very thought of the silent, cold look that he had turned upon her, and a tear trickled down her cheek.

She was helpless and at his mercy. At the mercy of the entire camp of loud, offensive men. She still had no idea why they had taken her, but she prayed as she paced that the awful ordeal might soon end.

Chapter Eight

Guardian

Laramie stacked enough wood against the wall of the cabin to keep the fire stoked for many days—even if the temperature continued to drop. Cautiously he surveyed the room with each trip he made. He noticed that the girl had very little in material comforts.

She had rinsed out the scrap of towel in the basin and hung it to dry by the iron stove. She must have brought a comb with her in that little bit of a cloth bag, for one lay on the shelf by the pitcher. There was no soap, no mirror, no garments, except for the heavy coat hanging on the peg, hat and gloves tucked up beside it. On the floor was a pair of fur moccasins. He was sure they were much too big for the small feet tucked under the table.

Apart from that, the room was bare. Bare and miserably dirty. His own stark quarters were in better shape. At least he could sweep them out and chase down the cobwebs with the broom.

For the rest of the day Laramie watched for an opportunity to speak with Sam alone. He would get no answers from his father—he knew that now—but Sam might be another matter.

He thought of Sam as a reasonable man, and had always been on good terms with him. It was Sam who had taught

Laramie his basic letters and sums. Laramie figured that Sam was likely the only one in camp who could have done so.

No, that wasn't true. Laramie remembered being surprised one time to find Shadow reading fluently. Who knew what other secrets the men of the camp might have? No one ever asked them to share about their past.

But Sam, as his father's right hand, might have some valuable information. If Laramie could just ease it from him.

It was almost sundown before Laramie found himself alone with the little man. They were both in the crude barn, preferring the company of their mounts to the company of the men in the smoke-filled, smelly cabin.

Laramie let his eyes travel around the dark enclosure to be sure they were alone.

"Sam," he began, choosing his words carefully, "ya know I got me this here new duty."

Sam nodded and rubbed the curry comb over his horse's withers.

"Well—I don't rightly know how to take it on," went on Laramie.

He waited. There was no response.

"I don't know nothin' 'bout lookin' after . . . after a woman," he added. "Know far more about carin' fer a horse."

Sam chuckled, then said, straight-faced, "Reckon there's not much difference."

Laramie waited.

"Ya gotta feed 'em an' keep 'em warm and healthy," commented Sam.

Laramie stopped his brushing. "But—it's the healthy part what gets me," he observed in a soft drawl.

"Meanin'?" asked Sam, not missing a stroke.

"Well—fer starters—how long ya think she's gonna be here? Thet might have a heap to do with what she be needin' to stay healthy and all."

It didn't look as though Sam was going to be drawn in. He shook his head to indicate he had no information, or else would give none.

"Well, it seems to me thet she's needin' more'n a basin and a slop pail," argued Laramie.

Sam chewed on his mustache.

"Well—she did ask me fer a tub of some kind," he replied with little concern or emotion.

"A tub?"

"She wanted to bathe—wash her hair an' her clothes, she said. Womenfolk do thet. Right in the dead of winter," Sam noted with some astonishment.

Laramie nodded. He led the brush over the chest of his horse and on down the left front leg.

"Where we gonna git a tub?" he asked.

Sam shrugged. "I've no idee," he answered.

"But thet was what she asked fer—a tub?"

Sam nodded and spit into the straw at his feet.

"Then I guess I'll jest have to ride on out and find us a tub," mused Laramie to himself.

Sam's head came up. "Ya can't do thet," he exclaimed. "Yer pa'd have yer hide."

"He told me to take care of her," said Laramie, his hand continuing the even strokes with the brush.

"He said to guard her," growled Sam. "Not—fuss."

Laramie let Sam's words drift into the air of the steamy barn, and then he turned to the older man.

"I really don't see much difference," Laramie said softly, "her being a woman. Ya can't do the one without the other."

❧   ❧   ❧

Mrs. Benson rose from her knees and wiped her eyes one more time. One day had slowly passed into another, day after day, and still there was no trace of Ariana.

She had grieved and hoped and wept and fretted and prayed. She had tried with all of her heart to trust. She had pleaded with God. Had begged for His intervention. She had even bargained—offering her own life in the place of her daughter. Still, the searchers returned empty.

But this morning as she wept before the Lord, a strange peace had entered her aching heart. She couldn't explain it. Wasn't even yet sure if she could fully trust it. But something seemed to be assuring her that Ariana, wherever she was, was in God's care. Her mind had told her that ever since that first dreadful night, but now her heart was answering yes.

"God," she whispered softly into the quiet of the room, "help me to trust. Help me to go on with life. Help me to forgive those who have tried to find her and have now gone back to minding stores and caring for businesses. They tried, Lord. They tried everything they knew. They couldn't go on searching forever. They have lives—families of their own— to tend to. Help me to leave Ariana . . . in your hands."

She blew her nose and straightened bent shoulders. Somehow she would find the strength to go on. She knew that strength must come from God.

✤   ✤   ✤

"Where'd ya git thet thing?" asked Sam, his eyes round with amazement.

Laramie reined in his horse, bringing the pack horse to a halt as well. The tin tub bumped up against the outstretched boughs of a spruce tree, and Laramie pulled the lead to ease the horse over so there would be no chance of damage to his important cargo.

"Found it," he said simply as he swung lightly down from the saddle.

Sam lifted his hat and scratched his balding head.

"Yer gonna take a heap of teasin' iffen the fellas see ya with thet," he observed.

Laramie simply shrugged his wide shoulders and busied himself with untying the ropes that held the tub in place.

Sam chuckled. "Ain't seen nothin' like thet since I was a kid," he observed as he ran his hand over the cold metal.

"Can't figure how one carries it when it's full of water,"

mused Laramie as he lowered the tub to the snow. "It's heavy as is."

"Ya don't," explained Sam patiently. "Ya put it where ya want it an' then pour the water in."

Laramie looked surprised. "How do ya git the water outta it?" he asked innocently. "Thing ain't got no drain spout."

"Ya dip it out," Sam answered.

Laramie stood to his full height and rubbed the back of his hand across his brow.

"Seems like I got me a powerful amount of work here," he said softly. "Sure hope she don't count on using it too often."

Then he turned back to his saddlebags. "Got a few other things, too," he informed Sam in conspiratorial tones.

"Like?" asked Sam.

"Some soap. Couple towels. This here—what ya call it—wash towel."

"Washcloth," Sam corrected.

"Some hair soap."

"Where'd ya git all thet stuff?" asked Sam again.

Laramie gave the older man a smile. "You got yer secrets—I got mine," was all he would say.

"Seems ta me yer taking yer guardin' duties awful serious-like," muttered Sam.

Laramie made no comment.

☙ ☙ ☙

Ariana was both surprised and delighted when the tub arrived—without comment—in her small room and was deposited close to the big iron stove. Silently she watched as Laramie filled both the kettle and the basin and placed them on the stove. Then he emptied a saddlebag of its contents, spreading the small items on the table.

"Thank you," said Ariana softly.

Laramie picked up the pail to go for more water, outwardly calm, though inwardly in turmoil. He had never been thanked before in his life. Her words caught him off guard.

He nodded his head toward her but did not look her way. "I'll git more water," was his only comment.

After he left, Ariana moved to look at what he had left behind on the table. Soap, a hand mirror, towels, a couple of washcloths, a bottle of shampoo advertised to make "one's tresses silky and perfumed," and a pair of ivory-tipped manicure scissors. In spite of her circumstances, Ariana had to smile. At least these few things would help to make her feel more human.

On the other hand, the simple items brought new worry to her already troubled heart. It looked as though they were expecting her to occupy the cabin for some time to come. The very thought made Ariana want to put her head in her arms and weep. Instead, she stiffened her back and tried to turn her thoughts to other things.

❧   ❧   ❧

While Laramie was hauling and heating the water for her bath, Ariana was looking for some way to hang one of the towels over the fully exposed window. Even though the pane was so dirty one could hardly see out of it, she didn't want to take any chances with someone seeing in.

But there were no nails, no pegs, no way of assuring any privacy. She still stood there, a frown on her face and the towel in her hands, when Laramie rattled the door again. Along with the pail of water, he carried another dented kettle and a big pot. He added these items to the stove top and filled them from the pail. The little stove was now so crowded that Ariana feared to move any of the pots lest she send one of them tumbling to the floor.

He turned to leave again, water pail in hand.

"I . . ." dared Ariana, her voice tight with nervousness. "I was wondering . . ."

He turned back to her.

She pushed aside her fear with grim determination. "The window," she said, pointing to it, "is there . . . can we . . . it needs to be covered . . . someway. If I had a hammer and some nails . . ." She held up the towel in her hands.

He made no reply but seemed to understand her faltering words of concern. He nodded and left again.

When he returned he not only had another pail of water but a hammer and some rusty nails. He set the pail on the small shelf and proceeded to the window, where he pounded the nails into the dust-covered logs. Ariana watched silently. When he had completed the task, she handed him the towel, which he hooked in place, making a makeshift but workable curtain for her window. He stepped back and eyed it carefully; then seeming satisfied he nodded his head.

"I'll be back to put the water in the tub," he said as he was about to leave.

"I can do it," Ariana was quick to inform him.

He looked at the stove and then back to her. He nodded in agreement and turned to go.

"But—" Ariana's voice stopped him.

"Somethin' else?" he asked as he turned to her.

Ariana looked nervously from the young man to the door and back again.

"Could you . . . could you . . . knock . . . before coming in next time?" she asked timidly, and her chin lifted just a bit to bolster her courage.

It took a moment for the meaning of the words to register. Then his face flushed.

"Miss," he said, his hand raising unconsciously to tip back his Stetson, "I'll be knockin' every time."

Then he was gone.

❧   ❧   ❧

As much as she longed to linger in the warm, soapy water, Ariana hurried with her bath. It didn't seem quite safe to remain in the tub in spite of his promise to announce his coming.

She yearned to wash her filthy garments but had nothing

to change into. She thought of wrapping herself in the coarse blanket while her clothing dried, but under the circumstances it didn't seem like a good idea.

Reluctantly she put on the same skirt and shirtwaist that she had laid aside. They smelled of woodsmoke and room dust. She was glad the weather hadn't been such to cause perspiration odor as well.

Then she set about washing her hair. It felt so good to give her scalp a good scrubbing. The shampoo lived up to its boast. As her dark brown curls began to dry, they did feel silky again, and they did have a delightful scent—even in the dust and dirt of the dank cabin.

⚜   ⚜   ⚜

When he came with her evening meal, her hair still had not dried completely and hung about her shoulders like a soft mantle. He could smell the perfume of it as he set the tin plate on the bare table. He moved quickly away.

"Yer done with the tub?" he asked, for something to say.

"Yes—thank you," she responded.

He was surprised that she had dipped out most of the water. The slop pail was full, as were the basins and big pot he had brought. As far as her circumstances allowed, she was independent. He liked that, though he really couldn't have said why. He set about finishing emptying the bath water while she toyed with her supper.

He was carrying out the tub and its last bit of water when she spoke again. "Is that . . . is that someone else's tub?"

He looked at her, wondering just what she was asking.

"No," he said curtly.

"Then . . . do you mind . . . bringing it back in?" she asked him.

He stopped short. Surely she wasn't going to bathe again—so soon.

"It'll get very cold if it's left out . . . out in the elements," she explained. "When it's cold it cools the water too quickly."

He understood then and nodded his assent.

He brought the tub back into the room. He had to kick some clutter aside in order to make room for it against one wall of the cabin. He swore beneath his breath, ending his words with "filthy place."

"If I had some sort of broom I could sweep it out," she offered from where she sat.

He felt embarrassed that she had overheard him.

When he reached the door he hesitated. "Anything else?" he asked.

It was almost a smile she gave him—though it was checked and guarded. "You've been most helpful," she said quietly. "I appreciate it. Thank you."

Her words made him squirm with discomfort. A prisoner—voicing thanks.

He nodded and turned quickly to go. He could stand no more—niceness or womanliness or whatever it was. But he promised himself that the next time he came to the cabin, he'd bring his stub of a broom and sweep out the place.

❧　　❧　　❧

"I bin thinkin'," said Sam, throwing a card on the pile between him and the boss. "Haven't we still got us a trunk 'round here somewheres with woman clothes?"

Will looked up and squinted his dark eyes at his card partner. "Why ya askin'?"

"Jest thinkin'," Sam replied and studied the cards in his hand.

Will took a long drink from the bottle at his elbow.

"Been thinkin'," Sam went on slowly, "thet there little gal be in the same batch of clothes ever since we brung her in."

"So—?" responded the big man. "I ain't changed mine neither."

"Well—you an' me is a little different," Sam followed slowly. Then he added, "We wear 'em 'til they fall off—or crawl away." He chuckled softly at his own joke.

They played on in silence for several minutes. Sam waited. Would Will refuse to give consent—or even consideration to his casual remark?

"Ya think those clothes would fit her?" Will finally asked when Sam had about given up.

Sam shrugged. "No idee," he responded, "but guess ya could mention 'em to the Kid an' see iffen he wants a look at 'em."

The big man nodded. "Ya can dig 'em up and show 'im," he said.

The dim glow of the kerosene lamp did not give away the sparkle in Sam's eyes.

Chapter Nine

Early Trouble

"Where'd ya git this stuff?" Laramie asked Sam as the two of them ran rough hands over the soft garments.

Sam said nothing—just watched the young man sort idly through the clothes. What was he to say—and just how much?

"Yer pa thought the gal might be able to use something. Git herself cleaned up," Sam said instead.

"Where'd it come from?" Laramie insisted.

"Been here a long time," Sam answered.

"Some raid?" asked Laramie. He lifted another calico gown and laid it aside. Then his eyes opened wide and he reached again into the trunk. "This here's a baby—somethin'," he said, disbelief in his voice.

Sam nodded. He looked off into the distance, thinking back in time. He hadn't expected the trunk of laid-aside things to affect him so deeply.

"Sam!" prompted Laramie. "What are these clothes?" He lifted up the tiny soft nightgown and stared at the smallness of it in his man-sized hand.

Sam spit into the dust on the floor.

"Well, boy," he said when he could trust his voice. "Yers, I reckon."

Laramie stared. "Mine?"

"Yessir."

"You mean—?" Laramie turned back to the trunk of feminine attire. "You mean—this was my ma's trunk?"

Sam nodded again.

"You mean she—? Did she live here? Was—?"

Sam raised a hand. "Look, Kid," he said and his eyes had grown dark, "I've said all I intend to say. This was yer ma's trunk of things. That was yer baby do-dad. I—yer pa thought this here gal might use some of the"—Sam reached down a hand and lifted one of the garments and let it fall back into the trunk again—"fancies—an' thet's *thet* an' thet's all I'm gonna say."

He lifted himself awkwardly from his kneeling position on the floor and turned to stalk away.

"Ya do what ya wanna do," he flung back over his shoulder with a wave of his hand, indicating that he had washed his hands of the whole business.

❧ ❧ ❧

Laramie lingered over the trunk, staring at the tiny garments—his. And the other soft, feminine things—his mother's. Nothing—nothing in his life had ever given him cause to think about the fact that he'd had a mother. A mother. What had she been like? Who was she, anyway? How had she come to connect up with his father? The items in the trunk looked totally foreign to the world he knew.

He again lifted the small baby garment and looked at it long and hard. His. Made undoubtedly by the hands of his mother.

Laramie couldn't have said why, but after carefully returning the clothing to the trunk, he kept out the one small soft item and tucked it inside his shirt.

The next morning he had Sam help him take the trunk to the south cabin. "Thought there might be somethin' in here ya could use," was his only explanation.

As the trunk lid was lifted back to expose the contents,

he saw the girl's eyes light up. It gave him strange, unexpected pleasure.

❧   ❧   ❧

"I wonder . . ." mused Ariana as she went through the trunk, carefully lifting out item by item and examining them.

What she found was clothing that had belonged to a woman about her size—but they had been worn during a previous time. Styles had changed a bit, but she couldn't fault the material. Whoever had claimed ownership had been a woman of some means. Ariana could tell that by the soft cottons and fine linens.

They were not party clothes, not silks and satins—they were sensible, everyday, workable clothes, though of the best fabrics available. Ariana's puzzled frown deepened with each garment she drew out. "Who was she?" she kept asking herself.

Then another question brought a new frown. What had happened to this woman? Had she also been brought to the camp as a prisoner? Why was her clothing left behind? What had become of this woman of mystery?

Ariana had no answer to any of her questions.

She came upon a blanket, folded neatly as though making a division of the contents of the trunk. She lifted it and saw carefully folded baby garments comprising the bottom layer. She could tell at a glance they were not new items, but carefully laundered and folded.

She stared, openmouthed. Did Sam and . . . and that other man know the trunk held baby items as well? Who was this woman? This woman who obviously had prepared garments to welcome a baby. Had the baby arrived? What had become of the woman and her infant?

There was a great mystery hidden here somewhere.

Ariana left the folded baby things and let the blanket fall back into position. She did not wish to intrude further on the privacy of this unknown woman—but thankfully she would wear some of the fine garments her unknown benefactor had left behind.

❦   ❦   ❦

Laramie pulled his horse up in the shadow of the tall spruce and slipped silently to the ground. He left his mount ground-tied and moved stealthily through the trees. It would be impossible to hide his tracks in the snow—but he knew the area well. No outsider ever came to the hidden springs, and his own gang members were presently more interested in staying by the warm fire than venturing out.

He was in no danger. But the party he had plans to meet had to be a bit more cautious. He would not be welcomed should he be spotted by any of the other members of the camp, or by the sentry on duty. For that reason, Laramie hoped they would not be seen.

He was early—had planned it that way. He would just find a comfortable, hidden spot and wait.

He chose his place of concealment carefully, brushed the snow from the stump with the brim of his Stetson, and took a seat. He had no sooner settled himself than he heard a soft chuckle.

"You make noise like moose," came the soft, familiar voice.

Laramie whipped around. White Eagle stood a few feet away, grinning, his arms folded across his chest.

"Yer here," said Laramie, rising to his feet again.

White Eagle, the amused look still on his face, made no comment but crossed to where Laramie now stood.

"We meet here—no?"

It was Laramie's turn to smile. He reached out, and the two young men shook hands firmly.

"Yes, we were to meet here," he agreed. "It's been a long time," he continued, placing a hand on the young Indian's shoulder.

"Long," agreed White Eagle. He nodded his head to the stump Laramie had vacated and eased himself to the ground. Laramie returned to his seat.

For some minutes the two friends sat silently, their eyes traveling out over the expanse of the valley beneath them. White Eagle broke the stillness. "You call," he said simply, and Laramie understood his implied question.

He removed his hat and ran a finger through shaggy, heavy hair. "Yeah," Laramie admitted. "I had to talk to someone."

"Trouble?"

"Not . . . not really trouble. Jest . . ."

Laramie stopped and White Eagle waited for him to go on. It was some time before Laramie continued.

"My pa brought this here girl to the camp," he said, feeling that the spoken words sounded pretty silly.

White Eagle nodded solemnly. "Trouble!" he said softly.

"Well—no trouble yet," Laramie hurried to explain. "I mean she's just a . . . a young . . . not a troublemaker or anything like thet. She's off in a cabin all alone. The fellas don't even know she's there."

White Eagle waited.

"Pa gave me the . . . the chore of . . . of guardin' her," went on Laramie.

"Nice—chore," White Eagle said, his eyes glinting with amusement.

"No—it's not," quickly cut in Laramie. "She's . . . she's . . . it's not a nice job—at all."

"She mean squaw?" asked the Indian.

"No," Laramie said quickly. "Nothin' like thet. She's young an' she's scared an' I have no idea what she's there for. I mean—I don't know what Pa plans. I asked—an' he got mad. Wouldn't say nothin'. Jest says I gotta guard her."

White Eagle shrugged his shoulders and spread his palms upright as if to say that there was nothing he could do to help the situation.

"It's jest . . . well, I mean . . . you've lived in camp—with women—all yer life. I . . . I don't know a thing about women. What . . . what am I supposed to . . . how am I supposed to. . . ?"

White Eagle smiled. Yes, he knew about women. Elderly ones who, because of their years and wisdom, were the mothers of the tribe, wives of hunters who tanned the hides of the game the men brought in and tended the cooking pots. Younger women, eyes soft with love for their newborn papooses, maidens who modestly lowered their eyes when the young braves walked by, and then stole covert glances beneath long, dark lashes. Even the frolicking, playful little ones—on their way to "becoming." He knew about life surrounded by women.

"But," he went on to explain, "I have visited the white man's fort—a few times. The women there are different—very different—from the Indian women in my camp."

He shrugged again. "I know nothing—of white squaws," he said, and spread his hands again.

"But—"

White Eagle shrugged again. "Not same," he said as though that was final.

Laramie was agitated. White Eagle stared at him, looking both surprised and confused. Finally he asked, "Why such little bit of woman trouble so much?"

Laramie couldn't answer the question.

"What you do for her?" White Eagle asked, his tone indicating he was genuinely trying to help his friend.

"I jest . . . jest bring her wood an' water an' food an'—"

"Why she not get own wood and water?" questioned White Eagle.

"She's our prisoner," responded Laramie.

White Eagle nodded. Then he frowned. "White man not make prisoner work?" he asked.

"She's locked up," said Laramie.

White Eagle nodded again.

"So you not like . . . chore?" asked the young brave.

Laramie stood to his feet and began to pace. He reached

up to push his hat back a trace. "No," he said. "No, I don't like it. She shouldn't be there. Shouldn't be in the camp. It's gonna mean trouble. I can feel it in my bones."

"Maybe she . . . escape," observed the Indian with a knowing look.

"She'd never make it. She'd die—or be killed—or taken," declared Laramie. He continued to pace, his jaw set firmly, his blue eyes darkening.

"You . . . not want that?"

Laramie whirled around to face the young brave. He did not even offer an answer. Of course he did not want that.

"So . . . you not like . . . care for . . . but you want . . . keep," White Eagle continued, as though carefully sorting through Laramie's problem.

Laramie did speak then. "I don't want to keep—I jest want to—"

He broke off. How could he explain to the Pawnee what he was feeling? That it was all wrong to take another captive. That his father had broken some moral code in bringing the young girl into camp. That he knew, deep down inside, that this was totally against everything that a real man should stand for.

"I want her . . . back . . . where she belongs," he stumbled on awkwardly. "Only . . . I have no way to get her there . . . so . . . so I have to do my best to take care of her and I don't—"

"You got trouble," agreed the young Indian again. "Plenty trouble."

Laramie stopped his walking and stared out over the valley. Down below he could see the ramshackle buildings of the camp. From the high vantage point the crude shacks looked fairly organized, almost attractive. In the far distance he could see the rising smoke of a campfire. By the way the small column drifted, he guessed it to be an Indian hunting party who sat around its warmth.

"Yer men?" he asked White Eagle, nodding his head eastward.

"Three," said White Eagle in reply.

"Hope they got something," mused Laramie.

White Eagle nodded. "They did. Snow deep. Stop to roast meat for strength on home trail."

"I think I'll do a little huntin'," said Laramie. "We could do with some fresh meat."

The young Indian brave stood to his feet, his movements catlike with grace and strength.

He did not brush the snow from his leather garments but pulled down a branch of the spruce and brushed it back and forth across the ground where he had reclined, removing all trace that he had been there. At its release, the branch sprang back into position.

"Fresh meat," he echoed Laramie. "Make strong. If girl ever . . . escape . . . she need eat. Be strong."

The two young men looked at each other. A silent message passed between them. Even as the idea crossed Laramie's mind, he discarded it as preposterous.

"You make signal," said White Eagle, and Laramie understood the brief words as a promise that he would be there. He nodded.

Before his very eyes the young brave seemed to melt into the shadows of the forest.

🙶　　🙶　　🙶

"You should get some fresh air," said Laramie after he had knocked, then brought in the plate of food to his charge the next morning.

Ariana glanced at the heavy wooden door.

"After you've finished yer breakfast we'll go fer a walk," Laramie continued. He had done a lot of thinking throughout the night. White Eagle was right. He had to try to keep her strong. Keep her healthy. Who knew what the future might hold?

She nodded silently, but he thought he saw a little sparkle come to her eyes. Was it fear—or anticipation?

When he returned later he was surprised to see she had

eaten more than usual of what was on the plate. She stood, dressed in one of the calico gowns from the trunk, staring out of the window.

"It's rather cold," he observed. "You'll need all the warm clothes ya got." He hesitated, then pointed to the corner. "I would suggest thet ya wear those moccasins 'stead of those shoes."

She changed footwear quickly, her back to him. He walked to the window and stood looking out so she wouldn't be embarrassed by his presence.

She was soon bundled in her heavy coat, her hat firmly in place over her pinned-up curls. He knew the flimsy bit of felt and ribbon would be absolutely no protection against the elements, but he didn't say so.

He pushed the heavy door open and proceeded her out into the wintery sunshine. Though it was weak in warmth, it was bright as it reflected off the whiteness of the snow. He saw her squint against it and remembered it had been some time since she had seen the full light of day.

They had taken only a few steps when the door of the big cabin burst open and three of the gang members stepped out into the light and headed for the barn.

Instinctively Laramie glanced around for cover. There was none. There would be no way to avoid a meeting.

Laramie heard the rough words, the coarse laughs, and then three heads came up and three pairs of astonished eyes stared in his direction.

"Well I'll be—" exclaimed James and followed his comment with a muttered curse.

Curly, a bottle dangling from his limp hand, could only stare, openmouthed.

But it was Skidder who drew the attention of Laramie. After his initial shock, his eyes narrowed and an evil grin began to spread over his face. "A 'prisoner'?" he guffawed. He spilled out a stream of profanity. "Prisoner, ya call thet? I'd bet my Winchester thet Daddy done gone and got his boy a pretty little filly."

He hooted again and slapped his thigh.

Laramie felt the heat rushing to his face.

All three of the men grinned, James fidgeting nervously and Curly twisting his near-empty bottle in bare hands.

Laramie chided himself for his carelessness. He had stepped out of the cabin right into a nest of hornets. He glanced in silent apology at Ariana's downcast eyes and burning cheeks. Skidder, who was known to be drawn to women, was bound to make an issue over a girl being in camp. But how big an issue? Would he be smart enough to back off? Or would he force Laramie into unwanted action?

For the first time in his life Laramie felt his fingers itching for the security of the cold butt of his forty-four.

Chapter Ten

What Now?

Laramie had heard the girl's sharp intake of breath and sensed her stiffen at the crude comments of the men before them. It was all he could do to hold himself steady. Inwardly he willed Skidder to keep his head and just move on. What would he do if the rough outlaw decided to push further?

"Reckon you boys got business at the barn," Laramie drawled softly. But his hands hung loosely and his stance had changed.

For a few moments the whole winter world seemed to hold its breath. Skidder stood poised as though deciding whether to have a bit more fun at Laramie's expense, or get himself out of the area in one piece. Common sense finally won and he nodded, still leering, and moved off toward the barn.

Laramie waited until the three were several steps away before he relaxed, nodded to the girl, and motioned for her to continue.

Her face had blanched white; her large eyes had widened. He could see that she trembled slightly, and he knew she was fully aware of the danger that had just passed.

"I . . . I'm not sure . . ." she began in a trembling voice.

"He won't be back," he said with more confidence than he felt.

She looked unconvinced.

"I think I'd just like to stay in," she managed hesitantly.

He nodded. He would not argue further. It was unfortunate that they had been spotted. He should have been more cautious. Now the others knew there was a girl in the camp. Now there would be no rest—and sure trouble.

Secretly he wondered if she would even be safe in the cabin—but he didn't mention that to her as he led her back down the snowy trail.

He would do what he could.

🌿 🌿 🌿

Ariana was surprised later in the day when the young man returned and brought with him a hammer and a large hook and eye. He spoke not a word as he nailed the two pieces firmly in place. She watched from her spot at the table, her book open before her, but she said nothing.

When he had finished he lifted his eyes to hers. "Keep it locked," he said simply. "Don't ever open it—'less it's me—or Sam."

Ariana nodded at another reminder that she was constantly in danger.

She let her eyes fall back to the pages before her. "Trust in the Lord," she read—then reread—and it brought her a measure of comfort.

She had been going through the Bible since her time of captivity, selecting all the passages that confirmed that truth. She was amazed at how often she found them—and at the heartrending circumstances in which they were spoken. She was excited to read how God acted on the behalf of those folks long ago. Surely she had great reason to trust such a powerful and merciful God.

🌿 🌿 🌿

"What's yer name?"

The question surprised Ariana. The young man often came and went without any conversation taking place between the two of them. Now he was stacking an armload of wood inside her cabin. He wasn't even looking her direction.

"Ariana," she said after hesitating.

"Ariana," he repeated, and Ariana was surprised at how her name sounded on his tongue.

He continued to stack the logs by the cabin wall.

"And yours?" she dared to ask.

"Call me Laramie," he replied.

Ariana did not repeat his name aloud but she did mentally. In some strange way it seemed to suit him.

She watched the even flow of his movements as he tucked the logs in place. He looked ordinary—yet she could not forget the change she had seen—had felt—when they had been confronted on the trail. Here was a kind of man she knew absolutely nothing about. So different from those she knew in her own small town. The very thought made her tremble.

❧   ❧   ❧

Mrs. Benson put another check mark on the wall calender before she loosed her braid and shook the silvering hair out to spill down her back. How long had it been? Thirty-one days. Thirty-one days and no word—nothing. She knew everyone in town had already given up. She wondered if her husband had joined their ranks. But no—not yet. He still included his petition for the safety of their girl in each of his spoken prayers. And how many times each day, like she, did he send up silent but fervent petitions? They both still clung to hope.

Hope in a sovereign God—that was all they had.

But surely—that was enough.

❧   ❧   ❧

"You must be tired of reading the same book," Laramie

casually observed as he set the extra pail of water on the shelf for her weekly bath.

Ariana looked up. His words surprised her. He so seldom spoke to her—and she never initiated a conversation.

"It's the Bible," she said.

"The Bible?"

"One can read it over and over and over—and still never stop learning or run out of fresh truths," she dared to continue, sensing that he was puzzled by her answer.

"I see," he said, looking at her, but she felt that he really didn't.

He changed the topic with, "I'll bring yer supper. Ya want it after yer bath—or before?"

Ariana thought of the tasteless food. She took a deep breath, then dared to bring up what had been on her mind for the past several days. "If I had a couple of pots—and some supplies—I could do my own cooking and you wouldn't need to bother—"

"No bother," he cut in quickly.

She felt disappointment seep through her at her unsuccessful bid to prepare her own meals. She was sick of the sloppy beans and tasteless biscuits.

He seemed to reconsider.

" 'Course—iffen you'd like to do yer own cookin'—guess it wouldn't hurt none," he said tentatively.

Ariana almost smiled in her delight.

"Make out a list of what yer needin'," he invited.

Ariana was perplexed. "I . . . I don't have a pencil or . . ."

It was his turn to look frustrated.

"Reckon there ain't one in camp," he confessed. Then he shrugged broad shoulders. "Suppose ya need the usual grub stake. I've picked thet up plenty of times. I can git it for ya."

Ariana let her eyes travel to the trunk against the wall. "You don't suppose there is anything like . . . a pencil . . . in there?" she mused, nodding her head in its direction.

"Thought you'd looked."

Ariana shook her head. "No, not at everything. I . . . I felt like I was . . . intruding. I just looked partway and then I . . . I found . . . I felt that I . . . that it was . . . private."

He nodded, seeming to be pleased at her respect for privacy.

He crossed to the trunk and lifted up the lid. "Maybe we should look," he said. Ariana joined him as he began to lift out some of the dresses. "Never seen ya wear this one," he said of a blue check. "It looks kinda pretty," he added, almost to himself.

"No," said Ariana in a voice not much above a whisper. "I just took one . . . change of clothes. I . . . I use them . . . and my own, and wash them turn by turn. I . . . I . . . appreciate the chance to . . . change . . . but I didn't think that I should . . . use all her clothes."

He looked surprised but made no immediate comment.

"These were—my ma's, I'm told," he said frankly. He stopped in some confusion, then said, "She's gone an' won't be needin' 'em."

"I'm . . . so sorry," breathed Ariana.

He came to the blanket, lifted it up, and deposited it on the floor beside him. But Ariana could sense his surprise at the sight of all the baby garments.

Then rather roughly he began to lift out the tiny things and lay them on the floor beside the blanket. He stopped short again after lifting up another handful of small clothing.

He peered into the trunk. A little chest lay on the bottom, and beside it a book with a black cover.

"Look!" Ariana exclaimed excitedly. "A Bible."

But Laramie was looking at the chest.

Carefully he lifted it up and opened the lid. In it were a number of small items. Brooches—hankies with lace trim yellowed with age—a tintype—buttons—lace—little bits of this and that which he did not take time to sort. He closed the lid again.

"The little chest . . . it must have been . . . your mother's," she said softly. "You should . . . keep it. It's a treasure. . . ."

He looked uncomfortable. He abruptly put the box down on the floor by his knee.

"Didn't see any pencil or paper in there," he said gruffly. "Guess it's not much good to you."

She reached down into the trunk. Almost tenderly she lifted up the Bible. She could tell from the covers that it had been well used, but she did not open it.

"You must take this, too," she said in a whispery voice. "I know your mother would want you to have it."

He did not argue but watched as she placed the Bible on top of the little chest. She had known as soon as the chest appeared that he would take it—would need to take it.

Quickly he rummaged through the rest of the belongings, but there was nothing else among the baby garments. An impatience seemed to have taken hold of him.

Ariana understood his mood. She stepped back. "I'll put the things back," she offered. She was sure he couldn't wait to carefully study each item from the chest in private.

He nodded and picked up the newly discovered items, clearly anxious to be on his way.

❧　　❧　　❧

Laramie did not forget about the supplies. Sam brought her meal the next morning—thumping on the door and calling out in a louder than necessary voice to identify himself.

When she unhooked the latch to let him enter, he came in growling.

"Day not fit fer man or beast, yet he decides he has to run off. He'll freeze hisself to death, thet's what. You'd think there was a train of gold or a—"

He stopped and looked nervously toward the young girl as if he had said too much.

"Said he needed supplies," continued the man with another growl. "Don't know what he's needin' thet wouldn't wait."

He cast a glance at her and Ariana felt embarrassed. Was

he blaming her that Laramie had ridden off in the cold? Maybe he was right. She hadn't given any thought to the weather when she had made her request. She had been self-ish. She'd had no idea that the food staples would not be ob-tainable in the camp.

"Yer breakfast," said Sam more softly.

"Thank you," replied Ariana.

"Don't know why you'd thank me fer it," Sam said. "Thet stuff ain't hardly fit to eat. Ole Rawley ain't much of a cook. Beans an' biscuits. Beans an' biscuits. Thet's all we ever git— an' they ain't even good biscuits."

He set the plate on the table with a grimace and turned toward her. "See yer still readin' thet book. Must have it near worn out by now," he observed in a lighter tone.

Ariana managed a wobbly smile. "The pages—maybe," she said, "but the message—no."

"Message. Thet some secret code?"

Ariana smiled fully now. "Code? Not to a believer, it's not."

The old man frowned.

"It's the Bible," explained Ariana. When there was no re-sponse she continued. "God's words to His people."

"I know what the Bible is," the old man retorted sharply. "My ma—" He shuffled uncomfortably and said no more about it. "Well—ya jest et up—thet—poor excuse fer break-fast," said the man, "an' I'll be back fer the plate. How's yer firewood?"

He turned to study the pile. "Look's like the Kid got ya enough firewood to last 'til a week from Christmas," he noted, and Ariana thought he looked relieved. "Guess ya need some fresh water, though."

Then he looked at Ariana with some alarm. "Ya ain't plannin' on bathin' today, are ya?"

"No—not today," she replied, shaking her head.

"Good," he said with feeling. "I sure weren't anxious to do all thet haulin'."

He left with the pail, and Ariana crossed to latch her door before turning to the food.

As determined as she had been to keep her strength up, she found it difficult to make herself eat the tasteless fare.

🌢 🌢 🌢

It wasn't until the next afternoon that Laramie knocked on her door and identified himself.

Ariana hastened to answer. She was relieved to hear his voice and prayed as she lifted the hook that he wouldn't have suffered from the ride in the elements.

He looked fine. She sighed with relief.

He carried a burlap bag in each hand. "Hope I got what ya needed," he said matter-of-factly, "'cause I don't think I'll be welcomed back fer a while."

Ariana frowned at the words but couldn't sort out his meaning. He deposited both bags on the table.

"Got a couple pots and this here thing," he said, drawing a strange piece of metal from the closest bag. "It's a reflector of some kind. Supposed to make biscuits without an oven."

Ariana had never seen one before. She had no idea how to use it but determined to give it a try.

He had brought a nice selection of basic supplies. There wasn't much in the line of spices or flavorings, but at least she would be able to do her own cooking. Ariana was thankful.

"Now—if I just had some meat . . ." she mused.

"I'll git some," he promised simply and later kept his word, appearing at her door with some venison steak just before the winter sun dipped behind the nearby hills.

🌢 🌢 🌢

Ariana could not believe how good the stew tasted after her weeks of unsavory beans. She even enjoyed a second helping.

The biscuits hadn't done well. They were burned in spots—and undercooked in others. She would need to practice with the new reflector. Even so, they were definitely better than what she had been served from the gang's kitchen. Perhaps now she could regain some of the weight she knew she had lost and have more strength when the time came for her to escape from her captors.

For Ariana lived for the day when the weather would improve, and she would find a way to slip away from the four log walls that held her captive.

Chapter Eleven

An Ally

In the privacy of the small cabin he called his own, Laramie lifted the small items from the chest, one by one, and laid them on the rough board table. According to Sam, these were his mother's things. He felt a strange connection with them—a longing to know more about this woman he had never known. He appreciated Ariana's reluctance to disturb the contents of the trunk any more than necessary for her own survival.

The pin he studied was a cameo. It looked fragile and delicate—the white profile surrounded with intricate filigree. It seemed out of place in a rough camp of lawless men. Did she really wear it here? Had she truly ever been in residence in the camp? Laramie found it hard to believe, yet her trunk—her things—were in camp. It puzzled him.

He withdrew one of the lace hankies. The cloth was soft to his touch—fine and smooth. He had never handled such fabric before. It was embroidered with a little pattern in delicate work, and as he looked closer he could make out letters. *L-A-L.* He put the letters together and whispered them softly. "Lal." They spelled nothing as far as he knew. Yet he felt they held a secret. Lal. It was a strange word.

He tenderly lifted the other handkerchiefs and placed them all in a neat little pile.

Another pin. This one small, with a blue stone in the middle that caught the afternoon light.

Another hankie—then an oval on a long gold chain. He turned it this way and that as he surveyed it carefully. He noticed a little clasp. Carefully he pressed on it and it opened. It held a small lock of downy hair. Whose hair? Why had his mother carried it in this strange little oval? He studied it for a long time before he closed it and laid it aside.

A scrap of lace. He turned it over in his hands, discovering no purpose for the bit of cloth. Yet he did not discard it—but put it gently on the growing pile. Another hankie, elaborately embroidered. It looked like a pair of intertwining rings. What had that meant?

And then he was lifting the tintype. He turned it to catch all advantage of the light. It showed a woman. A woman whose face still shone out at him in spite of the fading of the years—whose eyes were turned lovingly upon a baby boy she held in her arms. Could it be him—with his mother?

Her face was so sweet—so gentle. He had never seen such an expression before. For long moments he studied the picture. Something about the woman's likeness reminded him of the girl in the cabin. What was it? Was it the expression? The features? Maybe the eyes.

Carefully he placed the tintype on the bottom of the small chest and began to return the other items. Then he went to the corner shelf, lifted up the tiny gown that Sam had said was his, and gently added it to the other items in the chest.

His whole being was shaken by the experience. And yet he knew so little. He understood even less. Who was his mother? What had happened to her? If she had remained with him, would his life have been different? Somehow he felt it would have been, even though he wasn't sure just how.

He closed the lid of the little box and turned his attention to the Bible. He opened the cover and read of one King James, who had authorized the version. It meant nothing to him. He continued to turn the pages.

He came to a page with a list of names, entered in precise

and careful penmanship. His eyes quickly scanned the contents. It looked like a family record of some kind. He checked the heading at the top of the page and saw that it was titled *Births*. He skimmed down the page and read the last few lines.

Tilford James Bradley, 1812–1816
Margaret Rose Bradley, 1814–1842
Weyburn Oliver Bradley, 1817
Mary Louise Bradley, 1820–1820
Lavina Ann Bradley, 1822
Conrad Timothy Bradley, 1823–1824
Ethan David Bradley, 1826

There was a space and then the line announcing,

Burke Timothy Lawrence, August 10, 1860

Laramie wondered about the last entry. Why so much later? Why a different name?

Laramie turned the page. The headline at the top announced *Marriages*.

Margaret Rose Bradley & Thomas Cullen Roberts,
1833
Lavina Ann Bradley & Turner Donair Lawrence III,
1840
Weyburn Oliver Bradley & Jane Titford Gray, 1841

Laramie flipped another page. This one was labeled *Deaths*, and he quickly let his eyes scan down the page, noting the names he had read previously, now with little notations behind the dates. Died of natural causes—in childbirth—whooping cough—pneumonia. It seemed that his forebears, if indeed that was the record he held in his hands, had more than a little difficulty.

He turned the page again and found a table of contents and then on into the printed pages of the book. But the pages held more than print. Here and there he found, in the same careful handwriting, brief notations or comments about passages. The truth dawned. The same person who had recorded the births, marriages, and deaths was the owner of the Bible. His mother? It was among her things. If he was to believe Sam, then this Bible had belonged to his mother and her name might appear in the book he held.

But it didn't add up. His name was Russell. Laramie Russell. His pa's name was Will Russell.

Then Laramie smiled a cynical smile. It would seem his pa had seen fit to change his name. Perhaps more than once. There was nothing new about that. Laramie supposed there wasn't a man in camp who went by his given name.

Was there a chance his pa had once answered to one of those other names?

"So he was once Bradley or Roberts or Lawrence or maybe Gray," he mused aloud. "Quite a different handle than Russell."

Laramie slowly closed the book and promised himself that he'd do some more investigating into what it held as soon as he had the time. His horses needed to be fed and rubbed down. He'd have to satisfy his profound curiosity later.

Carefully he picked up the well-worn volume and the chest. His eyes scanned the room quickly. Then he walked to his wooden bunk, lifted it over a way, and knelt on the floor. With a small amount of coaxing, one floorboard groaned reluctantly upward. He slipped his treasure into the hole beneath, beside his money poke and extra Colt. It wasn't safe. There was nothing safe in the camp. But it was the safest place he knew.

He moved the bunk back into position and picked up his Stetson, anxious to get his chores out of the way.

❧   ❧   ❧

Laramie had finished with the horses and would have returned to his cabin and lit the kerosene lamp, but hunger drove him toward the main bunkhouse.

As he passed the south cabin the smell of cooking food caused him to stop midstride. He decided to check on Ariana to see how she was managing with the provisions he had brought her. Perhaps there had been something he'd forgotten.

He knocked, then called out and heard her move to the door and unlatch the hook.

She looked surprised, since Laramie never came in the evening except to bring her plate of food—and now the arrangement was for her to make her own meals.

"Jest came to see how ya made out with the cookin'," he quickly explained.

"Fine," she responded, indicating the empty plate she had just left to answer the door.

He moved past her and into the room. "Smells good," he observed.

"Just stew," said Ariana, her heart thumping with uncertainty. What did he want? She saw his eyes wander to the biscuits still on the cooking sheet.

"They didn't turn out too well," Ariana confessed. "I need to practice with the reflector."

"They look a heap better than Rawley's," he observed.

Ariana noticed the slight twitch of his nose.

"Help yourself," she offered.

He did, without hesitation or apology.

"There's a little stew left—"

"Do ya mind?" he asked and glanced at the plate on the table.

"I'm sorry," she offered quickly. "I only have the one plate, but I'll wash it—"

"No need. I've et off worse things," he responded and picked up the plate. He moved to the stove, where the stew still simmered, and dished out the remainder of the contents.

Ariana stood mute as she watched him squat on the floor, his back up against the door.

"You can sit at the table," she said quickly. "I'll—I'm finished."

But he shook his head. "I'm used to sittin' most anywhere."

Ariana had never seen a man eat so hungrily. She found herself wondering when he had last had a decent meal. She roused herself and moved to rinse the one cup so she could pour him a cup of coffee.

"Thank you," he said, looking a little embarrassed at the unfamiliar courtesy.

"I'm sorry I didn't make more," Ariana apologized as he cleaned up the plate with a biscuit. "I didn't—I was trying to—to not use the supplies—"

"I can git more," he stated briefly.

"But you said—" began Ariana.

He smiled. A lazy, good-natured smile. "True," he replied, "but there are other stores."

Ariana still didn't understand his meaning, yet she couldn't help but wonder if the food had been obtained with the help of a pistol rather than a gold piece.

He set aside the emptied plate. Ariana supposed that he must still be hungry. She had eaten two servings herself.

"Do you want those other two biscuits?" she inquired.

He nodded and moved to get up, but she brought the biscuits to him. He washed them down with great gulps of coffee.

The warm food seemed to relax his usually tense body. He even lifted off the Stetson and placed it on the floor beside him. Ariana noticed that his hair was curly. He was also in need of a good haircut. Then her eyes noticed a scar on his forehead—just at his hairline. She was wondering about it when his words drew her attention.

"What does lal mean?" he asked her suddenly.

"Lal?" she echoed.

"Lal. Jest like thet. L-A-L."

"Where did you see it?" She was forgetting some of her caution.

"On one of them hankies in thet little box."

"Oh," said Ariana, "then it likely was a monogram."

"A monogram?" He sounded puzzled.

"One's initials."

The frown still puckered his brow.

"The first letters of your names," went on Ariana. "Mine would be AYB. Ariana Yvonne Benson."

He seemed to be pondering.

"You mean, the hankie has my ma's—what'd ya say—initials on it?"

"If it was truly your mother's hankie—then, yes," said Ariana.

"So her name was like thet. LAL?"

"That would be my guess," responded Ariana.

He stood suddenly. "Thet's right interestin'," he said as he picked up his hat with one hand, the empty plate with the other. "Want me to clean this off in the snow?" he asked her as he looked down at the plate and cup he held.

"No, no—I'll take care of it," she quickly answered.

He handed it to her. "Mighty obliged, miss," he said as he placed his hat back on his head. "Been a long time since I had something other than beans."

"I—would you—I mean, I could make a little extra tomorrow if . . ."

He smiled again and with his finger pushed back his hat. "Well, now," he said, "I'd like thet jest fine—but I'm not sure I'd be too smart—me comin' here to et. 'Course iffen I could come up with some plate, might be I could sneak a little out."

Ariana let her gaze travel to the room's one window.

"I'll see what I can do to free it up tomorrow," he said, reading her thoughts.

She nodded.

He left then. She heard the beam fall across the door, which meant she was again locked in. Then his voice reached her through the heavy timber. "Don't fergit to lock yer door."

Ariana reached up and slipped the hook quietly into the eye.

✢   ✢   ✢

Another week passed slowly by. Ariana continued to make stews and potpies. She practiced with the reflector in various positions, and her biscuits improved each time she made a batch. Laramie consumed them with unbelievable ease.

He had surreptitiously removed the nails from the window frame and replaced them with hooks so it now locked on both the inside and the outside. Each night he brought his plate around to the window and held it while Ariana filled it. Then he took it, along with biscuits and coffee, and hastened off toward his own tumbledown cabin.

He had been giving full attention to his mother's Bible. He didn't pretend to understand much of it, but the little notations in the margins often shed some light on what he was reading. Still, he had so many questions and he had no one to ask.

He had also found a name that matched the initials. LAL. Lavina Ann Lawrence. Was that his mother? Laramie wanted to believe it was. Somehow it gave him a strange connection with the woman in the picture, an identity he previously had not had. He looked at the picture night after night until he felt—something—for the unknown woman. Something he had never felt before.

✢   ✢   ✢

"Seems ya don't eat much anymore," observed Will as Laramie stepped inside the communal cabin. "Ya been dippin' in someone else's pot?"

The words brought loud guffaws from the men lounging about the room. By now everyone knew the prisoner was doing her own cooking. At times the fragrant smells coming from her cabin made stomachs growl in protest.

Laramie made no answer.

"Maybe he don't need to eat," snarled Skidder. "Maybe he lives on love."

More loud laughter.

"Ya ain't been round much a'tall lately," Will went on.

Laramie got the strange feeling his father was trying to start something.

"Been in my own cabin," he said offhandedly.

"Alone?" asked McDuff, and the whole group of men hooted in response.

"I sure know I wouldn't be iffen . . ." said Skidder with a knowing look, leaving his comment dangling.

There were more nods and hoots in general agreement.

Laramie felt the back of his neck crawl. He didn't like the talk. Didn't like the crude insinuations. "Anybody want a game of cards?" he asked, hoping to turn the attention of the cabin to other things.

His invitation was quickly accepted, and a group of the men pulled their log stools close to the rough-hewed table.

Laramie shuffled the cards, let Shadow cut, then began to deal.

"What say we up the ante," said Skidder with a leer. "Winner gits to guard the prisoner."

All eyes turned toward Laramie to catch his reaction. He never flinched. Never moved a muscle except for the ones needed to distribute the cards. Even his deep eyes did not betray him.

He nodded slowly. "'Bout time someone else took a turn— but assignments are up to the boss. He decides who does what," he answered easily.

"Ya wanna gamble the girl—thet's yer doin'," responded Will in his gravelly voice, "long as she stays in camp."

Laramie nodded his consent without giving his true feelings away. He studied the cards in his hand. He wished he hadn't gotten himself cornered. Now he was in deep, for sure. What would happen if—? No, he wouldn't even think about it. This was one card game he had no intention of losing— the stakes were too high.

❧　　❧　　❧

"Ya really think this is gonna work?" asked Sam after the cabin had cleared of all but him and his boss.

Will's chuckle was not a pleasant sound. "Ya saw 'im," he snorted. "He acted like he couldn'ta cared less—but I'm thinkin' thet if someone else had won thet card game, there'da been gunplay."

Sam was surprised. "An' you'd—you'd welcome thet?" he asked, dumbfounded.

"It wouldn'ta been the Kid we'd carried out," said Will simply.

"No—but it mighta been a good man. An' we got a little trip to make 'afore long, to my recollection."

The boss nodded.

"I want this here thing settled before we make the next raid," he said, scowling. "It's drug on far too long already."

Sam nodded. "The boys have been more patient then I woulda expected," he agreed.

"Mighta worked out a lot sooner iffen he didn't keep her hidden away in thet cabin," growled the big man. "No one even gits to see what she looks like."

"Tell 'im. Tell 'im. Yer the boss."

"Yeah, but what do I tell 'im? I told 'im to take care of her. The weather's been mean as a rattlesnake. What reason could I dream up for 'im to make her come out in the cold?"

"Well, the weather should be on the upturn anytime now. Been winter far too long," observed Sam.

"Hope so," exclaimed the boss. "I'm sick an' tired of these here beans."

Sam stopped chewing on his plug of tobacco long enough to give that some thought. "Ya reckon he eats with the girl?" he asked at last.

"I've watched him comin' an' goin'. He don't hang around there long enough to eat," growled Will. "He's in an' out like he was plumb scared of her or somethin'."

"Well—he don't seem to be losin' no weight," observed Sam. "Funny, ain't it?"

❧   ❧   ❧

"I've got to get her out of there," Laramie told White Eagle.

His tone of voice and eyes gave away his intense feelings, even though he worked to keep his face expressionless.

"Something wrong?" asked the young brave.

"Yeah . . . yeah, things are . . . are . . . I don't know. I can jest feel the tension mountin'. I . . . I can't keep her safe . . . there anymore. Even the lock . . ."

He began to pace again.

It wasn't just the banter of the boys. Something had been happening since Laramie had been spending his days and nights reading his mother's Bible. Something he didn't understand. It was just there—deep within him. He was beginning to see that this life of his—this way of living was all wrong. And bringing her to the camp and keeping her there against her will—that was about as far wrong as they could get.

"How?" asked White Eagle, his simple question forcing Laramie back to the present.

He stopped his pacing. "I'll need yer help," he said, looking straight into the eyes of his friend.

"White Brother have my help," promised the Indian solemnly.

"Look, White Eagle. This will be dangerous. I know that. You must know that. My pa—he'd shoot to kill. He said so. In front of the whole gang. He'd not hesitate—"

White Eagle nodded. "You have gun," he interjected.

Laramie was shocked. "But I couldn't use it—couldn't shoot my own pa," he said quickly.

White Eagle looked thoughtful. Then he nodded again. "You more Indian than White," he told Laramie. "Have honor."

But Laramie brushed aside the words. He was deeply sorry about the fact that White Eagle felt as he did about the white race, but perhaps some of the animosity had been deserved. He wished things had been different.

He took a deep breath. "I'm not asking you to risk your life," he continued.

"I owe White Brother," replied the brave.

"No. No," responded Laramie. "You don't owe me. Sure I helped you out—"

"You save my life."

"Okay—I saved yer life—but thet doesn't mean—"

"White Eagle owe," the brave said firmly.

Laramie thought on his words, then accepted them with a silent nod. He had to allow White Eagle his Indian ways. Had to give him an opportunity to repay whatever debt he felt he owed.

"I won't pretend I'm not grateful," he responded. "I don't think I could manage it alone."

White Eagle made no comment, but the expression in his eyes as they met Laramie's was as good as a covenant signed in blood.

Chapter Twelve

Explosion

Laramie was in a race against time. He could sense that whenever he entered the main cabin with its quarrelsome occupants. There was a tension in the air—a feeling of agitation. Perhaps it could be chalked up to the length of the winter and the fact that the men had been virtually prisoners together for such a long period of time. Tempers flared. Patience had run out. Intolerance was evident. Snarls and complaints filled the air along with dark curses. Something was about to happen. Someone was going to snap.

But Laramie said nothing of his forebodings. Not even to Ariana. Nor did he tell her of his plans to remove her from the premises before the "explosion" took place.

He was sure White Eagle was working on his part in the escape plan. The hidden cave would be prepared for Ariana by the time she needed its safety. When Laramie gave Ariana her instructions, he wanted every detail to be in place.

It was a fairly simple plot. White Eagle would wait just beyond the cabin for Ariana. Laramie would ease her out of the cabin's window and send her through the darkness to the young brave. White Eagle, with his Indian cunning, would spirit Ariana to the hidden cave and leave her, protected and sequestered, until such time as Laramie was able to come for her.

In the meantime, Laramie was to lay a false trail. Riding his buckskin and leading his big bay and the little roan, he would take off through the valley, following the banks of the frozen river. He would travel dangerously close to the Indian encampment, a fact that would cause the gang some concern. It would pose no threat to Laramie. White Eagle had enlisted the help of his father, Chief Half Moon, and the braves were told to ignore the lone white man. Those orders had not been extended to any men who might follow.

At the edge of the Indian camp the saddles were to be slipped off Laramie's horses and transferred to the backs of new mounts. This too was part of arrangements made by White Eagle. Then Laramie would send his own horses on without a rider. He hoped it would be some time before the trackers would discover that the horses were traveling alone. Laramie was counting on the big bay—stolen from a local ranch—deciding to return to its home.

With the gang off on a false trail, Laramie planned to double back, pick up Ariana, and head out in the opposite direction. With all his heart he hoped that the plan would work and that it would buy him enough time to make an escape.

"If I don't make it," he had told White Eagle reluctantly, "try to take the girl back to your camp. Better she be the captive wife of one man than to be left at the mercy of the gang."

White Eagle nodded.

The two friends shook hands solemnly. Both knew the explosive nature of what they were attempting to do.

"You could die, my friend," said White Eagle.

Laramie nodded.

"That may be necessary," he said without emotion, then added thoughtfully, "But I plan to stay alive. A dead man won't be of much help to her."

White Eagle said nothing.

"I think all is ready," Laramie concluded.

"Must be soon," said White Eagle. "Spring stirring. Soon snow go. Ground go soft. Travel be hard."

"Three risings of the sun," agreed Laramie. "We should

have everything in place by then. Three days. I'll have her come to you."

"She wear buckskins."

"I'll be sure. I'll git to her the things you provided."

"Three sun risings."

Laramie agreed and the two friends parted.

❦   ❦   ❦

Only two of those sun risings had passed when Laramie's worst fears were upon him. It all started innocently enough. The men had just lined up in the chow line to fill their plates with Rawley's beans and biscuits, and Skidder took a sniff of the mess and turned up his nose.

Laramie, who was eating again with the men so as not to draw undue attention, saw the scowling face but thought little of it. The men often complained about the fare.

But Rawley was in no mood to have his food insulted.

"What's the matter," he snapped, "ya expecting ham hock and sweet taters?"

"Well—iffen I was, I sure ain't now," said Skidder with a snarl.

"Iffen ya think ya can do better, why don't you fix the food—"

"Food?" snorted Skidder. "Ya call this food? Pig wouldn't et this slop."

"Pig? Guess it would too. You've been ettin' it fer a fair piece now."

Laramie saw Skidder's face and knew that trouble was coming. The others saw it too. There was a changing of positions as everyone eased out of the line of fire.

Will intervened. "You fellas have a burr under yer saddle, take it outside," was all he said.

Skidder, the plate of food still in his hand and a mean look on his face, nodded his head toward the door.

Laramie hoped Rawley would let it pass. Would just turn his back on the testy gun-toter. Everyone in the room knew that Rawley was no match for Skidder.

But Rawley was not looking for a way to back off. With one quick flick of his hand he upended the extended plate, splashing its contents over Skidder's face and down the front of his leather vest.

The fight did not make it outside. A hand flashed, Skidder's gun flamed, and Rawley fell forward, clutching his chest. A movement in the corner brought Skidder spinning around just as James, Rawley's sidekick, cleared the gun from his holster.

It was too slow. Skidder's second shot caught the man in the abdomen before he could even pull the trigger.

"Drop it," roared Will, his chair falling to the floor with a crash as he leaped to his feet.

Skidder let his gun hand lower to his side. But the defiance did not leave his eyes.

"I don't take kindly to a man shootin' up my quarters," the boss said, menace in his voice. "An' I don't take kindly to losin' two good men jest before a planned job. Seems to me ya coulda et yer beans an' kept yer mouth shut—like the rest of us. Now wipe 'em off yer face and tend to those men."

Will picked up his chair, swore when he saw the broken leg, and jerked forward a log stool.

"Broke the only chair in the place," he mumbled angrily, still glaring at Skidder.

From the corner of the room, Laramie heard a groan. He pushed his way through the cluster of milling men and bent over James. The man was still breathing, but he had been hit hard.

"Help me git this man to my cabin," he said to Curly.

Curly's hands shook as he set aside his bottle of whiskey and bent to help lift the man.

All through the evening hours Laramie tried to stop the bleeding. Outside he could hear the scrape of the shovel in frozen ground. Skidder had been given the job of digging the grave for Rawley. Laramie hoped there wouldn't be one needed for James as well. Once he thought of going for Ariana. Maybe she could at least say a prayer for the dying man.

But Laramie decided against it. It wouldn't be safe. Besides, a girl like Ariana shouldn't have to be exposed to such horrors. The men in the camp were used to seeing men die—it would be a totally new thing for the young girl. One that could fill her sleep with nightmares—like those kinds of events had done for Laramie when he was a kid.

He made James as comfortable as he could and hoped that the man would make it to see another morning. Then Laramie thought of his mother's Bible. Carefully he took it from its hiding place and thumbed through the pages. He found a spot heavily marked in his mother's handwriting and began to read, his voice low but clear.

The passage had nothing to do with death or dying—or of preparing oneself for the possibility. It was the story of Jesus calling the fishermen away from their nets. "Follow me," He had said, and his mother had, sometime in the past, written carefully beside the passage, "I have decided to follow Him, too. It has brought such peace and joy to my being."

After Laramie finished the story he read on, page after page. He didn't know if the man lying on his bed could hear the words, but he himself needed them, even if James did not.

This life, this way of living made no sense. No sense at all. He had always had questions about it. Now he was more sure than ever. He would have wanted out even if the girl hadn't come into the camp. He had always wanted out. He realized that now. He had never really fit. There was something that had always held him back.

A sudden idea occurred to him, making his spine tingle with the thought. Could it possibly be that this mother—this unknown person in his background—had somehow influenced his life? But how? Was this unseen, unknown God of hers holding him in check? He did not know. He wished he knew. He wished he knew more about this God. He was sure that Ariana had some of the answers, but he dared not go to her. He was sure to be watched. Everyone would be watched.

The whole camp was like a powder keg—about to explode. Given time they would all destroy one another—and the girl too.

Laramie turned back to the Book in his hand. It was the only thing that seemed to make any sense.

Along about midnight he heard footsteps on the path. He recognized Sam's step; then there was a bump at the door and Sam pushed his way in. Laramie was glad to see him. He welcomed the man's company.

"How's he doin'?" Sam asked simply.

Laramie nodded toward the man, whose breathing was becoming more shallow. He made no comment. Sam could see for himself.

Sam pulled up a stool and sat down.

Laramie let his gaze settle back on the man occupying his bed. "Was James his first name—or his last?" he asked quietly.

Sam shrugged. "I dunno," he replied—then gave a little snort. "Most likely weren't neither," he said. "Coulda took it jest 'cause he liked it. Maybe borrowed it offa Jesse. Mighta made him feel big."

Laramie looked back at the man. They really knew very little about him—except that he wasn't fast enough with a gun.

Silence.

"Ya been to see the girl?" asked Sam.

Laramie looked up in surprise and shook his head.

"Figure she might be scared blue," went on Sam. "Bound to have heard the shots."

"She'll be sleepin' now," remarked Laramie.

"Iffen she is, she's in better shape then the rest of us," replied Sam, reaching for his wad of chewing tobacco.

"Would ya mind lookin' in on her?" asked Laramie.

"Why don't you go?"

Laramie was silent for a number of minutes.

"Don't want to drag her in on this," he said finally. "Skidder's been lookin' fer a chance to draw on me fer months."

Sam chewed and spit.

"Yer faster," he said at last, avoiding Laramie's gaze.

His eyes narrowed. Was that the way Sam reasoned too? That a man, even a man like Skidder, had no value? That a snuffed-out life was nothing more than another grave to dig?

The thought troubled Laramie. He got up from his place by the bed and began to restlessly pace the cabin.

At last he wheeled to face the man he had known since he was old enough to recall anything at all.

"Is thet what this is all about?" he asked frankly. "Was thet girl brought in here to force a showdown 'tween Skidder an' me?"

Sam said nothing.

"Was it, Sam?" Laramie demanded. "Tell me. Was it?"

"Yer pa was jest anxious fer ya to . . . to act a man," replied Sam, and he spit into the corner.

Laramie's face blanched white. Then a red stain of anger began to flush his cheeks.

"Thet's 'bout the lowest thing I ever heard," he muttered angrily. "The lowest. To bring a girl—why didn't he jest call me out hisself?"

"Now, Kid—yer pa jest wanted ya to use yer gun 'cause he didn't want some low-liver shootin' ya in the back."

"Why? Why? Am I any better than—than Rawley—or James? Is my life worth more than—?"

"Don't go gittin' all in a knot. No harm—"

"No harm? What do you think this little scheme has done to her? Holed up all these months in the camp of—of no-good desperadoes? What do ya—?"

"Ya could have shortened it some," said Sam with no apologies.

Laramie just stood and stared.

"By killin' a man?" he demanded, his voice like steel. "I could have freed her up iffen I'd jest—pulled my Colt and killed a man? And what would thet have accomplished. Kill one—then there'd be another—an' another."

He lifted a hand and pushed his Stetson back in agitation.

Sam shrugged. "It gits easier," he said casually. "Jest the first one thet bothers a man much."

Laramie stared, anger making his eyes glitter.

"Yer pa was jest thinkin' of you. Didn't want ya leavin' a string of one-arm gunslingers to track ya down—"

"So I shoot 'em all?"

The words were spoken in vehemence. Sam did not respond. The silence hung heavy in the log cabin.

"I don't think so, Sam," Laramie finally went on evenly, his control back again. "I don't think so. I . . . I'm at the place where . . . I'd be willin' to die fer her, but I . . . I haven't come to the place where I'd be willin' to kill in cold blood fer her. An' the more I read in thet Bible, the more sure I am of thet fact."

Sam's eyes widened. It was clear to Laramie that the words surprised and shocked him. "Thet girl been fillin' ya with Bible talk?" he asked, and Laramie could tell he was upset.

"Not a'tall," he drawled. "Been readin' it fer myself—an' fer James here."

"Where'd you git a Bible?"

"You gave it to me."

Sam looked about to explode. "I never did no sech thing an' you know—"

"Sure you did," replied Laramie. "In thet trunk—of my ma's."

"Yer ma's Bible?"

Laramie only nodded.

Sam chewed on his mustache, then spit in the corner.

"So what can you tell me about her, Sam?" Laramie asked quietly.

Sam's head jerked up. "Oh no," he said with a wave of his hand. "I got nothin' to say. Nothin'. Ain't no business of mine. It's yer pa's place to—" He stopped, looked at Laramie, then spit again.

There was further silence as Sam continued working on his chaw of tobacco. At length he looked up. "So yer holdin' yer position?" he asked frankly.

Laramie nodded again, his eyes thoughtful, his jaw set.

"Well, Kid," Sam said as he slowly lifted himself from the chunk of log. "I wouldn't give her much chance of gittin' back to life as she knew it, then. Yer pa's 'bout got his mind made up—an' it's 'bout like a rusty steel trap. Once shut—never git it open."

A slight moan from the corner cot caught their attention. Even as Laramie moved toward the bed he saw that the wounded man had taken his last breath.

Laramie stood over him, feeling helpless and sick at his stomach. He never had been able to accept the sight of a man who'd died because of a bullet in his stomach.

He turned away from the bed, one hand raised to slowly tip back the brim of his Stetson. His knees felt weak, his thoughts were jumbled in anger and confusion. It was so senseless. So brutal.

He heard the sound of scraping as Sam pushed himself up from his block seat and onto his feet. Laramie wondered if the sight of the wasted man was making Sam feel sick inside also.

When he turned to look at the older man, Sam was already moving slowly toward the door. Just before he exited the cabin he turned and spit into the corner. "Guess I'd better tell Skidder to git his shovel out agin," he said. He left the room without further comment.

❧　　❧　　❧

Laramie longed to go to Ariana. Was she awake? Had she indeed heard the shouting and the shots? Surely she was frightened and filled with questions.

And he was the reason. He was the cause of her being dragged off from home and family to this terrible bandit outpost. He, unknowingly, had brought about this awful deed.

He buried his head in his hands and tried to address a God whom he did not know.

And then a new thought brought some peace to his heart. Ariana knew this God. He had seen the quiet confidence in her eyes as she spread the Book out before her. Even in the midst of her fear, she had shown unbelievable courage. It wasn't her own doing, he was sure of that now. It was because she had faith in the unseen God she trusted.

Chapter Thirteen

Escape

Laramie brought the wood earlier than usual the next morning. Ariana had washed herself in the basin and dressed in her own garments. She was spending time in early morning prayer. The events of the night before had upset her, so she had not been able to sleep. She had heard the angry shouts, the gunshots, and then the scraping of the shovel against the frozen ground and rocky soil. Something terrible had happened. She was sure of it. It brought her added terror. She had spent most of the night in prayer.

She had hoped that Laramie or Sam would come to her cabin and assure her that everything was all right—but at the same time she knew better. Never had she clung so tenaciously to the promises of God as she had through those long night hours.

When the little rap came on her door, she recognized it as Laramie's signal. Without understanding her intense relief that he hadn't been the one who was buried, she crossed to the door and quickly lifted the sturdy hook. As the door swung open she looked from his armload of wood to the stack against the wall. She was not in need of more firewood.

"Close the door," he whispered, and Ariana hastened to obey. Instinctively she knew something had changed—and not for the better. Her face paled. Her hands knotted against her calico front.

Laramie walked directly to the stack of wood and dropped his pile of logs. As he did so a package tumbled out and fell to the floor. Ariana stared.

"Come here," whispered Laramie, and Ariana woodenly obeyed.

"I haven't time to talk," said the man as he began to stack the firewood, making an unusual amount of noise as he did so.

"I'm gittin' you outta here. Sh-h. We might be spied on. I can't stay long enough to give ya all the details. But I've some things fer you to do."

He glanced around the room again and proceeded to lift stacked logs and bang them against one another as he re-stacked them by the wall.

"First—make a big batch of biscuits—all ya can—an' wrap 'em up—in two different bundles—maybe in those towels. Don't worry none about crushin'. Thet won't hurt 'em.

"Then, after supper—pack the things ya want to take—in as tight a bundle as ya can. I'll pick 'em up. Put on the clothes from this bundle and wait. Light yer lamp—as usual. Keep the big towel over the winda. I'll knock three little raps—then agin three—on yer winda, not yer door. You be ready." More logs crashed against the wall.

"I'll take ya to a friend of mine. He's Pawnee. He'll take ya where ya'll be safe. Trust 'im."

He stood and moved to the fire.

"Ya need more water?" he asked in a normal voice.

Ariana stood mute, staring at him. It was too much to take in all at once. She blinked. Her mouth opened but no words came. His hand gave her a little signal, and she swallowed hard and found her voice.

"Yes," she answered in as even a voice as she could manage. "Yes . . . I'd like some extra . . . if you have time. It's . . . it's the day for my bath."

He smiled softly and nodded his head as though to compliment her on her control. Then he went to fill the kettle and the basin from the pail and left the cabin with the empty bucket in his hand. Ariana put the hook firmly in place. Her hand was trembling so uncontrollably she could hardly manage the small task.

※　　※　　※

Ariana finally had a day that demanded action. Over and over in her mind she sorted through those things she was to do. She really did take a bath, thinking that it might well be her last one for some time to come. Then she got out her food supplies and baked biscuits as she had been ordered, until she had a large stack of them on her wooden table.

By the time she had finished her baking the sun was moving lower in the sky.

Ariana began to gather the things she planned to take with her. She was glad she had dressed in her own garments that morning so the things that had belonged to Laramie's mother could be freshly washed. They now hung on the hook on the wall. She crossed the small room, lifted down each item, and folded it carefully. It was the first time she had opened the lid of the trunk since Laramie himself had removed the small chest and worn Bible.

"I wonder if he ever reads?" she mused as she placed the items of clothing back on the top of the pile.

" 'Laramie's Mama,' " she whispered to the unknown woman, "I don't know anything about you . . . whether you are alive . . . or dead . . . but I do thank you . . . whoever you are, for the use of your things. I have tried to . . . to return them to you in the same condition . . . ."

Ariana let the words trail off. It did seem awfully silly to be talking to someone who was not there.

She closed the lid quietly, letting her hand rest upon it for several moments as she looked down at the metal top, the stained leather straps.

"If only you could talk," she whispered to the trunk. "I'm

sure you'd have secrets to share."

Then she turned her attention back to the task at hand. She had to be prepared, small bundle and baked biscuits wrapped securely for whatever lay ahead.

❦   ❦   ❦

As darkness fell, Ariana lit the kerosene lamp as she had been told and sat down in the unfamiliar buckskin clothing on the log stool by her table. Normally she would have spent her evening hours reading or memorizing from her Bible— but tonight her Bible, along with her few other possessions, was wrapped securely in the little bundle and waiting on the floor close to the room's window, along with the two packages of biscuits.

Ariana had also made up another small bundle with additional food supplies that could be carried on a pack animal. She had no idea how long the trip might take to get back home. The trip through the storm had seemed to take forever—but if she remembered correctly, they had made it in four days of travel.

More and more throughout the day, the truth of her circumstances had begun to sink in. This was no pleasure trip through the beauties of the woods. She was not going to be released—set free. She had been smuggled into the camp of lawless men—and she was to be smuggled out. Laramie had made that plain with his secrecy and carefully laid plans. It was going to be a dangerous mission. Not just for her, she surmised, but for the young man as well.

"Would they really kill one of their own?" she asked herself.

After the events of the night before—still unexplained to Ariana—she had no doubt of the answer. Yes. Laramie could be killed in his effort to free her from the camp and get her back to her own hometown.

Over and over Ariana offered intense little prayers.

And she waited—her whole body feeling rigid and trembly, her hands clasped in front of her on the wooden boards of the table, the simple buckskin garments feeling strange on her skin.

The tension within her grew and grew as the night hours moved slowly by. Had Laramie forgotten? No, surely not. Had something happened to him? That thought brought her to near panic. *Pray,* she ordered herself sternly. *Pray—and trust.*

Ariana tried hard to fight the waves of fear that swept through her. She had to be calm. She had to be in control. Her flight depended upon it. Without control she might make some very foolish mistake.

And then she heard the gentle rap at her window. Three times. She waited. A repeat of another three. Ariana rose from her seat and moved quickly to the window. Even in her excitement, she noted the silence of the moccasins that had been provided.

She lifted back the towel curtain and could just make out the dim outline of Laramie's face. He motioned for her to open the window, and she did so as quietly as she could.

Without a word, she passed the bundles out the window to his waiting hands, then climbed on the log stool that she had placed below the window earlier in the day.

Without a sound Laramie helped ease her body through the small opening and lowered her noiselessly to the ground. Taking her by the hand he began to lead her through the darkness. Ariana wondered how he could even find his way through the heavy growth of trees, but she followed wordlessly.

Before long they came to a small clearing. Three horses stood, stirring restlessly, anxious to be back in their warm stalls. A late spring storm was bringing snow, icy hard flakes, driven by a biting wind. Ariana felt a sick feeling in the pit of her stomach. Was this a repeat of the whole horrible nightmare?

As if born of the night, another man was suddenly beside her. He spoke not a word, just reached for her hand. The Indian Laramie had told her about.

At the same time the young brave took her left hand, Laramie released her right. She was being led off into the darkness without even a final word.

She looked back once and stumbled slightly. Laramie was tying the bundles she had given him to the pack saddle on one of the animals. All except for one of the towel-wrapped batches of biscuits. The young brave carried that in his other hand.

❧   ❧   ❧

"You safe here."

It was the first the Indian had spoken. Wordlessly he had led Ariana across the valley, through the deep darkness of the woods and into the hills. Now they were entering a cave. Ariana could not restrain a shudder. She hated caves. Was afraid of them. Had always been afraid of them—even as a young child.

And now she was to enter one. She did not like the idea. But perhaps—perhaps it was a little better than being in a camp of outlaws.

She steeled herself, took a deep breath, and followed her guide into the opening.

The man was leading her deeper and deeper into the cave. She wondered how he could possibly know where he was going. He stopped and used a flint to light a small lantern that must have been waiting for their arrival. Then they traveled on, winding this way and that, squeezing through small openings in the rocks, crawling through short tunnels, pushing their way through rubble.

Ariana stifled a scream that pressed at the back of her throat. She feared she would suffocate. She frantically wondered just how much more she could stand—and then they passed through a narrow opening and came out into a larger space. Ariana was faintly aware of the sound of dripping water.

"You safe here," the young brave said again.

Ariana let her gaze travel over the cave floor. Someone lived here. There were robes and blankets and supplies. Someone. . . . Who? The Indian? Surely she wasn't expected to share the dwelling with—

"It dry—safe," the young man said again. Ariana still did not move.

"You light candle—one," he ordered.

Ariana stiffly bent to pick up a candle. She noticed that there was a rather large pile of them on the floor. She held the candle to the wick of the lantern he held out to her. The candle sputtered, then raised a tiny, flickering flame. He set the bundle of biscuits on the floor by the other stores.

"You eat—one—each time you light new candle," he commanded her in his soft voice. Ariana nodded dumbly.

"Sleep," he said and pointed to the pile of skins and blankets in the corner.

Ariana nodded again and moved to place her candle in the wooden holder that had been left for it.

He stared at her candle for a long moment with an expression she could not read.

"Don't let candle die," he cautioned. "No more light."

Ariana's eyes widened. Being in this deep, dark cave was bad enough—but with no light. The very thought sent waves of panic through her.

"I not bring another," and he indicated the flint in his hand with some apology in his tone. "I need at front of cave for return." She stared dumbly at him.

"I go," announced the man and moved away before Ariana could respond. She was afraid he would fade into the very rocks of the walls.

"Wait," she cried after him.

He turned back. The flicker of the lantern he held cast eerie shadows on his bronze cheeks. His black eyes seemed to reflect the dancing light.

"Wait," Ariana implored again, reaching out a trembling hand.

He stood silently while she tried to untangle her thoughts and get them in order for expression.

"I . . . I need to know . . . I mean . . . Laramie said you'd tell me what I'm to do," she managed.

He nodded. "You wait," he said simply.

"But . . . in here . . . alone . . . for who . . . how long?" Her questions seemed to tumble over one another.

He came a step closer and set his lantern on the hard rock of the cave floor. Then he surprised her by lowering himself to a cross-legged sitting position. Ariana waited.

He nodded to her, and she understood that she was also to sit—on the pile in the corner that was meant for her bed.

Obediently she sat.

"Alone—here—yes," he began. "Do not leave—ever. We come."

He seemed to feel that was settled. She was to wait here—alone—until someone came for her.

"How many suns? Not know," he continued.

"But . . . who will come? Laramie said—"

"Laramie come," he nodded in assurance, and Ariana's troubled mind grasped at that promise.

But her sense of relief was short-lived.

"Maybe yes—maybe no," he went on calmly, making her heart race again.

"If not—I come," he finished, then sat quietly as though waiting to see if she had any more questions.

She sat trembling, looking down at her folded hands.

"Food," he said, pointing at the supply against the rock wall. "Water," he continued and pointed to the opposite wall and up against the ceiling. It was the first Ariana had noticed the little ledge and the small clay pot that sat on it. From somewhere above, water continued to drip, drip into the container. That was her water supply.

"Sleep," he said again, and he rose like a shadow and turned away from her again.

She knew better than to call a second time. She was alone in a deep, dark cave, somewhere in the bowels of the earth.

And she was to wait—just wait—silently—patiently—until someone came for her. Ariana felt terror rise in her throat until she felt she wouldn't be able to breathe.

⚜   ⚜   ⚜

All through the night Laramie pressed his mount forward, the two animals on their tethers following obediently at his heels.

At times he hid his trail by traveling along the sheltered rock shelves; at others he left deliberate little clues as to which way he was heading.

He was glad for the snow. By morning, and the discovery that they were gone, much of the trail would be covered— just as it had been when his pa and Sam had brought the girl to the camp.

Laramie smiled. It seemed rather ironic. A snowstorm had kept her would-be rescuers from finding her—and a snowstorm might also defeat her enemies.

Laramie pulled his hat down over his face to protect himself from the bite of the whirling ice crystals and urged the rangy buckskin on.

Chapter Fourteen

Waiting

"Lord, it's been seventy-two days," Laura Benson reminded God in a quiet conversation with Him as she rolled crusts for an apple pie. "Seventy-two days—without any word."

She blinked away tears that welled up in her eyes. "I've tried to be patient, Lord. Tried to trust . . . but sometimes . . . it gets so hard."

The tears refused to stay in check and squeezed out from under her blinking lids and rolled down her wrinkled cheeks. She reached for the hankie in her apron pocket and quickly dispensed with the telltale marks of weeping.

"They say no news is good news, Lord," she continued. "Help me to really believe that."

❧   ❧   ❧

Ariana huddled in her corner. She was thankful for the warm furs beneath her and the woolen blankets she could wrap her body in. She wasn't sure if she shook from the cold, dank interior of the cave or from sheer terror, but she trembled just the same.

"If only I had my Bible," she said to herself for the twentieth time.

But you do, an inner voice prompted. *Haven't you been busy with memorization for the past weeks? You have much of the Bible within you.*

With a start of surprise, Ariana realized it was so. She had memorized many sections of Scripture during her days of confinement. Perhaps the long stay in the small cabin would not be for nought.

She pulled the blanket more closely about her shoulders. "Where should I start?" she asked herself. "Well . . . why not at the beginning? I'll gradually work my way through the Bible, recalling every portion I have learned."

"Genesis, chapter one. In the beginning God . . ."

Ariana stopped. The few words had given her much to think about.

"In the beginning *God* . . ." she repeated slowly. The words seemed to echo off the dark walls of rock.

Ariana spoke them again. At least her own voice was something with which to fill the stillness.

"God . . . in the beginning . . . and always," she mused to herself. "Well . . . if He has always been—and I fully believe He has—then I guess He must know all there is to know about what's going on. Even now. Even in this cave."

The thought brought comfort to Ariana.

She reached down one hand to feel the softness of her bed. Someone had taken a good deal of trouble to prepare it for her. Spruce and pine branches intertwined to make a soft layer beneath her. Soft moss covered the boughs. Then the thick fur—likely buffalo, Ariana guessed—and then the warm, though scratchy, blankets of wool.

Yes, she could not complain about her bed. It was much more comfortable than the rough wood bunk in the cabin.

Ariana let her gaze travel to the little stock of supplies. Here again her needs had been met. True, it was not especially tasty food that had been stored in the cave. But it was palatable—and nourishing. Pemmican. Dried berries and fish. And her own biscuits—which would soon be as dry as the berries, she thought wryly.

And water. She had a good supply of water—though at first the constant drip, drip had threatened to drive her mad. But the water was cold and fresh, and she had no trouble convincing herself to drink straight from the small earthen pot.

Ariana looked at the little stack of candles. So far she had relit a new candle from the old one seven times. She had no idea how long one candle burned. She had no idea whether it was now day or night in the outside world. She had even less of an idea how many hours had crawled by since she had been brought to the cave. She only knew that it seemed like a very long time.

And now her thoughts turned again from the cave and back to the Scripture.

"In the beginning God . . ." she said again and smiled to herself. "And in the end, God as well," she went on. "And in the middle, and in the past, and in the future—God. For always and ever—what a wonderful truth."

"In the beginning God created. . . ." She stopped again and let her eyes drift over the eerie walls of the cave. The flickering candlelight cast funny dancing shapes over the roughness of the rock.

"You did this," she spoke to the God she knew shared her abode. "You made this. Why? Why this strange little room way back in the rocks? Did you know—even then—that someday. . . ?" Ariana let her voice fade. It was too big an idea to even think about.

Suddenly the cave no longer seemed menacing. It did not even seem as cold and clammy as before. Ariana had the comforting knowledge that she was not alone.

❧   ❧   ❧

The severity of the storm made travel more and more difficult for Laramie. At the same time, it would make his trail harder to follow. He began to wonder if he shouldn't change his plans and head straight for the cave and Ariana.

At length he decided against it. He and White Eagle had laid their plans carefully. To change now might mean a disruption that could be costly—even deadly.

Laramie pulled the collar of his heavy coat up more closely to his chin and nudged the buckskin with a blunted spur.

He lifted his face to try to judge the time of day. It was hard to tell with the sky so overcast. He turned his thoughts back to the camp behind him. Had they discovered his absence? How had his pa responded? Laramie could easily guess. Were they already on his trail?

Then his thoughts turned to Ariana. He had no reason to think that White Eagle would have had any trouble getting the girl to the safety of the hidden cave. The sentry posted on the ledge would not have been able to see the brave and the girl, and certainly would not have heard them creeping through the cover of darkness. The rest of the gang members would pose no threat. They much preferred their bunks or the card table during the hours of night.

It seemed to Laramie that the first part of the mission had gone as planned. The hardest part was still to come. He had to backtrack and lead the girl from the cave to further safety. That would mean getting her out almost beneath the noses of the gang, and they were bound to be stirring about like a nest of disturbed hornets.

Laramie set his jaw and pushed on. If only the second part of the plan worked as well as the first.

❧   ❧   ❧

Laramie watched as White Eagle separated himself from the overhanging spruce and moved forward. Without a word to the waiting brave, Laramie swung out of the saddle. Three ponies stood ground-tethered in the shadows. The horses exchanged whinnied greetings and stomped in impatience.

White Eagle began to undo the girth of the pack saddle even as Laramie began to uncinch the belly straps of the riding saddle, still warm from his body.

"Any signs?" asked White Eagle.

Laramie shook his head. "Didn't see a soul," he replied. "The storm made sight and sound nigh impossible."

"They follow," White Eagle informed him. "Five." He pointed his hand straight up, and Laramie understood that he was saying the five men had not ridden out of the camp until near noon. That had given him even more time than he had counted on. For one moment he wished his plans had not included the trip to the cave. He should have just taken the girl and headed right out. But how could he have known that a spring storm would move in? How could he have known that the camp would not stir and discover the missing horses, then the girl's empty cabin, until noon? No, it was better that they had played it safe. But now—?

"What do you think, White Eagle?" he asked his friend. "Do you think it is safe to keep on riding, or should we change horses as planned and wait?"

White Eagle looked at the clear sky overhead. Laramie followed his glance and knew what his friend was thinking. The storm was over. Now there would be no advantage of being hidden by a winter storm or of having the trail covered by falling snow. There would only be drifts of whiteness on the ground. It would be impossible to cover one's tracks.

"Wait," said the young brave. "Send horses. Wait."

In spite of his similar assessment, Laramie wanted to argue. He had hoped White Eagle would assure him that it would be days before the men at his back would be able to sort out his trail. After all, they would not be expecting him to head straight to the Indian village.

And he had hoped—had just hoped—that he might not have to lose his buckskin. He had a great deal of affection for the animal. He would have liked to have left the saddle on the horse's back and just ridden out of the encampment the way he had ridden in.

Besides—things looked good right now. But what if something happened they had not anticipated? It could mean a long delay. Ariana was waiting. She would be restless, fearful. Wondering.

He hated to wait.

"I watch," White Eagle spoke again. "I take you to hiding place. Then I watch."

"Do yer people know I'm here?" asked Laramie.

"They know," said White Eagle solemnly. "My father say, 'Leave to White Eagle white brother.' They know. You safe. But for other men—my people not like white man."

Laramie knew that to be an understatement. There had been bad blood between the little pockets of outlaws and the Indian people. Raids—especially of horses—took place back and forth and often resulted in bloodshed.

"What if someone else—from another tribe—discovers me?" he asked his friend.

White Eagle shook his head. "I take you to sacred mountain," he said in a conspiratorial tone. "No Indian go there. Afraid."

Laramie nodded and removed the bridle from the buckskin. Without comment he ran his hand over the soft neck, the sleek back of the horse. He sure would miss him. He hated to let him go.

"Take care, partner," he whispered under his breath, and then he gave the surprised mount a slap on the rump with the flat of his hand. The startled animal leaped forward at the same time as the big bay who had been turned loose by White Eagle. Both animals started off at a gallop, the little roan fast on their heels. The Indian ponies stamped in impatience, their heads tossed high, their nostrils flaring, and pulled against their tethers.

The two men stood and watched the driven horses gallop on through the woods.

"He go back to ranch?" asked the Indian about the big bay, who had quickly taken the lead.

"I shore do hope so. He's tried to head thet direction each time I take him out," replied Laramie.

"Maybe he go," nodded White Eagle.

As the three horses disappeared from sight, the two men turned their attention to the other mounts.

"These fellas broke to saddle?" inquired Laramie as he carried his saddle toward them.

For the first time, White Eagle laughed. "We see," was his response, and Laramie guessed they might have a bit of a rodeo show in store.

❧   ❧   ❧

Ariana had worked her way through Genesis. When she came to portions that she had not memorized, she filled in accounts with her own version of events. Then she moved on to Exodus—easily recalling many of the stories and even quoting some of the scriptures. She reviewed each of the Ten Commandments, studying thoughtfully each one in a way that she had not troubled to do in the past. On to Leviticus. She found she had a difficult time untangling the laws and rules for living, worship, and sacrifice. Numbers. Deuteronomy. "I'm going to have to study those books more," she chided. "I haven't paid close enough attention."

She began her mental journey through Joshua, marveling how God led His people to victory time after time—whenever they were walking in obedience.

Occasionally she stopped to wonder how many days had passed. How many more meals the little store would provide. How long her supply of candles would last. At times fear gripped her and she wanted to scream against the confines of her quarters. Was her present circumstance really that much better than her former state had been? At least in the cabin she had had the blessing of seeing daylight. At least she had known whether it was day or night.

Then she would determinedly force her thoughts to other things. It would not do for her to get despondent. To give up. She must keep fighting for survival. She must eat her daily rations—must light her candle. And she must fight the urge to stumble her way out of the dark cave and into the sunlight. Her very life depended upon it.

⚜   ⚜   ⚜

Laramie chafed with the delay. It wasn't that he feared for his own safety. White Eagle had led him to a well-hidden spot close to the Indian settlement. It was not likely that the men from the gang would search for him here, and White Eagle had assured him that Indian braves stayed well away from the "place of the angry gods."

Still he paced restlessly. Shouldn't he be on the trail? Shouldn't he have picked up Ariana and galloped off while the men searched for him in the other direction? What was keeping White Eagle? Had something happened to the young brave?

It was all Laramie could do to hold his post. His agitation seemed to take hold of his very being. He had never been so troubled before.

Would Ariana be facing the same doubts? Would she be as restless? As irritated? Would her impatience drive her to do something foolish?

Laramie had to hold himself in check. He felt it would be easier to face a herd of stampeding buffalo—a nest of rattlers—than just to sit and wait. At least then he would feel that his destiny, to some measure, was in his own hands.

Just as he was about to explode from the tension, White Eagle slipped quietly into the little camp.

Chapter Fifteen

Terror

Laramie moved eagerly forward to meet the young Pawnee. "What's the news?" he asked impatiently.

White Eagle shook his head, and Laramie feared the word was not good.

"Red horse not go," he answered evenly.

Laramie stopped midstride. "Did they find 'im?" was his next question.

White Eagle nodded in reply.

Laramie licked his lips. He felt confused—betrayed by the animal.

"What happened?" he asked.

"They backtrack—close to village," responded White Eagle.

"They think yer people captured us?"

"Maybe yes," said White Eagle. "Maybe no."

Laramie waited. He was sure White Eagle had more to report.

"They know Indian not let horse go," said White Eagle simply.

Laramie thought on that and then nodded. It was true. The Indians would not have released the horses.

"So they know it's a false trail," he admitted aloud.

"They wait—just outside village—in draw."

"Are they still there?" asked Laramie.

"Had to tell Father to stop young braves," went on White Eagle. "They want to raid. Like horses. They wait now."

Laramie nodded.

There was silence as the young men pondered their situation.

White Eagle spoke. "You want braves attack?" he asked simply.

Laramie shook his head. He could not utter the order that would surely send the gang members to their death—including his own father. Nor did he wish to cause danger to the Indian braves—though he imagined the chief was having difficulty holding his men in check. They would have welcomed an opportunity to attack the little camp of desperadoes and plunder their supplies and their horses.

"No. No, don't attack. We'll wait."

But at the same time he still hated the thought of waiting.

"One thing more," said White Eagle thoughtfully.

Laramie turned to him.

"One sentry. One. He sits by big rock on hill."

Laramie waited.

"Leaning Tree, brave man. He like big red horse."

Laramie still waited patiently.

At last White Eagle continued. "Leaning Tree will silence sentry. Me take horses."

Laramie's eyes grew serious. "Kill the sentry?" he asked. He wanted no part of killing if there was another way out.

"Maybe yes. Maybe no," said White Eagle.

"Tell him no," said Laramie. "Take his guns. Leave him tied if you have to."

White Eagle looked dubious but nodded. "Leaning Tree not like this. . . ." He shrugged his shoulders when Laramie did not change his mind.

White Eagle spoke again. "Leaning Tree get big red horse. You—buckskin. Me—rest."

Laramie nodded. It would make White Eagle a very

wealthy young brave. He would be able to pick from all the maidens of the village.

"Wait," said Laramie, raising his hand to show that the deal had not been completed.

White Eagle watched his face closely.

"I get back the buckskin—and the roan," said Laramie, remembering the excitement when he first had put his saddle on the Indian pony White Eagle had provided. "You git yer mustangs back."

White Eagle looked amused. Then nodded in agreement. "Come," he said simply. "I take you to girl."

"Now?" Laramie was both surprised and excited.

"Now. You must be ready to ride tomorrow when horses come."

Laramie nodded. It sounded reasonable. After all, the whole gang that sought his hiding place would then be on foot.

☙   ☙   ☙

Ariana paced the small hideout. She told herself she had to keep limber—but in truth she knew she was just restless.

She had been in this hole in the rocks for such a long time. She didn't know how much longer she could endure it. Even the reciting of scriptures failed to quiet her troubled spirit.

She walked back and forth—back and forth.

Now and then her eyes traveled to her little stack of supplies. She had already eaten all the biscuits and the dried fruit. Only pemmican remained. Ariana was not sure just how long she could stretch it out. She was drinking more and more water in order to keep her stomach from gnawing with hunger.

Her pile of candles was being quickly used up too. Ariana would not let herself think about being left in the dark. She simply would not be able to endure it. She would bolt for sure. But did she know her way out? The young Indian had turned this way and that, selecting one tunnel over another—and he had a lantern. She would get lost in the labyrinth for sure without any light. She might wander forever and never find her way to daylight. The mere idea was more than she could bear.

"Sleep," she told herself. "Sleep. Time will pass more quickly. Surely he will come soon. Surely..."

She checked the candle to make sure it had plenty of burning time left and eased onto the bed of fur. She tucked the blanket firmly about her and closed her eyes. The constant dripping of water distracted her, but she fought against it. She found a hymn whose beat kept time with the dripping and sang it over in her mind. Over and over—until it was almost hypnotic. Finally she drifted off into a troubled sleep.

⚜   ⚜   ⚜

Ariana awoke, fighting for full consciousness. Something was wrong. She knew it—but in her state of drowsiness she was unable to reason it through.

She listened, straining to hear in the darkness. Nothing. Nothing but the soft drip of the seeping water.

Then if a noise had not disturbed her—what had?

She groped to pull the blanket more closely about her chin. Something was wrong. She could feel it.

And then the truth hit her full force. There was no light! Her candle was no longer burning. What had happened? What had put out the flicker of light?

It took several minutes before Ariana could gather enough courage to reach out in the darkness. The place where the candle had been was just a sticky spot on the wooden holder. She had slept too long. Her candle had burned out.

"Oh no," she cried out. "No." Her voice echoed around her.

Panic nearly suffocated her. She would never be able to stand it alone in the dark. Never. She wouldn't be able to find her food. Her water. She'd die. She'd surely die.

A feeling of total desperation overtook her. She found herself praying that she might die quickly. Then Ariana buried her face in the warm fur, and for the first time since the early days of her capture, she wept uncontrollably.

☙ ☙ ☙

"Ya sure we won't be spotted?" Laramie asked as he followed White Eagle along an unmarked trail.

"Leaning Tree watch," replied the brave.

The answer satisfied Laramie and he picked up the pace. Each man led one of the mustangs, saddles again in place after a struggle to get the horses to accept them. But White Eagle insisted it would be safer for them to walk through the trees rather than to ride. The horses had now quieted to the saddle, but accepting a rider in the saddle would start the battle all over again. They had no time to lose.

As it was, it was getting dark by the time White Eagle pushed aside a small bramble bush and motioned Laramie into the mouth of a hidden cave.

They had moved in a short distance when White Eagle stopped and lifted a lantern from a hidden place in the rocks. Silently he lit it and then moved stealthily on.

Deeper and deeper into the cavern they went, winding first one way and then angling back another. Laramie was counting on his friend to eventually get them to the right place—and to make sure they would find their way out again.

They had walked what seemed to be a long way when White Eagle stopped and put a hand to Laramie's chest.

"What is it?" Laramie whispered, the hair on the back of his neck lifting eerily.

"No light," responded White Eagle.

"No light?"

"No candle," repeated White Eagle.

Laramie felt his whole body tremble. Had something happened to Ariana? Was the whole effort in vain? He closed his eyes and willed strength back into his body. White Eagle began to move forward again.

They pushed their way through one last opening and entered a wider hole in the rocks. Laramie could see the pile of furs and blankets in the corner. Were they too late?

Then the blankets shifted. And she was looking at him, her eyes wide and terrified, pale cheeks stained from the cave dust mingled with her tears. Her hair hung about her shoulders in a tangled mass of uncombed curls, and her face looked gaunt.

"My candle went out," she gasped, then with a look like a wild thing, she turned her face back into the furs and began to weep again, her whole body shaking.

"I had to crawl about in the dark to—" she continued along with the sobs. "I had to—"

But she could not go on. The two men exchanged glances. One felt as helpless as the other. What could they do to comfort her? How did one reassure a distraught woman? What unspeakable terrors had she experienced in the darkness of the cave?

It was White Eagle who moved forward, handing the lantern to a stunned Laramie.

He knelt on the rock floor beside her bed and reached out one hand to her shaking shoulder. "It's over," he crooned softly. "Over. Soon you go. Soon. You safe now. Alone no more. Safe now."

As he talked he patted her shoulder rather clumsily and pushed back her hair. It reminded Laramie of one gentling a terror-stricken horse. Gradually the words and the human contact brought calm to the frightened girl. The sobs lessened. The shoulders stopped their shaking. Ariana began to fight for control.

"We light two candles," offered White Eagle. "Three candles. We light whole cave."

Ariana giggled—somewhat giddily—accompanied by hiccups. She forced her way up from the blankets and furs and dabbed at her face with a corner of the woolen throw.

"I was so scared," she admitted, apologetically, without looking up. "I had waited so long—I didn't know the way out—I thought you'd never come. Never."

"We come," said White Eagle—and he lit a fourth candle for good measure. "Tomorrow you go."

Ariana seemed to ponder his statement. For the first time she lifted her eyes to Laramie. Her face was still pale, her cheeks smeared, her hair in tangles. "Is it true?" she asked simply.

He nodded. He was still afraid to speak. He had never seen anyone look so desperate before.

Self-consciously she pushed hair away from her face. For the first time she seemed to realize her present state of disarray.

"I can't believe it," she said at last, her hands fluttering nervously. "I . . . I thought I'd never see the light of day again."

Laramie finally found his legs—and his voice. He moved forward with the lantern and set it on a small ledge of rock. The light spilled out in fanciful splashes, joining with the candles in lighting up the rock walls of the cave, making deeper shadows where the light did not reach.

"We'll leave in the morning," he promised her.

She fidgeted nervously and cast her eyes about the cave. "I . . . I guess I can stand . . . one more night," she finally managed and swallowed hard.

"I'll stay," said Laramie quickly, though he had intended to guard the cave's mouth and watch for signals from the valley.

White Eagle nodded. He seemed to understand.

"Both sleep," he said. "Long ride with new sun."

White Eagle gathered his lantern and left them, admonishing them again to get a good sleep in preparation for the next day's hard riding.

Laramie had nodded in agreement, but he wondered just how much sleep they would manage.

"When did you eat last?" he asked her.

Ariana looked puzzled. "I'm not sure," she replied honestly. "I . . . I lose track of time."

He nodded, then crossed to the food supply. It was almost gone.

"You'd better eat," he said and handed her a piece of the pemmican, then went for the little pot of water.

She appeared calm now. He marveled at the difference in her as he watched her dutifully chew away at the tough meat.

"I'm sorry it took so long," he began. "It didn't work like we'd planned."

She sat silently.

"It must have been . . ." He couldn't finish the thought. He didn't really know what to say.

She looked up then. Her big eyes had lost their terror.

"I was fine until the candle went out," she informed him. "At least . . . pretty good. I . . . I recited Scripture and prayed. I even sang . . . a little bit. But . . . after I lost the light . . ."

She shuddered and did not finish the comment.

"I'm sorry," he said softly.

They sat silently. She was the first to speak.

"I can't believe it . . . after all this time," she began. "I can't believe that I'm going home."

He began to say something and then quickly closed his mouth.

"My mama will be so . . . so . . ." She lifted her head, framed by her tangled hair. In the near darkness her eyes looked deep and shining. She pulled up her knees and wrapped both arms around them. The candlelight caught her face, making her eyes sparkle. Her soft buckskin clothing blended into the shadows of the walls. She could have been an Indian princess as she sat regally on her bed of furs.

Laramie cleared his throat. He hated to break the spell. Wasn't quite sure what he should say and how he should say it.

At last he took a deep breath and spoke with all of the gentleness he possessed.

"Ariana?"

It was the first time anyone had spoken her name in such a long time. She turned her full attention on his face.

He swallowed again.

"We won't be going home," he managed.

He winced at the look that came into her eyes.

Chapter Sixteen

At Last!

"What do you mean?" The words seemed to break as they rushed from her lips.

Laramie wanted to go to her—as White Eagle had done—but he did not stir. He was not sure he could have moved. Her eyes seemed to pin him to the spot.

"We can't," he managed, his own voice hoarse with emotion.

"But I thought—"

"I know, I know," he quickly cut in, "an' I wish it was thet way but—"

He did move then—but not toward her. He could not bear the look on her face. He turned his back slightly, his hand stealing up to push at the Stetson. When he had better control he turned back to face her again.

"I wouldn't dare take ya home," he said evenly. "Thet is the first place they'll look. And they will continue to watch an' wait for many days to come. I know—"

"But . . . what about . . . my folks?" Her voice still quivered.

"Once we're out we'll git word to them," he said simply.

He thought he saw tears slide down her cheeks in the light of the fluttering candles, but he wasn't sure.

She drew her knees closer to her chest and hugged them

to her. Her head lowered toward them until he could no longer see her face. The tangled hair spilled about her, providing her with privacy in her deep hurt at his words.

"I'm sorry," he managed.

He saw her shoulders tremble as she sat in silence—and then she seemed to give her shoulders a little shake. Her head came up again, and though he was sure now that he saw tears on her cheeks, her eyes looked at him frankly.

"What is the plan?" she asked. Her inner strength had returned.

Laramie felt more confused by her calm than he had been by her agitation.

What was the plan? Beyond the fact that he needed to get her out—away from the band that had confined her—what then? Edginess suddenly took hold of him. He had been so busy preparing for the escape that he had not thought much further.

"Is there anywhere—anyone else—that you know?" The idea came to him suddenly. He would have to take her to someone. He couldn't just free her from her prisoners and leave her alone in a hostile world.

She seemed to give his question deep consideration. At length she answered, hesitantly at first, and then the words poured out.

"An uncle—my father's brother—and his wife. I'm not sure—I've never met them—but Papa spoke of them. In Montana. Farmers. They live near a little town called . . . oh, dear . . . what is it now . . . Preston? Princeton? Oh, dear. It'll come to me . . . I just—"

"Montana," Laramie repeated. "Thet's a fair piece away."

Ariana looked apologetic. "They're the only ones I can think of. I—"

He cut in quickly so she wouldn't feel he had vetoed her suggestion. "Montana. Might be a good place to start over."

The silence stretched out between them for several minutes. It was not an awkward moment. Each was busy with personal thoughts. The other was content to let it be so.

Laramie spoke again. "You should git some sleep. It'll be a long day tomorrow."

Ariana stirred.

She let her eyes travel around the small cave. Three tunnels led off from it. One had been the entrance through which the Indian had brought her in. One was simply a closet-sized addition to the room she used now. She had made use of it over the days of her confinement. She had no idea about the third opening. Perhaps it led to a bigger cave. Perhaps it wound this way and that, twisting deeper into the rocks of the mountain. Maybe it ended abruptly, going nowhere.

"You need sleep too," she answered simply. "Here, take some of the bedding."

She stood to her feet and began to separate the furs and blankets. He started to protest and then realized how tired he was. Besides, it was easy to see that White Eagle had done his job well. The stack in the corner would serve more than one bed.

"This is plenty," he said as he lifted a heavy buffalo robe.

"Take this blanket too," she insisted, so he did.

He placed the robe on the rock floor and lowered himself to it. It really wasn't much harder than the wood bunk he was used to. He pulled the blanket firmly about himself and settled for the night.

He heard her stirring and turned so he could look at her. She was lighting a fresh candle.

꙰   ꙰   ꙰

He was awakened by a touch on his shoulder. White Eagle bent over him, his lantern held high in his other hand.

"You sleep like old bear," he said with a glint in his eyes.

Laramie stirred, chiding himself that he had not heard White Eagle approach. He quickly laid aside the self-incrimination. White Eagle moved like a shadow. No mortal man would have heard him enter the cavern.

His eyes asked the question that he did not voice. White Eagle responded.

"You have horse," he said simply.

Relief swept through Laramie's whole body. He freed himself of the blanket and sat up. "Then I guess I have a trip to take," he replied.

In the corner Ariana began to stir. Sleepily she opened her eyes and then quickly jerked to full wakefulness. "Did it work?" she asked before she even had time to stir from her blankets.

Laramie could not hide his smile. She was like a small child in her eagerness. "It worked," he replied, and Ariana began to push the blanket back as she unwound herself from the bedding and sleep.

"We must hurry," she exclaimed excitedly, and set about gathering together the last of the supplies in a little heap on her deserted bed.

Laramie and White Eagle exchanged glances. Their plan was working. They would get her out.

꙳   ꙳   ꙳

Will Russell was in a sour mood. First, his well-laid strategy had not worked out right. Instead of the girl bringing about the change in Laramie he had desired, she had been the final straw in breaking Laramie from the gang completely. Will's sense of loss was exceeded only by his great rage. Sam's knowing looks and mumbled pronouncements had not helped to appease his anger.

When the discovery had not been made until noon, Will knew Laramie had worked it out so that he had a long head start. With the snow falling, it had been hard to pick up the trail, but Will knew the direction that must be taken to get the girl back home.

He'd had the boys saddle up and they rode out, leaving only Skidder behind to guard the camp. Will had not wanted Skidder in their little posse. He knew the man would use any possible excuse to put a bullet in Laramie's back.

At first they had ridden hard, direct as the crow flies, toward the small town from which Ariana had been taken. Just before they were forced to make camp for the night, they came upon three horses, feeding casually in a small meadow. Laramie's mounts.

Will's first thought had been that the young man and his prisoner had run headlong into a small band of Pawnee. But that didn't add up. The Indians would have kept the horses. So what had really happened? Will was left scratching his head.

It was clear Laramie had made other plans. But what? Where could he get on foot? Had he changed horses? But why? His own mounts were still fresh. It hadn't appeared that they had been ridden hard. The whole thing had him puzzling.

"Set up camp," Will had growled to his men.

So they set up camp.

The next morning the gang expected an order to break camp, but Will looked in no hurry to leave. Instead, he had sent out scouts to scour the nearby countryside.

"See anything—fire three shots," they had been ordered. At the end of the day they had returned with nothing to report.

"Well—we jest sit here an' wait. He'll hafta crawl out sometime," Will had growled.

In the days that followed, the same procedure was repeated. Sam began to question how long they were to sit and wait—so close to the Indian settlement. Will just growled and said he figured he was still the boss. He'd give the orders.

But a nighttime Indian raid had changed his plans. The braves took all their horses—all the saddles. Even the small grub stake right from the center of the camp, as though to mock the little band of outlaws. Will was glad to be left with his scalp, though he would not have admitted it to his men.

The air was blue with curses directed at the "red savages." But Will knew many of them would have been directed at him had his men been expressing their true feelings.

So they were all on foot, tramping their way home. The warm spring sun turned the trail into slush, and then mud. They slipped and slid their way up the winding trail and forded waist-deep creek water.

No, they were not a happy group of travelers. The next raid had been carefully planned to take place in just three days—and here they were with no mounts except for a couple of scraggly animals back at the corral—and those without saddles for riding. Their supplies, even back at the base camp, were dangerously low.

As Will Russell trudged through the sloppiness of spring thaw, he kept checking over his shoulder. Men had been known to mutiny for less reason. He was glad he could count on Sam—who was dutifully bringing up the rear of the straggling band of reluctant hikers. Sam's loose hand was never far from his gun holster.

❧   ❧   ❧

"Do you have any idea what day it is?" Ariana asked as she raised a tired hand to push windblown hair back from her face.

"I know we've been ridin' fer eight days," replied Laramie.

"Where are we?"

"We've a good piece to go yet," was his simple answer as they plodded on.

Ariana felt like groaning. Her whole body ached. It felt as though they had spent those entire eight days in the saddle. Laramie had pushed them hard. He was intent on putting as many miles as possible between them and the camp in the hidden valley. He had not even allowed them the comfort of an open fire.

Ariana did groan, just thinking about it. The nights had been cold, and the scant blanket she clutched to her shivering body did very little to keep out the wind.

They had outridden the snow. The late spring storm that had swept through their area, giving them cover for their escape, had been followed by a bright warm sun that melted the small drifts and set the creeks to singing.

Ariana welcomed the feeling of warm rays on her back. At least there was one spot of her that was not still shivering from the cold night.

Ariana was surprised when Laramie reined in the buckskin. As soon as his horse stopped, Ariana's roan pulled up beside it, nuzzling the buckskin's lathered neck with its nose.

Laramie said nothing. Just sat his saddle as though born to it, studying Ariana with intent eyes. Ariana shifted uncomfortably. There were times when she felt he looked into her very soul.

"Little town up ahead—'bout a mile," he offered. "We're in need of some more supplies."

Ariana's eyes widened. "Have you been . . . way up here . . . before?" she asked incredulously.

"No," he answered with a shake of his head.

"Then how. . . ?" she began but didn't finish.

He smiled then, a lazy, easy smile. He nodded his head toward the north. "It's stickin' out—plain as day—on thet hillside."

Ariana flushed and shaded her eyes with her hands so she could stare off into the distance. Sure enough, she could make out buildings against the backdrop of trees and rock.

"We're going to stop?" she asked, hoping the eagerness was not too evident in her voice.

He nodded again. "We'll stop," he promised.

Suddenly Ariana felt she had new strength in her weary bones. She straightened in her saddle and gave her mount a heel. If they were going to be stopping, she was anxious to get there.

※　　※　　※

The small town had a rooming house, and Laramie ordered a room and a hot bath for Ariana before he went to the stables to arrange for the horses' care. They had pushed the animals hard. Laramie wanted time to check them thoroughly, searching for chipped hooves or sore muscles. He had always made a habit of checking the mounts at the end of each day and had noticed nothing seriously amiss, but the little roan had seemed to have a sensitive spot on her right shoulder. He decided on a little liniment and put on some warm compresses.

By the time Laramie had finished at the stable, the sun was setting. He looked down at his trail-soiled clothes and decided he could sure use a bath himself.

The doors of the town's one store were still open, so Laramie made his way into the building. All sorts of goods lined the shelves and formed stacks of deep piles anywhere the owner could find room.

"Howdy," greeted Laramie.

"Howdy," replied the man, letting his eyes travel up and down the newcomer as if to gather all the information he could in one glance.

"Ridin' through?" he asked casually, but Laramie knew the question was far from casual.

"Thet's right," he replied, his voice just as relaxed and off-handed. He began to finger one of the shirts in a nearby stack.

Both men waited.

"Wouldn't have supposed there'd be call fer this much merchandise in such a small town," observed Laramie. "Business must either be powerful good—or a sight poor."

The man responded with a hard laugh. "Where you been, cowboy?" he answered. "Don't ya know there's gold in them hills?" He jerked his head toward the northwest. "Been pouring through here a dozen a day—an' more on the way. I'm the last store between here an' the strike."

Laramie's head came up. "Ya don't say," he said with interest.

Silence again as Laramie went back to eyeing the merchandise.

"Ya fixin' on minin'?" asked the man, breaking the code of the West to wait until the information was freely given.

"Me?" Laramie's head came up. "Naw—I don't reckon. Had never thought on it." He hesitated a minute while he turned a black Stetson over and over in his hands.

The man looked disappointed. Laramie let him wait.

At last he looked up and gave a bit of a nod. "Do need me a bit of a grub stake, though," he announced. "Takin' my sister on up to stay with our kin."

Even as he spoke the words, his face flushed slightly. He had read in his mother's Bible an account of someone named Abraham making the same false statement regarding his wife Sarah, many, many years ago.

But the man behind the counter did not seem to question the remark. Perhaps his thoughts ran only to the sale.

"You jest pick out what ya want—an' show me hard cash, mister," he replied.

Laramie thought the merchant looked as though he was having a hard time keeping from rubbing his hands together in anticipation.

"Usual grub stake," Laramie said. "I'll be by to pick it up in the mornin'."

He hesitated. He had a bag full of stolen coins in the small saddlebag he kept with him, but he was reluctant to squander any of it. Actually, he was feeling uncomfortable even having the ill-gotten money. Still, they needed food and he did need a change of clothes. "An' you can add this to the list," he went on, selecting the articles of clothing. "Pay ya fer 'em right now."

❧   ❧   ❧

Laramie felt much better after he'd had a bath and dressed in the clean clothes. He even thought about getting his hair cut but decided against it. He didn't want to scatter too much money about the little town. There was no use starting tongues to wagging.

As soon as he had finished his simple grooming, he placed the new black Stetson on his head and picked up his money bag. He tied it carefully around his body under his shirt and strapped on his guns. Then he set off down the hall to see if Ariana was ready to try to find a place that served up supper.

᭥   ᭥   ᭥

Ariana waited impatiently, one small foot tapping the worn carpet. She was starved. She had lingered in the hot bath, enjoying the soothing warmth on her aching muscles. Then she had toweled herself dry and dressed in her own clothing from the pack-sack Laramie had left behind for her. The garments had felt strange at first after so many days in the buckskins, and she did deplore the fact of the many wrinkles. Still, she felt a little more herself as she pinned her hair carefully and surveyed her image in the darkened mirror in the room. Now she had been waiting for what seemed hours. Her patience was wearing thin. Had Laramie just dumped her and expected her to fend for herself? Was she to find her own supper—or just do without? He knew she had no money with which to make purchases.

And then a horrid thought raced through Ariana's mind. Did Laramie have money? Were they penniless? Would they need to *steal* their way to Montana—like Laramie had been doing all his life? What if—what if he had been—raiding— and something had gone wrong? He could have been thrown in jail. Been shot and wounded. She might be on her own in this strange little town. Miles from her parents. Miles from the uncle and aunt she did not know.

Ariana felt the panic rising in her chest. Should she go look for him? Should she deny ever having known him, if he'd been caught? Should she seek out a lawman and explain her dilemma?

A lawman? Strange. Ariana had not thought of that. Certainly it would be the reasonable thing to do now that she was in friendly environs. Surely this little town had law of some sort. They would help her. After all, Laramie was—was an outlaw.

Ariana hated to think of him in that fashion. But it was true. True. He was an outlaw. Why had she felt she could trust him?

She began to tremble. Her face paled. Her eyes widened with fear and concern. "Oh, God," she prayed, covering her face with her shaking hands. "What do I do? Should I . . . it would be proper to . . . escape . . . wouldn't it?"

Chapter Seventeen

End of Journey

Ariana rose shakily to her feet. She lifted her chin and looked about her. The room held very few of her personal items, but she carefully gathered them and bundled them into her little pack. Then she pinned her crushed hat carefully in place on her upswept hair and reached for her wrinkled coat and winter gloves. She would do it. It was the only reasonable thing to do.

She lifted her pack. It felt lighter now that she had emptied it of extra clothing and the heavy coat. There really wasn't much in it at all. Her few personal grooming aids. Her Bible. She let her eyes scan the room again to be sure she had missed nothing. The travel-worn buckskins were folded neatly and left on the chair, the moccasins placed on top of them.

Ariana took a deep breath to give herself courage and reached for the door handle. A sharp knock made her gasp and draw back quickly.

"Ariana," came Laramie's voice. "Ya ready?"

Ariana could not have said whether the intense feelings that passed through her were of regret or relief. Quietly she laid her little bundle on the floor behind the door, took a deep breath to calm herself, and reached to undo the lock.

Laramie stood there, clean-shaven and polished until he

fairly shone, his shirt still stiff with newness. Even the worn, droopy Stetson had been replaced. Ariana's little gasp caught in her throat. If he had been raiding it seemed he had covered a lot of ground in a big hurry.

He stood looking at her. Ariana looked down at her own faded, wrinkled garments. When she looked back up he gave her a slight nod as though to express his approval.

"Thought ya might be nigh starved," was his comment.

She swallowed and shifted uneasily. "Yes . . . yes, I am," she stammered. "I . . . I was beginning to think . . ."

But Ariana did not finish the statement. She wasn't sure how much she should say.

※　　※　　※

They left the town bright and early the next morning. Ariana was surprised when she went down to join Laramie that he had added another horse to the number. Bulging packs were secured to the pack saddle.

"Don't worry," he drawled, as though reading her mind. "It's all paid fer."

He did not explain how he had come by the money that paid the accounts.

Ariana was back in her buckskins, her dress repacked in the bundle she handed to Laramie. She noticed a slicker tied behind each saddle. His eyes followed hers. "Keeps out some of the wind and rain," he offered.

Laramie settled the bill with the woman who kept the rooming house, and he held Ariana's horse while she mounted, and they were on the trail once again.

It was almost a pleasant day. Ariana tried not to think of the little town they had left behind. She tried not to scold herself for not having attempted to find a lawman. She tried not to wonder if Laramie could really be trusted to deliver her to the home of her uncle in Montana. She pushed all of the troubling thoughts as far into the back of her mind as she could and tried to concentrate on prayer, even as she swayed slightly in the saddle.

Laramie was still pressing the mounts forward at a fast pace. Ariana had thought he would relax a bit. The spring sun was high in the sky before he took the first break. Ariana climbed down stiffly.

"Sorry to keep pushin'," he said in apology as he watched her dismount.

"I . . . just thought that . . . that we'd be . . . rather safe . . . now," she suggested.

He was squinting into the sunlight, studying every direction from their vantage point. At last he turned to her.

"Should be far enough ahead of . . . Pa," he conceded. "Don't s'pose he's on our tail but . . ." He let the words hang on the stillness of the spring day. Ariana waited.

"I've no idee who shares these hills," he finished at last.

That was a new and frightening thought to Ariana. Were they never to be out of danger?

"You mean. . . ?" she began but couldn't finish.

"Crow. Blackfoot. I don't know who ranges here." He hesitated for a few more moments and then went on soberly. "An' those hills yonder—bound to welcome stray pockets of malcontents."

So they had left one nest of robbers to be threatened by others. The thought was not a pleasant one.

"No need to tighten up," went on Laramie offhandedly, using an expression Ariana had not heard before. "Jest pays to keep a sharp eye—'specially at one's back—take stock now an' then."

Ariana nodded, but the fear that constricted her throat was not so easy to dismiss.

🌿 🌿 🌿

Gradually Ariana was beginning to think of Laramie not as her captor but as her deliverer. Without realizing why, she was able to relax in his company. She was learning to trust again.

When they stopped to make camp in the evenings, she was at ease enough to discuss little happenings from the day, to offer to share in camp chores, or to relate small events from her past.

Laramie responded in his easygoing way, even though she felt he never totally gave up his vigilance. He answered her questions, added comments to her chatter, and gladly shared the duties of preparing an evening meal and setting up camp.

"You know," said Ariana one evening as they cleaned up the tin dishes at a small stream trickling past their campsite, "I've totally lost track of time. I don't even know what day it is."

Laramie thought on her words and then drawled, "Does it matter?"

Ariana lifted her head, then laughed softly. "Guess not," she agreed. "Only it would be nice to know. If I were home . . ." She did not finish. If she were home it would be important for her to keep track of every passing day. To know school days and weekends, Saturdays and Sundays, holidays and birthdays. Yes, it would matter. It did matter.

"I don't even know if . . . if my mama's birthday is past," she went on wistfully.

"When's her birthday?" asked Laramie.

"May the second."

Laramie looked at the evening sun just dipping behind the distant hills.

"I don't think we're into May yet," he answered.

For some reason Ariana felt relieved. She would like to be home. . . . She let her thoughts drift. She wasn't going home. Well, she'd like to be at her aunt Molly's before her mother's birthday.

"When is your birthday?" she asked, turning her attention back to Laramie, who was rinsing the frying pan.

He shrugged.

"You don't know?" she asked candidly.

"I've no idee." He turned slightly toward her. "Never stopped to think about it, I guess. Maybe never cared. Should I?"

"Well . . . yes. Sort of. I mean . . . I'd want to know. Don't you?"

"Never thought on it," said Laramie as he swung the pan back and forth to dry it in the breeze.

"Didn't your father tell you?" asked Ariana.

Laramie let his eyes look out over the hills wrapped comfortably in gathering twilight. "Birthdays don't mean much in the camp," he said casually.

"Do you. . . ?" Ariana spoke hesitantly now. "Do you know . . . how old you are?"

Laramie turned back to her with seeming indifference. "I dunno. Somewhere around twenty, I guess."

He seemed totally unconcerned.

Ariana found it hard to accept his attitude. She was about to speak again when Laramie turned his face toward the west.

"Looks like it could blow in a bit of a storm," he observed. "We'll need to be sure things are rainproof tonight."

❧   ❧   ❧

"There's an outcroppin' of rock up ahead. We'll let the horses graze here and take our meal up there."

Ariana welcomed the opportunity. The view would be spectacular. Inwardly she knew it was not the view that interested Laramie. He saw the rocks as a lookout point.

They ate slowly, savoring the intensity of the sun, allowing its fingers of warmth to ease the aches from wearied muscles. Ariana began to feel drowsy. She wished she could stretch out and sleep—maybe forever.

Laramie seemed content to let her rest. The horses needed a break as much as their riders. He leaned against the rock at his back and pulled his old Stetson downward over his eyes. The new one rode proudly on the slicker behind his saddle.

But along with her sleepiness, Ariana also felt restless. They were getter closer and closer to their destination. She felt both excitement and reluctance. She could not unscramble her own thoughts or feelings.

Nor could she untangle her thoughts concerning Laramie. He was an outlaw—yet why had she learned to feel so secure, so safe with him?

She longed to study him, but she did not dare lest her searching eyes cause him to stir in recognition of her interest. She decided instead to rouse herself and take a walk.

She had only taken a few steps when his voice reached her. "Don't go far," he said lazily.

She did not even answer. Just continued to scramble up over the warm surface of the rocks. It was amazing what the sun could do to cold stone.

She found a spot just above him where she could see out over the whole valley. It was a magnificent sight. First the tall timbers of pine and spruce, dotted here and there with patches of birch and aspen just barely unrolling fresh spring leaves. Then the valley floor with its sparkling ribbon of river that curled and twisted through the greenness, being lost time and again in the lushness of the forest. Way beyond was a slim column of smoke. Ariana could not tell if it came from some small cabin's chimney or some wanderer's open fire. It really did not matter. It added something—mysterious—romantic—to the scene before her.

"Should be movin'," came Laramie's soft call.

Ariana breathed deeply, took one more longing look at the vista before her, and began to scramble back down over rocks to join him.

She was almost there when she was startled by a sharp command. "Don't move!"

Ariana jerked to a halt in unquestioned obedience, though she did not understand why.

Before she could even draw a breath, two shots rang out

through the day's stillness. Ariana was frozen to her spot.
Only her eyes dared move. Laramie was standing, guns in
hand, and they were pointed to the place where she stood.
Smoke drifted lazily from each barrel. Laramie's whole body
was tensed as though ready for further action.

Ariana became conscious of movement at her feet. She let
her gaze drop down and beheld the most hideous sight she
had ever seen. A snake was writhing just beyond her moc-
casined foot. What was left of its head was ragged raw flesh,
spurting blood. It splashed on the hem of her leather buckskin as it swished back and forth in the agony of death.

Ariana felt the world spinning round. She wanted to
scream. Wished to run—but she could do neither.

"Don't move," came Laramie's voice, but this time it was
controlled and gentle, though still urgent. "Where there is
one there is often more."

Ariana had no intention of moving. She was vaguely
aware that Laramie was moving toward her, the smoking
guns still in his hands as his eyes darted back and forth
among the rocks.

"Looks okay," he said at her elbow. "I don't see any more."

Ariana closed her eyes and sucked in her breath—but it
was too late. The whole world was quickly going black.

※   ※   ※

Laramie had caught her just before she hit the rocks.
Gently he carried the young woman down the slope of the hill
toward the waiting horses. He eased her down to the softness
of the new spring grass and went for the canteen that hung
on his saddle. Taking the bandana from his neck, he wet it
and began to sponge her pale face. She was so delicate—so
vulnerable. Then again he marveled at her strength. A lesser
person would have given in long ago under the horrible captivity, the dreadful wait in the cave, and the pressure of the
rigorous ride.

Anger gripped him as he thought of the injustice done to

her. Why had his father come up with such an unthinkable scheme? What had given him the right to so grossly interfere with the life of another?

He wet the kerchief again and ran the dampness over her forehead, smoothing back tendrils of wisping hair.

He had told Sam he would be willing to die for her. As he looked at her now, he knew he had spoken true words. She was something beautiful—precious. He wondered what his mother would have thought of her. Would she have loved her—like he did?

The unbidden acknowledgement startled him. What did he know about love? It was hate he had been raised to recognize and understand. Hate—and bitterness. Envy and greed. Those were the passions he had grown up with.

Yet as he bathed her face and ached for her to return to consciousness, he knew that what he was feeling was far from any of those emotions. Love her? Maybe. Maybe he did. But he had no right to love her—that much he knew. And the secret knowledge that he did was not going to make his job any easier, though it was certainly going to make it more intense.

He was relieved when she began to stir.

Her eyes fluttered open and she looked up at him, seeming puzzled by the fact that he knelt over her, supporting her head with one hand.

"A rattler," he explained to remind her. She looked as though she was about to faint again.

"It's okay," he soothed. "He's gone now."

She shut her eyes tightly against the memory of the headless, writhing snake. He remembered the blood on her buckskin skirt and wished he had thought to try to wash it away.

He eased back from her, but she reached out a trembling hand and clasped the front of his shirt. "Don't leave me," she begged him.

"I won't. I won't," he promised, and he pulled her close and held her until she stopped trembling.

"It was awful," she whispered against him.

"It's gone now," he reminded her.

"Its head—"

"I know. I know."

He patted her shoulder instinctively, pushed back the hair from her face. At last she opened her eyes. Her body still felt limp, but she had stopped shaking.

She pushed gently against him and he reluctantly released her. "We need to go," she said in a trembling voice.

"Not 'til yer ready," he assured her.

The color was returning to her cheeks. She swallowed hard. Then sat up.

"Could I have a drink of water, please?" she asked, her voice still trembling.

He reached for the canteen and held it for her. She drank, then reached a hand to brush a drop from her lips. He noticed the fullness of her mouth. He had never noticed it before.

"I think I'm okay now," she said with a nod, then flushed. "I'm . . . I'm sorry . . . I . . . it just caught me by surprise."

He longed to pull her close and hold her again. Instead, he reached out to help her to her feet. She stood shakily, still weak from the incident. She put out a hand to the trunk of the nearby birch for support. He moved back to hang the canteen on his saddle horn. He had to put some distance between them. He did not trust himself with his newfound knowledge.

"Whenever you feel ready," he said, his voice sounding stiff and forced.

"I'm fine—now," Ariana assured him.

He nodded. Perhaps. Perhaps she was. What about him? Would he ever be fine again?

❧   ❧   ❧

He allowed the building of a fire when they stopped each evening. He knew they needed to be cautious, but he felt he could not deny her any small comfort that was within his means to provide.

It was homey around the fire. Ariana always got out her Bible and read portions for her evening devotions. Rather hesitantly, he asked if she'd mind reading aloud. She nodded her assent, hoping her rapidly beating heart was not heard in the quiet of the still evening. Inwardly she prayed, over and over, that the words from the Book would be understood. That he might respond to the Gospel as it was given. Carefully she selected the portions for reading, praying that Laramie's heart would be responsive to the message.

As the evenings passed he seemed to be drawn in more and more. If he had questions, he asked, and she was patient as she explained her understanding of the passage. He began to look forward to those evenings and even thought of bringing out his mother's Bible so he might follow along. He wondered if the notations in the margins might be helpful to both of them. But he never had the courage to make the suggestion.

He had never been this intimate with anyone before. Sharing thoughts and feelings—and on occasion wishing he could also share his dreams. But he held them in check, for no matter how he fought against it, he could not envision his future without Ariana—yet that dream was an impossibility.

He was sure Ariana understood nothing of his discomfort. Nothing of the struggle going on within him. But Laramie was very aware of the conflict he felt within. On the one hand he was most anxious to deliver her to the safety of the unknown uncle. On the other hand, once he did, he would have lost her forever. He knew that. It made him somber, moody. Something he had never been.

❧   ❧   ❧

Ariana did not understand why, but she did notice the difference. She supposed she had inadvertently done something to annoy him. Or was it that he was feeling the break with his father?

She dared to broach the subject one night as they sat

around the open fire listening to the voices of the night creatures.

"What will you do after we get to my uncle's?"

The question brought his head up.

"Will you go back to . . . to. . . ?"

"Back? No . . . I won't go back," he said thoughtfully.

"I've . . . I've spoiled that for you . . . haven't I? I've made . . . a breach between you and your father," she went on, and there was apology in her voice.

At first he looked surprised and then he smiled his slow smile. "I reckon you have," he said frankly, "but not in the way you suppose."

She was puzzled but did not probe deeper.

"Do you miss . . . your . . . father?" she asked after a time of silence, finally getting to the question she had been longing to ask him.

"Miss 'im?" He stared into the fire a moment. "No," he said frankly.

She was sure her astonishment at his answer showed on her face.

"I . . . I think of him . . . wish things could be different . . . but I don't miss him," Laramie explained.

She drew up her knees in a manner he had come to recognize, and hugged them to her. "Oh . . . I miss my papa," she said with deep feeling. "And Mama . . . so much." A tear trickled down her cheek, exposed by the dancing firelight.

He made a move as if to come to her, but instead said, "We need to git some sleep. We got a long ride tomorra."

🌱   🌱   🌱

"I remember," called Ariana with excitement in her voice. "It's Pinewood."

Laramie turned back to look at her, puzzlement on his face.

"Pinewood," she repeated. "That's where Uncle Jake and Aunt Molly are. Near Pinewood."

He turned back to his mount. There—they had it. There would be no excuse to keep her with him now.

"Last name?" he called back to her.

"Benson. Benson—just like my father."

He guided his horse carefully over a fallen log.

"Pinewood," he repeated. "Guess we'd better stop first chance we git an' find out jest where thet is."

❧   ❧   ❧

When they finally found a farmstead, they were both amazed to discover how close they were to the little town of Pinewood.

"Happen to know Jake Benson?" Laramie asked the farmer.

"Jake? Sure I know Jake. Don't have many neighbors out here, so ya make it a point to get to know 'em," the man in the worn overalls stated. "Lives other side of town—'bout six hours from here."

Laramie was relieved to hear that they would have to share one more evening campfire, but he didn't say so. Nor did he tell the farmer they would be camping out again. He was afraid the man might, in his friendliness, take Ariana into the family's crowded cabin and offer Laramie the barn loft.

"Thank ya kindly," Laramie said with a tip of his head, and he led Ariana and the pack horse back out onto the dusty track that meant roads and civilization.

"We'll ride on fer an hour or two and then make camp," he said simply. "Shouldn't be much of a ride tomorra."

Ariana could hardly contain her excitement.

❧   ❧   ❧

Ariana trembled as she lifted her skirts and moved toward the farmhouse door. They had stopped back a piece, and Laramie had gone for a walk while Ariana took a quick dip in the cold waters of a small creek, then dressed hurriedly in her own clothes. She had not discarded the buckskins. Instead she'd folded them, almost tenderly, and put them in the bundle from which she had withdrawn her rumpled cotton. The buckskins had served her well. Calico or gingham would have worn through long ago on the endless trail.

Ariana looked down at her faded dress. She certainly was not coming to her kin looking pressed and proper. Hesitantly she lifted her hand to rap. Then she cast one more glance back over her shoulder to where Laramie stood holding the horses. The brim of his hat was shading his eyes, so she could not read his expression.

She took a deep breath and knocked on the wood. The door was soon opened by an elderly woman, a dish towel still in her hand.

"Yes?" she said, then blessed Ariana with a smile. "Come in," she welcomed and waved Ariana into the humble home. "You must be new here. Are you from the place down on Cedar Creek?"

"No . . . no . . . I . . ." Ariana took a deep breath. "Molly Benson?" she asked tentatively. "Are you Aunt Molly?"

The woman nodded her agreement but looked puzzled by the question.

"I'm . . . I'm Ariana," the girl managed. "George and Laura's daughter."

For a moment the woman stood silent, her face showing shock. Then with one quick movement she gathered Ariana into her arms, holding her close as she laughed and wept in unison.

"Ariana? Oh, God be praised. We all feared you were dead."

Chapter Eighteen

A Joyous Hello and a Painful Goodbye

"Oh, Aunt Molly," Ariana said through her own tears and laughter, "I was afraid we'd never find you." She realized that her long ordeal was finally over. She was back with those she loved. Her life could go on again.

"What are you doing here, child? How'd you get here?" the woman quizzed excitedly.

Ariana moved back out to the porch, drawing her Aunt Molly with her. She nodded toward Laramie, who stood with the horses.

"It's a long story—one I promise to tell—someday. It wasn't safe for me to go back home. But we must let Mama know. And Papa. We must."

"You sit right there." The woman pointed at a small bench in the shade of the porch. "I'm going for your uncle." She started off toward a nearby field, removing her apron as she bustled along. Ariana watched as she ran, waving the apron in the air to get the man's attention.

"It seems you've caused quite a stir."

Laramie stood close behind Ariana. She brushed at the tears on her cheeks.

"You know, I don't think I really believed it would happen. Oh . . . I tried to have faith. I prayed. But it . . . it seemed so

. . . so impossible at times. I don't think I really thought that . . . that it would ever end."

He was silent for several minutes as they watched her aunt draw near to her uncle, arms waving, fingers pointing back at the house. Ariana could almost guess her words.

"It's been hard for you," said Laramie simply. "I'm glad it's over."

Ariana turned to him, her eyes brimming, her face flushed. "I . . . I can never thank you enough. Never," she said with conviction. "If it hadn't been for you . . ."

Laramie shuffled uncomfortably. He reached up to push at the brim of his hat. At last his eyes lifted. "If it hadn't been for me you'd still be in your own hometown," he said huskily.

Ariana's eyes clouded. "What do you mean?" she asked him.

He took her elbow and steered her to the porch bench, out of the bright rays of the sun.

"I don't know if you've guessed . . . if you've really understood it all . . . but you were brought to the camp . . . because of me."

Ariana was still confused.

"I . . . I wasn't quite . . . shapin' up . . . like my pa . . . had planned. You see . . ." He hesitated, then swallowed. "I had never . . . killed a man."

"Killed a man?" she whispered. "I don't understand. That . . . is a fault?"

"In Pa's eyes," he said simply.

Ariana shivered.

"But I don't understand. What did that have to do with me?"

He took a deep breath. "Pa figured I'd . . . I'd be forced to . . . to . . . git into a fight over you . . . an' have to use my gun."

"But I—"

"You had nothin' to do with it—directly. Only indirectly. Pa knew thet there'd be other fellas who would . . . anyway, he figured there'd be a showdown—likely with Skidder—"

"Skidder?" said Ariana with a shiver. "Is he the one who said those awful things?"

Laramie nodded.

"But why would Skidder—? Why would you—?"

"Pa thought I'd fall in love with you." He said the words hurriedly as he watched the man and woman scurry up the lane.

She was shocked. "But that's—preposterous," she exclaimed.

He started to say something, then stopped.

Then her eyes softened. "I'm sorry," she whispered to him. "I didn't know. I've been the cause of . . . a lot of trouble between you and your father."

His face showed his surprise at her words.

"But I am glad—and I cannot deny it. Glad—and thankful—that you never . . . never killed. I . . . I just . . . don't think you are that kind of man."

"Ariana, I'm an outlaw," he reminded her.

"Not anymore you're not," she said quickly. "And I don't believe for a moment you ever would have been if you'd been given the choice. I've seen . . . enough . . . to believe that you—you're not like that."

By now the man and woman were rushing into the yard, panting from the hurried trip from the field. The short, private conversation was over. All Laramie could manage was a quiet "thank you."

Then her uncle was rushing toward Ariana, his arms open.

❦   ❦   ❦

Everything seemed in turmoil after the quiet days on the trail. Jake Benson hitched a team to the wagon and hurried off to town to send a wire to Ariana's parents. Molly fluttered about the kitchen, laughing, praising the Lord, and crying by turn. Ariana, flushed and excited, talked more in a few short hours than she had during the last four months.

Laramie withdrew from all the commotion, not used to the intensity of emotions, the free expressions of love and tenderness between Ariana and her family. He spent his time at the corral tending to the horses.

Slowly he unpacked the pack horse, lifting aside Ariana's small bundle. His job was over. He had delivered her safely to her aunt and uncle. They would take over now.

So what was he going to do? He had not thought about it. He could not turn around and go back. He wouldn't have wanted to, even if that was possible. Yet he had no particular skills—other than with a gun. Had never really worked. He was adrift. Freed from a world he had never felt a part of, to enter a world where he did not fit. What would he do?

He climbed up on the rail of the corral to watch the horses and ponder the question. He'd have to find work—somewhere. Maybe he should go back to the small town on the side of the hill, buy himself a grub stake, and try his hand at finding gold. Maybe he could look up a ranch and hire himself out as a cowpoke. He was good with horses. He might work fine with cattle, too. Maybe he should—

But every idea that came to him brought little inner response. Nothing seemed to connect with him. Yet here he was—for the first time in his life—free to make his own decisions.

He couldn't understand his mood.

"Aw, it's jest the letdown after all the days of tension," he tried to tell himself. But down deep inside he knew the real reason. It was Ariana. Once he left her, he would never see her again. His pa had been right. Loving a girl could nearly ruin a man.

❧   ❧   ❧

"Hungry?"

Laramie's head jerked up as Ariana came up beside him. "Aunt Molly has fixed tea," she announced.

At the look on Laramie's face she began to laugh. A soft,

joyful laugh. It was the first Laramie had heard her laugh so freely in all the months he had known her. It was a reminder of how much they had taken from her in holding her captive in such a degrading way.

"You don't have to drink tea," she said with a sparkle in her eyes. "I'll fix you some coffee."

Laramie supposed he should be hungry, but he really had little appetite.

"It's not the tea," he was quick to inform her, not wanting to be uncivil. "It's just that—" He let his gaze drop to his trail-dusty attire. "I'm not really fit company an' I—"

"Oh, come on," she coaxed. "Uncle Jake and Aunt Molly are just ordinary folk. Farmers. Uncle Jake didn't change out of his dusty overalls."

"It's not just the . . . clothes," he said, still hesitating. "I . . . hardly fit in with . . . proper company. I know little of— what do you call it?"

She smiled again. "Social graces? I promise we won't expect you to use one of those little teacups and eat bite-size sandwiches." Her eyes were twinkling again.

He was still uncomfortable.

"We're going to eat on the back porch," she continued.

He reached up one finger to tip back his new Stetson.

"You have to start sometime," she encouraged. "We won't be eating around a campfire anymore."

She had said "we." Was that just a slip? Surely she wasn't thinking that he intended to hang around.

"Come on. Aunt Molly is anxious to get to know you better. She's worried about letting you sleep in the loft. Says it's not really fixed for guests. I said, after where we've been sleeping—"

He stopped her. "You're not thinkin' I'll be stayin' here, are you?"

Her eyes widened. He could tell from her expression that it was exactly what she had been thinking.

"Where else—?"

"I can't." He shook his head.

The concern in her eyes deepened. She reached out and put a hand on his arm.

"But I thought—I mean, I never dreamed—that you wouldn't stay."

"I can't," he said again.

"But Papa and Mama will want to meet you."

"Your papa and mama? I thought they were back in Smithton."

"They are. But they'll come. Just as soon as they get the wire—they'll come."

He shook his head stubbornly. "I don't think they'll be wantin' to see the likes of me."

"What do you mean?"

"I was the reason . . . remember? I was your . . . prison guard."

She looked annoyed. "Can't you get past that?" she said tersely. "You brought me out. You risked your own life to help me get back to my folks. That's what they will think about and remember. That's what I remember."

He shuffled uncomfortably. She might forgive so easily—but could her parents?

"Come on," she coaxed. "We'll talk about that later. Come—have some sandwiches. Aunt Molly has them ready and Uncle Jake looks like he's about starved."

He was totally aware of the fact that she still had her hand on his arm.

"Sandwiches," he agreed and let her lead him toward the house.

❧   ❧   ❧

Ariana hummed as she prepared herself for the evening meal. She didn't remember when she had felt so light-hearted. *It is so wonderful to be free,* she exulted inwardly. It almost made her giddy.

But it was more than that. Perhaps it was because she now knew the real difference between imprisonment and freedom—fear and security. Perhaps it was because all the bottled tension of the past months was seeping slowly from her, making room for happiness to spill back in. Perhaps it was the loving welcome that her uncle and aunt had so willingly extended, making her feel so loved and accepted.

Perhaps it was—Laramie.

Ariana blushed, even though she was alone in the room.

What were her feelings concerning Laramie? She didn't know if she could answer the question—even in her own heart. But she did realize that her feelings had gone about a slow change during the days they had traveled to freedom together.

At first he had been her captor, and she had feared him just as she had every aspect of camp life. She was confused and lonely and terribly frightened. He had seemed civil enough. But he was the one guarding her as prisoner, and so she had remained aloof, on guard, watchful for any sign that might show his true colors.

Then he had become her liberator. She knew enough to know it had been daring on his part. Dangerous. His own father would have had no mercy had they been caught. But even in this role, Ariana had been cautious. Guarded. He was, after all, an outlaw. How could she know what strange and warped behavior might lurk beneath the seemingly controlled exterior?

But now something had changed. Ariana felt that it had something to do with the snake incident. She blushed again at the thought of it.

It wasn't that he had killed the snake. No, it was more than that. Something—that she found hard to define. Hard to think through. But it was there—between them. She saw it in his eyes as he bent over her, holding her head, wiping her face with his bandana. There was compassion reflected there. Tenderness. There was nothing evil in those eyes. Had he changed? Or was this what he had always been? Would have been, had his circumstances been different?

Ariana did not know. But in some unexplainable way she

felt in her heart that they were rather on even ground. Laramie had rescued her from her captors—and she, in some strange and unplanned way, had rescued him from his.

And he had listened to her read from the Bible—with such interest. Surely, surely, given a little time, he would understand its message and seek out God's forgiveness for his past. She prayed for that with an impatience and urgency she had never brought to prayer before. And she felt confident her prayer would soon be answered.

So she hummed, her heart light. Life held so much promise. She could hardly wait for what each new day would reveal.

❧   ❧   ❧

Ariana slipped up beside Laramie as he stood leaning against the corral fence, watching the horses feed from the overflowing manger of hay.

"You look very serious," she said in a teasing tone. "Was it really that hard to sit up to a table with a checkered tablecloth?"

Laramie smiled. "I plumb enjoyed it," he admitted. "Especially the apple pie."

Ariana stood beside him and placed her hands on the top rail. They remained silent for a number of minutes, each deep in thought.

In the distance a coyote howled and the farm dog answered in protest.

"Two different worlds," mused Laramie.

Ariana looked puzzled.

"The coyote and the dog," he explained. "Same family—yet two different worlds."

Ariana gave a slight shrug. "Guess either one of them might adjust—if they had to."

Laramie did not answer.

Silence again. The horses continued to feed, their energetic chewing reaching the ears of the two silent people.

"Which one would find it hardest, do you think?" wondered Ariana.

Laramie looked toward the horses. Ariana wondered if he had already forgotten the conversation of a few moments before.

"The dog—or the coyote?" she reminded him.

He seemed to be thinking on it.

"Would it be hardest for the tame animal to adjust to the wild—or the wild animal to adjust to being tamed?" she persisted.

"I couldn't say," he responded, but his voice sounded wistful.

Ariana waited before she spoke again. "Do you mind if I ask you something?"

He seemed to consider it a moment. At last he nodded. "Go ahead," he invited. "I'll answer, if I can."

"That scar—just at your hairline—how'd you get it? I noticed it before—when you took your hat off in the cave—and when you came in—"

"Now—thet I can't answer," he said with good humor. "It's been there fer as long as I can remember. All I know is thet jest a bit shows—but it reaches back further. Jest can't see it—with all my mane. Gotta find some place to git me a haircut. Surprised yer kin even let me in the house."

Ariana laughed softly. He smiled in response.

They fell silent again.

Then Laramie picked up the thread of the conversation. "I was jest thinkin'—'fore ya came out," he said. "You interested in keepin' thet little roan? Seems ya got on quite well. . . ."

Even in the gathering twilight he could see her eyes darken.

"You're still planning to go . . . aren't you?" she said quietly.

He nodded. He hated to see the hurt look on her face. If only she understood his impossible situation.

"I'm sorry," she whispered into the soft darkness. "I was hoping you'd want to stay."

Her words tore at Laramie's soul.

"Ariana . . . you know . . . I can't," he argued, his voice husky with his emotions. "I can't."

"But—"

"We don't even know for sure . . . who I am," he continued, turning toward her.

"But we do. Your mother's Bible—"

"It might not even be my ma's. We are just goin' on Sam's say-so—an' Sam ain't exactly one ya'd stake yer life on."

"But—"

"I might be thet . . . thet person named there. She might have been my ma . . . but I've still got lots of questions. I mean . . . she . . . she jest don't seem to fit . . . with him. The picture . . . the pretty things . . . the Bible."

"Maybe we can find the answers—together."

He took her by the shoulders and turned her toward him.

"I'm a wanted man," he reminded her.

He could see the tears spring into her eyes and slip unbidden down her cheeks.

"That doesn't matter," she whispered intensely.

For one moment he looked deeply into her eyes. "It does to me," he answered, and his words were spoken with finality. "It matters a whole lot to me. I . . . I'm not a free man. I'm . . ."

A sigh from somewhere deep within him stopped his words. He took another deep breath and contiued.

"I'll be leavin' before sunup." The words sounded blunt. Harsh.

She looked hurt—and angry. She pushed his hands off her shoulders. "Go then—go if you must."

She took two steps back from him and stood silently. He could see her shoulders lift and fall.

When she lifted her face the tears were falling freely. Her chin quivered. But her voice was now soft.

"I'm sorry," she apologized. "I had no right . . . I had hoped that . . . you'd wish to . . ."

She lifted her head and stared into his face, her eyes pleading.

"What I want has nothin'—" he began quickly, but he couldn't finish. The unvoiced thoughts seemed to tear at his very being.

Ariana stood before him, paying no heed to the tears that wet her cheeks. "Nothing will change your mind, will it?" she managed to say barely above a whisper. "Please, please— just promise me one thing," she implored. "When you've sorted it out—please—come back."

And then she was gone—and a big part of Laramie went with her.

Chapter Nineteen

Adjustments

When Ariana opened her eyes the next morning, her first thought was of Laramie. Did he really mean to do what he had insisted on the night before? Surely—surely he had changed his mind. He wouldn't just ride out of her life. Leaving her—alone again.

She scrambled from the bed and crossed quickly to the window, lifting back the curtain and peering out. Her heart was racing as she looked toward the corrals. "Please, God—" she whispered, but even before she could finish her prayer her eyes fell on the little roan, his head extended over the top rail of the corral fence as he gazed off down the rutted country road toward the distant hills. He had been left alone. The buckskin and the black pack animal were gone. With them had gone Laramie.

Ariana felt like the pony. Deserted. Alone. She returned to the bed, where she threw herself down and wept.

❧   ❧   ❧

Laramie rode all day. He wasn't sure where he was going. Wasn't sure what he would do when he got there, but he knew one thing. He had to put some miles between himself and Ariana. Had to be sure that he couldn't give in to impulse—to turn around and head back to her. He had no right. No right to love such a girl. He wasn't sure just who he was, but he was a wanted man. He knew that. Raids. Robbery. Rustling. He didn't know what the penalty might be for his crimes. He had even shot a few men. True, one could argue self-defense—and he'd never shot to kill. But he'd used his gun. What would that mean? Imprisonment? Hanging? He had no idea. But he was sure he'd better stay well away from any lawmen—and Ariana.

His life looked bleak. He was a man on the run.

❧   ❧   ❧

Ariana moved woodenly through the days. She spent hours with the little roan. They had been left, but they were together. Now they needed to start to rebuild their lives.

The fact that Ariana's father and mother were coming helped her to look forward. Each day she checked off one more day on the calendar. But she was restless. Cut adrift. She couldn't slip back into the same comfortable rut—nor did she seem to be able to slide into a new one. It was difficult.

If I could have gone back home, it would have been different, she told herself. *I could have gone back to my teaching . . . to the church . . . and life could have picked up where it left off. But this . . . I don't know where I fit. Don't know how I should fit. I'm floundering.*

Ariana busied herself with helping her aunt Molly. She even ran errands for her uncle Jake. They were soon declaring they didn't know how they'd ever gotten on without her. Still, she was restless and agitated.

Daily her thoughts went to Laramie. Where was he? Was he all right? Was he still looking for answers? Had he found at least some of them?

"Oh, God," she prayed over and over. "May he realize that you have the important answers. That you can forgive. That you love him, too."

Wisely, she turned to her Bible. Back to the wisdom and comfort of its pages. *I need to look up all those verses on trust again,* she told herself. *I thought I had learned that lesson . . . but I guess I need to start all over.*

So Ariana began again to explore the Scriptures.

᪐   ᪐   ᪐

The day finally arrived when the incoming stage brought the Bensons. Ariana's excitement was easily matched by her parents'. It was so wonderful to be held in her father's firm embrace, to hear his whispered words of love. Her mother's tears of joy, the familiar fussing over her, made them all laugh and cry and thank God together. Then they turned to having a good visit with Jake and Molly.

They had brought all of Ariana's things. "It wouldn't be safe for you to come home—not yet," Ariana's mother insisted, wiping away tears as she spoke.

"Who'll teach my students?" asked Ariana.

"They are looking for a new teacher for the fall," was the reply. "The children have already lost half the term."

"Why don't you teach here?" Aunt Molly asked.

"They need a teacher at a local school?"

"Well, we don't have a local school—yet—but we do have young'uns in the area," added Uncle Jake.

"Jake, why don't you talk to the neighbors at the next community gatherin'?" Aunt Molly went on, then she turned to her brother-in-law. "We don't have a church yet, but we meet for Bible lessons once a month—turnabout—in one of the neighbor's homes."

"Papa," cried Ariana, "why don't you start a church?"

Four pairs of eyes turned on George Benson. They all looked eager. Anxious.

He shook his head slowly. "I'd have to do a lot of praying about that," he said slowly. "God hasn't shown me that my work in Smithton is finished yet."

There were looks of disappointment, followed by nods of

assent. Certainly he had to follow the will of God.

"But we do need a school," went on Aunt Molly. "Jake, you talk to the neighbors."

Jake nodded. There was no harm in discussing it.

❧   ❧   ❧

"I can't believe you brought—*everything*," Ariana said to her mother as she carefully unpacked her belongings and stacked them in the chest of drawers Aunt Molly had provided.

"I didn't know when you . . . might be . . . home again," said her mother slowly. "I didn't want to put you in jeopardy."

"I really don't think they'd ever . . . take me again," said Ariana thoughtfully. "I mean . . . their reason is gone now."

"Reason—what was the reason? I never have understood it."

Ariana sat down, her eyes misty. She patted the bed beside her for her mother to join her.

"It's a long story," she managed. "You really want to hear it?"

Her mother nodded and took the seat on the bed.

"Well . . ." Ariana took a deep breath. She was finally going to get to tell her mother about Laramie. She welcomed the opportunity. They had always shared secrets. She could hardly wait to speak of him, for she knew instinctively that her mother would somehow understand the real man.

But even as she opened her mouth to begin, a little part of her held herself in check. What could she say to her mother? How much of her inner thoughts did she dare to reveal? Laramie was a wanted man. Yet Laramie was—a special man. Would she dare to confide in her mother that she thought—that she supposed she had fallen in love with her captor?

❧   ❧   ❧

"Why did you bring this?" asked Ariana, her eyes wide with question.

"It's yours," answered her mother simply.

"But I don't need it—now," returned Ariana.

She heard her mother sigh. "Ariana," she said, "I'm not sure when I will be able to make this trip again. And when a girl reaches your age . . . then . . . one never knows just when—"

Ariana was not sure how she should respond. She was saved by the bedroom door opening. Aunt Molly stuck her head in.

"Tea's ready," she called merrily. Then she saw the gown in Ariana's hands. She pushed the door open and stepped in.

"What a beautiful dress!" she exclaimed. "Oh—my. Where'd you ever get it?"

Ariana let her hand slide over the material. It was beautiful. The most beautiful thing she had ever seen.

"It was my mama's wedding gown," Ariana answered simply.

Aunt Molly turned her eyes toward her sister-in-law.

"Oh, not mine," Laura Benson was quick to explain. "Ariana's birth mama. It was rescued from the wagon train after the raid. Ariana's second mama—Lucy Millard—saved it for her. It was one of the few things . . ." Her voice trailed off.

Aunt Molly stared at her with horror-filled eyes. Then she turned back to the gown. "Well, it sure is a beautiful thing. I've never seen such a pretty dress in all my days."

"Yes," said Ariana softly. "It is beautiful. When I was little I used to dream about the day—" She stopped. She wasn't sure now if she ever wanted to wear the gown.

"What is it made of?" asked Aunt Molly.

"It's satin—satin overlaid with lace—Spanish lace, Aunt Lucy told me," replied Ariana. "It was imported. Brought over special. Just for the gown."

"One sleeve—" began Aunt Molly, reaching her hand out to the gown.

"One cuff is missing," Laura Benson filled in. "See the

way it is made—this big puffed sleeve nipped into this slender cuff that reaches to the wrist. This cuff—on this side—
buttons on with these tiny little buttons. That cuff must have
been lost at the time. . . . It'll need to be repaired before Ariana—"

"I wonder if one can find matching lace," began Aunt
Molly, who loved to sew.

"Oh, I don't think so," went on Laura Benson. "Lucy said
she watched for material—and I've looked too. Mind you, I've
not been to the bigger cities, but it was special material—
ordered just for that gown. Imported, like Ariana said. No, I
don't think one would ever match it."

"It's a shame," mused Aunt Molly, still studying the beautiful lace and the missing cuff.

"I've thought that one could just make two new cuffs—of
satin. It wouldn't be quite as elegant, but it would do just
fine. It's still the most beautiful wedding gown—"

"Well, there's plenty of time to be thinking on that," said
Ariana suddenly. "I have no plans."

She began to fold up the gown with trembling hands.

❧   ❧   ❧

"Is something wrong?"

Ariana stirred at the sound of her mother's voice. She did
not know how long she had been sitting, gazing off into
space, her thoughts far from the little log home that belonged
to her aunt and uncle.

"What do you mean?" she managed to reply.

"I don't know. You just seemed . . . miles away. Rather . . .
forlorn."

Ariana stirred listlessly again.

Her mother sat down beside her and placed a hand on her
arm.

"I've noticed—something—ever since we arrived. What is
it?"

"I'm . . . I'm not sure," Ariana began. "Perhaps I . . . just miss the school—the students. My friends from church. If I could have gone back home—"

"Maybe," replied her mother, not sounding too sure.

They continued to sit in silence, each occupied with her own thoughts.

"I thought you might be missing him," her mother finally commented.

Ariana swung around to face her, fully understanding her mother's remark. "He's an—"

But she couldn't say "outlaw."

"He's not . . . a believer," she said instead.

"I know. You told me," said her mother quietly. Her hand gently stroked the gingham sleeve. "That is what makes it difficult. You must dictate to your heart. You've made the right decision—but it isn't always easy to make the right decision—even when you know you must. Sometimes—sometimes—the heart needs some convincing, even though our faith says—"

"He was—"

"Your prison guard. I know. I've heard rather strange stories . . . about women and . . . and their captors. It really isn't at all unheard of for them to . . . to learn to love them."

Ariana brushed a hand nervously over her ginghamed lap. "Oh, Mother," she said quickly, "how could I? I mean, I was frightened of him—at first. I wanted the old man—Sam—to . . . to guard me. I certainly didn't—I mean, even after I . . . I thought of him as . . . safe . . . I still didn't—all the time at the camp—and even later on the trail I never—I mean, I never thought of him . . . in that way."

"And now?" prompted her mother. "Now that he is no longer your captor—but has become instead your liberator?"

Ariana shook her head and the tears began to fall, even though she fought against them.

"I don't know. I honestly don't know," she wept. "He was really . . . really a victim himself. He didn't choose that life. That way to live. His father . . . he was just raised to . . . and he had nothing to do with my . . . he didn't even know why I was there—at first. He really was ... quite. ... I ... I know I shouldn't. I know he still isn't a believer, so I can't ... but I ... I'm afraid ..."

She turned to her mother, the tears coming more quickly. "Well—it's a good thing he's gone," she blurted out and threw herself into her mother's arms.

The mother said nothing more, just held her daughter and patted her slender shoulder. It was as she thought. Ariana had indeed fallen in love with the young man. Her heart was still a prisoner—even though she had been set free.

🙦   🙦   🙦

Laramie managed to find work on a large ranch in the foothills. At first it seemed strange to have to report to the foreman, but he loved being out in the open. He even enjoyed working with the herd. And it was a new experience to line up once a month for his small stipend—earned wages—and know he had worked hard for what was rightfully his.

He didn't head for town and the saloon like the rest of the outfit. No one asked questions—though they must have wondered. Laramie didn't want to take any chances of being spotted by some lawman, though he was fairly sure he would not be known to anyone in the area as one of Will Russell's band.

Besides, he wished to save his money. Someday, he dared to dream, he'd have a little spread of his own.

🙦   🙦   🙦

"Preacher comin' to town," laughed one of the cowboys as he pulled off high-heeled boots and flopped down on his cot to sleep off the booze. "Can you imagine thet? A preacher. Here."

Hoots of laughter followed.

Soon snores replaced the coarse laughter. Except for

those who had duty riding herd, all would sleep for the rest of the day.

But Laramie was curious. Who was this preacher? When was he coming? And where?

He decided to saddle up and ride into town to see if he could find out.

❧   ❧   ❧

The neighbors were thrilled to hear of the possibility of their children being taught.

"We need to build a school," one big man proposed.

"Maybe we could use it for the Bible lessons," offered a small woman timidly.

"Shore—a school an' a church—all in one," someone from the back of the room called out.

Laura Benson smiled at Ariana as she laid a hand on her arm.

"Perhaps God brought you to this community for a purpose," she whispered and Ariana smiled in return. She fervently hoped they would hurry with the building. She was anxious to get back in the classroom again. Perhaps it would give her something else to think about. Something other than Laramie.

❧   ❧   ❧

Laramie looked up the preacher and was pleased to hear that the man was not just passing through the area. Laramie had lots of questions, and he was sure they couldn't be answered in a few short days. He began to attend the services whenever he was free. He even tucked his Bible in his saddlebag and took it with him as he rode the range. When he had a few moments as the herd contentedly grazed, he let his horse rest and feed while he sat in the shade and read the Bible, one eye on the lookout for trouble.

At last the pieces began to fall into place. He felt he was

beginning to understand what God had in mind for His creation—for him.

The sinner could be forgiven and the sin, not just forgiven, but forgotten, because of what Jesus Christ, the Redeemer, had done on the cross of Calvary. He had been the sacrifice—the atonement—for man's sin.

He, Laramie Russell, had to claim that gift of salvation—had to accept what had been done in his place. Had to vow to sin no more and make restitution—as far as possible—for sins of the past. Then he would be free to join one of the little groups that would be baptized at the small creek east of town.

It was not difficult for Laramie to acknowledge that he was a sinner. He had known that fact, deep down inside, for some time. Nor was it hard for him to ask for God's forgiveness. He had longed to be freed from his burden of guilt. It was going to be much more difficult to right past wrongs. He didn't quite know where and how to start.

Chapter Twenty

Truth

Ariana was thrilled when at long last the crude little schoolhouse was ready for use. Heart beating fast, she looked out over the small class of pioneer children. Their eyes shone with anticipation. Their faces looked to her with eagerness.

Perhaps Mama was right, she whispered to herself. *Maybe this whole chain of events was for this very purpose.*

It was nice to think that maybe there had been a reason—something good that could come out of the dreadful ordeal. *How wonderful to know that God never lost control*, she thought, *that He could be trusted even during the darkest times when there seemed to be no purpose to it at all.*

As Ariana looked into eleven pairs of eyes fixed on her face, she took a moment for a quick prayer. *Thank you, Father*, she whispered silently.

It was not much—but it came from an overflowing heart.

❧   ❧   ❧

Laramie felt torn in three directions.

His first desire was to return to Ariana. He was anxious to tell her about his Bible reading, his talks with the pastor, and the fact that he now understood her faith. Yet he hesitated. He had no right to expect acceptance from her or her family. He had a past. A past that had not been put to right.

His second choice seemed to be to stay where he was and continue to grow in his understanding of the words in his mother's Bible. He had been welcomed into the small Christian fellowship group. The minister was most willing to lead him in his new faith. Other church members greeted him warmly and made him feel one with the little congregation. In fact, the eldest of the minister's daughters seemed more than willing to move the friendship beyond that. Laramie noticed that she often tried to catch his eye, flirting just a bit, and took advantage of every opportunity to speak with him. Had it not been for his feeling for Ariana, he may have felt flattered and perhaps even responded. Laramie simply did not give the extra attention much thought.

Yet, as much as he longed to return to Ariana, and as much as he enjoyed the fellowship of the little church, Laramie concluded that the only honest choice was for him to pursue restitution for the past. It was not an easy decision and one that troubled his soul as he battled it through.

"I've got to go back."

Laramie came to the conclusion after a long struggle. He had wrestled with the problem for many weeks, trying to find a good excuse for avoiding the return. After all, the trip could well cost him his life. He would not be welcomed back to his father's camp. Nor would he be welcomed in any of the towns where he had been part of the gang's activities.

But there was no way to escape the urgings of his conscience. He had done wrong. He had been forgiven—but he must—as far as possible, make right the wrongs of his past.

❧   ❧   ❧

Laramie rapped loudly on the ranch house door and was admitted by the owner himself. The young man felt awkward and self-conscious as he stepped inside.

"Russell," the boss welcomed him and stepped aside for

him to enter. "Foreman says he's pleased with yer work. Know how to git the task done—without gripin' none. Been meanin' to have a chat."

Laramie removed his dust-covered hat.

"Jest came to thank ya for the opportunity of ridin' fer ya," he began. "I've appreciated it—but I have to be movin' on."

The older man looked puzzled.

"Somethin' happen?" he asked.

"Reckon it did," replied Laramie in his easy drawl. "Only—not here. Happened a long time ago."

The man waited.

"Ya see, sir," went on Laramie, fingering the hat in his hands, "I been ridin' under false colors. I . . . I'm wanted by the law."

The man shrugged careless shoulders. "So—" he said. "I don't ask no questions."

"No. No," agreed Laramie. "An' I appreciate it."

"Look," said the big man and took Laramie's arm to draw him farther into the room and toward a chair. "Likely ain't a cowpoke on the place thet ain't had a little run-in here or there. Thet doesn't mean the law's gonna catch up."

Laramie reluctantly took the seat, still twisting his Stetson in his hands.

"Ya heard somethin'? Somebody on yer tail?" the big man went on.

"No. Not thet I know of."

"There—ya see," said the rancher, looking relieved. "Likely no need to panic."

"Oh, I'm not panicky," said Laramie. "I jest want it cleared up. You see—I've been going to the little church— straightened out my life. Now—if I read my Bible right—I've got to do what I can to set the past straight. So—I've got to go back."

The big man looked shocked. "Ya mean yer walkin' right back into the hangman's noose?" he asked incredulously.

Laramie smiled and reached a hand up to the hat brim

that wasn't there. He scratched his head instead, feeling the scar that began on his forehead and stretched into the hairline.

"Well . . . now I don't know," he admitted. "I've no idea what my future holds. If I've got the hangman's noose to face . . . then I guess—"

"Don't do it, boy," the rancher said with great feeling. "It's a foolhardy thing. You'll never git a fair trial an' ya know it. It's good enough thet ya quit whatever it was ya was doin'. Thet's good enough." He put a hand up in some alarm. "Didn't kill a sheriff—or a marshal, did ya?"

"No," replied Laramie simply.

The rancher looked relieved. "There—ya see," he said, "likely nobody will even bother lookin' fer ya."

"You don't understand," said Laramie, and he stood to his feet. "The One who was looking fer me—the One thet really matters—He's already found me. An' He says yer sins will find ya out. He says, ya own up to 'em—make restitution, they call it—if it's possible. I plan to do that. An' I reckon what happens—well, thet's up to Him."

The rancher reached up to push back his thinning hair. He opened his mouth to speak and then closed it again, shaking his head.

He took a pace away from Laramie, then turned back to face him. "I think yer makin' a big mistake, boy," he said bluntly, then went on carefully. "But—iffen ya ever want to ride fer me agin—well you jest come on by."

"Thank you," said Laramie and he stretched out his hand.

"See the foreman. He'll settle yer wage." The two shook hands.

"I'll do thet, sir," replied Laramie. "I plan to leave before sunup."

❧ ❧ ❧

All during the long ride back over the country that Laramie had covered with Ariana, he thought and rethought his situation. How could he get into camp without being seen by the sentry from the ledge? Would he be gunned down before he even made it through the chasm in the rock walls? How would his father respond when he came with his apology? If it was accepted, would he expect Laramie to become part of the gang again? No, he couldn't do that. Not even if it meant his death.

Should he go to the law first? No, he might spend the rest of his days in prison. First he had to talk with his father. Had to ask his forgiveness. Had to tell him about the truths he had learned from his mother's Bible—if indeed it had been his mother's. His father needed to hear.

In the end it was White Eagle whom Laramie first contacted. The young brave seemed excited to see him.

"Thought you die," he said, thrusting out his hand to shake Laramie's, white-man fashion.

Laramie smiled. "Thought you would have moved," he responded. "It's been a long time."

"Move village many times. Back again," said White Eagle.

"What happened after we left?" Laramie had to know.

White Eagle laughed. "Like ants," he said. "Then—long walk. Mad." He laughed again, remembering.

"Your father's black, good horse," he said seriously. "Carry squaw."

Laramie spun around. "Whose squaw? Yours?" he asked.

White Eagle beamed his pleasure. Laramie could tell that his friend was now a family man.

"Naw," he said, slapping the young Pawnee on the shoulder. "Ya don't say? Any papoose?"

"Soon," said White Eagle. His eyes shone.

Laramie nodded, acknowledging the man's good fortune.

"How's everything?" Laramie asked, changing the tone of the conversation.

"Bad year," said White Eagle seriously. "Much sick. Little food. Bad year."

"I'm sorry to hear that," replied Laramie. "Anything I can do to help?"

"Pawnee do not need help," he said simply.

Laramie nodded.

"Still the same chief?"

"Father, Half Moon, die. New chief. Brother, Broken Tooth. Maybe trouble," said White Eagle.

Laramie let his gaze drift out over the valley that lay beneath them. Miles of timbered hills stretched all the way to vast prairies. But the scene included small farmsteads—ranches—even a couple of tiny towns. Many more campfires than the Indians' lifted smoke to the sky. What would be happening in the years to come? Could the white settlers and the Indian tribes live in peace?

"Have ya heard anythin' about . . . my pa?" asked Laramie, shifting his attention back to the man beside him.

White Eagle's eyes darkened.

"Not good news," he said.

Laramie turned toward him. "What do you mean?"

"They raid. Bank. Not good."

"You mean . . . some of them . . . didn't make it?"

White Eagle nodded.

"My pa?"

"I not know. Only know not good. Only two horse come back. Funny little man."

"Sam?"

"Man makes much spit." White Eagle spit in the dust to demonstrate.

"Sam," said Laramie.

"One more. Hurt bad. Not new horse of father."

Laramie felt a lump come into his throat. He knew with a certainty that he had to get to his father's camp—quickly. He began to gather the reins of the buckskin.

"How long ago?" he asked as he mounted.

"Two—maybe three moons," said White Eagle.

Laramie reached down to clasp the hand of his old friend one last time. He might never see him again. They looked at each other steadily, then without exchanging words, they both turned to go.

⚜   ⚜   ⚜

There was no man on the ledge that guarded the entrance to the camp. Laramie carefully studied the position before urging his mount forward.

As he rode into the little settlement he noticed how dilapidated the buildings all were. Bad before, they were even worse now. Everything seemed strangely deserted. Maybe there was no one around.

Then he noticed there were two horses in the corral. Someone must still live here.

He was dismounting when a shot rang out and splintered a pine bough just above his head. He dived for cover at the same moment that the buckskin reared and spun around, fear making the animal's nostrils flare.

Another shot. This one thumped into the tree behind which Laramie crouched. In the instant before Laramie ducked, he saw the shooter. It was Sam who leveled the rifle and was taking careful aim.

As soon as the echo stopped resounding off the rock walls of the valley, Laramie bellowed, "Sam. Sam, it's me. Laramie."

He waited.

"Show yerself," came a raspy voice.

Laramie wondered at the wisdom of obeying the command, but at last he eased out from behind the pine.

"Well, I'll be," said Sam, his rifle barrel gradually lowering. "It *is* Laramie."

Laramie looked around for his buckskin. The animal stood a few feet away, still appearing skitterish. The pack horse had run off several yards and was now feeding on the thick grass beneath a clump of birch.

Sam was walking toward him, his rifle lowered but still in his hand. His whiskered face was gaunt and his eyes dark and angry. "Ya got a nerve showin' up here," he growled.

It was not much different than Laramie had expected.

"I came back to see my pa," he said in explanation as he stooped to pick up his hat, which had landed in the dust.

"Yer pa," said Sam, and he spit in the dirt.

Laramie nodded and whipped the dust from his Stetson before putting it back on his head.

"Well—I'd say you were about three months too late," snapped Sam.

Laramie stared. "Ya mean—?"

"Dead! Like the rest of 'em. I'm the only one left." He spit again, his eyes glaring at Laramie.

The sudden pain in Laramie's heart was like a huge fist squeezing the life out of it. If only—

He turned away for a moment.

He turned back to Sam, swallowing hard. "Buried here?" he managed to ask.

Sam nodded. The gun had finally dropped down to his side. "Ya ain't brung a posse in here, have ya?" he asked gruffly.

Laramie's shock showed on his face. "Ya know better," he threw back at the old man.

Sam nodded his head toward one of the falling-down buildings. "Well—come in, then," he offered.

"I'll not be stoppin'," Laramie replied. "Just long enough to . . . pay my respects. . . ."

He gathered the reins of his mount and led him to a hitching post. The pack horse wouldn't wander far, he reasoned. Not with the other horses nearby.

"Now thet yer here, ya might as well come in," Sam said, spitting. Then he nodded toward the trees to their right. Laramie understood that his father had been buried there.

He found the grave. It was marked by a small homemade cross. On it had been written one word. "Boss." Laramie reached up and removed his hat. He felt choked. Saddened. He had wanted to talk to this man. To ask his forgiveness.

To tell of his newfound faith. And now he was gone. It was too late. Too late.

It was some time before Laramie felt ready to talk to Sam. He knew now that he would have to talk with him. He had so many questions. He needed some answers.

☙ ☙ ☙

Sam had brewed an awful pot of weak coffee. They sat sipping it slowly, each deep in thought. Sam chewed on his dirty mustache and spit frequently into the corner, and Laramie toyed with his Stetson and rubbed unconsciously at the scar on his forehead.

At last Laramie spoke. "How'd it happen?"

Sam spit again. "Robbery went sour," he said simply.

"Where?"

"Over to Elk River. Bank there."

"What happened?"

"Yer pa figured Skidder sold us out."

"Skidder?"

There was silence for some time.

"Skidder—is he—?" Laramie began to ask.

"Yer pa shot 'im. He'd turned sides."

Silence again.

"Yer pa got shot. His horse was shot right out from under 'im. He had no place to go. Caught two bullets. I . . . I got him out but he was hit bad. We grabbed another horse an' lit out. We made it back. But he only lasted a few hours."

Sam clamped his mouth shut and chewed on his mustache. He had said his piece. There was nothing more to say.

Laramie sat silently, letting all of the pieces fit together. White Eagle had said that it wasn't his pa's horse. He'd been right.

Laramie could imagine the scene of the robbery. He'd been there himself on more than one occasion in the past. But he had never walked into an ambush. A double cross of one of their own men.

"Why didn't ya put his name on the cross?" he asked Sam softly.

Sam snorted. "His name? Which name? Which one of the five or six I knowed about was I gonna put on there?"

Laramie nodded. He had not realized his pa had changed his name so many times. Maybe he was one of the men listed in his mother's Bible. For some reason he could not bring himself to ask.

He stood and set aside his cup. "I'd better git," he said. "I've some ridin' to do."

"What ya gonna do?" asked Sam. "Thought ya might stay. This is still the safest place—"

"Not lookin' fer a safe place," Laramie responded. "I'm fixin' to turn myself in."

Sam jerked upright. "Did you come here to—?"

"I said, myself. Not you. Not anyone else. I came here to see my pa—thet's all." He looked evenly at the older man. "I'm not runnin' anymore, Sam," he said quietly.

"They'll lock ya away—iffen they don't hang ya," Sam said brusquely.

Laramie nodded. "They likely will," he agreed.

"Yer crazy, boy," spat Sam. "Plumb crazy."

"I was sorta hopin' thet you'd decide to join me, Sam. I hate leavin' ya here—all alone."

Sam shook his head. "Got a feelin' I'd rather finish my days here then at the end of a rope," he said firmly.

"Maybe there wouldn't be a rope. Maybe—"

"They'd be a rope," said Sam, and he spit to the side of the coveted chair with its many-patched wobbly legs.

"Sheriff wouldn't be in his right mind iffen he let me go," went on Sam simply.

Laramie nodded. Maybe it was so. He hated to think of it. He hated to leave the aging man all alone in the forsaken camp. It didn't seem right. But Sam had chosen his life. There was little that Laramie could do to right the wrongs. Still, he did at least owe him a glimpse at the truth he had found. The man would have to make up his own mind.

"Ya know, Sam," he said softly as he lifted his hat and fingered the hatband, "when ya found thet there trunk of my ma's . . . ya opened a whole new world fer me. A world of . . . good. Of law and order and . . . faith in God. I didn't know where it would lead at the time, but I've followed the trail . . . an' it led me to . . . forgiveness. It feels good, Sam. It feels mighty good."

Sam only stared.

"An' thet's what I came back to speak to my pa about," Laramie finished. "Now thet he ain't here—not much reason fer me to stay. But I want you to know about it, too, Sam. It really works. God can forgive. He can turn a man's life around. One has to ask fer the pardon He offers. It's as simple as thet."

Sam said nothing. He spit again, the brown liquid making one more stain on the already darkened wood of the floor.

"Think on it, Sam," Laramie prompted gently.

Sam didn't even acknowledge the words that were spoken. Laramie rose to his feet. Reluctantly he moved to go. He nodded toward the older man. "Thanks, Sam . . . fer the coffee an' fer . . . carin' fer me . . . as a boy. An' fer . . . lookin' out fer my pa." His voice threatened to break on the last words. He settled his Stetson back on his thick hair and turned to leave.

Just as he was stepping through the door, Sam called out after him.

"He wasn't really yer pa, ya know."

Chapter Twenty-one

Reunion

Heart thudding in his chest, Laramie swung around. "What are you sayin'?"

Sam eyed him coolly. He took another cut from his chewing tobacco. "He weren't yer real pa," he repeated.

Laramie stepped back into the room, moving slowly toward the little man. "You knowin' somethin' ya haven't come clean on—or are ya jest talkin'?" he asked tersely.

"Oh, I knowed all right," replied Sam. "I was there."

Laramie felt the strength draining from him. He fought for control, easing himself back to one of the log stools that had served the camp for many years. Sam now claimed the boss's chair.

Laramie swallowed, his eyes intense.

"Are ya sayin' thet wasn't my ma's trunk?" he asked Sam.

Sam fingered the tobacco before returning it to his pocket, spit in the corner, and tipped his head. "Oh, thet were her trunk, right enough," he said slowly. "Not much doubt 'bout thet."

"Then—" prompted Laramie.

"Thet scar ya got—" said Sam with a careless wave of his jackknife.

Laramie waited.

"Thet came in an Indian raid. Reason yer pa hated the redskins so."

Unconsciously Laramie's hand reached to the scar. One finger traced it back into the depth of his hair.

"We'd been out on a raid," Sam went on, finally seeming to warm to his subject. "Came upon this wagon train. Jest been ambushed. They'd done a good job of it too. Everybody dead—all over the place. Men—womenfolk—kids—all dead. Scalps gone—faces slashed. It was an awful sight. Near made a grown man sick to his stomach.

"They'd set the wagons afire—but the rain stopped some of 'em from burning outright. Well, we didn't much like what we saw. Some of the fellas was pokin' through stuff—seein' iffen there was anythin' worth takin', an' then I heard this— little mew sound. Thought it was a wounded animal of some kind. I looked in this here wagon—an' there ya was—yer head split open by a tomahawk—yer clothes soaked in blood—but still alive.

"Well, I didn't know what to do. I called to yer pa and he come an' took a look. Then he—"

Sam stopped and seemed to choke on the next words.

"Anyway, he picked ya outta there. I asked iffen he'd lost his senses, but he said we couldn't jest leave ya there to die. He told the fellas to see what they could find—fer yer care, an' Rowdy found thet trunk. It had some things fer a young'un an' we figured thet it'd help—so yer pa ordered it brought. Near killed the pack horse gettin' it back to camp. We shoulda jest took the things ya'd need, but we didn't have time to sort through it there on the spot.

"Well—he brought ya home and patched ya up the best he could—an' ya made it."

Laramie's head was spinning. He could not take in all that the man was saying.

"I told yer pa you'd never make an outlaw," Sam went on as though in argument. "Ya jest—never had the stomach fer it—ya could see thet from when ya was a kid. I mean—" Sam waved the jackknife in the air. "Ya was always patching up

hurt things and cleanin' things an'—ya jest weren't made fer
it. But he said he'd make ya what he wanted ya to be. Thet
ya'd never survive elsewise. Someone would up and shoot ya
in the back, or somethin'. He says—"

"How old was I?" cut in Laramie.

Sam looked startled, then annoyed. "How should I know?
I don't know nothin' 'bout kids. Around two, I s'pose. What
difference—?"

Then Sam stopped and stared at the young man before
him. "Ya don't remember nothin'—?" he began, straightening
up in his chair.

"Nothin'," replied Laramie, a frown creasing his brow.

"Well—I ain't surprised. Ya was hurt real bad. Ya didn't
even start to talk fer a good piece after it. We wondered fer
a time iffen ya'd ever git any sense. Shock—yer pa said.
When ya came outta it—ya seemed bright enough."

"An' the trunk—?" insisted Laramie, leaning forward.

"Outta the same wagon."

Laramie managed to lift himself to his feet. "Is it still
here?" he asked hoarsely.

"In thet cabin—where the girl was."

Laramie nodded and left the room in a daze. Inwardly he
was being torn in two with separate identities. What could
he believe? Was Sam right? Was he really not the son of an
outlaw? Had his mother really been the sweet-looking
woman in the picture? Was he the little boy?

He pushed his way into the cabin, memories of Ariana
bending over her open Bible flooding through his mind. He
made his way to the trunk and slowly lifted back the lid. The
things were still all there. The garments that Ariana had
worn, carefully folded on the top. He lifted the gown and
stared long and hard. His mother's dress. She had been real.
She had loved him.

Laramie buried his face in the soft garment, and for the
first time since his babyhood he allowed himself the expression of tears.

❧   ❧   ❧

When his inner storm had passed, Laramie lifted himself from beside the trunk. It was over. He had emptied his soul of all bitterness, anxiety, and conflict. He was satisfied that he was who the book said he was. Burke Lawrence, son of Lavina and Turner Lawrence. He might never know more than that about his heritage—but at least he knew to whom he had belonged. It was something precious—a treasure to carry with him for the rest of his days.

He rose, folded the gown carefully, and placed it back in the trunk.

"Thank you, Mother," he whispered. "For yer . . . love. Yer prayers. I'm gonna be all right."

He closed the lid, gently, firmly, and left the room without looking back. He would call at his pa's—no—at his foster father's grave one more time. The man had saved him from certain death. He had raised him in the best way he knew how. He owed him respect—and one final goodbye.

❧   ❧   ❧

"Will Russell's gang, ya say?"

The crusty sheriff leaned back in his chair and lifted his feet up on the wooden desk.

Laramie nodded silently.

"Don't recall seeing ya when the bank got robbed," said the sheriff.

"I wasn't there," replied Laramie.

"Where was ya?"

"I had left—some time earlier."

The sheriff frowned. "Why?" he asked simply.

Laramie stirred. This was going to be harder than he had imagined. "There was a girl," he began. "She was kidnapped from Smithton. She was a prisoner in our camp. I took her—to her kin."

The sheriff's head lifted. He looked long and hard at Laramie, as though searching for his own answers, or looking for flaws. "What changed yer mind?"

Laramie frowned. "I never changed my mind—really," he replied. "I hadn't been in on the kidnapping."

"Who was?"

"My—the boss. Will Russell."

"What changed his mind?"

The man sure had a lot of questions. Laramie squirmed. Why didn't he just get on with it? Get a confession, or whatever it took, and lock him up.

The sheriff was still waiting for his reply.

"Well . . . he didn't change his mind . . . really. I . . . I took her without him knowin'," Laramie confessed.

"This girl—?" The sheriff's eyes narrowed and he lowered his feet. "Ya . . . harm her . . . in any way?"

"No, sir," Laramie was quick to reply. "I jest took her to her uncle's farm—in Montana."

The sheriff seemed to relax. "Why?" he asked as he lifted his feet again.

Laramie could feel the anger flushing his cheeks. He was annoyed with all the senseless questioning. "Because, sir," he said heatedly, "she didn't belong in a camp with a bunch of outlaws. She had done nothin' to deserve it. She was innocent and good and God-fearing. An' there was trouble brewin'."

He wondered if he had said too much. If he had become too vehement. He forced himself to cool down. He'd be getting the hangman's noose for sure with such action.

The sheriff looked at him steadily, then nodded, lifted his feet from the desk, and opened a drawer stuffed with papers. "Don't recall seein' yer picture," he mused.

"No, sir. Likely haven't," said Laramie in a softer tone.

"Why not?" asked the sheriff, putting his feet up again.

Laramie shuffled his feet uncomfortably. "Well . . . I reckon I haven't earned a poster, sir," he replied. "I was mostly left to hold the horses." He flushed as he spoke the words.

"So," said the sheriff, not looking up. "You haven't killed a man—you don't have a bounty on yer head—ya don't even have yer face on a poster?"

Laramie nodded.

The sheriff's feet returned to the floor with a heavy thump.

"Don't look like I got any reason to hold ya, then," he said simply.

It took Laramie a while to grasp the words.

"I don't understand," he said when he could speak. "I was a member of the gang. I—"

"Now, how am I s'pose to prove thet?" demanded the sheriff. "Ain't nobody claimed to have seen ya—ain't no poster. Nothin'."

"But I have admitted . . . my guilt," declared Laramie.

The feet lifted again. The sheriff leaned back and looked at Laramie. He chewed on a straw that he picked from his pant cuff. "So ya did," he observed. "They say thet confession is good fer the soul."

He stared into Laramie's eyes as though his words carried some secret message.

"Son," he said at last, "ain't ever' day thet anyone comes to me tellin' me of past sins. Now I'm takin' from this here—confession—thet ya ain't plannin' on being a part of such—action—agin. Thet right?"

Laramie nodded dumbly.

"Thet ole gang—it's been—what shall we say—dismembered. An' from our little conversation—I don't think thet you'll be pickin' up with another one. Right?"

Laramie nodded again.

"Then—I suggest thet our conversation is closed."

At the stunned look on Laramie's face he went on, pointing one long finger at Laramie's chest. "But let me tell ya this, son. You mess with me—you're gonna swing. Ya got thet?"

Laramie stood to his feet nodding. He swallowed again.

"There's one more thing, Sheriff," he managed.

The sheriff nodded, but he looked impatient. "Make it fast," he said. "The coffee's gittin' cold over at Evita's."

Laramie lifted the little leather bag. "Money," he said simply. "This is stolen money."

"Stolen from where?" asked the sheriff.

"I don't rightly know. Here an' there. Most anywhere. I . . . have no idea. It was always divided up evenly. I don't know where this came from."

The sheriff swore. "Then how'm I to know where to give it back?" he said gruffly.

"Well . . . what am I to do—?"

"Look," said the sheriff testily. "Thet's yer problem. Not mine. Ya don't know where to take it back—then it's yer burden. You figure it out. I dunno."

He walked away muttering to himself. "Outlaws," fumed the sheriff. "Got no business gittin' religion. Makes more trouble then it's worth."

Laramie, holding his leather pouch of gold coins, watched him go and then stepped from the office. It took several minutes for him to realize that he was a free man.

※　　※　　※

Carefully Laramie counted out the money he had earned honestly as a ranch hand. He had already been giving his tithe to the little church where he had attended. Now the small pile of coins that were left did not look like much. Laramie sighed. They'd never put a down payment on his own spread, that was a sure thing.

He had seen a little church just down the street. He made his way to it now. A surprised minister answered his knock.

"Do you . . . do you help out poor people and the like?" asked Laramie.

"We help when we can, son, but our funds are limited," said the man. "Don't know that we can do much but—what can I do for you?"

Laramie lifted the leather bag and poured its contents

out on the wooden desk. "I'd like to make a donation," he said simply. The shining gold pieces glimmered in the afternoon sunlight streaming through the window. The man stood and stared.

"It was not honest money, but I've no way to git it back to those it was taken from," Laramie admitted. "Maybe you can undo a bit of that by puttin' it to good use."

The man still stared.

Laramie tipped his hat in respect and moved toward the door. "May the Lord bless you—an' yer church," he said with deep feeling, and he was gone.

❧   ❧   ❧

Ariana moved about the schoolroom, cleaning the chalkboards, tidying the small desks, and putting the few books they possessed back on the one makeshift shelf.

She was finally able to hum again. It had taken many months for her to feel that the song was back in her heart. But the months had lessened her pain and disappointment—though she still prayed fervently for Laramie. God was in control. He had brought good from her ordeal. Never had she seen such eager students. And their enthusiasm for learning carried over into her Sunday school class, for most of them returned again on Sunday to have their Bible lessons in the same little building.

Ariana moved to put the last books on the shelf. It was a pleasant evening—with many promised hours of sunlight yet. She would have time to saddle the little roan and take a leisurely ride before Aunt Molly's supper was served.

A firm rap on the door brought Ariana to attention. She was not used to callers at the schoolhouse. Momentarily her heart began racing. She had not forgotten the men who had visited her over two years earlier and carried her captive. Ariana had a hard time finding her voice. She was not quite sure if she could bid the visitor enter.

The door opened—just a crack at first. Ariana watched

with her breath caught in her throat.

Then the door pushed open farther—and there stood Laramie.

He was clean-shaven with carefully trimmed hair. His clothes were not new but were clean and well kept. His eyes, which held a spark, seemed to look right into her soul.

She caught her breath again. One word escaped her lips. "Laramie."

He moved forward slowly, his black Stetson in his hands. "May I . . . come in?" he asked softly.

She nodded. She couldn't speak. He looked—the same— yet so different.

"You've come back," she managed to whisper.

He nodded. "You made me promise. Remember?"

"I . . . yes." Tears threatened to spill. He could see them coming.

He stopped a few feet in front of her. Just stopped and looked at her.

"You look . . . well," he observed.

She swallowed. "And you," she managed.

They stood in silence. Laramie struggled with words and then spoke softly. "You remember," he began, "that I was to . . . find some answers. Find myself."

She nodded.

"Well, I've done that," he said simply and then added, "an' in the process . . . I've found God, too."

She stood and looked at him and then the tears began to spill from her eyes. "Oh, Laramie . . . I've prayed and prayed. I was beginning to think—"

"I was . . . afraid thet . . . thet you'd have given up. Thet—"

She looked up into his face, her eyes shining in spite of the tears that still ran down her cheeks.

"Oh no," she said between tears and laughter. "I would have waited . . . forever . . . to hear those words, if need be. Nothing . . . could make me happier. We are . . . are . . . fellow believers now. Nothing . . . could bring me . . . more joy."

Laramie longed to reach for her. To brush the tears from her cheeks and bury his face in her hair. He did not dare. He knew he had no right to expect her to care for him in the way that he cared for her.

He swallowed hard and willed himself to remain at a distance.

Chapter Twenty-two

Adrift

Laramie found a job with a local rancher and settled into the community. He was welcomed into the small congregation that met at the schoolhouse, and Ariana saw to it that he was put to work. To his surprise, Ariana seemed to assume that the situation had now changed—that the past was forgiven and could also be forgotten. She even managed, in a subtle way, to convey the idea that she expected him to call.

Laramie was quick to oblige, and the young people were soon seen as a couple in the community. Even Uncle Jake and Aunt Molly expressed unspoken pleasure in the arrangement.

Laramie could not have expressed his deep joy. It seemed that his unthinkable dream might indeed come true. It was hard to keep his love for Ariana in check when she greeted him with sparkling eyes and welcomed, with open pleasure, his evening calls. They spent many pleasurable hours by the fireplace, sharing thoughts and dreams, talking about the events past and their dreams for the future.

❧   ❧   ❧

Ariana would have been happy to marry quickly, and though Laramie was also anxious, he held himself back.

"But why wait?" argued Ariana. "We both know that in our hearts we plan to—someday—marry."

"Not until I have earned enough money to at least provide us with some of the things we'll be needin'," he countered.

Ariana smiled. "There's little I need to make me happy," she insisted.

"But you would like a roof over yer head," he teased.

Ariana tipped her head and grinned saucily. "It might be fun to sleep under the stars."

"Until the first snowstorm."

"Perhaps we could borrow a tent—from White Eagle."

"White Eagle needs his tent. By now his papoose will have joined him. He is a true family man now."

Ariana smiled. She had never been happier. She wished White Eagle even a portion of the joy that she herself felt.

"We do need to set a date," she said, and she was no longer teasing. "I want Papa and Mama to be here. Papa will marry us, of course. An' Mama and Aunt Molly will arrange the dinner for family and friends. They will need to know so they can make plans."

Laramie agreed.

The summer was moving into autumn.

"How about a Christmas wedding?" he asked Ariana.

Ariana thought about it. It seemed a long time to wait. At last she smiled. A Christmas wedding would be just fine.

"I'll let them know," said Ariana. "I do hope they will come early."

Laramie reached out to smooth back her windblown hair. They had ridden out to the ridge overlooking the small farm that belonged to her uncle. The day was just warm enough to be comfortable. The last of the summer crops bowed their heads to the passing breezes. The birds filled the afternoon with spirited chatter.

"It's so peaceful here—I love it," mused Laramie in contentment.

"Can we live here—always?" asked Ariana dreamily.

"Always," he answered.

Ariana moved in closer to him until her shoulder was touching his chest. "I never dreamed I could be so . . . happy," she sighed.

His hand dropped to her arm and pulled her closer against him. He lowered his head to place a kiss on the top of her tousled hair. "It is still like a . . . a dream," he said.

"When did you first know?" she quizzed him.

He smiled and gave her a little squeeze. "Is that important?"

"Sort of. I just wondered."

"I . . . it was after I'd shot the snake. I was afraid. I suddenly realized thet if somethin' happened to you . . . thet I would . . . suffer terribly. Thet you were much more than a . . . prisoner thet I was bound to free. I loved you. I realized thet then."

Ariana stirred dreamily.

"That's when I first knew, too," she told him.

She turned and reached up to run a finger gently along the scar. "And to think that I might have never met you. That you could have died . . . as a baby. You know, I owe Will Russell so much. For saving you, then for . . . for kidnapping me."

She giggled. "That sounds like a silly thing to say, doesn't it? But it . . . it turned out very well . . . don't you think?"

He nodded, his heart too full for an answer.

"You know," went on Ariana, "our backgrounds really aren't that different. Both orphans. Both lost our folks in an Indian raid. Rather ironic—or coincidental—don't you think?"

Laramie nodded, his head bent over Ariana's.

"Well, all that's behind us. Now . . . now we have the whole future ahead of us. We can . . . can make up for all the past . . . in the years ahead." She sighed deeply.

"God has been good," said Laramie.

"He has. Laramie—" Ariana caught herself and laughed softly. "You know," she hastened on, "it's hard for me to . . . to switch to Burke. I like that name. Burke. It's just that I've always thought of you as . . . Laramie. Will you mind if I slip now and then?"

Laramie smiled good-naturedly. "It's hard fer me, too," he admitted. "It takes some gettin' used to. I still have to stop and think when I go to sign my name or even when someone speaks to me. I guess we'll get used to it in time."

Ariana nodded. "It's hard to make a change—as an adult."

They stood in silence for a few minutes and then Laramie spoke. "What if we keep the Laramie? It seems thet . . . well thet I owe thet much to my . . . pa. He did do his best. He could have jest left me to die. It must have been an awful nuisance fer a man like him . . . to raise a child."

Ariana smiled. "Mrs. Laramie Burke Lawrence," she said softly. "It sounds just fine to me."

❧   ❧   ❧

Laramie worked hard and saved his money for his upcoming marriage. They would not be wealthy—but neither was anyone else on the prairies. At least they would be together.

Ariana, too, was saving each penny she could from her small stipend as a schoolteacher. She was certain they would manage just fine. Her uncle Jake had given them a small parcel of land down by the creek and neighbors had promised a house raising just as soon as the crops were out of the fields. Ariana was fully confident they would have a snug little dwelling all their own by the time their important day in December arrived.

❧   ❧   ❧

Her mother and father arrived two weeks before the wedding. Ariana was so excited when she met their stage that she thought she was acting like one of her first-graders.

"Oh, I'm so anxious for you to meet him," she bubbled. "I

know that you're going to love him just as much—well, almost as much as I do."

Her papa smiled and her mama held her close. "I knew it," she insisted. "I could sense you were in love with him when we were here before."

"Oh, Mama," laughed Ariana. "I scarcely admitted it myself then."

"Well, I knew it. You can't hide the look of a girl in love."

Ariana laughed joyfully. "We're going to need to fix that gown," she reminded her mother. "Did you bring the satin?"

"Oh yes. I didn't forget. Perhaps Molly will do the sewing. She is much better with a needle than I am."

Ariana fairly skipped her way back to the house. In only two short weeks she would finally be Mrs. Laramie Burke Lawrence. It still seemed like an impossible, beautiful dream.

❧   ❧   ❧

"Ariana?"

It was Laramie who called.

"In here," she answered, her cheeks flushing with pleasure. She and her aunt Molly were busy at the kitchen table, studying the lace wedding gown, figuring just how to cut the satin for the new cuffs.

"I suppose we could undo this cuff and see just how it is put together. We would then have a pattern," Aunt Molly was saying.

Laramie stood in the doorway. Ariana looked up and smiled.

"It's okay," she assured him. "I'm not superstitious. You can see the gown before the wedding day."

He moved forward then. He knew nothing about gowns—but the gown that hung before him looked beautiful.

"You'll be . . . wearing that?" he questioned, his eyes traveling from the gown to Ariana and then back again.

She nodded, excitement flushing her cheeks and making her eyes shine.

He reached for her hand. "I had no idea—I mean, I've never seen a wedding gown before. I had no idea they were so . . . so . . ."

Ariana laughed joyfully. "They aren't—always," she admitted. "It just happens that you are seeing the . . . the most beautiful gown in all the Americas." She laughed again. "It's special—even for a wedding gown. Imported lace—right from Spain. Isn't it gorgeous?"

He nodded. "I can hardly wait to see you in it," he said quietly.

"Well, first, we have this little problem," stated Ariana.

"What is that?"

"This sleeve. See how that other cuff is? It buttons on. This one is missing."

"Can you make another?" Laramie inquired with a shrug of his shoulders.

"Not to match. We'd never match the lace. So we have to make two new ones—out of the satin. We're just trying to figure out if the cut is on the bias or—"

Laramie leaned closer and took another look. He frowned.

"Wait a minute," he said as he reached to finger the material. "I jest might have something to help you. I'm almost sure—"

Ariana looked at him in surprise.

"In my ma's little chest. I saw a scrap of material—almost like that. I don't think someone would notice any little bit of difference."

Ariana's eyes took on a shine.

"Could you get it?" she asked hurriedly. "It would be wonderful if we could keep the cuffs—"

"I'll go home and pick it up," he assured her. "I'll be back in an hour or so."

⚜   ⚜   ⚜

Laramie retrieved the small chest from its place of safety and flipped up the lid. He was anxious to get back to Ariana.

Hurriedly he put aside the small baby gown and fumbled through the hankies, searching for the bit of material he had seen in the box. He did hope that he hadn't inadvertently lost it.

He was almost at the bottom of the box before he found it. He smiled with relief and drew it forth.

Yes. He had been right. The lace looked very much like the lace of Ariana's gown. He smiled again. She would be so pleased.

Laramie was about to tuck the scrap of material in his shirt pocket when something caught his eye. A tiny button.

His eyes widened and he brought the material closer. Another button. And another.

He stared, not able to believe what his eyes were seeing. In his hand he held the missing cuff. It could only mean one thing.

ⵜ   ⵜ   ⵜ

His legs gave out on him and Laramie lowered himself to his bunk, his face in his hands. A wave of nausea passed through him, making him feel sick inside. Did he and Ariana share the same mother? It couldn't be. It just couldn't be. He loved Ariana. They were to be married. He felt inner pain as he had never felt before in his entire life.

His first temptation was to destroy the little cuff and say it had been lost.

But reason and honesty won the battle. That would not be fair. It would not be right. He could never live with the fact. Nor would Ariana ever forgive him if he tried.

One simply could not marry one's own sister. He lifted his head and stared—unseeing—before him. He would have to tell her. Would have to tell them all.

He hated the thought of the whole ordeal.

Why? Why? When everything seemed to have finally worked out for good?

Laramie dropped his head in his hands again and groaned. *Where are you, God? How could you let this happen? Why didn't you let us know we were brother and sister right from the start? Then our relationship could have been thet of family—good and proper.*

Laramie groaned again. He had never, in his lifetime, been struck such a cruel blow.

❧   ❧   ❧

Ariana paced back and forth on the porch of her aunt's farm home. Laramie was taking longer than she had expected. Was he having trouble finding the material? It would be so nice to have the cuffs matching—or even nearly matching. It would be so nice to keep the dress as close as possible to the gown her mother had worn. She did hope that Laramie was right. That the cuff would not need to be changed to satin.

She hesitated and looked out over the country road in the gathering twilight. Laramie was still not in sight.

She sighed and paced some more.

She hoped nothing bad had happened. What if his horse had spooked? What if the law had suddenly appeared? No, that was silly. Laramie had said that he had confessed and been pardoned. Nothing like that would happen now.

Just as Ariana felt she could stand the uncertainty no longer, she saw Laramie's buckskin appear around the bend in the road. In her agitation she felt like running out to meet him. But that would be silly. She held herself in check. He would be with her soon enough.

She tapped one foot against the porch boards, impatience making it hard for her to wait. The warm evening breeze played with her hair, wisping it about her oval face.

At last Laramie pulled up and threw the reins over the

hitching rail. He came toward her. Ariana beamed and moved to meet him.

"Will it work? Is the lace pattern close enough?" she called as the distance between them closed.

In the semidarkness Ariana could barely see his face. When he drew near enough she saw he was pale and drawn. Something had happened. Ariana felt her heart beat faster. Was it just his disappointment that the lace wasn't right?

He said nothing—just reached out his hand to her. In his palm was the bit of lace. Ariana took it and turned it over in her fingers.

"It doesn't matter if it doesn't match," she began. "Don't feel badly if—"

Ariana looked more closely.

"It looks—very close," she said and looked up at Laramie. He still was ashen—silent. She could not understand.

"Ariana . . . it doesn't just . . . match the cuff," he said softly in a choked, forced voice. "It *is* the cuff."

Her eyes widened. She looked into his face with disbelief.

"It *is* the cuff," he repeated. "Look. It has the tiny buttons."

Ariana's gaze went back to the bit of lace. She turned it over and over. First unbelief, then delight, filled her eyes.

"Why, that's wonderful!" she exclaimed. "Who would have ever believed it? Who would have ever imagined? The real missing cuff. Isn't it wonderful! Isn't God good!"

She threw her arms around Laramie's neck. Her warm tears of joy fell on his cheek.

Gently he pushed her from him. "Ariana . . . listen to me."

She looked at him, shock in her eyes. What had happened? What was wrong?

"I found the cuff . . . in my mother's box."

She nodded.

"My . . . *mother's.*"

She looked puzzled.

"It matches your mother's dress. Exactly."

She took one tiny step backward, still staring at him.

"You don't mean—?" she began, but she did not finish.
He nodded.

"But it can't be," she almost screamed at him. "It—can't
be."

"Ariana—"

She looked at him for one moment, her eyes wild and denying. His own tears were tracing the pattern on his cheek
where Ariana's tears had been such a short while ago.

"It has to be," he said simply, looking away from the pain
in her eyes.

"I don't want a brother," she cried. "I—want—" and then
she turned from him and ran toward the house.

❧   ❧   ❧

Dear Ariana,

*I am leaving. I hope someday to return when I can
think of you as a sister. I have decided that it is too hard
for us to see each other now. I will pray for you. I will
love you always, but that love must change now. Perhaps someday we will be able to say that God has
worked it for good.*

Love, Laramie

Ariana held the letter in a trembling hand, tears flowing
freely down her cheeks. Across the room she could see the
lovely gown of Spanish lace—its second cuff now securely in
its place.

"I will never wear it," she whispered to herself. "Never! I
loved him so."

She stirred and looked at the gown again, brushing at the
tears on her cheek with the back of her hand.

"If only I had *known* he was my brother. We could have
. . . have shared so many things. Learned to love each other
. . . in a different way. But this? This is so . . . cruel. I will
never be able to . . . to accept him as a brother. Never. I love
him far too deeply."

Ariana began to weep again.

Her eyes fell back to the final words of Laramie's note. "Perhaps someday we will be able to say that God has worked it for good." That seemed impossible. Impossible. God seemed . . . seemed so far away. So . . . beyond her reach.

Trust, came the quiet message to Ariana's heart—but at the moment she found it beyond her capability.

Chapter Twenty-three

The Diary

For the first week Laramie just drifted in a daze, except for the pain deep inside that constantly reminded him he was still alive. Even when he would rather not be.

It had all been so unexpected. Though looking back, Laramie wondered why he hadn't begun to put some of the pieces together much earlier.

The wagon train. The massacre and burning. The fact that both of them were without their real parents. Yes—it should have made him wonder. Yet who would have thought?

Laramie looked at the small chest with a mixture of love and hate. It had held one too many secrets. One that had torn his world apart.

"It was best that we know," he told himself over and over. "It would have been a dreadful thing if . . ." But secretly, Laramie wondered.

He found it hard to pray—so he read. At least he could still manage to concentrate when reading his mother's Bible. *Our mother's Bible,* he corrected himself. Perhaps someday—with a lot of help from the Lord—he and Ariana would be able to read it together.

No. No, he concluded. I just can't—can't think of her as a sister. I just can't.

After a week had passed, Laramie mentally took stock.

"I've got to get out of these doldrums," he told himself. "I've got to go on with my life."

At first he had a hard time deciding what he would do, and then he remembered the rancher. The man had said if he ever wanted a job—well, he needed a job now. Laramie saddled up his mount, tied the bundles to the pack saddle, and headed off.

When he rapped on the ranch house door, Laramie was welcomed.

"Hopin' ya'd come on back," said the big man. "'Bout given up on ya. But it couldn't have been at a better time. Foreman jest quit. Fixin' to have his own spread. None of those yahoos I got out there is worth their salt. I was afraid I'd have to be my own foreman. Hate the thought of all thet ridin'."

He stopped for breath and looked at Laramie. "Ya want the job, it's yers."

Laramie nodded. It was the only contract needed.

"The foreman has his own bunk," the man went on. "Thet little shack down the lane. Throw yer bedroll in there."

Laramie was thankful to be on his own. He much preferred it to bunking in with a bunch of card-playing, snuff-chewing, booze-drinking cowhands.

"Maybe I'm jest a coward," he chided himself, "but I sure don't feel ready to socialize yet."

He tossed his bedroll on the bunk, unpacked his few belongings, turned his horses into the corral, and went to look for some kind of a broom. The small shack was a mess. He planned to clean it thoroughly before claiming it as his own.

❧   ❧   ❧

Ariana stumbled through one long day after another. She previously had quit her position in the little school, so there wasn't even that to think about. Besides—it was the Christmas break. She wouldn't have been teaching anyway. She would have been getting married.

Now there was no wedding to think about. She didn't even want to think about Christmas. It was going to be very empty—meaningless.

Ariana shook her head. No, she mustn't think like that. She mustn't. Christmas would still have the same meaning as always. It was Christ's birth they celebrated. Nothing in her circumstances had changed that.

But as Ariana looked at the pocket watch she had purchased for Laramie, she found it hard to feel in the Christmas spirit.

She had to do something. Something to take control of her life again. She couldn't just stay in her room and weep and mope. That was not honoring to her Lord.

Two days before Christmas, she donned her nicest gown, bathed the puffiness from her eyes, and joined the family at the breakfast table.

Everyone seemed to hold a collective breath. Dared they speak? What topics were safe to address? What meaningless comment might start the tears flowing again?

Ariana managed a wobbly smile. She reached over and took her mother's hand.

"I've made a decision," she said simply. "I'm coming home with you."

Everyone at the table looked surprised. Four pairs of eyes turned toward her to see if she was in her right mind.

"It only makes sense," she went on calmly. "With the gang gone, there is no reason for me to hide myself away here. I've resigned from the school. They already have a new teacher engaged. I . . . I'll just go on home with you."

Gradually those at the table began to see that she was thinking quite clearly. Quite capable of making a decision. Her mother squeezed her hand. Her father beamed his pleasure. Her aunt Molly looked about to weep, while her uncle Jake just cleared his throat noisily.

"We'll miss you, dear," said Aunt Molly.

"It will be so good to have you home again. I've been so lonely," her mother admitted.

"You leave on the third," Ariana went on. "I will have no problem being ready." Her eyes clouded.

"There is only one thing I haven't figured out," she went on.

Her mother's hand tightened on hers. She was afraid there might be tears again.

"The little roan," went on Ariana, and though her voice cracked slightly, she did not begin to cry.

Her uncle Jake was quick to speak. Perhaps he feared a fresh outburst of tears as well. "Happy to keep him here— until such time as you can get him," he said, and then cleared his throat again.

Ariana smiled softly in appreciation. "Thank you, Uncle Jake," she said evenly.

The matter seemed to be closed.

❧   ❧   ❧

Laramie settled into his new responsibilities. For the first months, through the last of winter and into spring, he spent his days in the saddle from sunup to sundown. He wanted to discover the lay of the land—to survey the entire ranch and know thoroughly each draw, each hill, each valley. He checked the water supply, the grass supply, each head that grazed, each new calf that arrived. He could not manage well what he did not know well, he reasoned, and his boss took great pleasure in watching him take the job so seriously.

"Make a good rancher," he informed his elderly wife. "Too bad he don't have a spread of his own."

"He's young," his wife reminded him. "He has lots of time fer thet."

As the days lengthened, Laramie felt well enough in control to assign the range riders the tasks that needed to be done.

That gave him more free time—something he did not welcome.

He resumed his worship in the small church, and the

preacher's daughter took up her role of flirting again. Laramie tried to avoid direct contact with her. He was sure she was a fine young woman, but he just wasn't interested.

He began to look for things to do. They were not always easy to find. He spent more time reading his mother's Bible. The lessons he learned helped him get hold of his life again—but he still could not forget Ariana. He still was not able to think of her as his sister. He began to wonder just how long it was going to take.

One day, in his loneliness, he drew out his mother's little chest. Would he find healing there? Would he find the link that would finally enable him to think of Ariana as a part of his family?

Listlessly he turned over each hankie, each button, each little memento. There was nothing. Nothing that changed the feelings in his heart.

He had emptied the little chest and was about to put all of the contents back in place when he noticed that a bit of the lining was coming loose.

He wasn't skilled in mending and fixing, but he wondered if there was some way he could repair it so the little chest wouldn't continue to come apart.

He ran one finger along the spot and felt something he had not noticed before. He lifted the box for a closer look. To his amazement there was a little clasp hidden from casual view. He pushed on it. Wiggled it gently and pushed again. Then he lifted it—up and in. To his surprise the bottom of the chest flipped upward on a small spring. There was a false bottom to the small chest.

Laramie could not believe what greeted his eyes. The whole bottom of the small box was covered with bills. Money. Stacked thick—though crisp with age. Strange money. He was not familiar with it. But it was money, of that he was sure.

"I don't believe this," he said to himself. "Mama had a whole stash here."

He looked over his shoulder. He did not wish to be observed. The door was closed. He moved to pull the curtain over the one window. Then he sat back down at the table and began to lift out the crinkled bills.

At the bottom of the pile he discovered a small book. Was this her record of account? Laramie lifted the book and flipped the pages. No. There were no numbers. Simply writing. Some sort of—record. Or journal. He laid the book aside and began to count the money.

There were thousands of dollars. Enough for a ranch of his own. Enough to give Ariana—

His thoughts stopped there. When would he ever stop thinking of Ariana?

He stirred from the table and paced about the small cabin. The money had lost all its appeal. What good was it?

Yet it was there. He should do something with it. He placed it, all but a single bill, rather roughly back in the secret compartment and carefully fastened the false bottom into place. He did not return the little book. He laid it in with the hankies and buttons and brooches. He should send the things to Ariana. They were more suitable for a lady than for a man.

Laramie put the chest back in its hiding place, opened the covering on the window, and checked his hair in the cracked mirror on the wall. He would just ride on into town and visit the banker. Perhaps the man could shed some light on the strange currency.

❧   ❧   ❧

"Where'd you get this?" asked the cigar-chewing man behind the desk.

"My mama left me a box," replied Laramie. "I didn't realize it had a false bottom in it—until today."

"This was in it?"

Laramie nodded. There was no need to tell the man that the bill was only one of many.

"Haven't seen these for some while," said the banker as

he turned the bill over and over in his hand.

"Real money?" asked Laramie.

The man twirled his cigar with his tongue. He looked up and smiled in an amused fashion.

"Real money, all right," he said, and Laramie was about to let his breath out with relief when he continued. "Ain't worth a lick, though. Confederate. Union decided it's not legal tender. Might as well use it to start yer fire in the morning."

❦   ❦   ❦

So Mama's box held no treasure after all, Laramie thought to himself as he rode home. It had been a disappointment—but after what he had already been through, it didn't matter all that much.

He let his mount pick his own gait. He was not in a hurry to get anywhere. What was there to do when he did get home? Nothing? Perhaps he'd ride on out and check the west spring. Or maybe he'd see how that new colt in the east pasture was doing. Or maybe he'd just loaf. He didn't know—he didn't really care.

And then he remembered the little book. *Maybe I should take a look at it,* he concluded. *Looked like a woman's writing. Maybe it's Mama's. If it was her diary—it might hold some information. Maybe even some answers.*

Laramie urged the buckskin forward at a faster pace. He was rather in a hurry after all.

Chapter Twenty-four

The Answers

By the time Laramie reached the ranch he was anxious to get his saddle horse put up for the night so he could get to the small journal. His inner tension had been mounting with each mile he traveled.

He could hardly wait to discover just what the little book was. What secrets of his past—Ariana's past—it might hold.

He entered his small abode and shut the door against the noise and dust of the day. It was rather dark after he had pulled his curtain firmly across the little window, so he lit his lamp before lifting the small chest from its hiding place, withdrawing the small book, and settling himself at the wooden table.

He flipped open the first page.

"To my dear daughter Lavina Ann Bradley on the occasion of her fourteenth birthday. July 10, 1836," it read in a crisp script. Beneath the penned inscription were the words, "Always be the godly woman admonished by Scripture in 1 Peter 3:4. Your loving father, Winston P. Bradley."

Laramie turned to the next page. The writing had changed. He could almost envision a young girl sitting at a polished writing desk, her smooth brow puckered in concentration.

"July 10, 1836. Today is my fourteenth birthday. I cannot

believe it. Mama gave me the most beautiful blue gown. It is my first real grown-up dress with charming puffed sleeves and a full skirt with lots of petticoats, and blue ruffles upon beautiful blue ruffles. She also said that when I wear it I will be able to pin up my hair. Imagine. Me—grown-up. Papa gave me that horse I have been teasing for and a sidesaddle so that I might ride her in ladylike fashion. He also gave me this book. To keep a diary, he said. I think that he feels I am terribly impulsive and he hopes that it will teach me a bit of discipline. (He wishes me to write an account in it daily, but that seems like a very big chore. Almost like a school assignment. I think that I shall write in it only when something very important happens.) Like today. Today has been so exciting. Even Ethan shared in my joy. And brothers do not do that very often."

Laramie turned the page.

"July 11, 1836. I wasn't going to write in my diary today, but Papa asked me at the breakfast table if I had. Since I had not, I assured him quickly that I would. He seemed satisfied. But I really have nothing important to write about. It looks to be an ordinary day, and after having such an exciting day yesterday, it is difficult to endure. And it is so miserably hot and stuffy. I think that I shall die of the heat. I have asked Papa if we might go to our house in Charleston, where the ocean breezes help to make things a bit more bearable. He wouldn't give his answer.

"July 12, 1836. It is still hot and miserable. Even Mama is annoyed with the heat. I hope that she joins me in persuading Papa. Perhaps then he will take us to Charleston.

"July 13, 1836. We are going to Charleston. Oh, joy! I can hardly wait. Mama said that she simply could not endure the swampy heat of the plantation. I will take along my new blue gown and pray for a party so I may wear it. Ethan is fussing because Papa said that he cannot go. He has to stay home and help with the plantation. Papa says that is a man's duty. I don't think Ethan enjoys being a man—at sixteen."

The next date was not until September 29, 1836.

"It has been wonderful in Charleston. Every day there are new people to meet. I have never been to so many parties—but Mama is well-known here. Papa went directly back to the plantation. Mama has added more gowns to my wardrobe. She says that a young lady must be properly attired. I cannot believe how grown-up I now look, in just one short summer. I feel grown-up too, and I have had many nice compliments from the young gentlemen. Mama still will not allow me to have callers. She says I must wait until next year. That seems a long time to wait. We must leave for home tomorrow. It will seem very quiet and boring after life in the city.

"February 15, 1838. A most wonderful thing happened to me today. I had always thought that the most exciting thing that could ever happen to a young lady would be a proposal of marriage. Well, I was wrong. I discovered another love. All of my life my parents have been very diligent in making me attend services in our local church, in reading portions of the Scripture before our breakfast, in insisting that I read sections on my own and memorize the same. I had always accepted their faith as a matter of course. But today, today I understood the truth of God's Word for the first time. I really understood—with my heart as well as my head. I prayed the prayer of repentance, and such peace and joy flooded my heart. I will never be the same again—nor do I wish to be.

"March 2, 1838. My faith has continued to grow. It fills me with overwhelming joy—at the same time that it breaks my heart. I can't help but grieve for all of those who have not yet heard and believed. I have Papa's permission to start a little class of Bible lessons for the children of the slaves. They are so sweet and so quick to pick up the truths that I was so slow in learning.

"March 22, 1838. My first little 'black sheep' accepted the teaching of Scripture. What a joy it was to lead this little one in a prayer of repentance. I think that her mammy had already prepared her heart.

"September 12, 1838. I have just met the most wonderful

young man. Maybe I should have noticed him long ago. His father owns the plantation across the river from us. We have known the family for years and I do recall him faintly—but I had never really noticed him before—in this way. He's tall and very nice looking, with the most gentlemanly manner. I am quite taken with him. I am not sure how he feels about me. I have added him to my lengthy prayers. God knows what is right for me. I must learn to trust Him in this matter as well.

"April 4, 1839. Turner Lawrence III asked my papa for permission to call—and was wholeheartedly accepted. I am so thankful. I can scarcely believe my good fortune. (Papa says I am not to use that term. It is not good fortune for one of God's children—it is the grace of God.)

"July 19, 1839. We are leaving for Charleston as we do each summer, but this year I hate to go. I have enjoyed getting to know Turner. Our conversations have shown me that we are of one heart and mind. He, too, deplores the ownership of slaves. He says if he had any say in the matter, he would free his. His father still runs the plantation, though. Turner lost his mother to the swamp fever when he was only eight. How sad for a child to be raised without a mother. He does love his nurse. She is a big woman, with love for all God's children. I can understand why Turner feels the way he does about her.

"December 8, 1839. Papa has agreed to a spring wedding. I am so happy. I never knew that one's heart could be so full.

"May 10, 1840. Today is my wedding day. Papa sent to Spain for the lace for my gown, and Mama had it sewn in Charleston. It is the most elegant thing I have ever seen. It is ivory satin, overlaid with this gorgeous lace. The sleeves are full and puffed, nipped in with soft satin bows, with slender long cuffs buttoned underneath and reaching to each wrist. The skirts are full at the back with yards of bustle. The bodice is fitted with the lace gently sculpturing the natural lines. The neckline is high and simple and will show off the new sapphire and diamond pendant that Papa has given me.

Someday I will pass this beautiful dress on to my daughter to wear at her own wedding. I can almost see her walking down the aisle."

Laramie stirred restlessly in his chair. In his mind he was seeing Ariana in that same lovely gown, walking the aisle of the little church to join him at the altar. It was all he could do to continue reading.

"Mama is sure that all of Charleston will rave about the gown and the wedding, and I have a secret feeling that is important to Mama. I certainly would be ungrateful if I did not appreciate all that Papa and Mama are doing for us— but I would have been quite happy to just marry my Turner. He is so wonderful. This promises to be the beginning of a wonderful life. We have prayed together, many times, asking God to bless our union—to make us truly one in Him.

"Papa's gift to me was a new family Bible. He was so sweet as he gave it to me. 'Every home must have a Bible,' he said. 'A home cannot be safely built on any other foundation—no matter how much love is shared by the homeowners.' He also flipped to the pages for records and advised me to be diligent in keeping my posting up to date. I promised him that I would.

"August 15, 1840. I am a wife. I still find it hard to believe. After a wonderful trip abroad we settled into life at Roseberne plantation. Turner's father has informed me that I am the full mistress of the manor now. I am thankful that Mama took her teaching duties seriously and I know how to go about the task. Nevertheless, I am still a bit nervous. Turner is wonderfully reassuring.

"December 2, 1853. Today was a very difficult and sad day. Father Lawrence passed away suddenly last evening. The doctor said it was his heart. Turner feels it deeply. Though he has not always agreed with his father, he loved him dearly. I'm not sure what the future holds for us now.

"September 5, 1854. It has been decided. Turner is selling Roseberne. He cannot bear the thought of owning slaves— yet the plantation could never be run without them. It is an untenable situation. However, he refused to sell the slaves along with the property but granted them full freedom and gave them each an amount of cash to get established elsewhere. It was a sad time. We all cried together. I struggled with the decision. I do not like slavery either, but I could not but fear for our future. Turner is confident. We are to move. He has picked St. Louis. He does not like the unrest that is sweeping the South. He is afraid there will be war. He tried to talk to Papa and Ethan about it, but they both are adamant in their resolve to stay as they are. I feel so mixed up and confused—but Turner constantly reminds me that God will lead us.

"June 6, 1855. We are well settled in St. Louis. It is a fine little city, though it cannot compare in any way to Charleston. I miss the plantation life and I dearly miss my family. Sometimes I wonder if we have done the right thing. But rumors keep circulating. Turner is sure it will end in war. I pray that he is wrong.

"I had hoped to be a mother long before now, but that has not been. Turner keeps reminding me that God can still answer our prayers. It seems that each year that passes just breaks my heart a little bit more. It is hard to be patient.

"February 3, 1860. I cannot believe it. I am to be a mother. I had almost given up. At age thirty-seven it seemed that motherhood had passed me by. (I will be thirty-eight by the time our little one joins us.) I can only bow my head and my heart and thank God.

"August 10, 1860. The miracle has actually happened. I am a mother. What joy I feel! Our son arrived at ten o'clock this morning. I cried as I held him. He is beautiful. I think he will be a big man, like his father. But Turner insists he will have my eyes. He has only just arrived—and yet I would gladly give my life for him. God has been so good.

"January 2, 1861. Christmas was so special this year. Little Burke has given us the true meaning for all of life, but the thought filling my heart was that of the great love of God the Father. How could He love me enough to give His Son?

It is a love I cannot comprehend as I look at my own precious baby boy. To love enough to die for him—yes—a thousand times, yes. But to love enough to send him to die—I never could love that purely—that strongly. What a magnificent love is the Love of God! I pray that God will keep my boy safe—protected and in His care—always."

Laramie felt his eyes dampening. His mother was speaking of him. How he wished he could have known her. How he longed to feel the beat of her mother-heart.

The next page was not dated. The usual even script looked hurried, agitated.

"It is as we feared. Our beloved country is at war. North against South. Brother against brother. Ethan has gone. Mama says it was his duty. I don't understand about duty that would lead a man to fight his own countrymen. My heart is grieved. I am glad I didn't have a son earlier. He, too, might need to fight. Little Burke is still safe in his cradle. I pray that the day may never come when he has to use a gun to save his own life.

"October 14, 1861. Turner has decided we will move farther west. He is afraid that the effects of the war will even touch St. Louis. I pray that he is wrong but I have not argued. I am willing to go wherever he sees as best. Little Burke is my only thought. My only joy. He is growing so quickly. Turner was right. He does have my eyes.

"November 18, 1861. Turner has located a group of people who are planning to move west. He is making arrangements for us to join the train. I went with him to one of the meetings. He insisted. He did not want me to feel pressured into going farther west if I was against it. I was favorably impressed. They seem to be a kind, God-fearing group of people. The wagon master and his trail riders seem to be competent. I will feel quite safe in their company.

"November 26, 1861. We had another meeting of the people from the train. I met the sweetest young woman. Her name is Morgan Oliver. She and the man she plans to marry will be joining the train next spring as well. She is so anxious to marry her Preston that she reminds me of myself several years ago when I was all starry-eyed about my Turner. But she does not have a mother to help her with her wedding plans as I did. She would like to be married on Christmas Eve. I have told her that I would help in any way I can.

"December 25, 1861. What a lovely wedding we attended last evening. There was only a small gathering in the local church. The guests were mostly the people of the wagon train who are busy preparing for the spring trip to the West. Morgan married her Preston Whitehall. She was a radiant bride. I was glad that I had thought to offer her the use of my gown. I am sure my future daughter will not mind that we shared the dress with another. Morgan is such a sweet little thing. I am looking forward to having her on the train for those long, tiring days of travel.

"March 4, 1862. The war still rages. News is not good. Mama tries to keep us posted—but each letter that makes it through breaks our hearts a little more. I fear for the safety of my family. Turner was right. I am so thankful we have left so that Burke might be kept safe. Each time I look at him my heart swells with love.

"March 6, 1862. Morgan came by today with some delightful news. She is expecting a baby. We are both praying that our trip might go well and that we will have arrived and become settled before the little one is born. What a delight it would be if it is a boy. It would be wonderful to have a playmate for Burke. True—Burke would be two years older, but two years will not seem like much in years to come. I am praying daily for Morgan. I feel I am uniquely sharing her joy.

"June 4, 1862. Next week we begin our long trek west. Our days will be filled with all of the last-minute purchases, sales, packing, and planning. Turner has secured two sturdy wagons and an additional driver so that I can take some of my treasured possessions with me. He says that there is no need for me to feel I have forsaken civilization. He wants his son to grow up to have the social graces of a southern gentleman even though we have been forced to leave the South.

"I suffered a deep disappointment yesterday. The doctor has confirmed that I will not be able to have another child. I wept well into the evening, even though Turner tried to sweetly comfort me. Then I looked at Burke. I chastised myself. God has already blessed me much beyond what I have deserved."

I don't understand, mused Laramie. *How could that be? What about Ariana?* Laramie turned his eyes back to the book in his hands and read on. The doctor must have been proven wrong.

"August 16, 1862. We have been on the trail for what seems forever. Sometimes I wonder how much more I will be able to stand. I was not prepared for this. It has been much more difficult than I would have guessed. Bad weather has kept us from making the progress we had hoped. I worry for Morgan. She is due in September, but the trip has been hard for her. I fear that the rumbling wagons might bring the baby earlier than it is supposed to come. Each day I include her in my petitions. It seems that we keep God so busy with our many prayers. I am glad He is able.

"August 29, 1862. Morgan's baby arrived last night. She is a good two weeks early, and though she is small she is wiry and seems strong. Thanks to God. Morgan is so excited. I know the feeling. I felt the same way when Burke arrived.

"September 17, 1862. We had hoped to have reached our 'Promised Land' by now, but more bad weather has delayed us. However, Turner assures me we are getting close. I am concerned about Morgan. She does not seem to be getting back her strength as quickly as she should. A dear woman who lost her husband in a horrid drowning at a river crossing, Mrs. Millard, is helping her. We are constantly reminded that we are in Indian country, but our wagon master assures us we have little cause to worry. I keep reminding myself of the verse that I have carried with me, 'Trust in the Lord with all thine heart.' Sometimes that is all I have to cling to. I am not afraid for myself. I just pray that Burke will be kept from the evil of the world. He is all that matters. I pray each day that God will protect him.

"September 26, 1862. Morgan was up today but she is still weak. I pray that God will give her strength. We have decided to meet each day, in the time that we have left together, to pray for our babies. Their safety. Their futures. But most of all, that God will keep their hearts open to His voice and protect them from the sinful ways of the world. The West seems so frighteningly crude to me that I sometimes fear for my son. But God kept the young Moses. Surely I can trust Him with my precious Burke.

"We are soon to come to the parting of our ways. The Whitehalls plan to head south, while Turner has decided that we will travel north. I was so disappointed I wept for most of the day. I tried not to let Turner know—but I fear he guessed. I have made a decision. I will give Morgan the wedding dress."

Laramie's heart quickened and he hurried on.

"September 27, 1862. I bundled up my beautiful gown and took it to Morgan today. This is the last night that we are to be together. Tomorrow we are to go our separate ways. She was so touched when I made my little presentation that she wept and I wept right along with her. I had already shed tears alone. It seemed that I was giving away not just a dress, but my memories and my future hopes and dreams. However, I am not sorry. I will never have a daughter to wear it, and little Ariana seems almost like a daughter to me. I know that someday she will make a beautiful bride."

Laramie, breathing heavily, read the passage again. Ariana. Ariana was Morgan's baby. Morgan's daughter. She was not his sister. Could it be? Was the book telling the truth? He turned back anxiously to the little diary.

"I was disappointed to discover that one of the cuffs was missing. At first I was mystified and then I remembered that I had noticed one of the tiny buttons was loose. I laid the cuff aside until I could fix it. I can't recall where I put it unless it is in my little chest in my trunk.

"Later. I found the cuff. It was in the small chest that holds my 'treasures'—including this diary—between my recording days. (I haven't been as faithful as Papa would have liked, but I do see this little book as something very precious—even though I don't fully understand what gives it such value.) I fixed the button, so I'll be able to deliver the cuff to Morgan in the morning before she leaves."

There were only empty pages following the notation. He looked back at the last date entered.

Morning had never come for his mother. At sunrise the Indians had attacked.

Laramie felt physically sick. His mother—his dear mother—she who had loved him and wrapped him securely in her daily prayers—had not lived to see another day. He could not even think of it. And Ariana—she had lost her mother, too. Morgan. Morgan Whitehall. They both had been left orphans—Ariana hidden by the widowed lady whom she lovingly called her second mama.

Laramie stirred from his reverie.

Ariana. *Ariana needs to know.*

His thoughts moved from the horror of the wagon massacre to the fact that Ariana was not his sister. They had two different mothers—women joined only by friendship and the sharing of a beautiful wedding gown. It was a miracle. A little miracle. No, a great big, wondrous miracle. The secret compartment of the little chest had held a treasure far more precious than confederate money. It held the key to the secret of his past. Of Ariana's past.

He shoved the book into his pocket and began to pack a saddlebag. He could not wait to get to Ariana. Could not wait to share the knowledge the little book held. They were free. They were not bound by kinship. They were not brother and sister. They were free to join in marriage. They were free to love each other as husband and wife.

❧   ❧   ❧

Ariana stood with one hand on the window ledge and looked out at the young squirrels frisking about on the grass in the backyard. They looked so playful, so filled with energy. In spite of her still-heavy heart, she could not hide a smile.

"Ariana," her mother called from the front of the house. "You have a caller." Her voice sounded excited. Ariana wondered about it as she turned from the window and let the curtain fall back into place.

She walked down the hall to the parlor expecting to see one of her Sunday school class members or perhaps, she thought, with a quickening of her pulse, the school board chairman. Maybe they had found they could use her in the local school after all. She did hope that it wasn't Bernard Dikerson. He had been making a nuisance of himself ever since her return.

But it was a tall young man who stood there, hat in hand. Ariana could not have mistaken his identity, even though his face was shadowed.

"Laramie!" she gasped.

Her head began to spin. He had said he would be back when they could accept the brother-sister relationship. If he had worked it through, he was much ahead of her, she decided. She still was not ready to see him as the brother she had never known.

He stepped forward and reached for her hand, but Ariana drew it back. She wasn't prepared for this. She wasn't. She cast a look over her shoulder, willing her mother to interfere, to support her in some way. Her mother was nowhere to be seen. Ariana felt a moment of panic.

He did not try to reach for her again, though his eyes showed—what?

"I found something," he said, pulling the small book from his pocket. "I thought I would explode before reaching you. I traveled first to your uncle's. I—"

Ariana let her gaze look out the window. His buckskin and a pack animal stood tethered to the hitching rail, and by their side stood the little roan pony. Yes, he had been up to her uncle's. Tears began to form in her eyes. She turned back to him. But she still couldn't comprehend what he was saying.

"It's all in here," he began, his voice full of excitement as he tapped the small book he still held in his hand. "It's—"

He stopped and looked at her longingly.

Ariana slowly shook her head. "You said you wouldn't come until—" She stopped and licked her lips. "I'm sorry," she continued in a shaky voice. "I . . . I'm not ready . . ."

He moved forward then and placed his hands on her arms. "You don't need to be," he hurried to say. "This book. It gives the whole story. We are *not* brother and sister. Our parents—two totally different families."

Ariana drew back and looked at him with wide, startled eyes. She could not speak.

"Honest!" he continued. "Our mothers—our families—were not the same. It's all in here."

She was in a total daze.

"You're sure?" she managed to whisper.

"I'm sure. Honest."

And then she was in his arms, weeping against the pocket that had held the small diary with its precious secret.

"I can't believe—" she began, but her tears stopped the words.

"It's true—it's true. Our mothers' prayers have—kept us—fer . . . fer some special reason. I . . . I feel thet. I'm not sure jest what—yet. But we'll find it. We are free to serve Him—together—now. Honest."

His arms tightened around her and he lowered his face to bury it in her hair.

"Mama's book said it, too," he whispered. "Thet special verse of yers—'Trust in the Lord with all thine heart.' She said it, too."

Ariana lifted a smiling but still tear-stained face to Laramie, and he drew her closer and bent his head to kiss her moistened cheek.

Two hearts lifted in deep thankfulness to God. They were not brother and sister. They would soon be husband and wife.